"For decades Richard Horsley has been a leading figure in reassessing the roles of Pharisees and scribal groups in the politics of ancient Judaism. These essays—all engaging and accessible—trace his investigations and will be welcomed by both the student and the scholar. The history of the Pharisees and their relation to early Christianity will be much discussed topics for years to come, and Horsley's voice has been absolutely central to the ongoing debates."

—Lawrence M. Wills
Instructor of Religious Studies and Theology, Stonehill College

"Through a fine-grained analysis of Josephus and other ancient sources, Horsley challenges common assumptions about the Pharisees, describing them as a scribal group active in both the political and religious affairs of the Judean temple-state. Their status as 'legal-intellectual retainers' who advised the high priestly rulers ended with the Roman destruction of Jerusalem in 70 CE. Building and expanding upon his previous work, Horsley presents a paradigm-shifting synthesis of the history of the Pharisees."

—Jodi Magness
Kenan Distinguished Professor, University of North Carolina at Chapel Hill

"In The Pharisees, Jesus, and the Politics of Roman Palestine, renowned scholar Richard Horsley draws on six decades of research to build new understanding of the Pharisees' documented actions for two centuries within an unstable imperial environment. After tracing the evolution of both New Testament studies and his own intellectual journey, Horsley reconstructs the Pharisees' complex political, economic, and religious role in the Judean temple-state through close and innovative analysis of ancient narratives, especially the works of Josephus, the Jewish priest who was not a Pharisee. Volume 1 stands as a vital companion to recent scholarship and paves the way for Volume 2, which will examine the Gospels in depth to complete Horsley's fascinating study of the Pharisees, the most prominent pre-70 CE Jewish group whose legacy remains misunderstood and misrepresented to this day."

—Honora Howell Chapman
Dean, College of Arts and Humanities, California State University, Fresno

The Pharisees, Jesus, *and the* Politics *of* Roman Palestine

VOLUME 1:
Pharisees and Scribes
in the Politics of Roman Palestine

The Pharisees, Jesus, and the Politics of Roman Palestine

VOLUME 1:
Pharisees and Scribes
in the Politics of Roman Palestine

RICHARD A. HORSLEY

CASCADE Books • Eugene, Oregon

THE PHARISEES, JESUS, AND THE POLITICS OF ROMAN PALESTINE
Volume 1: Pharisees and Scribes in the Politics of Roman Palestine

Copyright © 2025 Richard A. Horsley. All rights reserved. Except for brief quotations in critical publications or reviews, no part of this book may be reproduced in any manner without prior written permission from the publisher. Write: Permissions, Wipf and Stock Publishers, 199 W. 8th Ave., Suite 3, Eugene, OR 97401.

Cascade Books
An Imprint of Wipf and Stock Publishers
199 W. 8th Ave., Suite 3
Eugene, OR 97401

www.wipfandstock.com

PAPERBACK ISBN: 979-8-3852-2169-1
HARDCOVER ISBN: 979-8-3852-2170-7
EBOOK ISBN: 979-8-3852-2171-4

Cataloguing-in-Publication data:

Names: Horsley, Richard A., author.

Title: The Pharisees, Jesus, and the politics of Roman Palestine , volume 1 : Pharisees and Scribes in the politics of Roman Palestine / Richard A. Horsley.

Description: Eugene, OR: Cascade Books, 2025. | Includes bibliographical references and index.

Identifiers: ISBN 979-8-3852-2169-1 (paperback). | ISBN 979-8-3852-2170-7 (hardcover). | ISBN 979-8-3852-2171-4 (ebook).

Subjects: LCSH: Galilee (Israel)—History. | Jews—History—To 70 A.D. | Hasmoneans. | Herod. | Josephus, Flavius.

Classification: BM175 H641 2025 (print). | BM175 (ebook).

VERSION NUMBER 103125

Contents

Preface | vii
List of Abbreviations | xii

Introduction | 1

1. Conflict and Crisis in the Judean Temple-State under Imperial Rule | 23
2. Implications of Recent Research for Understanding the Pharisees and the Law | 58
3. Laws/Customs, Politeia, and Traditions of the Judeans | 78
4. The Political Prominence of the Pharisees at Mid-First Century CE | 106
5. The Pharisees under the Hasmoneans | 126
6. The Pharisees under Roman and Herod's Rule | 168
7. The Pharisees and Other Scribal Groups under the High Priests and Roman Governors | 206
8. The Pharisees and the Politics of Roman Palestine | 236

Bibliography | 247
Index of Ancient Documents | 257
Author Index | 269

Preface

Several aspects of biblical studies bothered me as a student in theological school in the early 1960s and especially as a doctoral student in the later 1960s.

In history courses and tutorials in college we read whole texts (documents, treatises, letters, declarations, etc.) as sources. In biblical studies courses, however, we were taught to focus on tiny text-fragments, such as verses, sayings, even particular words, as the sources for "biblical" figures or ideas or doctrines. But how could particular words or sentences or sayings be understood separated from literary context, which might have been the only guide to the historical context?

We were supposedly being trained in the "historical-critical" approach. But this approach seemed neither historical nor critical. The controlling concepts in biblical studies, moreover, deeply rooted in Christian theology (of which biblical studies was a division), seemed inappropriate to the texts we were interpreting and the historical context in which the texts were to be interpreted.

I was particularly distressed by the obvious Christian anti-Judaism in biblical studies, especially New Testament studies. The controlling "paradigm" or grand scheme of "Christian origins" was how a new, more universal and spiritual religion (Christianity) originated in and then split away from an older, more parochial, political, and legalistic religion (Judaism). Supposedly this dramatic "breakthrough" could be seen in the conflict between Jesus and the Pharisees in many Gospel fragments. Jesus' sayings and fragments from Paul's letters were standardly interpreted over against Judaism, of which the Pharisees were supposedly the key representatives.

In my own research and teaching, however, I continued to read whole texts, declining professors' suggestions to focus on "word-studies" that were supposedly more manageable. And reading Josephus' histories, for example, despite his blatant elitist perspective, opened toward recognition of the historical context of other texts. Neither those histories nor other texts mentioned "Judaism" or "Christianity."

Instead what opened up was the conflictual history of Judeans and Samaritans and Galileans under the imperial rule of the Hellenistic empires and then of Rome. Josephus and other sources made clear that the empires ruled through client rulers, the Judean high priestly aristocracy and Herodian kings. The textual sources also indicated that the Galilean, Samaritan, and especially the Judean people mounted protests, movements, and even revolts against their rulers. Critical analysis of Josephus' accounts of these movements and revolts, moreover, suggested that they were rooted in Israelite tradition cultivated in village communities parallel to the elite Judean culture cultivated in scribal circles of the temple-state. In addition to the more frequent popular protests and movements, Josephus describes several protests by scribal groups, against the Romans and/or Herod or high priestly rulers. There was no indication that a religious dimension was separate from the political-economic dimension of these symptoms of the structural conflict and dynamics between the people and their rulers. These were the historical realities that I researched and laid out in a series of articles in the late 1970s and 1980s.

In a parallel project during the 1970s and early 1980s I was working toward a more critical understanding of the historical Jesus in historical context. I realized that New Testament scholars were woefully unprepared to even begin understanding Jesus in his historical context. The few previous presentations of the historical Jesus in mainstream scholarship simply left unaddressed many aspects both of the portrayal of Jesus-in-interaction in the Gospel sources and of the indications of historical context evident in both the Gospels and other sources. New Testament scholars understood Jesus as a narrowly individualistic religious figure, mainly a teacher unengaged in social relations. It was a puzzle how scholars supposedly aiming to discern and understand Jesus as a historical figure could pay so little attention to the historical context.

Not surprisingly, my research on popular movements and revolts and scribal protests informed my developing understanding of the historical Jesus in historical context. It appeared clear from the Gospel sources that Jesus' mission, like other popular protests and movements, was opposed not to Judaism but to the Roman and high priestly rulers. Jesus and his movement(s), moreover, were rooted in Israelite tradition, indeed appeared to be a renewal of the Mosaic covenant and other Israelite traditions in the village communities in which the vast majority of Galileans and Judeans lived.

I had intended the project on Jesus' mission in historical context to include a more critical consideration of the scribes and Pharisees and their conflict with Jesus in more sustained Gospel accounts. Previous treatment, based on text-fragments and questionable concepts had set them up as a stereotypical legalistic foil for Jesus' teaching. So it seemed important to focus directly on the important role of scribes and Pharisees in the Judean temple-state, with sympathy for the Pharisees, before focusing on the "controversy stories" in Mark and Jesus' woes against them in Matthew and Luke (and in "Q"). In the introductory chapter of *Jesus and the Spiral of Violence* I explained that in the social structure of the traditional agrarian society of Judea the Pharisees and scribes were intellectual-legal retainers of the ruling high priests who owed their position to the imperial rulers. I realized, however, that, like other New Testament scholars, I was woefully unprepared to treat the Pharisees and scribes adequately. So I simply left unaddressed the conflict between Jesus and the Pharisees in the 1987 book on Jesus in historical context.

At the time, however, I fully intended to launch a focused inquiry in the next few years. I even obtained a contract for a volume on the Pharisees and Jesus in the early 1990s. And I began wider and deeper research into second-temple Judean and later rabbinic texts, read widely in scholarly treatments of the Pharisees and of Qumran texts, and produced some papers and articles on the Pharisees.

It soon became evident, however, that it was necessary to deal with other problems in New Testament studies that stood in the way of understanding scribes and Pharisees and their conflict with Jesus appropriately. Some colleagues and I had begun borrowing from the field of sociology. It seemed clear, however, that this was being done uncritically. This called for a critical review of the problems with the structural-functional approach that had been largely abandoned by sociologists in the 1970s, but was being borrowed uncritically by biblical scholars in the 1970s and 1980s. Other colleagues were turning attention to Galilee, but again uncritically, ignoring its very different history compared with that of Judea and Samaria. In *Antiquities* Josephus offers at least a brief account of how Hasmonean high priests had taken over Galilee only about a century before the lifetime of Jesus. He then indicates that the Hasmoneans and Herod had ruled the Galileans through garrisons in several fortresses, especially at Sepphoris. It seemed clear that in order to understand Jesus and Jesus-movements in historical context, it was necessary to research a critical understanding that was both more comprehensive and more precise than those then available.

Also in the 1990s it was still troubling that the dominant Christian scheme of "Christian origins" that understood both Jesus and Paul in opposition to Judaism indirectly and often directly fostered the anti-Judaism implicit in New Testament studies. The 1987 book had laid out how the mission of Jesus, far from being opposed to Judaism and the Law, belonged among a variety of popular movements among Judeans and Galileans rooted in Israelite tradition that all opposed rule by the Romans and the client high priestly rulers they imposed. In the context of what seemed like an imminent invasion of Iraq by the United States, it seemed timely to show more explicitly how Jesus' mission was opposed, not to Judaism and the Law, but to the Roman imperial order, and to make more explicit how it was grounded in Israelite tradition, especially the Mosaic covenant.

Meanwhile, although historical Jesus scholars remained stuck in their focus on separate individual sayings of Jesus that reduced him to a "talking head," Gospel scholars had discovered that the Gospels were sustained stories. But they were historical stories, and not similar to modern prose fiction with its focus on "character-development." Although historical Jesus scholars of my generation never did "wake up" to this discovery and its implications, it was clear to me that the sources for investigation of the historical Jesus were not separate sayings but Gospel stories and narratives more broadly. It would be necessary to "back up" to the extended Gospel stories as the sources for investigation into Jesus-in-interaction—hence serious critical investigation of each Gospel story and set of speeches.

While working on understanding whole Gospel narratives in historical context, moreover, I became aware of and involved in several (largely separate) new lines of research into ancient communications media. At first only a small cadre of us were pursuing one or another of these lines of research and considering the implications for use of what evidently had been orally performed texts as sources. Having become involved in several of these lines of new research, however, I was persuaded that they were closely related, both in ancient social life and in their implications for appreciation and use of texts as sources. It was becoming clear that not only were the sources for the historical Jesus the sustained Gospels stories (and speeches), but that those stories (and speeches), in their historical context in which oral communication was dominant, were "oral-derived" stories (and speeches), stories and a series of speeches in oral performance in communities for which they were foundational. This recognition led me to the projects of critical analysis of the series of Jesus-speeches known as "Q," the Markan story, and the Johannine story, along with books and many articles focused on social memory, oral performance, scribal training and practice, and Israelite popular tradition.

Involvement in these (interrelated!) lines of research into ancient communications media, moreover, led to recognition of how they had serious implications for how we understand and work with texts produced by scribes (that is, most of the Judean texts from second temple times). Literacy was severely limited in ancient Judean society, mainly to scribal circles. Recent studies of scribal training, however, indicate that educated scribes learned texts (of torah and of prophecies) by repeated recitation, so that they were "inscribed on the tablet of their heart," that is, in their individual and collective memory. Clearly these researches require some rethinking of how we understand the important role of scribes in ancient Judea. That literacy was evidently confined largely to scribal circles, moreover, suggests that non-literate people's knowledge of Israelite tradition did not come from inscribed scrolls that they could not have read.

This broad range of new research and book projects in the 1990s and since meant extended delays in finally getting back to what might be a more satisfactory project of investigating the historical Jesus-in-interaction-in-context and, as I am now projecting the project, a complex critical investigation of "the Pharisees—and Jesus—and the Politics of Roman Palestine." In retrospect, however, it is fortunate that I did not proceed with the project of researching and discussing the Pharisees and their conflict with Jesus as originally planned in the early 1990s. For it is only during the last three decades that lines of new research have opened toward recognition of further complexities and conflicts in the historical context, of the sustained Gospel stories and speeches as sources, and of the oral and scribal communication media that require us to stop projecting anachronistic print-cultural assumptions and constructs onto ancient texts and history. The ground may now have been prepared for understanding the historical role of scribes and Pharisees in the temple-state of ancient Judea and the Gospels' portrayal of their conflict with Jesus.

Because of the complexity and length of the study, this project will appear in two volumes: because the Pharisees and other scribal groups were active in Judea long before Jesus and the Gospel stories, priority goes to them in the first volume, *The Pharisees and the Politics of Roman Palestine*. The critical examination of the historical context, origin, and history of the Pharisees and other scribal groups in Volume 1 provides much of the background and context for a critical examination of the conflict between the Pharisees and scribes and Jesus attested in the Gospel stories and speeches in Volume 2.

Abbreviations

Dead Sea Scrolls

1QpHab	Habakkuk Pesher from Qumran Cave 1
1QS	Community Rule from Qumran Cave 1
1QSa	Rule of the Congregation from Qumran Cave 1 (1Q28a)
4Q169	Nahum Pesher from Qumran Cave 4
4Q171	Psalms Pesher^a from Qumran Cave 4
4Q173	Psalms Pesher^b from Qumran Cave 4
4QMMT	Halakhic Letter from Qumran Cave 4
11QT	Temple Scroll from Qumran Cave 11
CD	Damascus Document

Josephus

Ag. Ap.	Josephus, *Against Apion*
Ant.	Josephus, *Antiquities of the Judeans*
War	Josephus, *War of the Judeans*

Rabbinic Works

b.	Babylonian Talmud tractates
m.	Mishnah tractates
t.	Tosefta tractates

Introduction

The purpose of this complex project is two-fold. The first is to critically and sympathetically understand the position and role of the Pharisees and scribes in their historical context, which was the Judean temple-state under the Hasmonean rulers and Roman imperial rule, drawing on the principal sources critically understood. The second is to investigate the social location and mission of Jesus in historical context, the villages of Galilee under Roman and Herodian client rulers and then the Jerusalem temple-state under the oversight of Roman governors. This two-fold investigation opens up an understanding of the conflict between Jesus and the Pharisees and scribes as between a popular prophet engaged in the renewal of Israel in its village communities and the representatives of the Jerusalem temple-state as the recognized experts on the *politeia* and laws according to which it operated.

Because of the complexity and length of the project, it will appear in two volumes that are meant to be read in tandem. Investigation of the Pharisees and other scribal groups in historical context commands priority of attention for several interrelated reasons. The Pharisees, understood as the leaders or principal sect of Judaism, have long been the "lightning rod" that took the brunt of charges leveled by Christian anti-Judaism. Embarrassed by how the latter was implicated in the Holocaust, Christian theologians and biblical scholars have "bent over backwards" in a rather superficial way of insisting that Jesus was a Jew, even a Pharisee or rabbi. But neither Christian nor Jewish interpreters have more critically investigated the social-political position and role of the Pharisees in their historical context, the temple-state headed by the high priesthood in late second temple times. The Pharisees and other scribal groups were playing an important mediating role between the rulers and the people and became a moderating influence on the worst abuses by the Roman and high priestly rulers, as will be evident mainly from a careful reading of Josephus' histories.

A closely related second reason is to reverse the usual priority of investigation by New Testament scholars. In their role as representatives of Christian culture and institutions that have been historically dominant, they gave priority to investigation of New Testament texts, "(early) Christianity" and the figures of Jesus and Paul. The Pharisees and Jewish texts were secondary, often understood merely as "background." But historically the Pharisees *were there first*. They had been engaged in the struggles between the rulers and the people of Jerusalem (and possibly Judean villagers as well) for almost two centuries.

A closely related third reason is to generate an understanding of the Pharisees in historical political-economic-religious context more adequate to the textual sources, critically evaluated.

Volume 2 will build on the closer consideration of the historical context laid out in the later chapters of Volume 1, which focuses mostly on the history of the Judean temple-state that had extended its rule to Galilee, but then had to yield control to Herod Antipas, appointed its new ruler by the Romans in 4 BCE. It will be necessary also to explore the local forms of village life and the people's cultivation of Israelite popular tradition that paralleled the cultivation of Judean scribal culture in Jerusalem. These village communities and their Israelite popular culture comprised the concrete context in which Jesus carried out his mission. Since previously standard interpretation of Jesus has been so individualistic and has focused so narrowly on separate sayings taken out of narrative context and historical context, it will be necessary also to develop a far more adequate approach to Jesus-in-interaction-in-historical context. This will require focusing on the sustained narratives of the Gospel stories before attempting to critically assess the social memory behind the Gospel stories.

Toward a More Appropriate and More Comprehensive Approach

Investigation of the Pharisees and Jesus in the politics of the temple-state under imperial rule moves beyond previously standard investigations in three major ways.

First: Previous investigations of the Pharisees and those of "the historical Jesus" and of the conflict between them have focused on text-fragments such as sayings and anecdotes as the sources. This narrow conception of what constitute the sources has gone together with the assumption that the context is (early) Judaism and/or (early) Christianity and the nascent tension between them. These controlling fundamental constructs in the fields of ancient Jewish history and New Testament studies, however, tend to block recognition of structural and other conflicts in the historical context that were integral in the dynamics of political-economic-religious institutions and interactions. These conflicts can often be discerned only by reading more broadly and extensively in the textual sources in which fragments or anecdotes directly focused on the Pharisees or Jesus' conflict with them appear in narrative context.

Critical evaluation and use of texts as sources require a sense of what they are *about*. The histories of Josephus are about the high priestly and Herodian rulers of the Judeans, and later also of the Galileans, and their dependency on their Roman overlords. The Pharisees and scribal groups are "bit-players" as representatives (or dissident resistors) of the rulers in Jerusalem and/or Galilee. Previously unknown texts from Qumran that mention "the seekers of smooth things," thought to be a reference to the Pharisees, are about the priestly-scribal community of a renewed Mosaic covenant that rejected the upstart Hasmonean high priests and moved out into the wilderness in protest. The Gospel stories are about Jesus as a popular (Israelite) prophet engaged in a renewal of the people of Israel in their constituent village communities in opposition to and by the high priestly and Roman rulers. The Pharisees and scribes appear in the Gospel stories as representatives of the high priestly rulers.

Second: Recognition of what these sources are about requires more comprehensive and more precise investigation of the turbulent history of the people and rulers of Judea and Galilee in the second-temple period, including the institutional forms by which the people were ruled and the conflicts within those institutions and their conflicts with the people they ruled. From Josephus' histories and texts such as Nehemiah it is clear that the Jerusalem temple-state was the institutional form of rule in Judea sponsored by and representative of a sequence of imperial rulers. It was not simply "religious," but was inseparably political-economic-religious. This recognition leads to a critical re-reading of other texts, such as Sirach, that offer information about the social-political structure and relations in the Judean temple-state, including the position and role of learned scribes as servants of the high priestly rulers. This information facilitates a critical re-reading of Josephus' accounts of the Pharisees and Sadducees and other scribal groups in his histories of the struggles of and within the Judean temple-state under the Hasmoneans and Roman imperial rule. Recognition of what the Gospel stories are about requires more precise investigation of the distinctive history of the Galileans, which differed considerably from that of the Judeans. And recognition of the distinctive history of the Galileans facilitates a more historically informed reading of the story of Jesus' mission and his conflict with the Pharisees and scribes.

Third: During the last several decades a number of lines of new research have developed into ancient communications media. Each of these largely independent lines of research poses challenges to standard concepts in the fields of ancient Jewish history and biblical studies. These researches, moreover, turn out to be interrelated, and if brought together, undermine long-standing basic assumptions as well as controlling constructs in the two interrelated fields. Most fundamental are the findings that communications in the ancient world were predominantly oral. Literacy was severely limited, to around 10% in the Roman Empire and mainly to scribal circles (at roughly 3%) in Palestine.

These findings are compounded by recent research into scribal training and practice: even scribes, who were trained in writing and reading, learned texts by repeated recitation, so that texts were "written on the tablet of their heart" (that is, their memory). Close text-critical examination of the MSS of books later included in the Hebrew Bible that were found among the DSS found (1) that there were multiple versions of these books and (2) that each version was still developing in late second-temple times.[1] The challenges to fundamental assumptions in these scholarly fields are profound: there were evidently no standardized texts of what were thought to be already standard "biblical" books. We can no longer simply assume that "the Jews" in Judea, most of whom could not read anyhow, were familiar with the Torah. The books of the Pentateuch can no longer be taken as evidence for what Judeans in general believed and practiced. It will be necessary in Volume 1, therefore, to investigate how some of the interrelated lines of new research challenge standard assumptions (1) about Judean texts that supposedly already had the singular authority of Scripture in late second temple times and (2) about the role of the Pharisees and scribes in what we think of generally as Judaism.[2] Correspondingly, it will be necessary in Volume 2, on

1. See Ulrich, *Dead Sea Scrolls*.

2. Meeting the challenges posed by the lines of recent research into ancient communication media, we face a problem of changing or at least adjusting some of the terms/concepts in the fields of biblical studies and ancient Judean history that are embedded in modern print-culture. The term "text" standardly refers to a written text (that must be read). Ancient Judean scribes, having learned texts by repeated recitation, thought of the texts as "written on the tablet of their heart" (Prov 3:3), that is, "inscribed" in their memory—as well as inscribed on heavy and cumbersome scrolls of parchment or papyrus. At least provisionally I am choosing to use "text" for a story or psalm or saga, etc., that was written and/or oral-memorial, recited from memory on occasion. It is standard in these fields to think of the Bible/Scriptures as books. But "book" is at best a metaphor when applied to a written text in the ancient world. As a reminder of this I will often place the term in quote marks, "book." Further clarification will be necessary as we take the recent researches into ancient communications media into account in the chapters below. See the highly suggestive analysis of Eva Mroczek, "Thinking Digitally

the basis of these lines of new research, to reason toward what may now be valid assumptions about the culture of Jesus and the villagers among whom he worked and the way in which that may affect how we can understand his conflict with the Pharisees and scribes.

Review of Changes in Recent Scholarship on the Pharisees

The last fifty years have experienced vigorous discussion and debate about the Pharisees in late second-temple Judean life. This has been a dramatic change from the previous century.

From the mid-nineteenth century to the mid-twentieth century, most Jewish and non-Jewish scholars believed that Pharisaism was dominant in (Palestinian) Judaism during the late second-temple period.[3] This understanding was based partly on a certain reading of some text-fragments from Josephus (esp. *Ant.* 13.288, 298, 401–402; 18.15), that the Pharisees were "popular" with "the masses," which enabled them to impose their views even on the high priestly "leaders" in the period before the destruction of Jerusalem and the temple. Among the three "sects" (or "philosophies") of Judaism, the Pharisees were dominant and the only one to survive the Roman destruction of Jerusalem and the temple. Thus the Pharisees became determinative of "normative" Judaism.

This was closely interrelated with the assumption of direct continuity from the Pharisees to the rabbis. Accordingly fragments from rabbinic texts were assumed to provide good evidence for the views of the Pharisees and were the primary source for the Pharisees and for Judaism generally. Gradually it was recognized that extracts from Josephus' histories and text-fragments from the New Testament texts were also sources for the Pharisees. The Gospels, of course, had long been a principal basis of Christian theological stereotypes of the Pharisees and of Christian anti-Judaism. Scholarly studies of the Pharisees, however, proceeded by combining text-fragments and anecdotes from one or more of these three general sources into composite portrayals. The principal debate was over the extent to which the Pharisees were overly legalistic and obsessed with ritual law, a debate focused mainly on text-fragments of the Mishnah that were sometimes compared with fragments from the Gospels, all taken at more or less face value.

About the Dead Sea Scrolls."

3. Among the many reviews of the older consensus view of the Pharisees and how it began to change, a concise summary with references is D. R. Schwartz, "MMT, Josephus, and the Pharisees," 67–69.

The Sources and the Development of a More Critical Approach

The development of ever more critical approaches to the three general sources for the Pharisees—rabbinic texts, the works of Josephus, and the New Testament—and for the conflict between the Pharisees and Jesus has been the principal factor leading to significant shifts in Jewish and Christian understanding of them.

By the 1970s scholars were developing more critical approaches to the textual sources, recognizing that text fragments reflected the perspective and agendas of their producers. They saw that the fragments from different sources presented different understandings of the Pharisees and this led to debates about their role and influence, while not changing the assumption that the overall context was ancient/early Judaism.

In a short but broad, sweeping article on "Palestinian Judaism in the First Century" (1956), Morton Smith had asserted that Judaism was swarming with sects. The Pharisees, while influential, were only one of the sects and had no real hold on either the masses or the high priestly "government."[4] Rabbinic literature is biased in favor of them and Josephus' histories are inconsistent. The few passages in the earlier *Jewish War,* (supposedly) more historically reliable, say nothing about their supposed influence. The few passages in the later *Jewish Antiquities*, however, are propaganda to persuade the Romans to entrust the leadership of the post-70 Jewish population in Judea to the Pharisees.[5] After Smith's student Jacob Neusner brought this thesis to wider scholarly attention it gained influence.[6]

More important for its impact on interpretation of the Pharisees, meanwhile, Neusner developed a sophisticated method for reading rabbinic texts. In the early 1970s he applied this to the rabbinic traditions of the Pharisees in ways that decisively undermined the earlier consensus assumption of considerable continuity between the Pharisees of the second temple period and the later rabbis.[7] Rabbinic texts were compiled centuries after

---

4. Smith, "Palestinian Judaism in the First Century," 81.

5. Smith, "Palestinian Judaism in the First Century," 74–77.

6. Neusner, *From Politics to Piety*, 45–66; and repeated in subsequent publications, such as Neusner, "Josephus's Pharisees." Goodblatt, "The Place of the Pharisees in First Century Judaism," provides a careful critical review of the debate over Smith's thesis and Neusner's variation. As Goodblatt notes (40), Neusner's argument consists mainly of quotations in English translation of passages from Josephus.

7. Neusner, *The Rabbinic Traditions about the Pharisees before 70*; Neusner, *From Politics to Piety*. Significant criticism in D. R. Schwartz, "Josephus and Nicolaus on the Pharisees"; and A. I. Baumgarten, "Rivkin and Neusner on the Pharisees." As Baumgarten states (117), the crucial lasting effect of the Smith-Neusner approach is that the rabbis are no longer "assumed simply to equal Pharisees."

the time of the Pharisees. They have their own perspectives and agenda. They provide information about their own concerns more than accurate historical information about the Pharisees in earlier generations.[8] No longer could even early rabbinic references to or citations of (presumed) Pharisees be taken as evidence without systematic critical analysis.[9]

Neusner's work also raised awareness that the other two general sources for the Pharisees, Josephus' histories and New Testament texts, were composed after the Great Revolt and the Roman destruction of the Jerusalem temple. Passages about the Pharisees had been shaped by later concerns. His pioneering work was also instrumental in beginning to deal with the fragments or anecdotes in each of the general sources separately before then moving to conclusions about the history of the Pharisees.

Neusner's work also contributed to the growing critical recognition that we have not just general sources (in which relevant fragments are found), broadly speaking, but *sets* of sources. The much later and voluminous rabbinic texts are an extraordinarily complex set of compilations of traditions with earlier layers in the many tractates of the Mishnah and Tosefta and later layers in the Talmuds that build on the earlier ones. Josephus produced two different sustained historical works, decades apart, each with its own agenda and emphases, and the *Life* as an apparent appendix to the later *Antiquities*. There are four different Gospel stories of the mission of Jesus, each evidently produced by a different Jesus movement with its own perspective and agenda. Scholars came to recognize that each text in a set of sources might have a distinctive perspective and agenda that affect the relevant fragments or anecdotes.

Christian interpreters of the Gospels generated studies of the portrayal of the Pharisees in particular Gospels.[10] Some of these exposed how the castigation of the scribes and Pharisees as "hypocrites" were the bases of developing Christian anti-Judaism. On the accounts from Josephus, Steve Mason

---

8. The Holocaust led Jewish scholars to greater awareness that the Roman destruction of Judea had been a massive catastrophe that would have made impossible a simple continuity from Pharisees to rabbinic Judaism. Also the Holocaust decisively delegitimated anti-Semitism and forced Christian scholars to deal with the implications of Jesus' attacks on the Pharisees and the tragic influence of the Gospels' accounts. This further motivated Jesus- and gospel-scholars to distance the attacks in the Gospels from the "historical Jesus." Another effect was the virtual disappearance of the topic of "Jesus and the Pharisees" in the surge of books and articles on the historical Jesus in the 1990s.

9. This gave Christian interpreters, already woefully unprepared to deal with rabbinic texts, an excuse to give even less attention to rabbinic texts that might be pertinent to the Pharisees—and just read Neusner's conclusions.

10. With the effect (and aim?) of relieving Jesus of responsibility for anti-Judaism in the aftermath of the Holocaust.

took an important next step toward a more critical approach by focusing on the passages mentioning the Pharisees in each of the different works of Josephus, the earlier *Jewish War* and the later *Antiquities* and the *Life*. He attempted to discern the significant features and Josephus' perspective in each work.[11] Mason's distinctive contribution was his recognition of the Flavian imperial patronage of Josephus and the imperial cultural context in Rome where he was writing that compounded and complicated his perspective as a wealthy Judean priest and his proud claim of Hasmonean descent. He insisted on the important procedural principle of investigating the perspective and view of each source in general; then he focused on the few fragments that mention the Pharisees. He was reluctant to move to reconstruction of historical relations and events on the basis of those fragments.

Meanwhile, the discovery of the Dead Sea Scrolls and the reconstruction, translation, and interpretation of key previously unknown texts have added a fourth set of sources for the Pharisees. Some passages in the *pesherim* to certain prophetic texts (applications of passages or terms to the situation of the people who produced the *pesherim*) offer confirmation of some of Josephus' accounts. More important, perhaps, are a wider range of previously unknown texts that indicate how a scribal-priestly community contemporary with the early Pharisees appropriated texts of torah.[12]

Characteristic of the scholarly use of all these sets of sources was the deeply ingrained habit of focusing on the limited passages or text-fragments that pertained to the Pharisees or the Pharisees and Jesus taken out of broader literary (narrative and rhetorical) context. Fragments or "data" from one source were then compared and/or combined with those from other sources to establish some point about or view of the Pharisees. It only gradually occurred to scholars that *the sets of sources*, and perhaps particular sources within a set, *might have been interested in different aspects of the Pharisees*. While including consideration of the (supposed) perspective of Josephus or of a particular Gospel, however, both Mason and Gospel scholars continued in the standard procedural habit of focusing on the passages or text-fragments directly pertinent to the Pharisees without attending to the broader narratives and attempting to discern what the overall narratives are about.

---

11. Mason, *Flavius Josephus on the Pharisees*; Mason lays out his aims and procedure on pp. 40–43.

12. See further the summary of the implication of the texts from Qumran by D. R. Schwartz, "MMT, Josephus, and the Pharisees," 72–80.

A More Complex Approach Adequate to the Sources

The steps taken in recent decades toward a more critical approach to the sources for the Pharisees have been crucial, but stop well short of a more complex approach adequate to the sources. It is important to know the dates, the perspectives, agenda, and bias of particular texts. It is helpful to discern Josephus' viewpoint and rhetorical judgments in his short accounts about the Pharisees in the *War* and *Antiquities*, respectively. As scholars in the fields of Jewish history and biblical studies begin to work more and more as historians of antiquity, however, it is important to critically assess the sources more comprehensively. As the fields of ancient Jewish history and biblical studies have diversified they have tended to become an array of separate subfields of research, knowledge, and interpretation devoted to particular "books," figures, issues, or "criticisms." Specialists in particular subfields find it difficult to "keep up" with developments in others. More comprehensive understanding of the Pharisees in historical context, however, may depend on bringing together the developing specialties.

Discovering the Narrative Contexts of Text-Fragments

The 1980s and 1990s saw increasing recognition that many texts used as historical sources are sustained narratives. To understand particular passages that pertain to the Pharisees it is essential to appreciate both the sustained narrative and the narrative sequence in sources leading to and following pertinent passages as the contexts in which they can be understood. This has not yet made much headway in use of the sources for the Pharisees.[13]

Considering the wider narrative contexts of Josephus' presentations of the Hasmoneans and their interaction with the Pharisees, for example, would result in a broader critical grasp of the information Josephus may provide on the Pharisees in their interaction with the Hasmoneans. In both the *War* and the *Antiquities*, his sustained narrative of the rise, decline, and disintegration of the Hasmonean dynasty of high priests is a major step in the overall historical narrative. His focus is always mainly on the rulers of the Judeans, with the Pharisees as mere "bit-players."

Still following the standard approach focused more narrowly on the passages that mention the Pharisees, Mason found that in the *Antiquities*

---

13. Interpretation of Josephus passages is not unique. Many studies focusing on or using sayings of Jesus against the scribes and/or Pharisees in a particular Gospel have not yet considered even the immediate narrative context, much less the broader context of the Gospel story as a whole.

as well as in the *War* Josephus is sharply critical of the Pharisees. He concluded that Josephus blames the Pharisees as power-hungry meddlers who weakened the Hasmonean rulers.[14] Recognition of Josephus' anti-Pharisee polemics is surely useful to historians attempting to evaluate sources and move toward historical reconstruction. The motives that Josephus polemically attributes to the Pharisees, however, should not be mistaken as the sole cause of a sequence of events. Consideration of the broader narrative would likely help supply the contributing factors in a multi-factor and multi-causal historical sequence recounted in the narrative. In the narratives prior and subsequent to passages on the Pharisees, Josephus recounts actions by Hasmonean high priests that would have motivated the Pharisees' actions that would have been blameworthy only to a partisan of Hasmonean and other rulers. Awareness of this more extensive narrative would be even more helpful to historians for historical reconstruction.

Yet another factor in the critical approach to the sources for the Pharisees that must be considered in appreciating Josephus' accounts as sources is his reliance on earlier sources. This makes it all the more important not to focus on text-fragments (which might be from earlier sources) without considering the wider narratives. Ancient historians, including Josephus, relied heavily on earlier historians and other texts. Among the sources on which Josephus had drawn heavily was Nicolaus of Damascus, historian in the court of Herod the Great, who evidently had reasons to be critical of the Pharisees.[15]

A far-reaching development in New Testament studies was the "discovery" of the Gospels as stories, as sustained narratives with plots and subplots of interrelated episodes.[16] Two aspects of the discovery that the Gospels are narratives have significant implications for understanding them as sources for the Pharisees and for the Pharisees' conflict with Jesus.[17] One would be the immediate narrative sequence of fragments on the scribes and/or Pharisees. In the Markan story, for example, Jesus' indictment of the scribes for "devouring widows' houses" is followed immediately by the

---

14. Mason, *Josephus on the Pharisees*, esp. 251, 253, 258–59. As A. I. Baumgarten, "Rivkin and Neusner," 124n39, notes, "Mason consistently tries to portray the Pharisees in an unfavorable light (an understatement). But, Josephus' position, in my view, is too complex to be explained by any such simple solution."

15. D. R. Schwartz, in "Josephus and Nicolaus on the Pharisees," argued that the key passages in the *Antiquities* that (supposedly) presented the Pharisees as influential with the masses in ways that might lead to resistance to rulers (13.288; 13.401–402; 17.401–402) were derived from Nicolaus. Josephus' treatment of the Pharisees was more complex than it appears in the Smith-Neusner thesis.

16. Kelber, *Mark's Story of Jesus*.

17. Provisional treatment in Horsley, *Hearing the Whole Story*.

poor widow giving the last coppers of her "living" to the temple, followed by Jesus' declaration that the temple is about to be destroyed. The other would be a critical reading of the overall narrative. In the Markan story the scribes and Pharisees appear again and again as the representatives of the high priestly heads of the temple-state who "come down from (their base in) Jerusalem." An early episode has the Pharisees conspiring with the Herodians to destroy Jesus. Then in Jesus' climactic confrontation with the high priestly rulers in Jerusalem the Pharisees' and Herodians' attempt to entrap Jesus with the question whether it is "lawful" to yield up tribute to the divine Caesar. The overall Markan story has the Pharisees and scribes concerned about far more weighty (political-economic) matters than eating with sinners and hand-washing before meals. The same is true of the other Gospel stories. Yet another aspect of the discovery of the Gospels as stories is that they may include rhetorical touches such as irony, humor, and mockery. Touches of mockery, for example, need to be critically discerned in order to understand the principal concerns of a story.

Political Forms, Structure, and Relations Evident in the Sources

Insofar as interpreters were thinking of the Pharisees in the general amorphous context of Judaism, it rarely occurred to them to consider their social-political position and role(s) in relation to other Judeans or the broader political structure of Judean society that is often indicated in the sources. For starters, this could be as simple as critical consideration of what particular terms in the sources were referring to. Mason's work on his dissertation and first book pointed to one way this might be possible. He took good advantage of the recent compilation of a concordance to Josephus' works that made possible focused "word-studies" of key terms in each work and in all of his works that help clarify the meaning and references of those terms in particular passages.

His word-studies, however, did not extend to terms for social-political relations in ancient Jerusalem and Judea. As Mason points out about Josephus scholarship in general, previous interpreters had been heavily dependent on and influenced by Thackeray's (1927) translation of the *War*. His translation often exacerbated Josephus' elitist attitudes toward ordinary people. Josephus himself clearly despised ordinary people. Often exaggerating Josephus' attitude, Thackeray further demeaned them, evidently without critical consideration of how Josephus used key terms and what they refer to. As a wealthy priest active in Jerusalem who would have been familiar with the social structure of Judea, however, Josephus is fairly consistent in using two particular terms alternately for the people of the temple-city, *demos/ demotikos* and *plethos*. Thackeray often translates these as "the masses" or even "the mob" in accounts that include statements of how the Pharisees had influence with the populace, evidently referring to the people of the city, not Judeans generally.[18] Josephus has other terms or phrases for the people of the countryside, villagers who were physically and socially removed from the more intense interaction between the high priestly rulers and the Pharisees (and/or Sadducees) and the people of the temple-city. At the beginning of the Hasmonean dynasty, of course, the population of Jerusalem would still have been so small that it is difficult to imagine there could have been "masses" of people.

The Gospels of Mark and Matthew have the scribes and Pharisees appear in Galilean villages to which they "come down" from their base in Jerusalem. Toward the beginning of the Lukan Gospel story (5:17) "Pharisees and teachers of the law (torah?) come from every village in Galilee and Judea" as well as from Jerusalem. As will be discussed in Volume 2, this Lukan passage appears to be a later projection onto the mission of Jesus in Galilee. More dependable historically are Josephus' texts that represent the Pharisees as active only in Jerusalem. A more critical sense of how he portrays their relations with the people of the city might enable us to make more informed critical judgment about whether they would have visited villages in Judea and, even less likely, later in Galilee, ninety miles from their base in Jerusalem.[19] During the lifetime and mission of Jesus Herod Antipas was the Rome-imposed ruler in Galilee, and the Jerusalem temple-state presumably no longer had jurisdiction there. Standard assumptions about the Pharisees as active in Galilee in late second temple times may have been influenced by rabbinic circles having relocated there following the devastation of Judea in the Roman suppression of the Bar Kokhba Revolt.

Rabbinic texts offer less by way of direct information about social relations in second temple times. The texts do, however, include legendary memories of "Pharisees" and "Sadducees" or of the high priestly families' exploitation and abuse of the people. They also include what appear to be foundational legends of the rabbinic movement in the rabbinic academy or council at Yavneh. While these legends have been generally accepted as reliable accounts, there have been critical studies of the legends about the

---

18. The elitist perspective of scholars thus compounds the elitist perspective of ancient intellectuals and blocks information the latter indicate in the terms they use.

19. The three Pharisees in the delegation sent by the high priestly council in Jerusalem to "recall" Josephus as their military officer charged with controlling the revolt in Galilee in 66–67 CE are hardly evidence for Pharisees regularly visiting the villages of Galilee.

"academy" at Yavneh.[20] There are also studies of whether and when rabbinic circles were attempting to influence the lives of the people in towns and villages, particularly in Galilee where rabbinic circles and their leaders had located.[21]

In order to read and evaluate the sources for the Pharisees in literary context, however, it is important but not enough to discern their respective perspectives and agendas and carry out rhetorical criticism. It is also important to read and analyze Josephus' histories and the Gospels with at least an elementary sense of the political-economic-religious structure and dynamics of the society headed by the temple-state that Josephus or a Gospel is portraying. Then these more comprehensive readings can become additional bases for moving from critical evaluation of the sources to better informed construction of the social-political position and role of the Pharisees in the temple-state that ruled the temple city and the countryside.

Conceptualizing the Pharisees and Their Historical Context

It has long been standard in the fields of Jewish history and biblical studies to understand the Pharisees (and the Pharisees and Jesus) and their context in terms of religion, without critical consideration of the concrete historical (i.e. political-economic-religious) context in which the sources portray them. In both fields the Pharisees are understood as the leaders of Judaism and/or a religious sect in Judaism in the late second temple period.

In modern Western culture it has become a standard assumption that religion is separate from political-economic reality and that religion in a historical situation can be understood in separation from the politics—or better, the political-economic structure and dynamics—of that situation. This separation has been institutionally reinforced by the "separation of church and state" in the United States and several other countries. The separation became further institutionalized in the historical development of the academic "division of labor" in which biblical texts and related matters were studied in Christian theological schools and Jewish institutions of learning. From those evolved the departments of Jewish studies and religion in colleges and universities. The separation is further institutionalized in the Library of Congress system of classification and in the agenda of professional

---

20. Saldarini, "Johanan ben Zakkai's Escape from Jerusalem"; Schaefer, "Die Flucht Rabban Johanan b. Zakkais"; Levine, *Rabbinic Class of Roman Palestine*.

21. Brief treatment in Cohen, *From the Maccabees to the Mishnah*, esp. 221–24; more extensive studies are Levine, *Rabbinic Class of Roman Palestine*; and Hezser, *Social Structure of the Rabbinic Movement*.

associations such as the Society of Biblical Literature, in which many program units have names that include the synthetic constructs "early Judaism" and "early Christianity." All such institutional arrangements confirm and confine: what is being studied is religion. Thus (early) Judaism and its twin, (early) Christianity, have long been basic controlling constructs in the fields of Jewish history and biblical studies. It has long been simply assumed that the "books" of the Hebrew Bible (Old Testament) were the Scripture of Judaism and the "books" of the New Testament were expressions of early Christianity.

In ancient life, however, whether in village communities, societies headed by city-states or temple-states, and/or empires, religion and politics and economics were not separate and cannot be appropriately understood in separation.[22] Thus the lumping together of different texts and movements and figures and institutions into the constructs of "(early) Judaism" and "(early) Christianity" creates serious limitations, distortion, and confusion for historical understanding.[23] These constructs simply block discernment of different institutions, diverse groups and movements, social-political-economic relations of power, and structural and other conflicts.

In attempting to understand the Pharisees in their historical context it seems only appropriate to ask *what the (now four) principal sets of sources are about*. And in investigation and reconstruction of the Pharisees in their historical context it would be appropriate that our guiding terms and concepts be appropriate to what the sources are about, and not broad synthetic constructs into which anything and everything from late second-temple times are lumped together. We may well be suspicious of "models" built up from a broad range of comparative studies. But comparisons with sources from and for other, comparable societies and historical situations might be helpful.

From the perspective of a wealthy Judean priest who had become a protege of the Flavian dynasty in Rome, Josephus focuses his histories on the interaction of the high priestly and Herodian rulers of late second-temple Judea and the imperial warlords and rulers who installed them and maintained them in power. The first books of his earlier *War* are about the

---

22. Goodblatt, in "The Pharisees in First Century Judaism," 24–25, was one of the few scholars who recognized the problem of academic discussion of the Pharisees as a (sect of) religion: "Did ancient Judaism allow for a sharp separation between religion and politics . . . ?"

23. Boyarin, *Judaism*, 17–22, suggests avoiding or discarding the later construct of Judaism. This would enable us to be both more comprehensive and more precise in references to particular texts, events, locations, institutions, power-relations, and political conflicts.

rise and disintegration of the Hasmonean dynasty, in which the Pharisees play a short-term role in the Hasmonean administration, and then the rise and the Roman appointment of the military strong-man Herod as king, in which the Pharisees make an appearance. The second book of the *War* focuses on high priestly rule of Judea under the oversight of Roman governors that deteriorates into turmoil, and then the eruption of revolt in Jerusalem followed by the widespread revolt by the Judeans and the Galileans in the countryside. Books three through seven then recount at length the course of the Great Revolt, largely of Galilean and Judean peasants, Josephus' own exploits in supposedly organizing the people's defenses against the anticipated Roman attack, and the stages of the systematic Roman reconquest and destruction of Jerusalem and the temple.

When the much longer *Antiquities* comes to the second-temple period, it is about high priestly rulers of the temple-state under a succession of imperial regimes and then about the tyrannical rule of Herod and the exploitative high priestly aristocracy and the often disruptive Roman governors. Josephus presents the Pharisees in a significant role in the Hasmonean regime and under the later high priestly rule, but only cameo resistance under Herod. And he mentions protests by other scribal groups as well as several popular revolts and movements that the rulers suppressed militarily. The *Life*, following a brief account of Josephus' own ancestry and early life, focuses on the origins of the popular revolt and mostly on his few months of command in Galilee attempting to control the revolt by "the Galileans." He devotes much of his narrative to the attempt by the Jerusalem council of high priests and leading Pharisees to replace him. In sum, Josephus' histories of the later second-temple period focus on the high priestly rulers and their relations with the Hellenistic and Roman rulers. They include several occasional short accounts or references to (the) Pharisees, usually in connection with the operations of the temple-state, often in conflict with the rulers, from the rise of the Hasmoneans to the Great Revolt.

Not only is there no term or concept that might be translated "Judaism" in these lengthy texts. It is also unclear how the construct Judaism might help us understand these accounts of the history of the Jerusalem temple-state and of the Judeans and the Galileans in Roman-ruled Palestine during these centuries. At certain points in his narrative in *War* and again in *Antiquities* Josephus inserts digressions on how there were three main "philosophies" of the Judeans, the Pharisees, the Sadducees, and the Essenes (and in one digression he adds "the Fourth Philosophy"). These are clearly apologetic passages aimed at explaining the way of life and customs of what can be recognized as the educated scribal-priestly elite of the Judeans to his elite Hellenistic audience in terms with which they are familiar. But there is nothing in these descriptions that suggests they were all somehow *sects* of *Judaism*, as they continue to be conceptualized and classified in standard scholarly discussion.[24]

Key texts of the Qumran community are about a priestly and scribal group's withdrawal from the temple-state in protest of the "Wicked Priest," who had taken control of it, to form a new exodus and renewed covenantal community in the wilderness. A few passages refer to "seekers of smooth things" (presumably the Pharisees). On the one hand, they are castigated as closely associated with the "Wicked Priest," who presumably headed the temple-state. On the other hand, the "seekers of smooth things" are killed by "the young Lion," evidently the High Priest Alexander Jannaeus, for summoning the Seleucid ruler Demetrius for aid in opposing him.

The Gospel stories, like other texts later collected in the New Testament, have standardly been classified as "Christian," expressions of Christianity, as opposed to Judaism. More recent critical examination of particular Gospel stories, however, recognize that they are deeply rooted in Israelite tradition. Indeed, they present Jesus' mission and the resulting Jesus movements among the Galilean and nearby villagers as a continuation of Israelite tradition/history. The Markan and Matthean stories, perhaps also the Lukan and Johannine, present themselves and their communities of origin as still

---

24. A. I. Baumgarten, *Flourishing of Jewish Sects*, presents a comprehensive summary of social-scientific studies of sects from the 1970s and 1980s and then draws both analogies and contrasts with how he understands the Pharisees, Sadducees, the Essenes, and the Qumran community. He defines a sect as "a *voluntary association of protest, which utilizes boundary marking mechanisms . . . to distinguish between its own members and those otherwise normally regarded as belonging to the same national or religious entity*" (7). Sects "*cut themselves off* from the larger institutions of their society." According to the somewhat limited sources for these Jewish "philosophies," however, while the Essenes/Qumran community might fit the definition, the Pharisees and the Sadducees do not, insofar as they did not "cut themselves off" from the Jerusalem temple-state. The Pharisees did resist some of the Hasmonean high priests and the violations and repressions of Herod. Baumgarten does discern a number of important distinguishing features of these groups, for example, that they "inhabited the same intellectual and religious universe of discourse" (34; cf. 64). That feature, along with their focus on the laws, suggests rather that they were the among the educated elite in Judean society in which literacy was extremely limited, as he noted in chap. 3. These aspects suggest that these groups served, or had formerly served, the same functions in the temple-state as had earlier scribes/sages, such as Ben Sira. In "Emergence of Jewish Sectarianism," Shemaryahu Talmon provides a very helpful critical review of the sociology of Max Weber and its application to "ancient Judaism." As Talmon lays out, Weber's conceptualization of religion and society, which must have been based mainly on European "society" as he knew it a century ago, simply does not apply to what can be known from critical reading of textual and other sources available since then (see esp. 597–605, 607–10).

belonging to the people of Israel.²⁵ The opposition in the Gospel stories is not between Jesus and Judaism but between Jesus-and-movement and the rulers, that is, the Roman governor, the Roman-client high priestly rulers, and their scribal and Pharisaic representatives. In his prophetic statements Jesus indicts the Pharisees for their actions in connection with their role in the operations of the temple-state. As in the histories of Josephus, so also in the Gospel stories, there is no term and concept for "Judaism." The Gospel stories are about the conflict between the mission and movement(s) of Jesus among villagers and the high priestly rulers in Jerusalem and their Pharisaic and scribal representatives, and not about a conflict between Jesus and the Pharisees as representatives of Judaism.

By contrast to the histories of Josephus and the Gospel stories of Jesus' mission among villagers, the rabbinic texts compiled long after the temple had been destroyed consist of thousands of rulings (with some anecdotes) of sages that they taught to their circles of students generation after generation, arranged by subjects. One late rabbinic memory about "King Yannai" offers a parallel to a story that Josephus tells about the Pharisees and John Hyrcanus. But only a small number of the rabbinic rulings purport to be from earlier figures thought to have been Pharisees, with more being differing rulings reportedly from the two Pharisaic schools of Hillel and Shammai. Critical rabbinic scholars conclude that the rabbis and their rulings did not have much presence—much less influence—in local village and town synagogues until centuries later.²⁶ That is when the rabbinic teachings began to serve as the more communal basis for a wider rabbinic Judaism.

This brief survey of the principal sources for the Pharisees (and the Pharisees and Jesus) indicates that the historical context was the history of the unstable temple-state in Jerusalem headed by the high priests who were attempting to control the Judeans and other peoples, while themselves negotiating with unstable imperial regimes.²⁷ The principal division and conflict indicated in both Josephus' works and the Gospels stories was between the high priestly rulers (and later the Herodian rulers) and the Judeans and other peoples they ruled (and in some cases had conquered).

25. Discussed, for example, in Saldarini, *Matthew's Christian-Jewish Community*; Horsley, *Hearing the Whole Story*; Horsley and Thatcher, *John, Jesus, and the Renewal of Israel*; provisional treatment of the Lukan story in Horsley, *Empowering the People*, chap. 10.

26. E.g., Cohen, *From Maccabees to Mishnah*, 221; S. Schwartz, *Imperialism and Jewish Society*.

27. It is the recognition and investigation of their interactions with the high priests at the head of the temple-state in Jerusalem that has been missing in studies of the Pharisees. I attempted to fill this lacuna in research in a series of papers and articles from 1991 to 2007, now collected in *The Pharisees and the Temple-State of Judea*.

This continuing division appeared dramatically in the Maccabean Revolt (160s BCE), the persistent resistance to the Rome-designated king Herod's conquest of his future subjects (40–37 BCE), the widespread revolts by Galileans and Judeans at Herod's death (4 BCE), and the Great Revolt against the high priests and the Romans (66–70 CE).[28] The Pharisees themselves appear as advisers of the high priestly rulers and administrators of the temple-state who at points were rejected by or resisted the high priestly rulers or the rule of the King Herod. At crisis points in the conflictual history Josephus also mentions resistance to the rulers by (other) scribal groups whom he describes in terms similar to his portrayal of the Pharisees.

In the last several decades a number of critical historical investigations have sought more comprehensive and precise knowledge of the history of the people and the rulers and their regimes in Palestine under the Hellenistic and early Roman empires—knowledge that includes the structural conflicts and dynamics, the regional differences, the changing institutional forms and arrangements, the function of scribal circles, and the forms of popular protests and movements.[29] These studies have helped clear the way for taking into consideration the concrete structural conflicts and dynamics of the changing institutional forms and arrangements in late second temple times in which the Pharisees functioned, according to the sources. On this basis it may be possible to discern the role and function of the Pharisees and other circles of learned scribes or sages and to better understand the conflict between the Pharisees and Jesus' mission.

The Chapters of Volume 1

The histories of Josephus, the principal sources for the position, role, and history of the Pharisees and (other) scribes, are about the struggles of the

---

28. Other evidence includes the two kinds of popular movements mentioned by Josephus that took distinctively Israelite form, the movements led by popularly acclaimed "kings" in the revolts of 4 BCE and 67–70 CE and the movements led by popular prophets (like Moses-Joshua) in mid-first century. See Horsley with J. S. Hanson, *Bandits, Prophets, and Messiahs*, more fully documented with analysis in the series of my articles behind the book. These articles are now accessible, collected in *Politics, Conflict, and Movements in First Century Palestine*.

29. For example, Goodman, *Ruling Class of Judea*; Horsley, "High Priests and the Politics of Roman Palestine"; Horsley with J. S. Hanson, *Bandits, Prophets, and Messiahs*; Horsley, *Jesus and the Spiral of Violence*; Horsley, *Galilee: History, Politics, People*; Horsley, *Jesus and the Politics of Roman Palestine*; and S. Schwartz, *Imperialism and Jewish Society*. Such studies offer alternatives to the previously standard synthetic constructs that have been blocking recognition of the complexity, diversity, and conflict in historical events and developments.

high priestly rulers as heads of the Judean temple-state in their shifting relations with their imperial patrons, on the one hand, and the people they ruled, on the other, as noted above. The limited accounts of the Pharisees present them as advisors and administrators of the high priestly aristocracy and/or as dissidents who resist the high priestly rulers. So it would presumably be helpful in understanding the origin and function of the Pharisees under the Hasmoneans to know what had been the traditional political-economic-religious structure of the Judean temple-state and the society it ruled, and the position and function of learned scribes (sages) in particular.

Chapter 1 discusses Judean society headed by the High Priest, the temple-state, and the role of learned scribes as represented in the instructional speeches of the famous Jerusalem scribe Jesus ben Sira just prior to the severe crisis of the Hellenizing reform and the Maccabean Revolt. This is followed by an account of the reaction to the Seleucid invasion to enforce the Hellenizing reform by some scribal circles who believed the dominant high priests leading the Hellenizing reform were abandoning the traditional Judean covenantal law (as portrayed in the so-called "apocalyptic" texts of Dan 7, 8, 10–12; and 1 Enoch 85–90). This chapter is intended to set the stage for chapters 4 through 7 that explore the history of the restored temple-state and the Pharisees' and scribes' role in, and at times resistance to, the high priestly and Roman rulers.

Since Josephus presents the Pharisees as experts in the laws and it became a standard generalization that they were the principal interpreters of the laws, it seems important to investigate how scribes learned and cultivated the laws and what all may have been included in the laws in late second-temple times.[30] Several lines of recent research into ancient communications media are now undermining what have been the standard assumption in biblical studies so deeply rooted in modern print-culture. Chapter 2 summarizes these lines of recent research, particularly the recent studies of scribal training and practice, and their implications for the Pharisees and scribes and their expertise in the laws. Some of these recent researches and the texts discovered in the Dead Sea Scrolls are challenging the long-standing assumption that the Torah, in the five books of the Pentateuch, had become (the sole authoritative) Scripture already in late second temple times. Chapter 3 will explore this challenge and examine what all may have been included in the laws and customs and ancestral traditions in which the Pharisees and other scribes were known for their expertise.

---

30. See in the collection of incisive essays in Kelber, *Imprints, Voiceprint, and Footprints of Memory*, 434–40.

The ensuing chapters in Volume 1 that have been set up by chapter 1 will then focus on the historical context of successive rulers and the role that the Pharisees and certain groups of (other) scribes played in the temple-state under the rule of the high priests and Herod and the Romans.

The examination will start in chapter 4 at the end of the Pharisees' history of involvement in the Jerusalem temple-state as the Great Revolt against Roman rule erupted, after which they disappeared from history with the Roman destruction of the temple and the temple-state. The point of beginning at the end is to show that, contrary to earlier claims, the Pharisees had not withdrawn from politics and become a mere "eating club." In fact Josephus, who was a participant in the events of the beginning of the Great Revolt describes how "the leading Pharisees" worked closely with the leading high priests who remained in Jerusalem at the outbreak of the revolt in a ruling council that attempted to hold the lid on the revolt. For the leading Pharisees to have been so prominent as the partners of the high priests in the attempt to control the revolt means that they must have effectively consolidated their position in the temple-state in the preceding decades. Chapter 4 also includes an important critical review of Josephus' opening autobiographical statement (in *Life* 12) that has been misread as an indication that he was himself a Pharisee. He states rather that as he became involved in political life in Jerusalem he had to recognize that it operated according to the views of the Pharisees.

Chapters 5 through 7 then examine closely the history of the Pharisees and scribes under successive earlier rulers, the Hasmoneans, Herod, and the high priests in the first century CE. Chapter 5 attempts to sort through the accounts in 1 Maccabees and especially Josephus' account in *Antiquities* to reconstruct the first steps in the restoration of the temple-state by Jonathan and Simon. Josephus' accounts suggest that the Pharisees as well as the Sadducees and Essenes originated in this general situation. Combining several clues in Josephus' accounts with a sense of how the temple-state had operated according to Ben Sira, it is possible to surmise that the early Hasmonean high priests, illegitimate as upstart common priests, would have needed the expertise of a circle of trained scribes to lend them some legitimacy and provide knowledge for the operation of the temple-state. As the Hasmonean high priests consolidated their power and launched their wars of expansion, according to Josephus' histories, we can then trace John Hyrcanus switching from the moderate Pharisees to the aristocratic Sadducees as his advisers.

In the midst of increasing popular protest expanding into active resistance, the Pharisees then evidently joined the popular revolt against Alexander Jannaeus, who brutally killed many, evidently including Pharisees, and drove many into exile. In a dramatic reversal, his wife and successor, Alexandra Salome, restored them as "the true administrators" of the temple-state, who sought to bring Jannaeus' military officers to justice for their role in the killings. For her part, the queen attempted to appease the military officers under the leadership of her more war-like older son, Aristobulus, by allowing them to "withdraw" to the fortresses throughout the expanded territory ruled by Jerusalem—which only led to civil war between the rival Hasmonean factions and the Roman invasion to impose order.

After many years of Hasmonean civil war compounded by the Empire-wide Roman civil war, the Roman Senate imposed the Idumean military strong-man Herod as "King of the Judeans." While making his realm a showcase of Roman imperial rule with temples and whole cities in honor of Rome and Caesar, Herod retained the temple-state as an instrument of his own rule. He massively rebuilt the Jerusalem temple in grand Hellenistic style and appointed his own creatures, some from the diaspora, as high priests, thus expanding the high priestly aristocracy. By examining the few, uncertain, and very fragmentary accounts in Josephus' histories chapter 6 focuses on the Pharisees' attempt to mediate and mitigate the severely repressive rule of Herod. Recognizing the overwhelming military power of the Romans and their client king, they advised the people of Jerusalem to acquiesce in Herod's rule. The Pharisees' role had clearly been diminished with the temple-state subordinated to the king's regime. Yet Herod appears to have recognized that they were useful in the operation of temple affairs and, in effect, mediating his rule. But they refused to sign the loyalty oath(s) he imposed on the people, and midst the turmoil of his later reign, even entered into a palace intrigue to subvert his rule.

As Herod lay dying, other scribal teachers and their students finally dared to stage a bold protest, cutting down the golden Roman eagle that Herod had erected over a gate of the temple. These scribes and their protégés did not accept the blatant imposition of Roman rule of Judeans symbolized by the symbol of Roman power over the very entrance into the temple. Also, at some point during the repressive reign of Herod, another circle of scribes composed a series of psalms (the Psalms of Solomon), which were previously attributed to Pharisaic authorship) that condemned both the rule of the Hasmonean high priests and the Roman conquest and imposition of Herod.

Ten years later the Romans restored the high priestly aristocracy heading the temple-state to rule Judea, still including Samaria and Idumea, but not Galilee (over which they had appointed Herod Antipas), under the oversight of a Roman governor based in Caesarea. They again imposed the tribute to Caesar, to be collected by the high priests. Chapter 7 focuses on the scribal role in and resistance to the Roman imperial order in Judea. Although Josephus provides only inferences and hints, they are sufficient to detect continued Pharisaic presence. Other scribal groups, perhaps interrelated with the Pharisees, however, actively protested and began plotting against what they saw as an unacceptable political situation. Almost immediately this touched off a campaign to refuse to "render unto Caesar" led by the scribal teacher Judas from Gamla and the Pharisee Saddok. Josephus states explicitly that they agreed with the Pharisees on all matters, except that they were bolder in taking action. That they were talked down by the High Priest, Joazar, however, indicates that such scribal circles were still serving in the temple-state. From the evidence surveyed in chapter 4, during the decades leading up to the outbreak of the Great Revolt, the main body of Pharisees must have been gaining influence in the temple-state. The "leading Pharisees" immediately became prominent in the "provisional government" that attempted to control the revolt, in which Josephus himself was involved. That the Pharisees disappear from history with the Roman destruction of the Jerusalem temple is yet another indication that historically they had been the advisers and representatives of the temple-state under the expansionist Hasmonean high priests and then under Herodian and Roman rule. For the preceding two-hundred years, however, the Pharisees were actively, usually centrally, involved in the politics of the temple-state under imperial rule.

1

Conflict and Crisis in the Judean Temple-State under Imperial Rule

The learned scribe Yeshua ben Sira celebrates the grand ceremony of the High Priest Simon son of Onias presiding at festival services in the Jerusalem temple:

> When he received the portions from the hands of the priests,
>   as he stood by the hearth of the altar
>   with a garland of brothers around him,
> He was like a young cedar on Lebanon
>   surrounded by the trunks of palm trees.
> All the sons of Aaron in their splendor
>   held the Lord's offering in their hands
>   before the whole congregation of Israel . . .
> Arranging the offering to the Most High, the Almighty,
>   he poured a drink offering of the blood of the grape;
>   a pleasing odor to the Most High, the king of all.
> Then the sons of Aaron shouted;
>   . . . they sounded a mighty fanfare . . .
> Then all the people . . . fell to the ground on their faces
>   to worship their Lord, the Almighty, God Most High.
> Then the singers praised him with their voices . . .
> And the people of the Lord Most High offered their prayers . . .
> (Sir 50:12–19)

Ben Sira portrays the temple as the sanctuary where the High Priest and other "sons of Aaron" sacrificed to the Most High God before the people with great pomp and circumstance. This fits well with our modern understanding of religion and the standard scholarly picture of early Judaism as centered on sacrifice and ceremony in the temple.

The sources for ancient Judean history, however, tell of other aspects of the central institutions of temple and high priesthood. As illustrations we may take, first, one that involved the people's economic support necessary for and inseparable from the ostensibly religious institutions and, second, the political conflict that emerged in the expansionist operation of the temple-state centuries later and erupted even in a sacred ceremony in the temple itself. These illustrate that the religious aspect of the temple and high priesthood was inseparable from the economic and political aspects in ancient Judea.

Prophets active at the time the Jerusalem temple was rebuilt centuries before Ben Sira placed considerable emphasis on the economic support and function of the nascent temple-state. "Bring the full tithe into the storehouse, so that there may be food in my house," said God, according to Malachi. Whatever daily or weekly rituals and festival ceremonies might be conducted from time to time, the temple was a storehouse for agricultural produce. In fact, the people bringing a percentage of their crops to the temple was God's price, as it were, for providing rain, hence fertility, to the soil for subsequent crops (Mal 3:10; cf. Zech 8:9–13). Responding to the people's resistance to the demands for revenues and labor to support the building and operations of the temple, Haggai's prophetic pleas sound like what could only be called religious-economic extortion: if you don't render up revenues to support the temple, God will cause your crops to fail (Hag 1:7–11).[1] Haggai projected a grandiose vision, indeed an imperial scenario: "the treasure (silver and gold) of all peoples will come, and I will fill this house with splendor, says Yahweh of hosts" (Hag 2:6–9).

Moreover, the "memoirs" that in previously standard biblical scholarship constituted the very charter of Judaism, the books of Ezra and (particularly) Nehemiah, include repeated discussions of the chambers in the temple to which the inhabitants of Yehud are to bring their first fruits, tithes, and other taxes in kind to be received by the priests and Levites, stored, and then distributed to the priests and Levites (Neh 10:32–39; 12:44–47; 13:4–14). The temple-officers also played a role in the collection, storage, and transmission of the "tribute" (*midda*), the "head tax" (*belo*), and the "land tax" (*halak*) rendered up to the Persian imperial regime (Ezra 4:13, 20; 7:24;

---

1. Malachi and Haggai thus make God resemble the Ba'al that Elijah and the bands of prophets had battled back in the days of the attempt by Ahab and Jezebel to replace loyalty to Yahweh with service of the fertility-forces of the Canaanite kingships.

cf. Neh 10:36–37).² The imperial tribute was enforced so seriously that in order to pay it hungry peasants were forced into debt and debt-slavery to exploitative wealthy creditors (Neh 5:4). Besides being the sacred site where the high priests presided in grand ceremonies, the temple was the center of a temple economy over which the priestly aristocracy presided and served as an integral instrument of the overall imperial political economy.

Centuries later the High Priest Alexander Jannaeus, grandson of one of the Maccabean heroes who led the guerrilla warfare against the Seleucid imperial armies attempting to enforce suppression of the traditional Judean way of life, conquered more and more of the surrounding cities and territories with his mercenary armies. "His own people," however, "aroused against him, pelted him with citrons at the festival [of tabernacles] as he stood beside the altar ready to sacrifice." In retaliation, "he killed some six thousand of them, and placed a wooden barrier about the altar . . . to block the people's access to him," according to the account by the wealthy priest and historian Josephus (*Ant.* 13.372–373). Later, when thousands of Judeans who were fighting against him fell into his hands, "he ordered some eight hundred of them to be crucified, and slaughtered their children and wives before the eyes of the still living wretches" (13.379–380). Many of the remaining opponents, "some eight thousand, fled by night and remained in exile so long as Alexander lived" (*Ant.* 13.372–373, 379–380, 383). The temple was a place for political protest, even in the middle of the reigning High Priest's leading the sacrifices. And the relation between High Priest and people involved politics, including some rather gruesome violence. It seems clear from Josephus' accounts that the mystifying pomp and ceremony could not sustain legitimation of such naked exercise of brutal repressive violence.

As the accounts of Josephus attest, second-temple Judea was not a cohesive monolithic society, unified by temple and torah, as often assumed in biblical studies. In fact, the central controlling concepts of biblical studies such as "Judaism" (and "the Bible/biblical") tend to hide the key interrelated political-economic-religious institutions evident in the sources that determined life and historical developments in the tiny out-of-the-way territory of Judea. In particular, they have hidden the multilevel conflicts that led to the crisis that threatened the continued existence of the temple-state in the early second century BCE, the crisis that became the watershed of the subsequent history of conflict and crisis in the temple-state under imperial rule.

---

2. The priests, Levites, singers, doorkeepers, and other servants in the Jerusalem temple themselves may have been exempt. See the fuller analysis and explanation by Schaper, "Jerusalem Temple as an Instrument," 535–37.

From extensive new criticism of the limited sources in the last several decades it has become clear that the temple-state in Jerusalem that ruled and exploited Judea was the creature of a succession of empires. The Persians did not install a temple-state in Jerusalem immediately upon taking over control of the Babylonian empire. The territory of Judea may well have been administered mainly by officials based in Ramat Rahel, just south of Jerusalem, for a few generations. But according to sources such as Ezra-Nehemiah, the Persian regime had sponsored the rebuilding of the temple in Jerusalem and, through repeated interventions by Persian governors, enabled an emerging aristocracy of priestly families, in conflict with local "big men" in the area, to gradually consolidate their power.[3] Subsequent imperial regimes, from the successors of Alexander the Great to the Romans, perpetuated the temple and high priesthood as the ruling institutions of Judea.

Contrary to constructs of a unified and monolithic Judaism, both the temple and high priesthood were periodically contested. Incumbents took measures to consolidate their power. But rival priestly groups periodically challenged incumbents for position and power in Jerusalem. The fortunes of incumbents and challengers, moreover, often depended on shifts in imperial policy and power and/or rival factions in the imperial regime and/or rival imperial regimes vying for control of Palestine. The resilience and persistence of the temple-state headed by the High Priest and priestly aristocracy as the controlling political-economic-religious institution in Judea is indicated in its survival after what were two historical self-destructions of the priestly aristocracy. In the early second century BCE the Hellenizing "reform" by the dominant high priestly faction purposely replaced the

---

3. I drew on the upsurge of critical historical probes into the rebuilding of the temple by a colony of the descendants of previously deported Jerusalem elite and the collection of traditional Judean/Israelite laws sponsored or at least encouraged by the Persian imperial regime in a provisional historical reconstruction of the unstable affairs in Persian Yehud in *Scribes, Visionaries*, chaps. 1–2. Some years earlier, S. Schwartz, in *Imperialism and Jewish Society*, 20–21, argued that "it is nearly certain that the Jerusalem Temple was built under the aegis of the Achaemenids, and likely too that some version of the Torah became the authorized law of the Jews in the same period." His comment that "we may wonder why the Persian emperors should have been interested in imposing Judaism on the Jews" anticipated his later observations that Judaism was (created by) the Judean oligarchy that headed the Temple and "sub-elite" of priests and scribes who cultivated and applied the Torah (whatever it was at the time). In the course of chaps. 1 and 2, however, Schwartz then includes anything and everything that crops up in the sources under the construct Judaism, which suggests that his structural-functional sociology obscures the concrete political-economic-religious conflicts that appear in the limited sources throughout the second-temple period. Nevertheless, Schwartz's caustic comments about conflicts (the seriousness of which he downplays) are a refreshing change from much of the historiography of second temple Judean history (usually conceptualized as Judaism).

temple-state with the Hellenistic *polis* of Antioch-in-Jerusalem. But that touched off widespread resistance and revolt in the early second century, and the temple-state was restored to power through the machinations of the Hasmoneans (who had led the Maccabean Revolt) by maneuvering between the two rival factions of the weakened Seleucid imperial regime. Little more than a century later rival Hasmonean claimants to the high priesthood engaged in self-destructive warfare mixed up with the Roman conquest of Palestine. But this led the Romans to install the military strong-man Herod as king, who massively rebuilt the temple and expanded the high priestly families as instruments of his rule. Then, after his death, the Romans restored high priestly control of the temple-state.

Interrelated with such struggles at the top were various factions or circles of learned scribes (sages) who served as administrative-intellectual-legal retainers of the ruling aristocratic families. Only in the late third and early second centuries do we have enough textual sources to discern how these scribal circles became significant players in the political-religious conflicts of the Jerusalem temple-state under the increasingly invasive rival Ptolemaic and Seleucid imperial regimes. The book of Sirach offers a rich array of the instructional speeches and songs of Yeshua ben Sira from which we can derive a fairly clear picture of the political-economic-religious structure and dynamics of Judean society as of the early second century BCE: a ruling priestly aristocracy, the learned scribes who served in the temple-state, the artisans and others of the people of Jerusalem who supplied the needs and desires of the temple and aristocracy, the Judean peasantry whose crops supported the whole, and the often conflictual political-economic-relations between them.

Ben Sira, however, somehow ignores that the Jerusalem temple-state was subjected to the Seleucid imperial regime that had recently wrested control militarily from the rival Ptolemaic regime. For the repeated conflict between the rival imperial regimes and the corresponding rivalry for control of the temple-state between factions among the priestly aristocracy, we are dependent on the *Antiquities* of the Judean historian Josephus. His accounts help explain how Judea and Judeans had suffered intensified military invasion and economic exploitation in the course of the third century and then in the early second century a Hellenizing "reform," that is, a "hostile takeover" by a high priestly faction that abandoned the traditional Judean covenantal polity and way of life. Josephus and the book of 1 Maccabees on which he depends present accounts of how these events led to the popular resistance, the (Maccabean-led) guerrilla warfare that fought the Seleucid armies to a standoff. This produced a great crisis, breakdown, and watershed in the history of the Jerusalem temple-state.

Ben Sira's instructional speeches and hymnic wisdom offer a rich illustration of how learned scribes serving in the temple-state supplied supportive propaganda that helped legitimate the temple-state generally and the high priesthood in particular, whatever their misgivings and complaints. By contrast, although previously undiscerned or ignored, contemporary texts standardly classified as "apocalyptic" supply evidence of other circles of learned Judean scribes who sharply opposed the "reform" carried out by the high priestly rulers and the increasingly violent invasion of Seleucid imperial forces. These circles played a significant role in the resistance that brought the escalating conflict to a head, including the production of texts of visionary histories of the events in which they themselves were involved.[4]

Social Structure and Social Dynamics on the Eve of the Reform and Revolt

While the wisdom included in Sirach is of several different types, most of the book consists of Yeshua Ben Sira's instructional speeches addressed to his "sons," or students in his "house of instruction."[5] These speeches contain telling information about the high priestly rulers who exploit the poor (peasants) and warnings to fledgling scribes to "watch their back" when dealing with the rulers whom they serve but who have power over them.

One relatively long speech that boasts of the important role of the learned scribe (or sage) also sketches the principal supporting social roles and social relations in the temple-city itself (38:24—39:5). In a sequence of stanzas Ben Sira describes the tasks of agricultural workers and urban artisans. It is somewhat unclear whether his lines about those who handle the plow and tend the cattle refer to the peasantry generally or perhaps rather to workers on lands around Jerusalem controlled by the temple and/or the high priests. In poetic lines he lauds the work of the artisans who design and cut seals, the smiths who devote hard labor to their craft, and the potters who carefully mold clay and glaze their pots. He then comments appreciatively that "all of these rely on their hands, and are skillful in their

---

4. Their critical perspective on the events of the crisis and their own "action" has been blocked from view by the synthetic modern scholarly construct of "apocalypticism." See the analysis of Daniel and "Enoch" texts in Horsley, *Scribes, Visionaries*, chaps. 8–9, and on Daniel, in Portier-Young, *Apocalypse Against Empire*.

5. Much of the previous interpretive literature on Sirach/Ben Sira assumed that most of the book consisted of largely separate maxims, wisdom sayings. Those maxims, however, are components of instructional wisdom speeches. See the analysis in Horsley, *Scribes, Visionaries*, chap. 7; and Horsley "Oral Composition and Performance of the Instructional Speeches of Ben Sira," in *Text and Tradition*, chap. 4.

work; without them no city can be inhabited." Focused on their trade, these artisans "maintain the fabric of the world" (38:31–32, 34). By contrast with all of these workers who rely on their hands, the scribe is sought out for the council of the people and attains eminence in the assembly; since he understands the decisions of courts, he can sit in the judge's seat; since he can expound sound discipline and wise judgment, he is found among the rulers (32–33). "He serves among the great ones and appears before rulers" and even travels (on state embassies) in foreign lands (39:4). These lines boasting about the importance of the learned scribe(s) also indicate that overall control is exercised by the rulers in their council and assemblies.

To flesh out a more complete sketch of the fundamental political-economic-religious structure and dynamics and social roles and relations, Ben Sira's speech can be supplemented by a near contemporary decree of the restoration of the temple in Jerusalem by the Seleucid Emperor Antiochus III (*Ant.* 12.138-144). After granting the Judeans permission to conduct their affairs according to their ancestral laws, the decree gives special tax-relief (that is, of payments to the imperial court) to a specific list of "the senate of elders and the priests and the scribes of the temple and the temple-singers" (12.142). This is a list of functionaries of the temple, arranged from highest rank to lowest. *Gerousia* is simply the Hellenistic Greek term for what appears to the imperial regime as the council of elders that heads the Jerusalem temple-state.[6] "The scribes of the temple" are the scribes Ben Sira boasted served in the council and assemblies of the rulers. To Ben Sira's list must be added the ordinary "priests of the temple" and "the temple singers" who both served in the sacrifices and other ceremonies in the temple itself. That only these privileged groups received relief from (certain) imperial taxes indicates that others remained subject to them. That is, the peasant villagers, who comprised the vast majority of the Judean people, were still expected to render up resources to the Seleucid regime from their crops (in addition to the tithes and offerings required to support the temple and

6. The Greek translation in the book of Sirach does not use the term *gerousia* either with reference to the "brothers" of Simon, son of Onias, or with reference to the group of "great ones, nobles, judges, etc." In Ben Sira's instructional speeches the Hebrew *edah*, translated by *laos* ("people") or *synagoge* ("assembly"), and *qahal*, consistently translated by *ekklesia* ("assembly"), generally refer to the (assembled) people (of Jerusalem, understood as representative of "Judeans" or of "Israel"). He does, however, refer to a "gathering/council (*plethos*) of "nobles/elders" (*sarim, presbuteron*), a council in which he and other sages/scribes were (sometimes) present (Sir 6:34; 7:14; i.e., the same *sarim* or "nobles" that the sages serve, as in 8:8). It may be significant that *sarim* can be understood as "elders," as in the *gerousia* in the decree Antiochus III. Modern interpreters' reading of the *gerousia* as a purely lay body, such as Hengel, *Judaism and Hellenism*, 1.26, appears to be determined by the modern western assumption of the separation of religion and politics.

priesthood). Unclear is the form of taxes that the urban artisans and others in the city of Jerusalem may have been expected to continue paying to their imperial masters.

From the plethora of Ben Sira's instructional speeches and his praise of the ancestors it should be possible to gain a fuller sense of the fairly well-defined political-economic-religious roles and power relations in Judea under the Jerusalem temple-state.[7] A critical assessment of the explicit indications and suggestive clues in Ben Sira's descriptions leads to discernment of the inherent tensions and potential conflicts between the priestly aristocracy and the Judean people they ruled: the peasantry in the countryside, the artisans and others in the city, and the learned scribes who advised and assisted them in the operations of the temple-state. With Ben Sira's picture of the overall structure of Judean society in mind we can further explore particular social relations and potential conflicts by focusing on the key roles of the aristocracy, the peasantry, the people of Jerusalem, and the scribes, our special concern in this volume.[8]

The High Priesthood and Ruling Aristocracy

In the early second century Ben Sira and other sources indicate clearly that the temple-state and the Judean people were ruled by a High Priest at the

---

7. The following is heavily dependent on the critical analysis and discussion in Horsley, *Scribes, Visionaries*, esp. chaps. 3–5 and 7, and in turn chap. 3 is dependent on research and analysis done some years before together with Patrick Tiller, eventually published in "Ben Sira and the Sociology of the Second Temple." I am deeply indebted to Tiller particularly for his philological expertise and his close critical analysis of key passages in Sirach.

8. There has been a great deal of interest among biblical scholars in the last generation in applying social-science models to "biblical" texts, society, and history. The historical sociology of advanced agrarian societies by Gerhard Lenski, laid out in *Power and Privilege*, has been the most suggestive in several respects. Perhaps the major problem with Lenski's model of advanced agrarian societies, as well as the main reason it does not fit second-temple Judea, is that his elaborate scheme of social stratification (the predilection of much American sociology) tends to obscure how social dynamics and conflict are rooted in the structure of power-relations. So instead of applying an unhistorical twelve-class stratification it makes sense to focus on the fundamental political-economic-religious power relations between the high priestly rulers and the peasantry and the people of Jerusalem, and particularly on the relations the high priestly rulers and the learned scribes/sages who served the temple-state as legal-clerical "retainers" who assisted in the governing of Judean society. The comparative studies on which Lenski draws, however, have proven useful in certain connections, so it may be pertinent to comment on aspects of Lenski's treatment in subsequent notes.

head of a priestly aristocracy.⁹ This could not be more vividly portrayed than in the Jerusalem scribe's fawning description of a festal celebration at the altar at the climax of his long paean of praise of the ancestral rulers (Sir 44–50). Some modern interpreters have simply assumed that there was a lay aristocracy as well as the priestly aristocracy, the Aaronid priesthood, that had "authority over" and a special "inheritance in" the people.¹⁰ The still small size of the territory and population of Judea, however, placed a limit on the size of aristocracy that could be supported economically. It is not surprising that the conservative and learned Judean scribe in his instructional speeches uses traditional terms (derived from the earlier monarchic period) that had become standardized in earlier wisdom-teaching, such as "the great, rulers, princes, judges, nobles, elders, etc." that were virtually interchangeable and synonymous. He refers several times, for example, to scribes standing in gatherings or assemblies of the rulers/great ones/princes/elders (6:34; 7:14).¹¹ All such references, however, suggest that these terms refer to the same aristocratic figures who had collective authority, exercised various functions, and operated collectively in relation to scribes and to the people (9:17; 10:1–3; [30:27]; 33:19; 39:4).¹² Perhaps the key indication is that with regard to both "the sons of Aaron" and "the great/rulers/princes" Ben Sira's portrayal of economic revenues is the same: the tithes, offerings, and sacrifices brought to the priests/rulers in the temple. Another indication that the Judean aristocracy was priestly is that the ambitious Tobiads, sheiks in the trans-Jordan area, repeatedly married into the high priestly family, presumably as the way they could enhance their influence in the temple-state.

9. Here is a prime illustration of how Lenski's model of an advanced agrarian society, with its proliferation of different vertical "classes," does not apply to the Judean temple-state. In his delineation of the "priestly class" as separate and different from "the ruler," the "governing class," and the "retainer class," Lenski was apparently making the western differentiation between religious and political roles and institutions normative for his model. In much if not most of his materials, however, these dimensions of life have not been separated, or have been unevenly divided at different levels.

10. It has been assumed that the priestly aristocracy of the second temple was Zadokite, although Ben Sira does not mention this. Perhaps not even all of the Zadokites would have been among the ruling aristocracy. And perhaps not all members of the aristocracy were Zadokite priests.

11. Since *sarim* frequently occurs in the plural in Hebrew texts, suggesting that such "princes" or "nobles" operated in a group, *presbuteron* in 7:14 would be an understandable translation in Greek.

12. Some members of the priestly aristocracy may have held a particular office; Josephus refers to a "temple captain" in later centuries. But we should not imagine that all members held the "portfolio" of a particular "ministry," as in the cabinets of modern governments.

The central figure and institution in the aristocracy, as well as symbolic head of the temple-state and Judean society as a whole, was the High Priest. In order to understand how the whole political-economic-religious system of second-temple Judaea worked, we must devote more attention to the religious dimension focused on the high priesthood. The people are to fear and to serve "the Most High," who is explicitly understood as "the king of all." Correspondingly, the whole temple-state apparatus is structured ostensibly toward the service of God. The priesthood headed by the High Priest, established by everlasting covenant and given "authority and statutes and judgments" over the people, is the people's representative to God as well as God's representative to the people. This is why the people (are to) 'honor the priest' with their tithes and offerings: yielding up such resources, in the economics of the system, was the way of "fearing the Lord" (see esp. Sir 7:29–31; 45:15–21).

Ben Sira thus presents a "proprietary theory of the state," but in a combination of theocratic and hierocratic terms.[13] God, as the ostensible "head of state," is the "proprietor" of the land, with the (high) priesthood as regent and actual head of (temple) state-and-economy. In that position (the eponymous ancestor) Aaron was granted a "heritage" but no "inheritance" among the people/land (45:20–21). The priesthood (supposedly, at least) has no land of its own because as the head of the whole it receives a (special) heritage of "first fruits and sacrifices." Ben Sira's speeches on topics such as the relations of the rich and the poor and the obligation to pay tithes and offerings (7:29–31; 35:6–12) indicate clearly that the High Priest and the priestly aristocracy derived their economic support in just these forms from the villagers in the countryside. Ideologically at least, the high priest(hood) and priests have no individual or personal wealth and power separate from their wealth and power as public figure(s) representative of the whole. The High Priest and other members of the priestly aristocracy may well have used their public wealth and power as a means of generating what

---

13. Lenski, *Power and Privilege*, 215–16, suggests "a proprietary theory of the state": common or corporate "ownership" can be understood as vested in the head of state. "*All agrarian rulers enjoyed significant proprietary rights in . . . the land in their domains*" (italics Lenski's). The "proprietary theory of the state," however, does not yet help us understand second-temple Judea and other temple-states. Lenski does not discuss the mechanism by which such "proprietary rights" are legitimated for the monarchs or aristocracies of traditional agrarian societies. He focuses almost exclusively on the material level, while the *dialectical materialist* Karl Marx takes the religious dimension more fully into account. Marx recognizes more generally that in such societies it is by virtue of being the symbol of the society as a whole, the head of the whole body, that the god or the god's regent (priest-king or High Priest or priestly aristocracy) is the controller (and beneficiary) of the tribute or tithes taken from the members of the social body.

would appear as private wealth or property, e.g., by charging interest on loans made from the stores/wealth they controlled (as representatives of the whole). But the basis of their wealth, power, and privilege was their position as the representative head(s) of Judean society as a whole.[14] This particular hierocratic ideology was essential to the working of the Judean temple-state, both in its internal power-relations and as a component political-economic unit of the reigning empire. Therein lay also the potential for conflict, both within the temple-state and between tradition-minded Judeans and the ruling imperial regime. Ben Sira, however, studiously ignores that the temple-state was subordinated to, indeed the creature of the imperial regimes, first the Persian and then the rival Hellenistic empires of the Ptolemies and the Seleucids.[15]

Insofar as the (high) priesthood was representative of and had authority over the whole, then it both claimed support from the agricultural producers and commanded the loyalty of the governing apparatus it developed in addition to the priesthood itself, such as scribal advisers and administrators. So long as the traditional Judean hierocratic ideology and institutional forms were left intact, the Judean temple-state could operate in a semi-autonomous way, with the high priesthood serving its traditional function as representative of the Judean people focused on God, temple and high priesthood, while simultaneously serving as representative of the imperial regime, maintaining the imperial as well as domestic order.

Judging from other sources, such as 1 Maccabees and Dan 10–12, however, when (a leading faction of) the ruling aristocracy compromised with

---

14. For how this worked in practice toward the end of the second temple period, see the article about the "temple economy" by Broshi, "The Role of the Temple in the Herodian Economy."

15. Perhaps because of its part in his overall evolutionary scheme, Lenski's model does not take into account the fact that most concrete examples of agrarian societies are parts of larger agrarian empires. This is a serious omission that makes the model all the more inapplicable to the states and temple-states subjected to the successions of empires in the ancient Near East/SW Asia. As Kautsky explains in *The Politics of Aristocratic Empires*, 82, the aristocratic rulers of a large agrarian empire were usually the ruling elite of a different society from the peoples they dominated, and the rulers of subordinate states were often of different ethnic and cultural heritage from the people(s) they ruled. Since many large aristocratic empires ruled subject peoples indirectly through the native/local aristocracies or monarchies, the overall political-economic-religious system was far more complex than Lenski's model allows. This subordination of one society to another and one ruling class to another should then be juxtaposed with the social system that was held together by an ideology of a god and/or king/High Priest at its center as a symbol of the whole. This juxtaposition enables us to discern the interrelated issues of (a) the 'legitimacy' of the ruler(s), local and/or imperial, and (b) the potential conflict between the levels of rulers with different legitimating ideologies.

or appeared to abandon the traditional way of life in favor of the ideological and institutional forms of the imperial regime, it lost "legitimacy" among Judeans. This would have happened especially among those who strongly believed in and/or had a stake in the theocratic-hierocratic ideology. And such a compromise of Judean traditions and compromise with an alien culture would have affected Judeans according to their position and role in the social (political-economic-religious) structure of the temple-state. Adherence to the traditional hierocratic ideology could thus become an issue about which rival parties among the aristocracy and/or different circles of scribes might divide, or about which scribal circles might come into conflict with their patrons in the priestly aristocracy. The people of Jerusalem also may well have experienced a loss of a sense of the purpose of practicing their trade and if their rulers no longer had any use for their finished products, they may well have begun to "go hungry" (see again Sir 38:32).

The Judean Peasantry

Peasants, like women, have generally been "hidden from history." Typical of sources produced by the literate elite, Ben Sira does not give focused attention to the Judean peasantry. In his various instructional speeches, however, he does indicate how peasant producers in the villages of Judea supported the whole temple-state apparatus with their tithes and offerings (Sir 35:1–12) and first fruits, guilt offerings, and animal sacrifices sent as revenues to "honor the priest" (7:29–31; 45:20–22). Comparative studies suggest that since the level of agricultural production was traditionally low, the peasants had to comprise about 90% of the population in order to support the rest of the society as well as themselves with food. They generally lived at the subsistence level, constantly threatened with poverty and hunger since their "surplus" produce was being expropriated by their rulers.[16] In Ben Sira's speeches terms such as "poor," "hungry," "needy," and "desperate," apparently refer to a large proportion of villagers, not just exceptional cases (see, e.g., 4:1–10). Judean peasants were therefore chronically in need of alms (29:1–20) and susceptible to the predatory practices of the wealthy and powerful (34:24–27).[17] That "the poor" were the "feeding grounds of the

---

16. Lenski, *Power and Privilege*, 270, states the relationship of the peasantry and their rulers bluntly: "In short, . . . the political elite sought to use the energies of the peasantry to the full, while depriving them of all but the basic necessities of life."

17. Ben Sira (in 34:24–27) sounds like the prophet Amos (in 2:6–8) when he suggests that powerful creditors were taking advantage of vulnerable peasants who had fallen heavily into debt.

rich" (Sir 13:18–23) had evidently long since become a proverbial observation in the traditional agrarian society of Judea.

Discussion of the Judeans living in the many villages around the temple-state in Jerusalem should include the ordinary priests who conducted the day-to-day, week-to-week sacrifices and offerings in the temple. The decree of Antiochus III cited above gives tax-relief to "the priests . . . and the temple-singers," as well as "the senate of elders" and "the scribes of the temple." From several sources (e.g., Ezra and Nehemiah) we know that some of the tithes were intended as economic support for the priests and Levites. While some of the large number of ordinary priests lived in Jerusalem, others of them lived in the villages with other villagers. These ordinary priests were, like their fellow villagers, subject to the rule of the priestly aristocracy and shared common political-economic interests with their fellow villagers.

The fundamental structural opposition in the society between the ruling priestly aristocracy and the Judean villagers had potential for more overt class conflict. Studies of comparable agrarian societies and, more recently, of Israelite villagers find that they are deeply embedded in and committed to time-honored traditions, including their rights to land and at least a subsistence living and to collective mutual aid, particularly in times of need.[18] Because they are relatively powerless vis-à-vis their rulers, they tend to be remarkably long-suffering, unless pushed into desperation. Popular revolts are rare. Peasant resistance tends to be covert, in subtle forms.[19] Ben Sira's observations about the condition of Judean peasants, however, suggest that the threat to their traditional way of life, including their tenuous hold on ancestral land and a subsistence livelihood became a significant factor in one of those rare outbursts, the Maccabean Revolt of the mid-160s, a few decades after his own scribal career.

The People of Jerusalem

Except for his poetic appreciation of the artisans living in the city who "maintained the fabric of the world" and "without whom no city could be inhabited," Ben Sira offers little information about the people of Jerusalem. Yet some further aspects of their roles and social-economic relations can be

18. Such would be the implications of the extensive critical study of Israelite laws by Knight, *Law, Power, and Justice in Ancient Israel*. I attempted to draw out the implications of the Israelite popular tradition of village community customs and mechanisms that were evidently parallel to those of peasantries in other societies, such as those studied by J. C. Scott, *Moral Economy of the Peasant*. See Horsley, *Covenant Economics*, esp. chaps. 2–3.

19. J. C. Scott, *Weapons of the Weak*.

inferred from his instructional speeches (and from comparative studies). The "fabric of the world" in Jerusalem would have included implements and decor for the central operations of the temple *manufactured* by the hands of the smiths and artisans. The pots and jars molded by the hands of the potters would have included cooking pots and storage jars for grain, wine, and oil extracted from the peasantry. The people of the city were essential for the operations of the temple and they had a stake in its proper operations. If most of them had particular tasks and roles at which they worked and were not raising food themselves, then they must have been economically dependent on what the rulers extracted from the crops of the villagers. Ben Sira commented that wherever artisans and smiths and potters lived, "they would not go hungry" (38:32). So presumably those who needed what only the artisans could produce would generally have made sure they had at least a subsistence living. Comparative studies of the people in royal/capital cities find that they are committed to the operation of the capital city according to time-honored traditions. Also, even though they do not have a voice in those operations through an institution such as a popular assembly, they make their voices heard in the shouts and actions of "the urban mob."[20] In such circumstances, wise rulers will often simply let the mob express its concerns and not intervene to suppress their "riots." Intervention and suppression by rulers can aggravate the situation and cause the turmoil to escalate and spread.

Learned Scribes/Sages

The principal function of the learned scribes or sages in the temple-state, as repeatedly evident in Ben Sira's instructional wisdom generally, as in his proud reflection on the role of the sage, was "to serve the magnates/rulers" (*megistasin, sarim,* Sir 8:8). Their particular functions included service as advisers of the collective rulership in Jerusalem (6:34; 7:14; 15:5; 21:17; 38:32–34), as members (or advisers) of courts that heard cases (for they understood the decisions of courts and could expound judgments; 4:9; 11:7–9; 38:33; 42:2), and travel, perhaps on diplomatic missions (39:4). And there were other ways in which learned scribes served the priestly aristocracy of the temple-state. For example, scribes whose repertory included astronomical wisdom and observation of the heavens were instrumental to the rulers of the temple-state in formulating their lunar calendar as authoritative (e.g., 16:26–30; 42:15–25; esp. 43:1–33), which was fundamental for the temple

---

20. See the discussion of the crowd in Jerusalem in Horsley, *Jesus and the Spiral of Violence,* 90–99.

economy heavily dependent on harvest and other pilgrimage festivals. From Ben Sira's extensive reflections on his own and presumably others' activities it is clear that the scribes/sages were what sociologists and others have termed retainers, with legal-cultural functions.[21]

In his sustained poetic boast about the importance of the scribe for the operations of the temple-state, Ben Sira begins with his "opportunity for *leisure (schole,* in Greek)." In the temple-state what qualified the priests for service was their lineage; what qualified the artisans was their skills; what qualified the scribes was their learning. For the scribes to serve among the rulers, they required leisure for their learning. Specifically, he continues, the scribe devoted himself to learning the torah of the Most High, he cultivated prophecies, and he learned the wisdom of the ancients (39:1-4). This listing of the tri-partite curriculum of the scribes (torah, prophecies, and wisdom), has led some interpreters to imagine that scribes at the time of Ben Sira were studying the books of the Hebrew scriptures (or "Old Testament") that later comprised of the books of the Torah, the Prophets, and the (Wisdom) Writings. Ben Sira, however, is evidently referring to the much wider and deeper Judean scribal culture that was (already) understood to have the three segments of Mosaic torah, prophecies of various prophets, and wisdom of several particular types (to be discussed in chap. 2 below).

In order to perpetuate the service of scribes to the high priestly heads of the temple-state another role of a mature learned scribe was to train the next generation of scribes/sages. Much of the collection of Ben Sira's wisdom is devoted to just this. Recent studies have provided a much clearer and fuller sense of scribal training and scribal practices in the Jerusalem temple-state and the earlier Judahite monarchy, building on previous investigations

---

21. Learned scribes in Ben Sira's description clearly fit into Lenski's "retainer class," those who assisted the rulers in "governing" an agrarian society. The distinction between the scribal retainers and the rulers in Ben Sira's Judea was relatively clear, compared with other agrarian societies included in Lenski's synthetic study, where the boundary was "often fuzzy" (Lenski, *Power and* Privilege, 244). There must have been other retainers in the temple-state. Since the imperial regime would have kept a monopoly on military force, there were presumably no military forces at the command of the priestly aristocracy. Yet maintenance of the temple compound called for temple guards or "doorkeepers." The "physicians" admired by "the great ones" for their skills with healing and medicines (38:1-8) may have been more like retainers, serving the aristocracy directly, and less like the artisans, who were less directly in service to the elite. The regular priests and Levites would seem to have functioned somewhat as did the retainers Lenski describes in other agrarian societies, i.e., mediating between the high priestly rulers and the common people, including "effecting the transfer of the economic surplus from the producers to the political and religious elite" (Lenski, *Power and Privilege,* 246).

of scribal culture and training in ancient Egypt and Mesopotamia.[22] A substantial section of the next chapter will be devoted to recent investigations of scribal training, particularly to the cultivation of Judean scribal culture.

Insofar as learned scribes served the priestly aristocracy in various functions—and did not farm the land or work as potters or smiths—they appear to have been dependent economically on the rulers. The principal clue is Ben Sira's repeated warnings about their deference when in close contact with their powerful patrons. The sages must bow low to the ruler (4:7). When invited to dinner by rulers, they must know how to handle themselves prudently, so as not to give offense (13:8–11; 31:12–24).[23] His general exhortations about the importance of tithes and offerings to the priests evidently involved a certain self-interest.

The instructional wisdom of Ben Sira and particularly his proud boast about the important role of the sage in the temple-state, also make clear that, despite their economic dependence on the aristocracy, learned scribes had developed an authority of their own. At least in their own mind, their own authority stemmed from their knowledge of wisdom and their knowledge of and faithful adherence to the torah of the Most High. The high priesthood had its power, privilege, and authority from God through "an eternal covenant;" so also the sages had their own authority as the custodians of divine revelation in the torah of the Most High and prophecies which had come ultimately from God.[24] They themselves were the heirs of ancestral sages. Ben Sira even claims that his wisdom has a certain affinity with prophecy as well (24:33).

---

22. Extensive discussion in Carr, *Writing on the Tablet of the Heart*; and Horsley, *Scribes, Visionaries*, chap. 4.

23. The scribes' vulnerability in their relations with their aristocratic patrons is reflected in Ben Sira's teaching about women, especially about wives. The fundamental social-economic form in ancient Judea, as in any traditional agrarian society, was the transgenerational patriarchal family headed by the husband-father as a petty monarch in the household. Ben Sira's instruction about women, however, strikes a tone even more negative and controlling about wives than already traditional proverbs and previous wisdom-teaching in Proverbs. See especially the extensive and insightful analysis of Camp, "Understanding a Patriarchy." Instructional speeches about women lay great stress on the stability and security of marriage and home and the respectability and obedience of wives and daughters (Sir 25:1, 8, 13–15, 16–26; 26:1–9, 13–18). The husband-father has a special concern about being completely in control and the strict obedience of wives (25:24–26). This need for security and control in the marriage and home is very likely related to scribes' lack of control in their relations with their superiors who exercised control over them.

24. In an excellent article on second temple history, Blenkinsopp, "Interpretation and the Tendency to Sectarianism," 16, states that "the scribal class must have consolidated its power and prestige during the long period from Ezra and Ben Sira."

Understood in the broader political-cultural context of the Hellenistic imperial situation in which they were operating, this dedication and sense of independent higher authority should alert us to the potential for overt as well as latent social-political conflict. Insofar as the scribes' professional role or function was the cultivation of the traditional Judean covenantal laws (often as official state law), their dedication to the covenant and these laws would have been far more than a matter of individual piety or morality (as often portrayed in biblical studies). The sages had a clear sense of their own understanding, independent of their priestly patrons, of how the temple-state should operate, i.e., in accordance with the covenant and commandments as they understood them.

The learned scribes' strong personal and professional dedication to the Mosaic covenantal commandments, along with the independent authority they claimed on that basis, may also have contributed to their concern for the poor, judging from Ben Sira's instructional speeches. His exhortations include not only admonitions of personal ethics to "stretch out your hand to the poor" (7:32), but also what look like instructions to other scribes not to "cheat the poor" or to "reject the supplicant" and even, more actively, to "rescue the oppressed from the oppressor," presumably in their official or professional capacities (4:1–10). Clearly Ben Sira's view of the learned scribes' function in society included more than simply an obligation to his aristocratic patrons. It also included a perceived obligation to God to mitigate the abuses of the poor by the powerful.[25]

Presumably the high priestly rulers accepted this semi-independent role of the scribes because their claim to divine authority enabled the scribes to produce the ideological basis for the priests' rule. Ben Sira provides a prime example of how a staunchly partisan scribe could play this role faithfully, despite his complaints about the abuse of the poor by the powerful wealthy and his warnings to his proteges that the rulers could not be trusted. Several of Ben Sira's poems and hymns articulate cosmological wisdom and/or reflective wisdom, most strikingly hymns of praise of the personified transcendent heavenly Wisdom. In an astounding claim, he declares that the Creator has assigned Wisdom, the divine ordering force of the universe,

---

25. In both their potential opposition to certain actions or policies of the high priestly rulers and their concern for the poor ancient Judean scribes display similarities to the clergy in medieval Europe described by Lenski. But their social structural position was quite different. The medieval Christian clergy was "a specially protected class," economically and politically separate and independent, whereas the second-temple scribes were economically dependent and politically-religiously subordinate. Yet the sense of direct divine authority independent of the rulers is clearly evident in Ben Sira, who was representative of other learned scribes, and perhaps helped set a precedent for what the Christian church eventually institutionalized more securely centuries later.

a domain (in the temple) in Zion (24:1–22). Even more remarkable is the long poetic praise of the ancestors (Sirach 44–50), the holders of the distinctively Israelite/Judean offices of prophecy, kingship, and especially the high priesthood, as represented by Aaron, Phinehas, and Simon son of Onias, in an everlasting covenant. In these hymns and poems a well-known learned scribe articulates the legitimating ideology of, indeed propaganda for, the temple and the high priestly rulers in the decades just prior to the major crisis in the history of the second temple and the Judean people.

Conflict and Crisis in the Early Second Century

The potential for conflict in the political-economic-religious relations between the priestly aristocratic rulers of the Judean temple-state and their scribal retainers came to a head in the late third and early second centuries. The key factors were two: (1) the conflict between the legitimating religious ideology of the temple-state and the dominant imperial culture into which the priestly aristocracy was drawn by their dual, and potentially conflictual, role as heads of the temple-state and agents of the imperial regime; and (2) the conflict between scribes loyal to the ancestral traditions of the Judean temple-state and high priestly factions prepared to compromise those traditions in their assimilation to the ways of the dominant imperial culture and politics.

While Ben Sira ignored that the Judean temple-state was subjected to imperial regimes and had been for centuries, other Judean sources are clear about this, fragmentary and unreliable on the details as they may be. If we avoid imposing the modern separation of the religious/cultural dimension from the political-economic dimension, it is clear from several sources how the subordination involved inherent tensions and potential conflict. The Persians had allowed or perhaps sent the descendants of the Jerusalem elite previously deported by the Babylonians back to Jerusalem, in effect, to colonize *Yehud*. They claimed to be the true *Yehudim* in distinction from the descendants of the people who had been left on the land. Some texts have the *Yehudim* and others rebuilding the temple and the walls of Jerusalem, under orders and supervision by Nehemiah, the Judean-Persian sent as governor of Judea. But according to imperial ideology in ancient SW Asia, it was kings who built temples. So in the book of Ezra, the Judean-Persian scribe the Persian court delegated to attend to affairs in Judea, it was King Cyrus of Persia who built the "house" for "the god who [was] in Jerusalem" and ordered that the cost be paid from the imperial treasury (Ezra 1:1–4; 6:1–5). The Persians thus (presumably) sponsored the "house" of "the god who was in Jerusalem" and symbol of Judean society as a whole so that Judeans were yielding up tithes and offerings (etc.) for their own Lord, the god of heaven, to the priestly regents in the temple. The priestly heads of the temple, however, were then responsible for sending some of the revenues collected from Judeans to the imperial regime as tribute. This basic arrangement was continued by the succession of empires that controlled Judea.

Even the ruling elite was not exactly happy about this arrangement, however. The long prayer of confession led by Ezra in Neh 9 ends with the lament: "Here we are, slaves to this day—slaves in the land that you gave to our ancestors to enjoy its fruit and its good gifts. Its rich yield goes to the kings whom you have set over us because of our sins; they have power also over our bodies and over our livestock at their pleasure, and we are in great distress" (Neh 9:36–37). Subservience to the Empire of course required an ideology that put a good face on it: the blame was placed on the people's disobedience.

The Ptolemaic and Seleucid imperial regimes initially left the Jerusalem temple-state intact with its traditional Judean cultural forms of temple, priesthood, and its authorizing traditional culture and covenantal customs and laws. But the newly established Hellenistic imperial regimes brought dramatic changes for the ruling priestly aristocracy and the Judean people.

First, after the conquests by Alexander's armies, which would have meant destruction and trauma for many subjected peoples, the successor Ptolemaic and Seleucid regimes founded Hellenistic *poleis* that comprised the new political-economic-cultural local institutions through which they controlled the territories and peoples they had subjected. Macedonian soldiers from the conquering armies and indigenous elites from the conquered principalities were "enrolled" as the citizen bodies of the *poleis* that thereby also became the new ruling class that controlled the villages in the surrounding countryside (*chora*). The Hellenistic regimes thus set up an often sharp divide between cities with their new Hellenistic (Greek) political-cultural forms and the peoples of the countryside still cultivating their traditional culture and language. The Jerusalem temple-state was thus left as a relatively isolated political-economic-religious island surrounded by numerous Hellenistic *poleis* to the north (Ptolemais and Scythopolis), the east (the Decapolis), and the west along the Mediterranean coast.

Second, the Ptolemaic regime that controlled Palestine for much of the third century BCE also set up an imperial economic system to maximize its revenues that, in Palestine at least, included opportunities for great economic gain by local opportunists ("entrepreneurs") to bid on the tax-collection for certain districts.[26] This also brought them into close interaction with the new Hellenistic political-culture of the imperial regime and of its *poleis*. The historical account of Josephus includes stories of how representatives of the Tobiad family, based in the trans-Jordan, who had been intermarrying with high priestly families for generations, became wealthy and very influential in the priestly aristocracy at the head of the temple-state (*Ant.* 12.154–236). The Tobiad Joseph in particular became involved in the more systematic Ptolemaic generation of revenue from subject peoples in which the priestly aristocracy, like other indigenous elites, collaborated in a more intensive exploitation of the villagers than before. Some among the Jerusalem priestly elite developed a taste for and intense interest in the new Hellenistic political-culture.

Third, continuing the Hellenistic imperial military conquests that had brought them to power, the rival Ptolemaic and Seleucid regimes fought periodic wars for control of Palestine. Although Jerusalem and Judea comprised only a tiny territory relatively "out of the way" of the usual routes of military clashes, they experienced some destruction and economic impact from these wars. In the fourth war the Seleucids were finally able to wrest control of Jerusalem from the Ptolemies, involving military invasion and considerable destruction and serious partisan struggles in Jerusalem. It was in the aftermath of these invasive conflicts and their destructive impact on Jerusalem and the temple, that the victorious Seleucid Antiochus III issued the decree about the repair of the temple and the exemptions of the priestly aristocracy (*gerousia*), the scribes of the temple, etc., from taxes: that is the restoration of the temple-state now as the representative of Seleucid imperial rule in Judea

Under the dramatic changes brought by the Hellenistic empires, the conflicts inherent in the Jerusalem temple-state under imperial rule intensified into a full-blown crisis. The ancient sources, 1 Maccabees, 2 Maccabees, and Josephus' histories disagree as to the relative roles of principal actors in the crisis and the sequence of events, and modern scholars have made different constructions of the relative roles of actors and the sequence of events.[27] The way the story of the historical crisis has been told tends to

26. A critical review of the Judean temple-state and ruling aristocracy in S. Schwartz, "On the Autonomy of Judaea," esp 163–68. Schwartz's hermeneutics of suspicion (see 167), however, had not yet extended to how "the fully-developed mythology of 1 Enoch 1–16" and the historical visions in 1 Enoch 85–90 and Dan 7–12) were responses to the Ptolemaic rule of Judea, subsequently discussed in Horsley, *Scribes, Visionaries*, chaps. 8–9, and later in this chapter.

27. The different constructions of Bickerman, in *From Ezra to the Last of the Maccabees* and *The God of the Maccabees*; and of Tcherikover, in *Hellenistic Civilization and the Jews*, were highly influential. Bickerman argued that the "reform" was the initiative

focus on the priestly aristocracy, particularly on what became the dominant faction. A substantial faction among the priestly aristocracy had become eager to participate in the new Hellenistic political culture of the *poleis*. After Antiochus IV Epiphanes became the emperor, in 175 BCE, Jason, the leader of the emerging dominant faction and brother of the High Priest Onias III, offered Antiochus 300 talents of silver for the high priesthood and promised more if he were authorized to change Jerusalem to "the Greek way of life" (2 Macc 4:7-10). This Hellenizing "reform" transformed the Jerusalem temple-state into the *polis* of Antioch-in-Jerusalem, thus in effect abandoning the traditional Judean covenantal way of life.[28] In the circumstances of this "reform," scribal circles who were rigorously loyal to the Judean cultural tradition of which they were the custodians would have been caught in an acute dilemma, torn between their loyalty to the traditional way of life and their dependence on the aristocracy they served.

Three years later another upstart priestly aristocrat, Menelaus, outbid Jason by another 300 talents for the high priesthood, thus touching off an armed struggle for control of Antioch (Jerusalem) between two "reforming" factions and their hangers-on. Antiochus, thinking Judea was in revolt, sent military forces to enforce the reform, plundered the temple of its silver, gold, sacred vessels, and lampstand, and profaned the altar. Then he launched a systematic persecution of those who insisted on the traditional Judean observances and way of life. All of this evoked a guerrilla rebellion of ordinary priests and other villagers led by the ordinary priestly family of Hasmoneans and in particular by Judas "the hammer." After years of guerrilla struggles, the Maccabean Revolt succeeded in taking control of Jerusalem and purifying the temple, at least temporarily.

It was evidently a dominant faction if not the majority of the priestly aristocracy who carried out the Hellenizing reform. On the other side it

---

of a dominant faction of the priestly aristocracy, while Tcherikover emphasized that Antiochus' edicts and invasion came in reaction to a rebellion in Jerusalem by opponents of the Hellenizing reformers who had taken control. The two explanations are not mutually exclusive. For a concise glowing assessment of Bickerman's work, see Himmelfarb, "Elias Bickerman on Judaism and Hellenism."

28. The careful concise discussion of "The Macedonian Conquest and Its Impact" by S. Schwartz, *Imperialism and Jewish Society*, esp. 27, places the Hellenizing reform in broader historical context: "nations (anachronistic concept) long in existence or established by the Persians might simply be willed out of existence by their upper classes' desire to be Greek, to reconstitute themselves as the citizen body of a Greek city. Indeed, such a process . . . may be precisely what occurred in Jerusalem and Shechem in the second century, precipitating the Maccabean revolt." My concern here is how threatening the abandonment of the traditional Judean *politeia* and (covenantal) way of life was to scribal circles, such as the *maskilim*, and the ordinary priests who served in the Jerusalem temple-state.

would have been at least a critical mass of villagers, rooted in the traditional covenantal Judean way of life, who mobilized to eventually fight the imperial troops to a standoff. These were the principal drivers and forces of the reform and the revolt, respectively, as represented in 1–2 Maccabees.

First Maccabees does suggest that, at the beginning of the revolt, some scribes may have been (among those) involved in "a company of Hasideans" (*hasidim* = "pious ones;" 1 Macc 2:42). The subsequent reference to "the Hasideans" seems to make them identical with "a group of scribes" who sought a truce. They trusted Alcimus, who had recently been made High Priest, because he had the necessary lineage as "a priest of the line of Aaron"—but he seized and killed sixty of them (1 Macc 7:12–16, an account that calls Alcimus a "godless renegade"). The standard presentation of the crisis of the reform and the Maccabean Revolt, however, leaves us wondering about the views and activities of other circles of scribes, the professional cultivators and guardians of Judean tradition, during the escalating conflict and then in the acute crisis of the reform and the revolt.

Interpretation of the Crisis and Active Resistance by Scribal Circles

The focus of scholarly analysis and reconstruction of the crisis of the temple-state has understandably been on the eventual invasion of Jerusalem and violence against the temple by Antiochus Epiphanes and on the Maccabean Revolt led by Judas "the Hammer" and the rededication of the temple in 164 BCE. Much less attention has been given to the reaction among Judean scribal circles to the wars between the Ptolemies and Seleucids that raged over control of Palestine and to the priestly aristocracy's relations with the Ptolemaic regime and the eventual Hellenizing reform.

Given the position and role of scribes/sages in the temple-state that can be learned from the instructional speeches of Ben Sira, they would have been concerned about and likely implicated in the emergence of factions among the priestly aristocracy in relation to the attractions of Hellenistic political culture and to the intensification of Ptolemaic and Seleucid military invasion of Palestine. Many of the Judean texts that are extant from this period were produced by Judean scribal circles and are focused directly on the intensifying conflicts and the major crisis of the reform under Antiochus Epiphanes that affected them directly and in which they were actively involved. But critical discernment of the contents and significance of these texts has, ironically, been blocked by the way in which they have been understood in established biblical studies.

Since at least the end of the nineteenth century, biblical scholars have classified the visionary reviews of history in Dan 7, 8, and 10–12, along with those in 1 Enoch 85–90 and the Testament of Moses, as "apocalyptic texts." These and related texts were thought to articulate "Jewish apocalypticism" that focused on the End of the World in the Last Judgment and a cosmic cataclysm. It was assumed, moreover, that this "apocalypticism" was an unprecedented theology that suddenly pervaded "Judaism" generally. Recent criticism of "apocalyptic texts," however, has argued that "apocalypticism" or "the apocalyptic scenario" is a modern scholarly (theological) concept constructed from fragments extracted from several different texts (ranging from the third century BCE to the second century CE)—without considering them in coordination with their particular historical context.[29] Upon close examination, however, none of the late second-temple Judean texts so classified actually attest the supposedly component themes of apocalypticism, much less the whole scenario.[30] To understand what have been labeled "apocalyptic" texts requires a more comprehensive critical review of learned scribal culture and scribal practice in the Jerusalem temple-state, including its background in scribal culture in the royal and imperial regimes of ancient southwest Asia.[31]

Ben Sira, in indicating the remarkable breadth of Judean scribal culture that included torah of the Most High, prophecies, and wisdom, did not exemplify the complete repertoire of scribal wisdom in his own remarkable learning and creativity. In addition to instructional wisdom that comprises much of his book, it also included cosmological wisdom and reflective wisdom (often in combination) in his many hymns. Included in cosmological wisdom was astronomical knowledge based on centuries of observation (exemplified in "the Book of Luminaries," 1 Enoch 72–82). Such knowledge was important for states and rulers for determination of their calendars, although it was a potential source of conflict depending on whether authority was attributed to the pattern of the sun or that of the moon (see Sir 43:2–5, 6–8, 9–12; 1 Enoch 72–82). Also, in scribal reflection heavenly bodies and natural elements might be personified, with wills to take certain actions (Sir 39:31; 42:16–17; 43:17).

---

29. See the critical analysis of "Enoch" texts and "Daniel" texts in Horsley, *Scribes and Visionaries*, chaps. 8 and 9; further analysis and discussion of a wider range of "apocalyptic" texts in Horsley, *Revolt of the Scribes*; and the analysis and discussion of Daniel texts in Portier-Young, *Apocalypse against Empire*.

30. Critical analysis of the second-temple Judean texts usually classified as "apocalyptic" in Horsley, *The Prophet Jesus and the Renewal of Israel*, chaps. 1–5.

31. Horsley, *Scribes, Visionaries*, is an attempt to begin just such a comprehensive critical review.

Sirach, however, did not include a fourth type of wisdom that had been cultivated by scribes in the earlier royal and imperial regimes in Mesopotamia; this has been labeled "mantic" wisdom.[32] Interpretation of dreams and omens was evidently being practiced by some Judean scribes. Abundant evidence indicates that interpretation of dreams and omens was particularly important to rulers in ancient SW Asia. The legendary figure of Daniel, the quintessential Judean sage in exile who had been trained in a wide repertoire of wisdom, was particularly skillful in interpretation of dreams and omens (such as the handwriting on the wall) in his service in imperial courts (Dan 1–6).

Another kind of wisdom has been identified as "secret but revealed." But it is difficult to distinguish from dream interpretation and cosmological wisdom. Ben Sira rejects divination and interpretation of dreams—unless of course they are divinely revealed (34:5–7). He also sends mixed signals about "revealed" wisdom. He warns about seeking "what is hidden," whether about the divine world or the future (42:18–19; 43:32–33). But he declares that heavenly Wisdom "reveals her secrets" to the wise (4:18, 21) and says that God "discloses what has been and what is to be, and reveals the traces of hidden things" (42:19), with the implication that they may be made known to the godly who have wisdom (43:32–33). In connection with Judean scribal cultivation of dream interpretation, moreover, Judean scribes also understood themselves to be the heirs of the prophets and their prophecies, as Ben Sira boasts (39:1–3). And although Ben Sira himself does not say much more, it is clear in extant prophetic texts that prophets experienced heavenly "auditions," even visions, as they were transposed to the divine heavenly court and heard voices of various heavenly spirits or even the voice of God (e.g., Micaiah ben Imlah in 1 Kgs 20; a disciple of "Isaiah" in Isa 40).

The (visionary) reviews of history in Dan 7, 8, and 10–12; 1 Enoch 85–90; and the Testament of Moses all originated in the midst of the escalating conflicts and the crisis of the Jerusalem temple-state in the early second century. Critical reading of these texts enables us to get underneath the veneer of scribal ideology from Ben Sira as well as underneath the modern scholarly construction of "apocalypticism" that blocked recognition of how other learned scribes were experiencing the more violently invasive and destructive Hellenistic imperial rule. In these visionary reviews of history different circles of learned scribes, adept in different kinds of wisdom, were attempting to discern what was happening to the Judean people under the attacks of the succession of imperial rulers and to imagine how the crisis

---

32. Discussion of the different kinds of wisdom in Horsley, *Scribes, Visionaries*, 126–28. A similar typology was laid out in John Collins, "Wisdom, Apocalypticism, and Generic Compatibility," 168.

would be resolved or end. Leading Judeans have abandoned the covenant and law, the traditional Judean way of life. But these scribal circles have steadfastly maintained their faith that the Most High is still ultimately in control of history despite the imperial attacks on the Judean people. Both the review of history in Dan 10–12 and the "Animal Vision" in 1 Enoch 85–90 indicate that at least some of the scribes from the circles that produced the texts even became actively involved in resistance to the invasion of Antiochus and to the Judeans who abandoned the covenant.

The surveys of history in Daniel 7, 8, and 10–12 take the form of visions followed by interpretations.[33] In Dan 7 and 8 the accounts begin with dream visions, followed by the "interpretation" given by an attendant in the heavenly court or the divine messenger Gabriel. The historical survey in Dan 11–12 consists of "what is inscribed in the book of truth" revealed by a heavenly figure (Gabriel?). The main concern of all of these visionary reviews of the history of the Judean people under a succession of empires is the overwhelming power of the empires, especially the horrendous violence and destruction wrought by the Hellenistic imperial regimes. The more detailed third survey, however, devotes considerable attention to the *maskilim*, a group of learned scribes (sages) who are among those who remain loyal to "the covenant." These are evidently the producers of the whole series of visions-and-interpretations. These visionary reviews of history articulate the sharply critical response of a significant circle of learned scribes to prolonged domination by imperial rule and offer their (somewhat veiled) account of their own resistance to the Hellenistic reform by the priestly aristocracy and the attacks by Antiochus Epiphanes.

In the famous dream-vision of four ferocious beasts in Dan 7 the fourth beast is dramatically more vicious and destructive than the preceding ones: "terrifying and dreadful . . . it had great iron teeth and was devouring and breaking in pieces, and stamping what was left with its feet" (7:7–8).[34] The

---

33. In ancient Judean texts (e.g., 4QFlor 2:4; Josephus, *Ant.* 10.266–268), Daniel was known as one of the prophets. The figure of Daniel in the book of Daniel is a Judean development of the prototypical sage in ancient Near Eastern scribal lore. In the Aramaic tales in Dan 1–6 he is trained as a learned scribe at the imperial court and then functions particularly as an interpreter of dreams. The interpretations of visions in Dan 7–12 are scribal developments of prophetic tradition. "Daniel" thus exemplifies the deep learning and cultivation of two of the principal segments of Judean culture that Judean scribes were responsible for, according to Ben Sira, prophecies and (various kinds of) wisdom.

34. Ferocious beasts and monsters had long been used as symbols of fearsome imperial military power by Assyrian, Babylonian, and Persian regimes, and imperial rulers represented as predatory animals in Israelite prophetic tradition. Horsley, *Revolt of the Scribes*, 86. While less predatory than the beasts in Dan 7 the two-horned ram and the goat with a horn between its eyes in Dan 8 are were also standard symbols of

interpreter explains that the fourth beast is the fourth empire that would be different from all the previous ones in "devouring the whole earth and trampling it down." Its ten horns were the ten kings that would arise. The dream image of the extremely violent fourth beast represented Alexander the Great's conquest of the whole Persian Empire and the succeeding Hellenistic empires that were far more violently invasive and oppressive than the previous empires. Most violent of all was the little horn that "made war with the holy ones and was prevailing over them." This was clearly a symbol for the emperor Antiochus Epiphanes who invaded Jerusalem "to change the sacred seasons and the law" and violently attacked the sacred site and ceremonies of the temple.

The invasive imperial violence and destruction is so overwhelming that it can be ended only by the Ancient One, appearing in heavenly judgment, to take away the dominion of the other beasts and destroy the little horn. The human-like figure who comes with the clouds of heaven and is given dominion so that all peoples should serve him is a symbol for "the holy ones of the Most High." This is interpreted to mean that Judeans, "the people of the holy ones of the Most High," currently still under attack by Antiochus Epiphanes, would receive the sovereignty and an everlasting kingdom when "the court shall sit in judgment."

The review of history in Dan 10–12 is a revelation from a heavenly figure (probably Gabriel) that offers a much more precise account of the military battles between the Ptolemaic and Seleucid regimes for control of Palestine. It is not difficult to imagine the destruction that these wars brought to the countryside and many villages and towns. More than half of the review focuses on "the contemptible" Antiochus Epiphanes' attacks on Jerusalem and the temple, its principal concern. The account becomes ever more specific about the relation between those who abandon the covenant and the attacks against Jerusalem to enforce the Hellenizing reform, and about "those who are loyal, stand firm, and take action."

"Those who forsook the covenant" would have been the Hellenizing reform party who had cut a deal with Antiochus to transform Jerusalem into a *polis*. Judging from the connections in which it is used in the narrative, "the holy covenant" probably referred generally to the "constitution" of Judean society, the cultural traditions, customs, and rituals that held together the temple-state and the people in their loyalty to the Most High. The Mosaic covenant and covenantal torah evidently formed the core of these bonds.

---

imperial military power.

"The people who know their God" who stand firm against "those who violate the covenant" probably referred to all those who remained faithful to the traditional way of life. But the *maskilim* appear to have understood themselves as at the center of the events. That they "stand firm *and take action*" indicates that adherence to the covenant meant resistance to Antiochus' attempts to enforce the reform and his attacks on the temple.

Understanding what it might have meant that the *maskilim* would "impart understanding to the many" requires a sense of the social relations in context. "The many" would have been ordinary Jerusalemites (that is, not including peasants in outlying villages). If Ben Sira is any guide, learned scribes saw looking out for ordinary people as part of their role. But they ordinarily communicated their wisdom mainly among other scribes or in councils of the aristocracy, not to artisans and others in Jerusalem. Given the crisis, however, they may have tried to explain the revelation they had received and to convince people that resistance was urgent and in their own self-interest.

That the *maskilim* would, for a prolonged period of time, "fall by sword and flame, and suffer captivity and plunder" indicates both that their resistance was persistent and that the imperial soldiers were hunting them down and killing them or taking them prisoner. Insofar as the Maccabean Revolt had not started yet, "(a) little help" cannot refer to Judas, its leader. Rather, the translation should be "they would receive little help," which fits with "many shall join them insincerely." That some of the *maskilim* would fall so that they would be purified and "made white" (cleansed) indicates that they were understood as martyrs for "standing firm" in defense of the holy covenant and "taking action" against Antiochus' prolonged attacks on the temple-state.

It is unclear how the brief statement of the deliverance and restoration of the Judeans (12:1–3) fits with the preceding narrative.[35] Michael, the "protector" of "Daniel's" people will finally "arise." But he had already supposedly been battling against "the prince of Persia" and then "the prince of

---

35. The reappearance of the heavenly figure clothed in linen and his final words in 12:5–13 constitute the ending of the vision from which "Daniel" received the revelation of the review of history in 10–11 (while it has evidently been adapted for an ending to the whole book of Daniel). Also, the encouraging explanation that the people loyal to the covenant are already half way through the severe imperial invasion and repression (12:11–12) fits the reassuring messages that the people have already endured half of the last week of the history of imperial domination and oppression in the preceding reviews ("a time, two times, and a half a time," etc. in 7:25; 8:13–14; 9:27). The vagueness of this timing suggests that these visions-and-interpretations were composed during the escalating repression by Antiochus Epiphanes, but prior to the emergence of the Maccabean Revolt.

Greece." After an unprecedented time of anguish, the Judean people would finally be delivered (from imperial attack and oppression). It would have been important that the restoration of the people would include those who had died. Accordingly in what had become a standard image of the restoration of the people (e.g., in the "valley of dead bones" that come to life again, in Ezek 37; cf. Isa 26:19), those who had "fallen asleep" in the earth will "awaken," the loyal to long life and the others to perpetual shame.[36]

As for the *maskilim*, particularly those who had become martyrs, "they will shine like the brightness of the sky, like the stars." This was an image that had evidently come to the fore in scribal circles that had been resisting domination in various ways, including the "Enoch" scribes: the oppressed righteous "will shine like the luminaries of heaven; . . . will be companions of the host of heaven" (1 Enoch 104:1–6). Such learned scribes/sages understood themselves to be in close communication with heavenly forces/figures such as Michael and Gabriel and other "holy ones." As a reward for their loyalty to the covenant, the martyred maskilim would be like the heavenly figures from whom they had received their wisdom.

The Animal Vision in 1 Enoch 85–90 is one of at least five texts attributed ultimately to the prototypical scribe Enoch (originally composed in Aramaic, then translated into Greek and then Ethiopic).[37] Although standardly categorized as "apocalyptic," these books present themselves as wisdom (of various types). Like Ben Sira and Daniel, Enoch is represented as a scribe: the "righteous scribe" (1 Enoch 12:3) and "the scribe of truth" (15:1).[38] In the texts attributed to him, the portrayal of Enoch's operation in the heavenly court reflects knowledge of how learned scribes functioned in an earthly court.[39] And his claims to have received his wisdom through heavenly communications media, both vision and words, probably indicate how the "Enoch"-scribes received the wisdom in 1 Enoch 85–90.

Like the *maskilim* in the visionary reviews of history in Dan 7, 8, and 10–12, the "Enoch"-scribes who produced the Animal Vision were focused

---

36. Daniel 12:2 has long been the key proof-text for the belief in the resurrection from the dead, often understood as resurrection of the individual; but Dan 12:2 is a statement about how the dead would be incorporated into the restoration of the Judean people.

37. On the texts included in 1 Enoch, see more fully Horsley, *Scribes, Visionaries*, chap. 9; On the "Animal Vision, see more fully *Revolt of the Scribes*, chap. 3.

38. The book of Jubilees indicates how prominent the role of the antedeluvian Enoch was in Judean scribal culture: "He was the first among humans . . . who learned writing and knowledge and wisdom . . . And . . . what was and will be he saw in a vision of his sleep; . . . and he saw and understood everything, and wrote his testimony, and placed [it] on earth . . . for all generations" (Jub. 4:15–19).

39. See *Revolt of the Scribes*, 48.

on their own situation in which they were resisting the violent attacks by Antiochus Epiphanes. While the *maskilim* sought the perspective of the experience of Judeans under the sequence of empires since the origins of the temple-state, the "Enoch"-scribes sought the perspective of history since the creation of the world and the origins of the Israelite people. If history was ultimately still under the control of the Most High God, then how had it become so completely out of control? How could it be symbolized that the Israelite/Judean people had suffered under such extremely violent military invasion and destruction and economic oppression of one empire after another? The "Enoch"-scribal circle had become so obsessed about imperial military violence and exploitation already in the third century under Ptolemaic domination that they sought to symbolize (or explain) the very origin of empires and their overwhelming and irresistible military power and economic oppression in "the Book of Watchers" that draws heavily on cosmological and astronomical wisdom in its speculation about origins.

The explanation must be a rebellion of some of the many heavenly forces in the divine governance of the history who generated a race of giants on earth who, in turn, generated empires with their iron and other weapons of violence. The Animal Vision seeks a similar explanation of the origins of empires in the first fifth of its allegory (85:3—89:8). Rebel stars generated gigantic beasts that gored and bit and devoured. In the rest of the allegorical survey the predatory animals and birds are transparent to the kings and empires of history that have attacked and devoured the "sheep," that is, the Israelites/Judeans, in the ups and downs of their relationship with their "shepherd."

In the second fifth of the account (89:9–38), after the Lord leads the sheep in escape from the wolves, they struggle to follow the path shown by the lead sheep and to coalesce in a "house," evidently the covenanted people. When the "sheep" stray and kill the prophets sent to them, the Lord abandons them to lions, leopards, and hyenas who "tear them to pieces, devour them, and carry them off."

Fully a third of the survey (89:59—90:19) is then devoted to the escalation of violent imperial domination under a succession of empires. The sheep having abandoned the house, the imperial Lord of history placed them under the domination of a sequence of seventy "shepherds" (heavenly imperial rulers) and their "subordinates." The extreme violence that the Judeans experienced, especially under the Ptolemies and Seleucids, is thus attributed to superhuman heavenly forces that stand behind and give orders to the predatory beasts and birds, that is, imperial regimes.

Significantly, the account of the Persian period focuses on the rebuilding of Judean society and the "tower." But now the tower is not "high," with the Lord standing on it (as the original tower had been, 89:50, 54, 56, 66). The account, moreover, states pointedly that the bread on the table before the tower "was polluted and not pure" and the sheep were blind (89:73–74). This is a serious indictment of the Jerusalem temple-state as problematic from its beginning. With escalated imagery the narrative then portrays the Ptolemaic regime as devastating for the Judeans. "The eagles and vultures . . . began to devour those sheep and peck out their eyes and devour their flesh . . . until only their bones remained" (90:2–4). The imagery of the imperial predators devouring the people's flesh suggests severe economic exploitation.

The allegorical narrative comes to its climax as some of the sheep become "awakened" (primarily the "Enoch" scribes themselves?). The last twelve shepherds, those in charge of the Hellenistic empires, "had destroyed more than those before them" (90:17). The narrative suddenly moves into more specific references to groups and struggles. Close examination of the duplication of certain terms and of conflicts in the narrative (90:6–19) indicates that the text as we have it has been "updated," with 90:9b–10 and 90:12–16 having been inserted into an earlier version in 90:6–9a, 11, 17–19.[40] The "great horn" that sprouted on one of the sheep" and "the horn of that ram" (90:9b) are obvious references to Judas, the charismatic leader of the Maccabean Revolt and the predatory birds (90:12–13, 16) represent the Seleucid armies' attempts to suppress the revolt.

Prior to the "updating," however, the narrative indicates earlier opposition to Hellenistic imperial rule and/or what the temple-state had become. The narrative of the crisis in 90:6–9, 11 appears to be a self-representation of the "Enoch"-scribes who produced the allegorical vision. "The lambs who began to open their eyes and to see" come to recognize just how oppressive and intolerable Hellenistic imperial rule had become. Their "crying out to the sheep" who did not listen suggests they appealed to other Judeans, who continued to acquiesce in the intensified imperial order. It is difficult to tell from the narrative when this "crying out to the sheep" had begun. It is conceivable that the "Enoch"-scribes had been "crying out" against Ptolemaic domination and the closer collaboration of (factions in) the priestly aristocracy in imperial rule already in the late third century.

In any case, it seems that the "Enoch"-scribes had started a sufficiently serious resistance to the Hellenizing "reform" that the imperial birds of prey attacked and seized the "lambs" (the "Enoch" scribes) and dismembered others of the "sheep." Then the emergence of "horns" on those lambs must refer to a more serious, organized, and perhaps militant resistance, and the

---

40. Nickelsburg, *1 Enoch 1*, 414–45.

ravens casting down their horns must be further imperial attacks to suppress their resistance, with the escalated attacks by all the birds of prey to devour the sheep indicating expanded measures to suppress resistance. There were thus at least two significant circles of scribes (the "Enoch"-scribes as well as the *maskilim*) engaged in active resistance to the Hellenizing reform and the imperial invasion to enforce it and suppress the resistance, evidently before ordinary priests and other villagers mounted their revolt.

The imagery becomes more fantastic as the narrative moves from recently experienced historical events to anticipated events in the near future. The action continues to take place at two interrelated levels: the Lord finally asserts sovereign control in the governance of history as the sheep wield the "large sword." The "Enoch" scribes here anticipate God's decisive action in support of their own resistance just when it seems hopeless.

The anticipated resolution of the historical crisis in 1 Enoch 85-90, however, is more concrete and elaborated as a restoration of the people in historical and not fantastic terms, not only free from imperial domination but without the temple and, presumably, the temple-state. The Lord executes judgment on the errant heavenly forces that had propagated the gigantic beasts of imperial violence and oppression and on the seventy shepherds who had exercised such severe imperial oppression of the Judeans, especially through the Hellenistic empires (90:20-25). That the blinded sheep who had opposed the awakened lambs (the priestly aristocracy that collaborated in Hellenizing rule and reform?) were also thrown into the abyss (90:26-27) suggests just how serious their actions had been in the view of the scribes who produced the allegorical narrative.

The divine judgment clears the way for the restoration of the people as a new house, larger and higher than the first one (90:28-29). But the house pointedly has no tower, that is, no temple—just as the original house had no tower (89:28-36). Once God was directly involved in the restoration of the people, there was no need for a tower.[41] Scribes who had come to oppose the temple-state as implicated in imperial domination and exploitation were focused on the renewal of the people freed of local as well as imperial rulers.

The visionary review of history in the Testament of Moses is an "updating" of the prophecy of Moses at the end of Deuteronomy (chaps. 31-34).[42] Anticipating his death. Moses commissions Joshua as his successor, commands the preservation of the "book" of covenantal teaching. "Moses" then narrates key events in Israel's history according to the pattern familiar from

---

41. This motif continues into the Apocalypse of John where there is no temple in the New Jerusalem that descends from heaven at the end of the narrative (Rev 21:1—22:5).

42. Fuller analysis and discussion in Horsley, *Revolt of the Scribes*, 76-79.

Deut 32 and the "book" of Judges of the people's breaking of the covenant and God's punishment, followed by the announcement of God's judgment of the enemies and deliverance of the people.[43] The text articulates the viewpoint of Judean priests and/or Levites and/or scribes attached to the temple as established by "those sent home to their own land" by a God-inspired emperor. They are facing a crisis that "those who are their leaders have abandoned justice, polluted the temple and altar, and serve other gods" (T. Mos. 5). The review of history evidently comes at the height of the crisis when Antiochus Epiphanes has instituted the forced abandonment of the traditional Judean commitment to the covenant, yet prior to the revolt led by Judas the Hammer. Midst this crisis, the review suddenly focuses on "a man from the tribe of Levi named Taxo and his sons" (T. Mos. 9). The Latin text carries over the name *Taxon* from the Greek, where it evidently translated the Hebrew *mehoqeq*, "staff." Keying from the Damascus Rule that takes "the staff" of Num 21:18 to signify "the expositor of the law," the leader who instructs the movement (CD 6:3–12), Taxo must be the scribal leader and his "sons" his disciples, that is, the "Moses"-scribes who composed the Testament of Moses. This priestly-Levitical-scribal group were committed to obedience to the covenantal commandments, in resistance to the decree of Antiochus, which presumably led to their martyrdom. Taxo insists that "our blood will be avenged before the Lord" (T. Mos. 9:7; cf. Deut 32:43). The historical review concludes with a prophetic oracle of God's appearance to judge the oppressive empires and renew Israel (T. Mos. 10). This theophany, with earthquake, solar eclipse, and astronomical disarray (10:3–7), continues a long prophetic tradition of the coming of God to judge oppressive king and to deliver the people (Mic 1:3–4; Isa 13; Jer 25).[44]

The Situation of the Temple-State as the Crisis Unfolded

By the beginning of the second century BCE the temple-state in Jerusalem had been subjected to the rival Hellenistic imperial regimes for over a century. The swift and complete conquest of ancient Southwest Asia by Alexander the Great and a century-long series of wars between Ptolemaic and Seleucid armies for control of Palestine meant that subject peoples such as the Judeans experienced a pronounced increase in destructive military

---

43. Interpreters have long recognized that chaps. 6 and 7 are later additions that "update" the history to Roman rule after the Hasmonean dynasty and the reign of Herod.

44. Earlier interpretations of the text as an "apocalypse" took the hyperbolic imagery somewhat literally as an expectation of "cosmic catastrophe."

violence. The effect of the destructive imperial invasions were exacerbated by the Ptolemaic system of maximizing the economic exploitation of subject peoples during most of the third century when they controlled Palestine. Their tax-farming practices offered opportunity for entrepreneurial "big-men" in the area but meant increased economic demands on the peasant producers.[45]

The ruling priestly aristocracy had to learn how to deal with very different imperial regimes with a new language and Hellenistic political culture. Besides the rivalry between the regimes there would have been rival factions in the imperial court of each, almost requiring subject rulers to maneuver between them. The Jerusalem temple-state ruled a relatively tiny territory in the Judean hill country. The Jerusalem priestly aristocracy that had been presiding in the now traditional Judean institutions, customs, and culture would have become aware of the newly founded Hellenistic *poleis* in which the previously indigenous elites had come to enjoy the power and privilege of the new Hellenistic imperial political culture. The so-called Tobiad romance recounted in the *Antiquities* of Josephus offers an illustration of both the attractions of the new imperial political culture and the entrepreneurial opportunities for the Judean priestly aristocracy.

As well attested in Ben Sira's instructional speeches and hymns, learned scribes were intellectual-legal retainers who served the temple-state and the presiding priests in the operations of temple affairs and the temple-state's rule of and gathering of revenues from Judean villagers. In preparation for their role in governing councils they had become the cultivators, the guardians, and probably the further developers of (elite) Judean culture, customs, and traditions: the torah of the Most High, the prophecies of earlier prophets, and various kinds of wisdom. They would also have developed a personal loyalty to and identification with Judean culture and traditions, and had developed a sense of their own authority, from the Most High, independent of the delegation of authority from the high priests. Insofar as some of the learned scribes knew about and even participated in the aristocracy's dealings with the imperial regimes, they would have been aware of what was happening in the wider empire and in the relations between their high priestly superiors and the imperial regime.

The brief reviews of Ben Sira's wisdom, Josephus' historical account, and some of the visionary histories leading up to the crisis of the temple-state under Antiochus Epiphanes have shown that different circles or factions of learned scribes had emerged and that they had different views of

---

45. Among historians with this assessment is Schäfer, *The History of the Jews in Antiquity*, 17–18.

and stances toward particular high priestly regimes. Ben Sira himself, while critical of the wealthy priestly aristocrats that he and other scribes served, was a propagandist for the Oniad priesthood (Simon II) of the early second century. The "Enoch"-scribes had come to be sharply critical of the whole temple-state institution at some point, at least by the late-third century. Indeed they seem to have been deeply concerned that history had become utterly out of (God's) control during the Ptolemaic imperial violence and exploitation (as indicated in the Book of Watchers and the Animal Vision). When a dominant faction of the priestly aristocracy mounted the Hellenizing reform in which they abandoned the traditional covenant by which the temple-state had operated, both the "Enoch"-scribes and the *maskilim* moved into active resistance to the dominant aristocracy and the attacks of Antiochus Epiphanes in his attempt to defend and further effect the "reform." If the *hasidim* mentioned in 1 Maccabees included yet another scribal circle who were allied with the Maccabean Revolt once it started, it evidently sought a truce once Antiochus appointed a new high priests, Alcimus, with the proper Aaronid lineage.

Once the Maccabean forces, in their guerrilla warfare, fought the imperial armies to a stand-off, and when Alcimus died, there was a hiatus in the line of high priests. It seems that the temple-state had disintegrated into factional fighting in and around Jerusalem. After further years of fighting with a weakened Seleucid regime that itself had split into rival factions, Jonathan, brother of Judas "the Hammer," maneuvered between Seleucid factions to gain recognition as the new High Priest in 152 BCE. Having been leading the revolt for the previous ten years, he had popular support and an experienced popular army. But how could he bring the temple-state back into effective operation? And, coming from the Hasmonean family of ordinary priests, how could he gain some legitimacy for the high priesthood of a warrior-priest? And given the role of learned scribes in the temple-state, how would those in the dissident scribal circles who had not been martyred and other circles of scribes of whom we have no evidence have responded to the situation once Jonathan had been recognized as the new High Priest by one of the rival Seleucid pretenders?

Chapter 5 below will attempt to address these questions, mainly from indications in 1 Maccabees and Josephus' account in the *Antiquities*. First, however, it is necessary to take into account how lines of recent research and discoveries of new sources undermine previous assumptions and standard constructs in the fields of Jewish history and biblical studies. These new researches and new sources seriously affect how we understand the Torah/Law of which the Pharisees were supposedly the principal interpreters. And they seriously affect how we understand and use the sources for the role of the Pharisees and the conflictual history of the Judean temple-state in which they served.

2

Implications of Recent Research for Understanding the Pharisees and the Law

In what has been the standard understanding of Judaism that prevailed in the fields of biblical studies and Jewish history, "the Torah/Law" was the basis of social-religious life and (thus) also the principal source for reconstructing it. Because these fields, like other modern academic fields, were rooted in the fundamental assumptions and controlling concepts of modern print-culture, "The Torah/Law" was understood to be the books of the Pentateuch. These books were assumed to have been composed or edited in writing in "exilic" or early "post-exilic" times. It was further assumed that (at least) by late second-temple times the Torah/Law had become Scripture, authoritative for all Jews, who were assumed to have known and observed its laws.

The Pharisees were assumed to have been the recognized experts in interpreting the Law/Torah. Interpretation and application of the Torah in *halakhah* was thought to be done by exegesis of Scripture, the Pharisees having begun the process of interpretation attested in later rabbinic texts. In a parallel and closely related construction, the Pharisees were understood to have a two-fold Law/Torah, the written laws of Moses and the Oral Torah also given to Moses at Sinai and then transmitted faithfully by ancestors, as in the sequence of pairs of sages in m. Pirke Abot 1–2.

This overall picture that was standard in the fields of Jewish history and biblical studies, however, is not attested in our sources for second-temple times, which are few and fragmentary, or in later rabbinic texts, which are extensive. The controlling concept of the two-fold Oral and Written Law, for example, turns out to be a modern scholarly construct that has been projected onto ancient sources. The scheme of the two-fold Law was compelling as a simple explanation of evidence of laws and customs that were not contained in the written books of the Torah/Law (Pentateuch), such as the regulations promulgated for the people by the Pharisees from the traditions of the ancestors, according to Josephus (*Ant.* 13.297), thought to be (the same as or) similar to the *paradosis* of the elders mentioned in Mark 7:1–13. Careful critical research into rabbinic texts, however, has shown that the Hebrew phrase and concept "torah in the mouth" (*torah she-ba'al peh*) did not become reflectively crystalized until Amoraic texts in late antiquity.[1]

The demise of the two-fold Law scheme, however, leaves us needing to understand that in late second temple times the Law or laws and customs functioning in Judean society—on which the Pharisees were supposedly the most accurate—were more, and more complex, than those included in the books of the Pentateuch. But the existence and function of texts of torah and traditional laws and customs were evidently obscured, even hidden, by standard controlling concepts in the fields of Jewish history and biblical studies. Probing this complex situation will require a loosening and perhaps abandonment of such concepts. And whether our focal concern is "the Law/Torah" or more narrowly the relation of the Pharisees and "the Law/Torah," it may be necessary to move beyond previously standard concepts and procedure.

Because of the complexities of the material that the fields of Jewish history and biblical studies are dealing with, it became standard scholarly practice to focus narrowly on the passages and text-fragments in sources that are (ostensibly) directly pertinent to particular subjects or issues. For research into the Pharisees and the Law/Torah, this meant focusing on the relatively few passages in Josephus' histories and in the Gospels that mention them and particular rabbinic traditions that mention or were thought to pertain to the Pharisees. Those particular passages, however, are fragmentary components of much longer texts that have broader concerns and implications and can only be understood in broader literary context (e.g., the agenda and perspective of those longer texts). Moreover, the Torah/Law and the Pharisees both functioned in a particular historical context bristling with divisions and conflicts. The limited number of references to the Pharisees, including their relation to the Torah/Law can be more fully and critically assessed only in the broader historical context of late second temple Judea.

---

1. See esp. the elaborate critical investigation by Jaffee, *Torah in the Mouth*.

Taking into Account New Lines of Research

The picture of "the Law/Torah" at the center of "Judaism" and of the Pharisees as its principal interpreters that has been standard is now being undermined and challenged by new developments and researches in the fields of Jewish history and biblical studies.

The Structure and Dynamics of the Changing Historical Context

In the last several decades the political-economic-religious structure and dynamics in second temple Palestine have been probed more precisely and comprehensively than before. Continuing discussion and debate about the Pharisees—and about the conflict between Pharisees and Jesus—have not paid close attention to these recent investigations of the historical context in which "the Law" and the Pharisees functioned. Like other academic fields, Jewish history and biblical studies have become increasingly diverse and specialized so that it is difficult for specialists in one area to stay abreast of developments in other areas. The result is that previously standard constructs and approaches continue to be projected onto second-temple texts and contexts. Taking the recent investigations of the historical context into account requires fresh critical reading of textual sources in their historical contexts. It also requires a more historical approach that considers the historical changes and conflicts in second-temple times.

With regard to "the Law/Torah" it has become evident that previous assumptions and broad generalizations no longer hold. As further attention is being given to the historical contexts, there is considerable debate and no consensus about the development of "the Law/Torah," much less about its functions. Anticipating the discussions in this chapter and the following, I will attempt to account for distinctions in the sources by using "the Torah/Law" with reference to the Pentateuch, the five "books" that became Scripture, evidently gradually and well after the second-temple period; but I will refer to the broader and deeper (scribal) repertoire of "torah/law" (laws, customs, practices) that included materials included in the Pentateuch but other laws/customs that appear in Jubilees and the Temple Scroll (11QT) and other (alternative) "texts of torah" and laws/customs that Josephus included in "the laws/customs" that Moses had supposedly taught but do not appear in the Pentateuch. The Pharisees' "traditions of the elders/ancestors" are included in this broader scribal repertoire. Periodically I will also mention "torah/teaching" (of Moses) as a reminder that "torah" meant "teaching."

With regard to the Pharisees, previous assumptions and concepts and the terms of debates may no longer apply. In order to gain at least some perspective on Judean torah/law(s) and its development and on the origin and role of the Pharisees, it will be necessary to consider critically a wider range of sources and to consider whole sources and not continue to depend on text-fragments taken out of literary and historical contexts.

Chapter 1 above includes an attempt to draw upon information from the instructional wisdom and other material in Sirach about the Judean temple-state and the key role of learned scribes in its operations at a point well into the Hellenistic period and just prior to the Hellenizing crisis early in the second century BCE. As the (only) Jerusalemites who had the leisure to become learned in the torah of the Most High, prophecies, and various kinds of wisdom, learned scribes (or sages) were obviously the cultivators of the (elite) Judean cultural repertoire and the composers and cultivators of texts of torah and prophecy as well as various kinds of wisdom. The structure and dynamics of the Jerusalem temple-state and the role of the scribes laid out in chapter 1 hopefully provides an appropriate beginning context in which to evaluate a wider range of texts pertinent to "the Torah/Law" in second temple times, in this chapter and the next. Chapter 1 also sketches the historical context that immediately preceded the origin and historical role of the Pharisees.

Because the historical context and conflicts became more complicated with the Hasmonean expansion of their control of other areas and people and the Roman conquest and imposition of client rulers, later chapters will draw upon broader recent historical studies.

Most important for understanding the stage of development of the "books" of the Torah/Law and the position and function of learned scribes, particularly the Pharisees, are the profound implications of the new lines of research into ancient communications media. It is necessary to come to grips with these implications before proceeding into other aspects of the Pharisees and scribes in the politics of the temple-state in Hasmonean and Roman times.

Several lines of recent research are exposing the controlling print-cultural assumptions on which the previously standard picture of Judaism, the Law/Torah, and the role of the Pharisees were based. These lines of research have been pursued largely independently. But they turn out to be interrelated, indeed overlapping, and their implications mutually reinforcing for a more appropriate understanding of cultural practices in second-temple Judea and the political-economic-religious institutions of the historical context. It is possible to bring them together in assessing their impact toward a more nuanced and historically appropriate understanding of the torah/

laws and customs) and of the role of the Pharisees in their cultivation in late second-temple times.[2]

Limited Literacy and the Dominance of Oral Communication

Perhaps the broadest challenge to the most important assumption of the fields of Jewish history and biblical studies comes from decades-long research demonstrating that communications in the ancient world were predominantly oral, with literacy severely limited.

Because the field of biblical studies is so deeply embedded in print-culture, it is important to recognize that in traditional societies communication proceeded orally in nearly all aspects of life, whether in village communities or in the ruling cities. Particularly important in sustaining personal and collective identity, social interaction, and cultural coherence over generations were the stories told and the songs sung and the rituals performed, all of which were known in the collective memory. Local or regional customs, such as how and when to redistribute land or how the village assembly or community elders should handle disputes were remembered by whole communities, perhaps especially by local elders.

Oral communication was clearly dominant throughout the Roman Empire, and literacy extremely limited, estimated at around 10%.[3] Writing functioned primarily as an instrument of power. For example, the "census" of how much tribute could be taken from the people of a given territory was kept in writing (cf. Luke 2:1). The rate of literacy in Roman Palestine was as low as three percent, as is now well-documented.[4] Judean and Galilean villagers and urban artisans communicated orally, with no need for writing. As in other areas of the Roman Empire, villagers and urban artisans in the areas of Palestine conducted transactions of all kinds orally, usually face to face. Local loans, for example, were agreed upon orally, often confirmed by

---

2. The following discussion builds on the ground-breaking and foundational investigations and reflections of Werner Kelber, particularly on the essays in *Imprints, Voiceprints, and Footprints of Memory*; and on my own earlier attempts to explore and bring together some of the separate lines of research into ancient communications media, particularly Horsley, *Scribes, Visionaries*, chaps. 4–6; and Horsley, *Text and Tradition in Performance and Writing*, chaps. 1–5.

3. The standard work is Harris, *Ancient Literacy*, on which the following sketch depends. Harris' analysis and conclusions are confirmed by other scholars' research and analysis, such as Mary Beard et al., *Literacy in the Roman World*; and Bowman and Woolf, eds., *Literacy and Power in the Ancient World*.

4. The extensive research in Hezser, *Jewish Literacy in Roman Palestine*, confirms and much more fully documents what several of us sketched earlier in articles and book chapters.

witnesses, the transfer of symbolic objects, and/or personal oaths. Such interactions were regulated by time-honored customs and rituals, with oaths and witnesses, judging from rabbinic references. Ordinary people thought that personal witnesses and testimony were far more trustworthy than written documents that could be manipulated by the literate for their own advantage. In fact, they were suspicious of writing, as in the popular attack on the archives in Jerusalem at the outset of the Great Revolt, "to destroy the money-lenders' bonds and prevent the recovery of debts" (Josephus, *War* 2.426–427).

Literacy in Roman Palestine was limited mainly to scribal circles in Jerusalem and later the nascent rabbinic circles. The situation was complicated by the different languages. The general impression and scholarly consensus are that Aramaic was the language spoken by the people, while only the scribal elite were trained in ("biblical") Hebrew.[5] The language of the wider Hellenistic and then Roman imperial context was Greek, which would also have been the language of some or many communities of Judeans living in cities of the Empire.

Insofar as modern biblical studies developed on the basis of print-culture and the field's purpose was to interpret *sacred written texts* (Scripture), it is perhaps understandable that even scholars who had become aware of the limited literacy continued to trust previously standard claims about general literacy among Judeans (who were supposedly a people of the book). "According to Josephus, in first century Judaism it was . . . a religious commandment that . . . children be taught to read . . . [R]abbinic sources suggest . . . that by the first century C.E. . . . . even small communities had elementary schools."[6] The key passages cited from Josephus, however, indicate not that children were taught to read but that the teaching and learning of "the laws" were done through public oral recitation (at Sabbath assemblies). In these boastful apologetic passages, Josephus is probably referring to Judeans in diaspora synagogues. Through recitation and hearing the laws would become "engraved on [the people's] souls . . . and guarded in their memory" (*Ant.* 4.210; 16.43; *Ag. Ap.* 2.175, 178, 204; cf. Philo, *Embassy* 115, 210). The rabbinic texts cited about "schools" refer rather to rabbinic circles themselves, a tiny segment of the population, not to schools among the wider population.

---

5. The basic picture has changed little following the study of Fitzmyer, "The Languages of Palestine in the First Century A.D." Poirier, "The Linguistic Situation in Jewish Palestine in Late Antiquity," updates Fitzmyer's survey, coming to roughly the same conclusions. See also the coverage of the expanded evidence in Smelick, "The Languages of Roman Palestine"; and critical review of the evidence, considering multiple factors, in Horsley, "The Languages of the Kingdom," 201–5.

6. Gamble, *Books and Readers in the Early Church*, 7.

And rabbinic sources cited as evidence of *reading* (e.g., m. Berakot 4:3; m. Bikkurim 3:7; m. Sukkah 3:10) refer rather to *recitation* of certain psalms and prayers from memory.

Historically, and varying from society to society and within societies, there have been different modes of oral communication and different literacies.[7] Practices of reading (or more likely recitation) and writing have been culturally embedded in the wider and deeper sea of oral communications and have expressed the interests usually of the literate elite. Ironically our only access to oral communications is through texts that are extant because they were written and rewritten, then in modern times "established" from manuscripts by text critics and, along with translations, set into print. Since we "biblical" scholars have been trained in a field that is deeply embedded in print-culture into which we have been socialized, moreover, much of our discussion of ancient texts is conducted in concepts derived from print-culture. Thus it is important not to uncritically impose modern typographical assumptions and concepts in which our scholarship is embedded onto ancient texts and the oral communication that might be discernible in or through the written texts that are the only remains visible of the much deeper "biosphere" of communication from which they grew.[8] It is important, therefore, to investigate specific social practices of communication and practices of reading and writing *and* practices of recitation and oral performance.[9]

Another line of largely independent recent research and analysis has been attempting to do just this: critical investigation of the practices of the learned scribes (sages) who produced and cultivated texts in the course of their service in the Judean temple-state.

The Oral-Written Training and Practice of Judean Scribes

For the field of biblical studies it is especially important to recognize how written texts were produced and cultivated prior to the rise of print-culture, along with their interface with oral communication, including the oral cultivation of texts. An obvious step therefore would be to attend to recent

---

7. For this reason I am attempting to avoid abstract "-ity" terms and concepts such as orality and textuality and focusing on particular modes of oral communication and different kinds and functions of writing.

8. See especially the call for the field to critically rethink its own birth and basis in print-culture by the pioneer in the study of orality, Werner Kelber, in "Jesus and Tradition" and other articles reprinted in *Imprints, Voiceprints*.

9. See further Street, *Literacy in Theory and Practice*, 2–3; Foley, *How to Read an Oral Poem*, 66–69.

research into the training and practices of ancient Judean scribes who were producing and cultivating the very texts that are studied and interpreted in biblical studies, including texts of torah.

Recent studies of the training of learned scribes for service in the Judean monarchy and temple-state[10] have been able to build on investigations of the training and functions of learned scribes in the imperial regimes in Egypt and Mesopotamia (for which sources are fairly plentiful). As noted in chapter 1, the purpose was to inculcate the personal discipline and obedience to higher authority suited for service in an imperial court or temple-state. The skills of reading and writing were fundamental, yet ancillary to the inculcation of culture and the learning of the cultural repertoire of knowledge of which the learned scribes were, over the generations, the cultivators and guardians. Studies of the training of scribes in ancient Egypt and Mesopotamia find that learning was done primarily through recitation or performance.[11] "Indeed, most of the core texts appear to have been composed for oral performance, with use of metrical, episodic, and repetitive structures that would cue a performer seeking oral mastery of the text."[12] Scribal training and practice should thus not be equated with writing and written texts. It was rather oral-written. While it included writing and reading, scribal learning proceeded mainly in an oral-aural mode, by recitation and hearing.[13] As in the imperial courts in Mesopotamia and Egypt, scribes in Judea learned texts in the Judean scribal repertoire by hearing them recited and then cultivated them in recitation or performance.

Scribal training took place in scribal families where the students were addressed as "my children," mainly "sons," whether actual sons or non-family members brought in as students. As important as the acquisition of skills and cultural content in the family apprenticeship, a principal function of scribal training was the inculcation of a conservative character appropriate to the scribes' sociocultural role. The qualities of character necessary for scribes' social-political-religious functions would have included patience with detail for lower-level administrative tasks and especially personal

---

10. Van der Toorn, *Scribal Culture and the Making of the Hebrew Bible*; and Carr, *Writing on the Tablet of the Heart*; on which I have drawn here, as in Horsley, *Scribes, Visionaries*, chaps. 4–6.

11. The Egyptian term *sdj* usually translated as "read," referred rather to performance. The voicing of the texts was often by singing or chanting. References and discussion in Carr, *Tablet of the Heart*, 72.

12. Carr, *Writing on the Tablet of the Heart*, 72, 78, who notes that Egyptologists take the fact that only consonants were represented in writing as another mark of the primacy of oral recitation in scribal training.

13. As stated repeatedly by Carr, *Writing on the Tablet of the Heart*, e.g., 21, 64, 73, 86.

discipline and obedience to higher authority. Parent-teachers/masters admonished their students/proteges repeatedly, by precept and example, to fear the Lord, guard their tongue, defer to their superiors, and to lead lives that were beyond reproach. In the course of this rigorous process of character-formation, scribes-in-training were shaped as the bearers of elite culture and character in the temple-state.

A deeply important aspect of the training of aspiring sages/scribes, one that has not received sufficient attention, was the close personal relationship between, indeed devotion of the student/protégé and the "father"-teacher/master. This may be because texts from earlier second-temple times do not reach into close personal relations. Not until rabbinic lore in late antiquity do we find indications of the deep attachment and devotion of students to their mentors.

But the close relationship in which the character-shaping power of the master's teaching was so effective because embodied in the master that Martin Jaffee[14] describes among the Amoraic discipleship communities in Galilee was surely already prefigured in the training of earlier Judean scribes, such as Ben Sira and his "sons." There are at least some indications of scribes/sages deeply honoring the great ancestral sages whose lives-and-teaching they themselves are continuing: The *maskilim* looked to the archetypal sage Daniel, the producers of "Enoch"-texts understood themselves as the students-progeny of the primordial scribe Enoch, taught by God himself. It should not be surprising that we find indications of the close personal teacher-student relations continuing among scribal teachers and students into Roman times: Josephus mentions that the sages/scribes (*sosphistai*) Judas son of Sepphoraeus and Matthias son of Margalus were widely revered in Jerusalem as the teachers of their young students. His account then indicates the students' faithful devotion to their teachers in their braving death in obedience to ancestral law that required cutting down the Roman eagle over the gate of the temple that symbolized Roman imperial rule in place of the rule of God (to be discussed in chap. 6).

While rare in other extant Judean texts, a rich array of indications of scribal training and practice appear in the instructional speeches of the prominent Jerusalem scribe Yeshua ben Sira.[15] Ben Sira admonished his protégés to fear the Lord, lead lives beyond reproach, and defer to their superiors (and patrons) in the Judean aristocracy. Writing was involved, but only ancillary to broader learning. He had "written" understanding "in

---

14. Jaffee, *Torah in the Mouth*, esp. chap. 7.

15. Fuller discussion in Horsley, *Scribes, Visionaries*, chaps. 3–5, 7, on which the following depends.

this writing" (50:27). In his "house of instruction," however, Ben Sira taught not by asking his students to "open a writing," but by "opening his mouth" (51:23–25). "For wisdom becomes known through speech" (4:24). Students would "learn how to serve princes" "from the discourse of the sages" (8:8–9). Nothing in Ben Sira's representation of learning suggests that written texts were involved.

In a speech boasting the importance of the scribe to the temple-state Ben Sira provides a fundamental description of the elite Judean culture of which he and others were the custodians. Basic in his outline of the curriculum of Judean scribal training were the principal forms of wisdom ("sayings of the famous, . . . parables, . . . proverbs," 39:2–3). But the curriculum also included the other segments of the Judean scribal repertoire, as the scribe also "held in mind the torah (teaching, laws) of the Most High" and was engaged "with prophecies" (39:1), as noted in chap 1. Scribes were trained to assume their important role in "the assemblies of the rulers," by oral-aural learning of the cultural repertoire of torah, wisdom, and prophecies (5:10–11; 5:13—6:1; 11:7–9; 15:5; 21:15–17; 23:7–12; 27:11–15; etc.). Scribes could then draw upon a deep reservoir of torah (teaching, laws) in their memory as occasions arose in the assemblies and councils in which they served as those who knew what particular torah/teachings/laws (or prophecies or proverbs) were applicable to issues that arose (38:32–34; 4:9; 6:34; 7:14; 11:7–9; 15:5; 21:17; 42:2).

Instruction in writing and responsibilities (of some) for copying and preserving written texts may have aided scribes' learning, effecting a certain stabilization of orally-cultivated texts. It is significant that Judean scribes, like their predecessors in Egyptian courts and temples, understood the internalization of texts in a chirographic metaphor: "written on the tablet of the heart" (Prov 3:3; 7:3).[16]

That metaphor points to the essential role and importance of *memory* in the cultivation of texts. "Inscription" on the memory happened in the process of oral recitation, hearing, and further recitation.[17] From the studies

---

16. As explained by Assmann, "Kulturelle und Literarische Texte," the same metaphor was used in ancient Egypt for the socialization of scribes into the ruling class, as (what he calls) "the cultural texts" became fixed firmly "in their hearts" (69–70). The *Satirical Polemic* 10/9—11/3 is rendered, "You are a skilled scribe at the head of his fellows and the teaching of every book is incised on your heart"—cited by Carr, *Writing on the Tablet of the Heart*, 64, 73; cf. 86, where again he emphasizes "orality and memorization" via "hearing."

17. Carr, *Writing on the Tablet of the Heart*, 86. Cribiore, in *Gymnastics of the Mind*, a study of the education of the Greek-speaking elite in Egypt, while still projecting print-cultural concepts such as writers, written books, and readers onto Greco-Roman antiquity, clearly recognizes the central importance of memory; see esp. 130, 149–51,

of scribal training and practice in Egypt and Mesopotamia and Judea, it is clear that the primary "place" for "storage" of texts was in the memory of those who had internalized them by repeated recitation.[18] A principal goal of scribal training and of continuing practice was memorized mastery of the repertoire of (scribal) culture-texts. The writing systems were extremely complex; scribes could not have read texts inscribed on scrolls unless they had already memorized them. In the imperial courts and temples of Mesopotamia and Egypt "scribes would not have worked with written scrolls on an everyday basis."[19] Similarly Judean scribes would not have needed to eye a written scroll in front of them either for recitation or for inscribing a new scroll. Having memorized (virtually but perhaps not verbatim) the (multiple) texts of the cultural repertoire they could either have recited (selections from) them (as appropriate) before an assembly of high priests or in instruction of their students and they could have dictated the text to another scribe (or mumbled it to themselves) in order to inscribe a new scroll.[20]

As we have learned again about the intellectual elites of antiquity and the middle ages, they had prodigious capacities for memory of long and complicated texts, with elaborate systems of memory that "stored" texts in various "locations," *topoi* (places, hence the term "topics").[21] This helps explain how the repertoire of authoritative Judean texts could include what seems like a collection and compendium of different smaller texts (for example, the "book" of Isaiah or of Jeremiah) *and* why we find in the horde of written texts at Qumran different versions of such a compendium. The composition and recomposition of such texts did not require visual copying of earlier written scrolls, but scribes working from their capacious memory.

The remarkable capacity of the memory of ancient cultural elites can be illustrated from two features of the continuation of Judean scribal training and practice in rabbinic circles. In reference to the texts of the (scribal) cultural repertoire, a distinction was made between "what was written" (*ketib*) and "what was recited" (*qere*).[22] "What was recited" was carried and

---

231–32.

18. Carr, *Writing on the Tablet of the Heart*, 82. The way scribal communication worked in oral communication, traditions and texts were recited orally, received aurally, with memory as the connector between ear and mouth, mouth and ear, as stated by Jaffee, *Torah in the Mouth*, 17–18.

19. Carr, *Writing on the Tablet of the Heart*, 75, 80, 82.

20. Carr, *Writing on the Tablet of the Heart*, 159–60; Horsley, *Scribes, Visionaries*, chaps. 5–6.

21. Carruthers, *The Book of Memory*. On storage in memory in antiquity, see Cribiore, *Gymnastics of Mind*, 149–51, 231–32.

22. See Green, "Writing with Scripture"; and the broader survey from "biblical"

repeatedly actualized from the rabbis' individual and collective memory. Also, as is well known, the rabbis taught their students the intricate debates about *halakhah* through recitation. They held that once students had heard a teaching or a traditional rabbinic debate about an issue recited several times, they should remember it.[23] It may not have been until the end of the second century CE that the tractates of the Mishnah and Tosefta were put into writing[24]—while the teaching continued in oral repetition, with the addition of ever more complexifying *gemara* that eventually was compiled in the respective Jerusalem and Babylonian Talmuds.[25]

In biblical studies, modern scholars have standardly projected their own practices of "reading," "studying," and "interpreting" scripture in standard translations and interpretations. A key passage in the Community Rule of the scribal-priestly community at Qumran, where written scrolls were kept and texts inscribed on new scrolls, provides an illustration of how it is necessary rather to recognize what Martin Jaffee calls the "oral-performative tradition" by which authoritative texts were appropriated, cultivated, and perpetuated in the oral-written communication environment of this Judean scribal-priestly community.[26]

> Where the ten are, there shall never lack a man among them who searches[27] the teaching [*dwrs btwrh*] day and night, concerning the right conduct of a man with his companion. And the many shall watch in community for a third of every night of the year, to recite the writing [*lqrw' bspr*] and to search the justice-ruling [*ldwrs mspt*] and to offer blessings communally [*lbrk byhd*]. (1QS 6:6-8)[28]

---

texts to ancient and medieval "reading" (i.e. recitation) practices by Boyarin, "Placing Reading."

23. See the more general discussion in Jaffee, *Torah in the Mouth*.

24. On the other hand, the very learned Saul Lieberman, *Hellenism in Jewish Palestine*, 87–91, suggested some time ago that the Mishnah was "published" not in written form but in the form of "a fixed text recited by the Tannaim" (the "repeaters" or "reciters"). "Evidently the Tanna was a living book" (90).

25. Later, in medieval European cultivation of important culture texts, memorial internalization and recitation were not differentiated. In ancient and medieval elite cultural circles, manuscripts were produced and maintained, but were "almost accidental" or "reference points" to the oral-memorial cycle of repeated recitation by which texts continued their life. See the discussion in Carruthers, *The Book of Memory*, 156.

26. Jaffee, *Torah in the Mouth*.

27. In Qumran usage *doresh* still had predominantly the meaning "to seek" or "to inquire," with only isolated instances of meaning "expounding."

28. Adapted from Vermes, *Complete Dead Sea Scrolls in English*.

All three of the activities mentioned, recitation, "searching," and uttering blessings, were clearly oral. The "writing" is usually assumed to have been a scroll of "the Torah," probably Deuteronomy, since it is the only one that claims to be a "book" and to prescribe its own periodic recitation (Deut 31:24–26; cf. 28:58–61). But even if a scroll of torah were open in front of the reciter(s), the recitation would have been from memory. The text was inscribed on the memory of the scribes and priests of the community. The function of the recitation of torah in the communities associated with the Dead Sea Scrolls, like the learning by recitation of texts by scribes-in-training, was not external study and interpretation but the (in this case, collective) internalization of spiritual-moral discipline.[29] The result would have been also the oral-memorial knowledge of many texts and of the wider and deeper cultural repertoire in which those texts were embedded.

Recent researches into ancient communication and into scribal training and practice are thus undermining the standard assumption in biblical studies that most Judeans would have known the Torah/Law by having read written texts (the Scriptures). Literacy was confined mainly to the scribes, but they learned texts by repeated recitation and not by reading cumbersome scrolls. The training and professional practice of scribes was devoted to learning and cultivating in memory the various texts of the cultural repertoire as well as cultivating an ability to recite those texts in appropriate occasions. If written texts were involved either as the source of scribal knowledge of a given text or as an aid in the recitation, they played (only) an instrumental role in a much more intensive process of oral learning, cultivation, and performance of cultural texts and their transmission to successive generations of scribes.[30]

---

29. See further Horsley, *Scribes, Visionaries,* chap. 5; as indicated in 1QS 6:6–8, the internalization of texts by recitation (oral performance) was collective as well as individual-personal. That the function of oral-memorial recitation was collective internalization of texts is confirmed by a Qumran scholar who discerns appropriation of texts via reading aloud in a "deeply social context;" see Popović, "Reading, Writing, and Memorizing Together," esp. 448, 453–56. More generally, see now the ground-breaking study by Miller, *Dead Sea Media.*

30. Carr, *Tablet of the Heart,* 4–9, and repeatedly through the book, stresses the central role of memory in the learning and recitation of cultural texts. As Redford, "Scribe and Speaker," 218, comments about the primacy of orality in learning and recitation of texts in Egypt, "all that the writer-scribe can do is to try to keep abreast of a genuinely oral tradition that enjoys its own vibrant life, and record its momentary stages."

Different Kinds of Writing

Closely related to the recent research on oral communication and the limits of literacy has been critical discernment of the different kinds of writing produced by scribes, who were virtually the only people trained in writing. The term *seper* in Hebrew was used for all sorts of writing, only some of which would be appropriately understood as written texts in the sense of "books" (the term "book" is a modern metaphor derived from print-culture).[31] In ancient Judea and other societies, writing functioned in ways quite different from those assumed in modern print culture. Most important is to recognize that by no means was all writing produced for reading to obtain information or for storage of knowledge. Some of the most important writing was iconic or monumental rather than informative.

Some "writings" were short and simple but powerful in their social impact. A prime example of such a brief "writing" is the *seper* of the purchase of land of his next-of-kin that Jeremiah and others signed (Jer 32:6–15). The scribe Baruch deposited both the sealed "deed" and the open copy in a pottery-jar for long-term preservation. This writing was thus clearly not intended as a record to be consulted or presented as proof of "ownership." It was rather a "pledge to posterity," an assurance of continuity under God's providence.[32] In this case the prophet Jeremiah made the "permanent" writing of the deed into a prophetic sign in the context of the imminent Babylonian conquest of Judah, a symbol of God's promise of continuity of Judean society and its tradition of ancestral land in each multigenerational family as a basis of their livelihood.

Another example of such a brief formulaic message that operated at a local level directly pertinent to the Pharisees' conflict with Jesus was a husband's *seper* of divorce placed in his wife's hand as he sent her out of the household (Deut 24:1–4).[33]

This *seper* of divorce is also an example of how, in a predominantly oral society where writing was rare, it could be particularly powerful. In religious ceremonies and sacred sites such as temples, writing exuded a special aura of authority. It was *numinous* in its power. The ultimate in such *numinous* writing was that of God. The covenant commandments, "words" in short formulaic phrases, were portrayed as not only delivered by Yahweh "in a

---

31. The discussion of different kinds of writing and how they are related to oral communication by Niditch, *Oral World*, is particularly illuminating.

32. See further Niditch, *Oral World*, 62–63. These simple messages were similar to the records from medieval England discussed by M. T. Clanchy, *From Memory to Written Record: England 1066–1307* (Cambridge: Harvard University Press, 1979), 125.

33. This will be discussed in Volume 2, chap. 3.

loud voice," but engraved on stone by the finger of God in the theophany at Sinai (Exod 24:12; 31:18; 32:16; Deut 4:13; 5:22; 9:10). This gave them awesome power and authority. Placing these tablets written by God into the ark of the covenant made it "electric" with divine power.

The divinely-derived "*seper* of the covenant/teaching (*berit/torah*)," besides being numinous, was also *monumental* writing. This is by far the most important writing mentioned in Judean texts, playing a prominent role in Exodus, Deuteronomy, Joshua, 2 Kings, and Nehemiah. The best-known examples of monumental writing in antiquity are the stele(s) of Hammurabi in Mesopotamia and the *Res gestae* of Augustus inscribed on triumphal arches in cities of the Roman Empire. Such monumental writings were not intended to be read cognitively by the (largely non-literate) people to learn the contents of the laws or the founding legend of the imperial regime.[34] They were rather inscriptions on awesome monuments to impress the people with the power of their rulers.

The "books" of Exodus, Deuteronomy, and Joshua present repeated accounts of "the *seper* of the torah or covenant" as a *monumental* writing. In the covenant-making ceremony on Mt. Sinai (Exod 24:3–7), "Moses wrote down all the words of Yahweh."[35] Again, after he had delivered an extended covenantal teaching (*torah*), Moses "wrote down in a *seper* the words of this teaching" and commanded the Levites to "place it beside the ark of the covenant of Yahweh... as a witness against you" (Deut 31:24–26; cf. 28:58–61). Leading a covenant renewal ceremony, Joshua, as instructed (in Deut 27:3–8), "wrote on the stones [of the altar he had built] ... a copy of the teaching of Moses, which he had written" (Josh 8:31–32). In a concluding ceremony of covenant renewal Joshua pointed to the covenantal laws written on a large stone as witness (Josh 24:25–27).[36] As symbolized

---

34. "Monuments are not to be read word for word to obtain information." Niditch, *Oral World*, 55.

35. Yahweh was understood as the people's ruler, their transcendent "king." This conception was central throughout the "books" of Torah and Prophets and will be throughout discussion in these chapters.

36. While discussing the writing of torah/covenant, we should note another aspect of these accounts that are directly relevant to understanding the Law/laws as cultivated by the Pharisees and others. The scribes who produced these accounts evidently just assumed that in successive "writings" of the torah the laws had multiplied and become more complex. Joshua and his contemporaries are represented as having "a copy of the teaching of Moses which he wrote" (8:32), presumably what Moses had received from God. "The document of the teaching (of Moses)" in Josh 8:30–35, and the teaching that Joshua wrote on stones in Josh 24:25–26, however, appear to be what was known to the later reciters/hearers of the book of Joshua (not to Joshua and the Israelites in the covenant ceremonies led by Joshua). Clearly the covenantal torah was undergoing some development from one "writing" to the next.

by its inscription on the stones, the *seper* of the covenant/teaching was a permanent *monumental* witness to the covenant with YHWH, who was understood as the people's ruler.

Such numinous writing full of divine presence and power came alive and became effective in speech, in its oral performance—in an integral relation between *what is written* and its oral performance that seems strange to modern people socialized into print culture. Yet that the "words" of YHWH were written made them all the more effective when proclaimed into the ears of the people ("all that Yahweh has spoken we will do"). But while the people internalized the covenantal text by hearing it performed, it continued as a monumental writing with an independent numinous existence over against them. Such a monumental writing of the covenant teaching (= *torah*) externalized and eternalized the covenant between Yahweh and Israel, guaranteeing its continuing force. It was not primarily a text from which the people could learn the content of the statues and ordinances or which priests and scribes could later consult.[37] And even its ceremonial recitation to the people was not primarily to help them learn the particular laws but to commit them to the covenantal relationship with Yahweh in a ceremonial re-enactment of the covenant.

Results of Close Study of Previously Unknown Texts and MSS from the Dead Sea Scrolls

Research into and critical analysis of the scrolls discovered seventy-some years ago in the wilderness of Judea are also undermining and challenging previous assumption and concepts in the fields of Jewish history and biblical studies. Particularly important are the MSS of books later included in the Hebrew Bible and previously unknown texts discovered at Qumran, including alternative texts of torah.

Found among the Dead Sea Scrolls at Qumran were scrolls of the "books" of the Torah/Pentateuch that were more than a thousand years older than the (medieval) MSS that had served as the basis of the *textus receptus* "established" (constructed) by earlier generations of text critics. These ancient MSS and the careful text-critical analysis of them during the last few decades pose the most direct challenge to what had been the standard understanding of the "books" of the Torah/Law as Scripture supposedly known by all or most Jews in late second-temple times. Widely

---

37. Cf. Niditch, *Oral World*, 83–88; Jaffee, *Torah in the Mouth*, 16: "Inscribed objects in general, and books in particular, commonly functioned as ritual objects whose iconic significance *transcended that of the information they preserved.*"

recognized text-critical authorities devoted their whole careers to patiently poring over these scrolls, comparing them to previously known MSS and recognized reconstructions of the Masoretic text, the text of the Samaritan Pentateuch, and the Hebrew *Vorlage* of the Septuagint. Eugene Ulrich, for example, concluded that among the Qumran scrolls of "books" that were later included in the Hebrew Bible there were evidently multiple versions of the texts; these versions did not correspond neatly to the textual versions known from later, medieval MSS. All of these versions, moreover, had still been undergoing changes during late second-temple times. There thus had been no standardized text (of the "books") of the Torah/Pentateuch. As Ulrich pointed out, there is no sense in speaking of late second-temple times as the "biblical world" since there was no Bible yet.

Also found among the DSS were previously unknown texts of torah, such as the Temple Scroll (11QT), and several copies of (parts of) the "book" of Jubilees. These texts and others such as the *Biblical Antiquities* of Pseudo-Philo included episodes and laws known from the books that were later included in the Bible. Scholars of the Dead Sea Scrolls previously referred to these texts as "rewritten Bible/Scripture." This label suggested that these texts were derivative from and secondary to the books of the Torah, leaving the prime authority of the latter intact as Scripture.

More critical examination, however, led to three recognitions that complicated developing understanding of the forms of torah and the function of torah in the Qumran community in particular and in the Judean temple-state more broadly.

First, the Temple Scroll and the copies of Jubilees were more complex than the concept of "rewritten Bible" allowed. The book of Jubilees takes its framework and much of its contents from the narrative in the beginning of Genesis to the covenant scene at Sinai in Exod 19. But the book does not include much that is contained in Genesis and Exodus, and includes figures, legends, and lore not included in those books. Most important with regard to torah/law, Jubilees systematically relocates torah familiar to us from passages in Leviticus, Numbers, and Deuteronomy to points in the patriarchal-matriarchal narratives where the issues addressed first appear— i.e., long before such torah is first revealed to Moses on Sinai (as in Exodus-Numbers-Leviticus). Jubilees, moreover, includes laws and rulings that do not appear in any of the "books" of the Pentateuch. The Temple Scroll is a utopian "charter" for the final temple that God would construct. The text draws on various traditions of the wilderness tabernacle, Solomon's temple, and the schematic temple of Ezekiel. It follows the 364–day calendar known also in Jubilees and 1 Enoch 72–82 and enhances festivals and sacrifices beyond what was prescribed in the books of the Pentateuch.

Second, the Temple Scroll and Jubilees claimed greater authority than the "books" of the Pentateuch insofar as they had supposedly come directly from God prior to the revelation to Moses. Torah revealed to Moses on Sinai had already been written on heavenly tablets. Jubilees has many instances of torah revealed to the patriarchs from the heavenly tablets long before they were revealed to Moses on Sinai. It even makes a distinction between itself and "(the book of) the first torah/law" (Jub. 2:24; 6:22; 30:10). Texts such as the Temple Scroll and Jubilees were thus evidently *alternative books of torah*. And the coexistence of these other texts of torah combined with the multiple versions of the "books" of the Pentateuch suggest that *all of them had (only) relative authority in late second-temple times*.[38]

Third, the Temple Scroll and Jubilees contained torah/teachings/laws that were not included in the "books" (Exodus, Leviticus, Numbers, Deuteronomy) that supposedly had already become *the* Scripture of Judaism. This suggests that the composers of texts such as the Temple Scroll and Jubilees knew a range of laws or teachings/torah that had not been included in the "books" of the Pentateuch. There was evidently a reservoir of torah (different, or different versions of, laws and customs and episodes) that had been functioning "underneath" what is known to us from previously known texts, some of this torah evidently not previously included in texts that were (also) written.

Implications for Understanding the Torah/Law and Pharisees

These heretofore largely separate lines of recent research into the historical context(s), aspects of ancient communications media, scribal training and practice, different kinds of writing, and the different versions of "biblical" books and alternative texts of torah found at Qumran all undermine one or more of the most basic assumptions and constructs of biblical studies. It is not surprising that established biblical studies, a product of modern print-culture and deeply rooted in its assumption, is threatened by these lines of research and has been resisting their implications. For example, it would be the most existential of threats to scholars who have dedicated their lives to interpretation of particular books of the Bible to recognize the findings of "revisionist" Hebrew Bible (Old Testament) text criticism that the diverse MSS of "books" of the Torah/Pentateuch found at Qumran indicate that there was no standardized text of those "books." More generally it makes

---

38. If the number of scrolls of particular books found at Qumran is an indication of their relative authority, then the 15 scrolls of Jubilees suggests that it rivaled Exodus, at 17 scrolls, and Leviticus, at 14 scrolls.

scholars dedicated to interpreting written texts, Holy Writ, uneasy to admit that communication of those who produced the "books" that later were recognized as Scripture was predominantly oral—even for the literate scribes, who learned texts by repeated recitation and not by reading scrolls.

Heretofore, however, these lines of research have been pursued separately. As is typical of the diversified field of biblical studies, specialists on one area or subject of study simply cannot keep up with developments in other specialized areas or subjects. The result is largely separate silos of special knowledge and analysis. As should be evident from the brief survey of the separate lines of research just above, however, the areas of these researches are closely related. Not only can they help illuminate one another's findings. But if these separate lines of research were brought together the implications pose more serious challenges to the assumptions and constructs of the fields of biblical studies and Jewish history.

If we bring them together the lines of recent research and the diverse manuscripts of "books" later included in the Hebrew Bible found at Qumran can help illuminate one another. That there were different versions of a text, as found by Ulrich and others, shows both that the text had a certain well-defined general outline and that it was still being developed. That scribes learned texts of torah (and other texts) by repeated recitation so that they became "written" in their memory means that the latter became a factor in the inscription of the text on new scrolls. The co-existence of different versions of authoritative texts of torah and prophets as well as other texts of torah (evidently also authoritative) strongly suggest that *the already defined texts were embedded in a broader and deeper repertoire of torah in Judean scribal culture,* just as there were different kinds of wisdom in the scribal repertoire of wisdom (as indicated in Sir 39:1–4).[39] In their training and practice, scribes would presumably have learned (internalized in their individual and collective memory) the broader and deeper repertoire of torah so that torah not already included in the "books" that later came to comprise the Torah/Pentateuch could play a role in the composition and development of new (alternative) texts of torah.

The implications of correlating these lines of new research thus undermine a fundamental assumption about "the Torah/Law" and its functioning in Judean society. Text-critics of the newly discovered scrolls have shown that there was no standard text (of the books) of the Torah but multiple

---

39. This is among the points developed in the multifaceted argument in Horsley, *Scribes, Visionaries,* chaps. 4–6. The flexibility and continuing development of Judean scribal texts of torah was anticipated in Najman, *Seconding Sinai,* particularly in her discussion of the gradual production of Deuteronomy (in chap. 1) and in the discussion of Jubilees and 11QTemple (in chap. 2).

versions of the different "books" of the Torah/Pentateuch. That there were also other, alternative "books" of torah suggests further that the "books" of the Pentateuch, while having authority, had authority relative to both the alternative texts of torah and the wider repertoire of torah cultivated in scribal circles. That literacy was severely limited, mainly to the scribes serving the temple-state, moreover, suggests that texts inscribed on scrolls and in the scribal memory had authority mainly in the scribal circles that cultivated them. All of the texts written on scrolls would have been confined to scribal circles or (probably) laid up in the temple.[40] The villagers who comprised the vast majority of the people and probably spoke dialects of Aramaic would likely have had no direct contact with these scrolls inscribed in "biblical" Hebrew and could not have read them anyhow.[41]

We should not imagine, however, that villagers/peasants had no knowledge of Israelite tradition because they were not literate. The people's very identity was embedded in the stories and legends of the exodus, wilderness wandering, and subsequent events in Israelite history. They would certainly have known and celebrated the exodus from Egypt at Passover. They would also have known the commandments of the Mosaic covenant that guided local social-economic interaction and time-honored customs such as making loans to one another without interest and leaving some grain and grapes in the fields for their needy neighbors to glean at harvest time. There are thus plenty of indications that the villagers of Judea and Galilee were rooted in and cultivated orally their own Israelite popular tradition, just as peasants in other agrarian societies lived out of what anthropologists have called a "little tradition" that is parallel to a corresponding "great tradition" that exists partly in written form.[42] It will be important for understanding the conflict between the Pharisees and Jesus to discuss the Israelite popular tradition in which villagers' life and identity were embedded in Volume 2.

---

40. The implications of these recent lines of research into scribal practices and text-criticism of recently discovered MSS of biblical books were prefigured and anticipated over a generation ago by the great rabbinics scholar, Saul Lieberman, in *Hellenism in Jewish Palestine*, 20–27, 83–99. It is unclear to me whether the reference to written texts deposited in the treasury of the temple in 1 Macc 14:48 might include sacred scrolls of torah or prophets.

41. An important implication of severely limited literacy in ancient Jewish Palestine is that the books that were later included in the Bible cannot be used as direct sources for village life (what the vast majority of Israelites who lived in village communities believed and practiced) in late second temple times, although they are essential as indirect sources.

42. Discussion in Horsley, "Contesting Authority," and more broadly the cross-cultural discussion in J. C. Scott, "Protest and Profanation."

3

Laws/Customs, *Politeia*, and Traditions of the Judeans

During the centuries preceding the Hellenizing "reform" and the Maccabean Revolt the temple-state in Jerusalem had become well-established as the ruling institution of the tiny territory of *Yehud,* under the overarching rule of a succession of empires. The restoration and continuation of the political-economic-religious institution in control of Judea and Judeans is often obscured by the continuing use of the synthetic construct of (early) Judaism. When the Hasmonean leaders of the revolt finally fought rival Seleucid regimes to a standstill in the 160s and 150s BCE, they reverted to the temple-state as the institutional form in which to exercise their rule. First Jonathan and then Simon negotiated with the weakened Seleucid regime(s) for recognition as High Priest. This indicates that the temple-state had become sufficiently well-rooted among Jerusalemites, and perhaps many Judean villagers as well, that they would at least accept the restoration of the temple-state despite the Hasmoneans being ordinary village priests, hence unqualified by their lineage to become the reigning high priests.

Drawing heavily on the instructional speeches of the distinguished Jerusalem sage/scribe Yeshua ben Sira, chapter 1 sketched the structure and dynamics of the temple-state and its operations in which learned scribes served as the intellectual-legal retainers. Chapter 2 summarized recent research into ancient communications media and the training and practice of learned scribes. As ben Sira explained, learned scribes had undergone a disciplined learning of the law/torah of the Most High, as well as prophecies and various kinds of wisdom, so that they could draw upon a deep Judean cultural repertoire in their service in the assemblies and courts of the high priestly rulers. The next step is to examine what the torah/law(s)/*politeia* of the Judean temple-state may have consisted of in late second-temple times.

Even though critical studies and discovery and analysis of new sources were raising challenging questions, the fields of Jewish history and biblical studies persisted in discussing the sources and their context in terms of "(early) Judaism" in which the "books" of the Torah/Law and other texts later included in the Hebrew Bible had already become canonized as the Scripture of Judaism. And it was standardly assumed that the Pharisees were principal interpreters of the Torah/Law. In the last few decades, however, as discussed in the previous chapter, several lines of new research into ancient communications media have undermined and challenged this fundamental conceptualization of Judaism and its Torah/Law. Chapter 2 also attempted, provisionally, to move toward a more appropriate conceptualization appropriate to the findings of these new lines of research and, with chapter 1, to a more comprehensive understanding of the historical context and structure of the temple-state. Text-critical examination of MSS of "books" of the Pentateuch, for example, concluded that there were different versions, all still developing, so that there was no standard textual tradition of these books. To call these books of the Bible or Scripture would appear to be somewhat anachronistic.

It is thus now becoming clear not only that the torah/law (teachings/laws/customs) was far more diverse than the previously standard conceptualization would allow, but also that texts of torah were only the most obvious components in a broader and deeper scribal repertoire of teachings (torah) and laws. Correspondingly, it is becoming unclear whether scribes and Pharisees were involved in *interpretation* of texts of torah whose dominant authority was supposedly already recognized. Thus the next step, in this chapter, will be to review texts from the second-temple period that present laws and/or information on torah, that is teachings/laws/customs that were operative in the temple-state, teachings/laws that the learned scribes would have learned and cultivated in their role in the temple-state.

Before proceeding further, the conceptual problem created by standard conventional translations should be addressed again. The term *law* in English and the term *nomos* in Greek are inadequate and at times inappropriate translations of *torah*. *Torah* would be more appropriately translated with *teaching*, which more easily accommodates the substantial proportion of legends and stories and ideological schemes included in the "books" of the Pentateuch. In his histories Josephus uses a variety of terms, such as *nomoi, nomima, ethe,* and *politeia* in referring to rules, practices, customs, etc., operative in the temple-state. It is quite unclear what all is included in his phrase, "the laws (*nomoi*) of the Judeans." The variety of terms and the unclarity of their referents creates a problem of nomenclature for the following discussions. Where the referents are indefinite, broad, and/or unclear, I will resort to using slashes between multiple terms, such as "torah/teaching(s)/laws/customs." In accounts where he is discussing the *politeia* (constitution) of the Judeans, a synonym for which is evidently *nomoi/nomima*, I will again use multiple terms with slashes. In Josephus' accounts or other primary or secondary sources where the referent appears to be the five "books" of the Torah, I will often use "the Pentateuch." And, to note what is perhaps obvious, I will place the term "book" in quotes to indicate that in the history of culture prior to the emergence of print culture, the term is a metaphor for a text inscribed on a scroll or codex.

The Teaching(s)/Law(s) in the "Books" later included in the Hebrew Bible

With considerably more critical and comparative understanding of law and collections of laws in ancient SW Asian civilizations, biblical scholars have devoted more critical attention to law-collections in the "books" later included in the Hebrew Bible. They recognized, for example, that these were not law-codes according to which law-courts functioned. The long-standing assumption that *torah* is appropriately translated and understood as law has been a major factor in the misunderstanding and misinterpretation of the "laws" included in the "books" of the Torah/Pentateuch. In the last generation, biblical scholars recognized that the collections of "biblical laws" in Exod 21–23; Lev 25; and Deut 12–26 were not law-codes that judges could apply to particular cases in court, as in modern societies.[1] This misunderstanding persisted, however, in recent analyses that ponder why, for example, Nehemiah did not appeal to particular laws as the basis of his "reforms." The appropriate analogies for these collections in the ancient Near Eastern context are rather the (monumental) decrees issued by emperors declaring that they would rule their subjects with nobility and equity, such as the collection inscribed on steles by Hammurabi.[2]

The standard approach in dealing with these "books" later included in the Hebrew Bible, moreover, was standardly based on the assumptions of

---

1. The critical essays in Watts, ed., *Persia and Torah*, offer new assessments of Judean laws influenced by the Persian imperial regime. Also important is the more general study of Israelite law and biblical law by Knight in *Law, Power, and Justice*.

2. See Bottero, "Le Code de Hammur-abi," 444; Finkelstein, "Ammisaduqa's Edict and the Babylonian Lawcodes"; and Knight, *Law, Power, and Justice*, 104.

print-culture in which biblical studies was deeply rooted. That is, scholars attempted to ascertain the authors and dates and circumstances of particular writings and sources and layers of writings. They typically looked for later writings' knowledge of and dependence on earlier writings, such as quotations.

The dawning recognition of ancient media of communication and scribal practices, however, leads to a more complex and flexible approach. The scribal cultivation of the torah/teaching of Moses and its customs and laws was much broader and deeper than the composition and/or editing of the extant written texts available to us. This basic starting assumption should replace the (print-cultural) assumption that Mosaic torah was confined to written texts known to us and perhaps a few others. The only sources we have to work with and through, however, are extant written texts (re-)constructed or "established" by generations of text-critics. We can take "soundings" from these texts, using our nascent knowledge of scribal practices, in order to understand how laws we know from these "books" may have functioned in the Judean temple-state.

The early development of the "books" of torah later included in the Hebrew Bible was closely related to Persian imperial rule. The Persians sponsored or at least permitted the repatriation of descendants of the previously deported Jerusalem elite who rebuilt the temple and established a temple-state that eventually consolidated power in Yehud. Scholars of these "books" continue to debate the extent to which the Persian imperial regime required or simply encouraged the collection of Judean customs, laws, and other traditions. Without attempting to determine the sequence in which "books" were composed, I will begin with two that appear directly pertinent to the temple-state and its operations in which learned scribes would have been involved.

The "Book" of Deuteronomy

The book of Deuteronomy as we have it is the teaching (torah) of Moses to "Israel" in three speeches. More specifically, it presents itself as, and has the overall and internal structure of the Mosaic Covenant. The Covenant in Deuteronomy exhibits a pattern of three component steps that is discernible in several other texts (such as Exod 20; Josh 24): a declaration of deliverance, covenantal demands (the central and most extensive component), and sanctions of blessings and curses. Deuteronomy includes a core Mosaic Covenant on Horeb that repeats and renews the original Covenant on Sinai (Deut 5:1–33) within a much more elaborate Mosaic Covenant (what is *in* and behind Deut 1–31, esp. the extended law-giving in Deut 12–26). After a review of the recent history of deliverance of the people and Moses' exhortation to the people to observe or practice the teaching (in order to be secure in the land God is providing them; Deut 1–4), Moses declares the ten "words"/commandments, which are prefaced by a[nother] brief declaration of the exodus event of deliverance (Deut 5). Keying on the first two commandments, which are demands for the people's exclusive loyalty to God, Moses delivers a speech elaborating the requirement of loyalty to God and obedience of the commandments as a long preamble (Deut 6–11) to the extensive pronouncement of laws in Deut 12–26. These are finally followed by a list of blessings and curses as sanctions on keeping the covenantal stipulations (Deut 28–29). "Appended" are "the Song of Moses" and "the blessings of Moses" (Deut 31; 32). The form and content of the Mosaic covenant so permeates the book as we have it, that it is difficult to imagine that earlier versions in the development of (the text of) this *seper* were not also Mosaic covenantal in form and substance.

The "ten words" in the Covenant within the Covenant are principles that would presumably have governed the relation of the people with YHWH/God and social-economic interaction in the village communities of an agrarian people. Observance of the commandments on social-economic interaction would seem to prevent any family from gaining political-economic leverage over other families in some sort of centralization of power. This intent or function of the Covenantal and its commandments is confirmed by other key traditions taken up into other texts of the Hebrew Bible, such as the reluctance of the prophet Samuel about giving the people a king to rule over them and his warning about what a centralized monarchy would mean (1 Sam 8:4–18).

The section of laws/teaching in the overall Covenant, Deut 12–26, however, deals with most of the major facets and institutions of public life in an agrarian society: rituals and festivals in the temple, the priesthood, justice in social-economic relations, courts, prophecy, kingship (albeit limited and constrained), and civil and family law. The covenantal torah (teaching) prescribes all of these in a way that specifies the centralization of power and administration in "the place that the Lord will choose" (that is, Jerusalem). The broader Mosaic Covenant in Deuteronomy thus established the temple-state in "the place that YHWH will choose" that was not included in the core Covenant of Deut 5.

Earlier scholars took this centralization as originating in the "reform" undertaken by King Josiah at the end of the seventh century (narrated in 2 Kgs 22–23), supposedly based on a venerable old writing of the torah/laws of Moses "found" in the temple. A more recent tendency has been to see

Deuteronomy taking more of its constitutive form in early second-temple times. Its provision for an extremely limited and constrained kingship fits well the situation of Yehud under the Persian imperial regime. With its set of laws regulating most areas of social-economic life and the principal political-economic institutions, Deuteronomy appears to be an appropriately designed "constitutional" text for the temple-state in which the priests have charge of the administration.[3] All sacrifices, offerings, and tithes are centralized in the temple (Deut 12). This includes the centralization of the Passover festival—originally a family-based celebration—in the Jerusalem temple.

Once we are aware of the different kinds of writings in ancient Judea it is important to inquire about the function of the "book" of Deuteronomy as the scribes serving in the temple-state understood it. In its self-presentation Deuteronomy is a *monumental* as well as *constitutional* writing (of hoary antiquity). At the conclusion of his long speech about the institutions and social-political relations of the centralized state, Moses and the elders of the people instruct the people to inscribe "all the words of this torah" very clearly on uncut stones covered with plaster, an altar on which burnt offering was made, in a covenant (renewal) ceremony (27:1–8). Then "all the words of this torah" were written on a *seper* (writing) that was given to the priests who carried the ark of the covenant (28:58; 29:1, 14–15; 31:9).[4] Considering that scholars have connected the book of Deuteronomy with the centralizing reform of Josiah and/or with the political-economic-religious centralization in the early temple-state, it would be an obvious step to associate this self-described monumental writing with the retrospective stories of the idealized ceremonies of centralization focused on monumental constitutional writings of covenantal teaching in 2 Kgs 22–23 and Neh 8. These two accounts strongly suggest that there was a collective memory of such a ceremony focused on the numinous constitutional writing, even if there is little evidence of its having been performed every seven years.

---

3. Davies, *Scribes*, 94–96, says Deuteronomy appears to have "the character of an ideal national constitution representing all the official institutions of the state: the monarchy, the judiciary, the priesthood, and prophecy." The term "national" seems anachronistic. Davies (*Scribes*, 96–99) suggests rather the document of an "immigrant group wedded to a central sanctuary," a "colonial program within a society of the people of the land. In the historical context of the Persian Empire, Deuteronomy would appear to be more a "constitution" for a subordinate temple-state. Versus Davies (*Scribes*, 96), neither Deuteronomy nor Leviticus articulate an "ethnic identity" of Israel.

4. In contrast with the function of books in print-culture (and now in culture of the internet), however, it was effective (only) in and through its oral performance. Laid up and stored out of sight (supposedly) in the ark as a numinous sacred object, it became effective (only) when performed in the ears of the Israelites (supposedly) every seventh year when they were assembled at the place that YHWH will choose during the festival of booths (Deut 31:9–13).

According to the story in 2 Kgs 22:8—23:3, a *seper* of the torah (that had presumably been previously deposited in the temple) found by the High Priest had a profound impact when recited to king Josiah. He in turn then "recited all the words of the writing of the covenant (*berit*)" in the ears of the assembled people and carried out a massive centralizing "reform, . . . as prescribed in this *seper* of the covenant" (2 Kgs 23:4–20, 21–23; cf. 23:24). This long-lost *"seper* of the torah (teaching)" found in the temple, hardly a dusty old manuscript, was a power-full monumental and *constitutional* writing that embodied the legitimating authority for Josiah's centralizing reform.[5] Accordingly, it included new torah, such as the requirement that celebration of the Passover be centralized in Jerusalem (2 Kgs 23:21–23, 24–25) that would presumably not have been in the teaching delivered by Moses on Mount Horeb. That "the book of the teaching" was found unexpectedly in the temple suggests that such a covenant document had been deposited in the temple but was not regularly consulted or brought out for periodic recitation to the assembled people. This *seper* was thus an iconic legal "monument for posterity," similar to writings placed in temples in Egypt and Mesopotamia and the earliest inscription of laws in Greek temples.[6]

A monumental document of sacred power is also clearly evident in the account of Ezra's presentation, opening, and recitation of "the document of the teaching of Moses" (Neh 8). This is the central event in the highly elaborate ceremony before the assembly of Judeans that formalized the re-formation of the Jerusalem temple-state. Ezra, flanked by other high-ranking figures, stood on a raised wooden platform constructed specially for the occasion. "Ezra opened the writing (presumably a huge heavy scroll) in the sight of all the people, for he was standing above all the people; and when he opened it, all the people stood up" (Neh 8:4–5). In antiphonal blessing and praise, the people answered, "'Amen, Amen,' lifting up their hands," then "bowing their heads and worshipping Yahweh with their faces to the ground" (8:6). "The scroll of the teaching of Moses" is clearly a numinous sacred object in the presence of which the people bow down.[7] It

---

5. Similarly in Egypt some texts claimed authority "by including accounts of how they were found—after long neglect—in a temple deposit," according to Carr, *Writing on the Tablet of the Heart*, 81. As Niditch remarks (*Oral World*, 103), the "found book" theme had to do with validation of political actions, as explained in Wolfgang Speyer, *Die literarische Faelschung im heidnischen und christlichen Altertum*. See also Horsley, "Origins of the Hebrew Scriptures under Imperial Rule," 33–41.

6. See, for example, Pedersén, *Archives and Libraries in the City of Assur*, 12–19; and Thomas, *Oral Tradition and Written Record in Classical Athens*, 31.

7. The awesome sacred aura evoked by the presentation and opening of "the document of the teaching of Moses" might be compared with Assyrian royal inscriptions, as discussed by Machinist, "Assyrians on Assyria in the First Millennium B.C.," 101.

is important to note further that the numinous "writing" comes alive and becomes effective in its display, worship, and formal performance.[8] Insofar as these accounts are suggestive of how the more elaborate "books" of torah such as Deuteronomy were composed, laid up in the temple, and performed before the people, such huge scrolls of the Torah were not records of laws to be read for information. They were rather iconic monumental writings that authorized and *constituted* the temple-state.[9]

It is possible, even likely, that written texts that were originally or principally monumental and/or constitutional could have acquired other functions as well. This could well have been the case with (proto) Deuteronomy. Assuming that in their early stages of development in scribal circles the contents were similar to what we find in the "book" included in the Hebrew Bible/Old Testament, those contents serve to "constitute" the Jerusalem temple-state and even to give instructions for its functions and its operations. It would have been obvious for this text to have assumed a prominent place in the curriculum of those training as scribes to serve in the temple-state and thus to have become "written" in their memory. The book of Deuteronomy as we have it has a strikingly didactic character. Might this suggest that at some point in its development it was further shaped in scribal circles into a *prescriptive* "constitutional" text? Given the paucity of extant written texts from early second temple times, however, it is quite unclear by when this would have happened so that the contents of proto-Deuteronomy became functionally part of the (scribal) repertoire of "the torah of the Most High" actively cultivated in scribal circles. Presumably there would have been no conflict between "the scroll of the torah" laid up in the temple or brought out on occasion as a numinous icon in a temple ceremony and the internalization of "the words of this teaching" in the memory of scribes (and

---

Van der Toorn, "The Iconic Book," compares the Torah, as in the presentation of the book of Mosaic covenant law presented by Ezra, to the images of the Babylonian gods that were worshipped as sacred objects.

8. The intention and function "the searching of the words of the torah (teaching)," in the ensuing account in Neh 8:13–18, is to authorize and gain acceptance and practice of the (evidently new) Festival of Booths by (the colony of) the returnees from exile in Babylon.

9. The large scrolls of the torah of Moses would thus have been somewhat analogous to the monuments in fifth and fourth century Athens on which the laws of the *polis* were engraved. This "publication" of the laws at a time when writing was becoming more widely used in ancient Greece was not so much a means of informing the Athenian public of the content of the laws (only a fraction of the populace was literate) or a way of recording the laws for future reference or administrative purposes. The inscription of public laws was rather basically "a monument or memorial whose public presence and very existence guarantee[d] the continuing force of the decision it record[ed]." Thomas, *Literacy and Orality in Ancient Greece*, 85; Thomas, "Literacy and the City-State," 39–43.

priests). In neither case would proto-Deuteronomy have been functioning as a written text to be read or consulted for information about Judean laws.

Leviticus

The book of Leviticus presents instructions (laws) for the priests for their conduct of sacrifices and other functions of the temple and their own discipline and economic support. The text represents the temple in archaic terms as "the tent of meeting" in the time of Israel's origins in the wilderness, following the exodus and assembly before God on Horeb/Sinai. The text is framed in *covenantal* terms as Yahweh's instruction to Moses (and Aaron) in two main sections. Leviticus 1–16 contains prescriptions for sacrifices and other rituals, consecration of and rules for priests, food laws, and instructions for priests on purification sacrifices (e.g., for cases of skin lesions) and the Day of Atonement rituals. In form and contents, "the Holiness Collection" (as noted, "Code" is somewhat of a misnomer) in Lev 17–26 stands in and further develops the Mosaic covenant tradition, with adapted formulation of many of the commandments in Lev 19 and blessings and curses in Lev 26. The collection includes requirement of the centralization of sacrifices in the tabernacle (temple), laws prohibiting sexual relations with certain close kin, a repetition of covenantal commandments, priestly restrictions and sacrificial rules, a calendar of festivals, laws of sabbatical release of debt slaves and "jubilee" return to family inheritance of land, and "blessings and curses" as sanction on the observance of all the laws. The text concludes with prescriptions for the economic support of the tabernacle and priests (Lev 27).

Critical analysis has shown that the text addresses the priests administering the temple (and temple-state) in the second temple period. The functional terms are not the traditional ones of kinship. For example, there is only one reference to *nasi'* (tribal chieftan, Lev 4:22–26), who is treated like any ordinary individual. The people are evidently a network of village communities engaged in agriculture, around the central temple, with the "administration" in the hands of the priests, headed by the High Priest (Lev 21:10; "the anointed priest," 4:3)—all under Persian and/or later Hellenistic imperial rule. The laws in Lev 25 indicate a significant political-economic-religious division: the wealthy and powerful few have gained economic power by manipulating the poor into debt, indenturing them, and gaining control of their land. The laws protect the economic interests of the priests and others who live in Jerusalem/the temple city.[10] The collection of laws in

---

10. The principal of interpretation here is that if there are laws or teachings against

(proto-)Leviticus appears to be an "updating" of the collection in Deuteronomy, making some significant changes in further centralization of sacrifices and social-economic administration in the temple and priesthood. In the laws in Lev 25, for example, it becomes clear that, even though family inheritances are supposedly inalienable to the people as the "tenants" of God, the "owner" of the land, the economic relief in the sabbatical year evident in the presumably earlier laws in Exod 21–23 and Deut 15 have been discontinued. The laws in Leviticus protect the interests of people who live in the temple-city (evidently mainly leading priestly families) at the expense of villagers and others who have become indebted. The collection of laws in (proto-)Leviticus as given through Moses in a covenant made on Horeb/Sinai is thus evidently a divine authorization of sacred political-economic order of the temple-state that legitimates operations by the priests and their economic support by the people.

The collections of laws in Leviticus appear to both reflect and prescribe priestly practice in the temple. They were inscribed on a scroll that would have "authorized" and legitimated the temple rituals and social administration of the temple-state by the priests (at least for the priests and scribes who knew of the existence of the scroll). But the hereditary priests would already have known the instructions from their habitual practice of them; that is, the instructions reflected existing priestly practice. It is quite unclear how the priests would have enforced some of the laws, laws that expected the people to come forth with the required sacrifices in order to remain in the temple-community. A principal function of a proto-Leviticus in second temple times would thus appear to have been a text in the scribal curriculum from which they would have known (in their memory) the prescriptions for procedures in the temple already or previously being practiced by the priests. As with the laws and teachings in a proto-Deuteronomy, it is difficult to find indications for when and how laws in (a proto-)Leviticus may have been functioning in scribal service in the temple-state.[11]

That the "book" of Deuteronomy and, to an extent, the "book" of Leviticus have the form and content of the Mosaic covenant suggest that Judean scribal torah and laws prominent in early second-temple times were Mosaic covenantal. Both Deuteronomy and Leviticus suggest that the distinctive Judean scribal conception and overall conceptual form of teaching and laws was in terms of the Mosaic covenant as adapted in support of the temple-state. This was a serious transformation of the Mosaic covenantal

---

something, it has become a problem in the society.

11. As will be discussed in Vol. 2, Jesus was remembered to have taken seriously the expectation of payment to the priest/temple for purification after skin-lesions and the expectation of sin offerings (Mark 1–2 and par.).

tradition to suit centralization of power in Jerusalem and legitimation and regulation of the priesthood and divine authorization of the temple-state.

Nehemiah and Ezra

Scholars have debated whether the books of Ezra and Nehemiah indicate knowledge and application of the teachings/laws of the Torah (Pentateuch).[12] What is clear from the accounts of Nehemiah and Ezra is that multiple conflicts had arisen in Yehud. These conflicts were sufficiently severe that the Persian regime sent Nehemiah as governor (with military forces) and later dispatched the priest and scribe Ezra as envoy to deal with them.

Both Nehemiah and Ezra issued decrees prohibiting intermarriage with other peoples and forced elite families into divorcing (putting away) their "foreign" spouses (Neh 10:30; Ezra 9:10–15; 10:1–44). Ezra 9:11–12 has been taken as a paraphrase of Lev 18:24–30 and Deut 7:3–4, supposedly indicating knowledge and application of laws in the Torah/Pentateuch. That Ezra 9:11–12 addresses the same issue as laws in Deuteronomy and the priestly laws, however, hardly indicates knowledge and use of the Pentateuch. Presumably cultivation of scribal culture had continued into fifth-fourth century Yehud. Insofar as intermarriage of elite Judean (priestly) families with prominent families in nearby areas would have been a continuing issue, prohibitions of them would have continued to be formulated and further developed in the scribal repertoire, including collections of laws and their further development.

In response to popular outcry protesting exploitation, Nehemiah called a "great assembly" and charged "the nobles" with unjustly manipulating Judean peasants into spiraling debt and indenturing them in debt-slavery (Neh 5:6–13). Knowing that this was a threat to the tax-base of the imperial court ("the king's tax"), the Persian governor had been loaning the people seed-grain for subsequent harvests, unsuccessfully attempting to sustain

---

12. See the articles collected in Watts, *Persia and Torah*. Blenkinsopp, 57–59, argues that the "author" of Ezra was familiar with what is now known as Deuteronomic and Priestly legislation and the Holiness code, and that the majority of scholars have concluded that Ezra's law corresponds to the legal content of the Pentateuch at a mature but not yet final stage of development. Continuing discussion is problematic in that it projects the assumptions and concepts of modern print culture onto ancient texts, imagining that "authors" had "written" the memoirs and edited written collections of laws, and that these were the only modes of cultivation of the Judean (scribal) cultural repertoire. In this connection, it is pertinent to note how few Judean texts seem to know of Ezra.

their viability on a subsistence basis. In the assembly, according to the account, he forced "the nobles and officers" to agree to stop taking interest on loans, to restore the people's fields, vineyards, olive orchards, and houses, and to stop demanding interest on loans of grain, wine, and oil (the staple crops and foods). He then made the priests take an oath to do as they had promised (an indication that the nobles were priestly aristocrats). Although as the imperial governor he did not provide relief from payment of "the king's tax," he did force economic reforms in the political-economic relations in the temple-state. The account gives no hint that he was drawing on or appealing to teachings as formulated in "the Covenant Collection" (Exod 21–23) and/or Deut 12–26 and/or the Holiness Collection (Lev 25), such as prohibitions of charging interest on loans and the requirement of sabbatical cancellation of debts. But it is evident that he knows and is drawing on (covenantal) customs in earlier Israelite tradition that we see were also adapted in those collections. The Judean nobles had displayed no regard for traditional Israelite customs. It took the imperial governor responsible to maintain the imperial as well as local "tax base," the productive peasantry, to forcibly insist on observance of what were evidently standard Israelite customs.[13]

In order to counteract violation of the sabbath by Jerusalemites eager to buy fish and other goods packed into the city by Tyrian and other merchants, Nehemiah simply ordered the gates of the Jerusalem be closed on the sabbath (Neh 13:19–21; cf. 10:32). It seems clear that he was attempting to enforce the keeping of the covenantal commandment to keep the sabbath, even though according to the account he did not appeal to it explicitly.

The accounts of Nehemiah's enforcement of previously instituted obligations of the people for tithes, first fruits, first-born livestock, and other economic support for the temple and its priests, Levites, and other personnel do not appeal to particular laws included in Leviticus (Neh 10:32–39; 13:10). Among the obligations to support the temple and its personnel, at least the one-third shekel due annually is a new tax, not mentioned in (supposedly earlier) collections of laws.

When recounting the measures taken by Nehemiah the narrative repeatedly provides authorization for the measures with "God's law that was given by Moses" (Neh 10:29) or "as it was written in the torah" (10:36) or "it was found written" (in the "book" of Moses (13:1). But the accounts do not cite or refer to particular laws or teachings from those written texts. There surely existed written texts that authorized the temple-state and reflected

---

13. It may have been Persian policy to foster observance of such customs, as discussed in recent scholarly debates; see e.g., Watts, ed., *Persia and Torah*.

or prescribed its personnel and practices. But these written texts were not understood and did not function as collections of particular rules, statutes, and ordinances that Nehemiah or others could refer to and enforce the obedience of. Rather they functioned as (sacred) authority in a general way for the commands given by Nehemiah to institute or return to particular practices. We cannot tell from these accounts whether or not Nehemiah or anyone else knew particular laws (or the gist of them in covenantal customs and teachings). Nehemiah evidently judged what was right to command or do in particular circumstances to further the stabilization of the temple-state as part of the Persian imperial order. His commands and actions then would have entered into the repertoire of temple-state law and teaching, cultivated by scribes and in this case were more formalized in the text of Ezra–Nehemiah.

Keeping the Covenant and the Law/Teaching of the Most High in Ben Sira

Given the paucity of extant texts in the centuries between Ezra-Nehemiah and the texts recently discovered at Qumran, the "book" of Sirach is particularly important for investigation of the functions of laws and teachings in the mid-to-late second temple period.

In his preface to the "book" Ben Sira's grandson declared that his grandfather Yeshua had "devoted himself to the reading of the Law and the Prophets and the other books of our ancestors and had acquired considerable proficiency in them." Taking the grandson's statement at face value, scholarly interpreters go even further, claiming that "Ben Sira cites or alludes to" nearly all the "biblical" books, and "often bases his didactic discourse on a single text from the Torah."[14] Ben Sira's relationship with "the Torah/Law," however, was more complicated than modern interpreters have allowed. As discussed just above, Judean scribal culture was much deeper and richer than its modern scholarly reduction to the books that later became biblical had allowed. Ben Sira's instructional wisdom includes an exhortation to his students in parallel clauses to "seek the torah/law and be

---

14. DiLella, "Wisdom of Ben Sira." The general scholarly tendency is to take any reference to the figures and events of Israelite tradition and especially any reference to a "book" as evidence for the existence and use of the Hebrew scriptures. Two representative examples are: "It is clear that by the writing of Ben Sira about 200 BCE the Pentateuch and the Prophets were more or less in the same shape as the present Hebrew canon" (Grabbe, "The Law of Moses in the Ezra Tradition," 99); and "Sirach was certainly familiar with the Torah in its written form (cf. 38:24)" (Collins, *Jewish Wisdom in the Hellenistic Age*, 52).

filled with it" and "kindle deeds of justice" (32:14—33:3). While his exhortation to seek the torah/law is rare, however, the learned Jerusalem scribe *repeatedly teaches obedience of the "covenant" and "commandments" of God* and often associates wisdom with the commandments. Ben Sira, however, simply does not cite particular laws or teachings from torah-texts such as Leviticus or Deuteronomy.[15] If he knows "the statutes and ordinances" in such "books" he certainly does not refer to them.[16] This leaves no basis for the standard claim that he was engaged in the interpretation of the (books of) the Pentateuch.

Although he does not quote particular laws from written texts, however, Ben Sira knows of a "'*Book* of the Covenant of the Most High God." Indeed he not only knows of its existence, but in his hymn of the self-praise of (personified) heavenly Wisdom (Sir 24), after God grants her a home in Jerusalem, (Ben Sira declares that) She is embodied in "the book of the Covenant of the Most High God, the law that Moses commanded" (24:23). Insofar as it is the only "book" of torah that identifies itself as "book" of torah, this is evidently (an early stage of) the "book" of Deuteronomy.[17] That "the book of the covenant . . . , the law that Moses commanded" is the embodiment of heavenly Wisdom that the Most High created in the beginning—an escalation in the numinous aura that has been "established in Zion"—makes it the ultimate in monumental texts that gives the temple divine authorization.[18] As the paean of praise continues, the book of the covenant "pours forth instruction" and Ben Sira even claims that he is the channel for its instruction as he "pours out teaching" for all generations. Moreover, the learned scribes of the temple-state find their own divine authorization as

15. As recognized by Collins, Ben Sira "does not cite biblical laws directly" and his teaching is "neither legal proclamation nor legal interpretation," *Jewish Wisdom in the Hellenistic Age*, 55, 45.

16. Ben Sira's instructional speech on economic relations and interaction in 29:1-13 offers an illustration of how his teaching (torah) may be rooted in but does not quote or reference Mosaic covenantal customs, commands, and exhortations that we are familiar with from "the Covenant Collection" (e.g., Exod 22:24) or Deuteronomy (15:1-10): "Lend to your neighbor in his time of need . . . Help the poor for the commandment's sake" (Sir 29:2, 9).

17. This may also be indicated by the lack of allusion in Sirach to any sort of cultic and dietary laws such as found in Leviticus, as suggested by Collins, *Jewish Wisdom in the Hellenistic Age*, 47, 57.

18. This would appear to be rooted in the kind of legitimating temple ceremony of the adoration and formal recitation of the numinous constitutional book described in the account in Neh 8 (discussed above). One could easily imagine this by an analogy: Ben Sira's remarkable psalm of praise of the great Israelite officeholders (ancestors, high priests, kings, prophets, Sir 44-49) comes to its climax in the portrayal of the august ceremonial appearance of the priestly aristocracy in Sir 50.

those who know the book of the Covenant. The book of the Covenant as the embodiment of heavenly Wisdom is thus far more than a written text that Ben Sira and other scribes read, cited, and interpreted.

The "book of the Covenant" (the monumental constitutional text of Deuteronomy), however, was not the sum total of the torah/law that Ben Sira was responsible for learning. As discussed in chapter 1 above, the broader torah/law that had first place in the curriculum of the learned scribes was "the torah/law of the Most High" (Sir 38:34—39:1). That the "torah/law of the Most High" has a broader reference than a particular "book" is suggested by the parallel lines that refer to the other divisions of the scribal curriculum in broad general terms ("the wisdom of all the ancients/ancestors," "prophecies" in general, and parables and proverbs in general). "The torah of the Most High" evidently refers to torah/law in general, in the comprehensive sense that Ben Sira and other scribes learned, held inscribed on the tablets of their heart, and could draw on in their service among the rulers of the temple-state.[19]

According to Ben Sira's ideology of the priesthood, God had given Moses the commandments face to face so that he could teach the covenant and its decrees to the people (45:5). He then gave Aaron (and the Aaronid priesthood) "authority and statutes and judgments to enlighten Israel with his torah" (45:17). In the evolution of Judean temple-state the learned scribes who served the high priesthood must have taken over this function and its authority. The learned scribes are the ones who learned as comprehensively as possible "the torah of the Most High" as part of their broader function as cultivators and guardians of Judean scribal culture in service of the rulers of the temple-state (38:34—39:4).

That Ben Sira focuses on the covenant and the commandments (and not so much on the laws) is suggestive for the way learned scribes may have been thinking of the temple-state and its laws/customs/ancestral traditions in the early second century BCE. It is all the more suggestive that in the visionary history in Dan 10–12, the narrative refers to the object of Antiochus Epiphanes' attack as "the holy covenant" (11:28–30) and to the high priests who had carried out the transformation of the Jerusalem temple-state into

---

19. Is a somewhat similar distinction being made in 1 Macc 1:57, between the torah/law in general being adhered to by those struggling against the Seleucid invasion and copies of "the book of the covenant" (Deuteronomy?) that some of the resistors possessed? Would "the 'books' (scrolls) of the torah/law" that the invading forces were burning (in 1:56) have referred to copies of Deuteronomy or other written 'books' of torah as well? And is a similar distinction made in 2 Macc 8:21–23, between "the laws" (in general) that the Judeans were ready to die for and "the holy book" that Eleazar read aloud to them, the latter presumably again being Deuteronomy insofar as Deut 20 has rules about (holy) war, including a priest's speech in preparation for battle?

a Hellenistic *polis* as "those who forsake/violate the covenant" (11:31–32). The circle of learned scribes known as the *maskilim* evidently did think of the temple-state (or its underlying "constitution") they had been serving as "the (holy) covenant," whether they were referring to the temple-state in Jerusalem or the Judean people more generally.

Forms and Functions of Texts of Torah at Qumran and in the Dead Sea Scrolls

The scrolls discovered in the wilderness of Judea are forcing serious questioning of standard assumptions and key controlling constructs in the fields of Jewish history and biblical studies, as discussed above. Among these are the assumption, rooted in modern print culture, that *the Torah* in its five books were already canonical Scripture of Judaism, recognized by the Jews generally. *The scrolls attest a broader range of texts of torah/law and a deeper repertoire of torah that Judean scribes would have been cultivating in late second-temple times.* The newly discovered scrolls, including previously unknown texts of considerable variety, provide evidence of at least three forms of torah/teaching and laws cultivated by Judean scribes in late second-temple times. They also provide a clearer sense of how texts of torah were functioning in scribal circles, that is, how they were being appropriated and cultivated among learned scribes.

First, as noted, among the Dead Sea Scrolls discovered in the wilderness of Judea were multiple scrolls of each of the "books" of the Pentateuch that were later included in the Hebrew Bible. These finds indicated decisively that the "books" of the Torah/Pentateuch later included in the Hebrew Scriptures not only existed by the second-century BCE but were used and copied repeatedly. To repeat text-critics' conclusions from chapter 2, careful text-criticism applied to these scrolls, however, showed that *there were in fact multiple versions of each "book," all of which were still being developed.* This means that *there was no standard stable "text" in the inscription of these texts on scrolls.* While these texts were evidently authoritative in scribal-priestly circles, they were not yet (part of) *the* Scripture of Judaism, at least in the sense previously assumed in biblical studies.

Second, again as noted above, the scrolls found at Qumran included what were evidently *alternative texts of torah* that claimed authority. This suggests that the "books" of the Torah/Pentateuch that were still developing had only relative authority in comparison with other texts, and that mainly in scribal-priestly circles.[20]

20. Already in 1972, in "The Unwritten Law," J. M. Baumgarten noted that in the

Third, these alternative texts of torah thus also give evidence of a considerable amount of tradition and torah that had not been included in the "books" of the Pentateuch. As suggested in Ben Sira's description of the scribe's learning of "the torah of the Most High," there was evidently a fairly deep and broad reservoir of torah/law in the repertoire of scribal culture that had not been included in previously composed texts.

Close study of the Scrolls, moreover, is resulting in two important recognitions about the functioning of the torah/teaching and laws in the scribal-priestly community.

First, even though the community (*yahad*) at Qumran understood itself as a renewed covenant, it did not look directly to the "books" of the Pentateuch for the rules and ordinances that guided its common life. Rather, the community at Qumran and satellite communities generated their own guidelines and prescriptions, as evident in the Community Rule and the Damascus Rule and other texts.

Despite the paucity of quotations from books of the Pentateuch in Qumran texts that have sections of rules for community life, earlier interpreters of the Scrolls often stated that the laws of the Qumran community were derived from (the texts of) the Torah in some way.[21] The key sections in the Community Rule (1QS) and the Damascus Rule (CD), however, do not support such a claim. Both the Community Rule and the Damascus Document are focused on the community they address as the Covenant community that is devoted to obedience to the Covenant and its commandments and laws. They call the faithful remnant of Israel to return to "the Covenant that Moses made with Israel, the Covenant to return to the *torah* of Moses" (CD 15:9–10; cf. 1QS 5:8–12).[22] The Covenant is more or less

---

Qumran community certain texts, such as the Damascus Rule and Temple Scroll, exhibit "unrestricted use of non-biblical writings" (9) and instructions (in 1QSa 1:3–8) to teach the members from the book of Hagu/Hagai as well as to read into their ears "all the laws of the covenant," a mix of "biblical" and "non-biblical" texts. That the book of Hagai was not identical with the Torah is indicated in CD 14:5–7. He also comments (10) that the Temple Scroll was thought by some Qumran scholars to have been considered part of the holy scriptures and that Jubilees was considered an authoritative supplement to the Torah.

21. A representative example is VanderKam, *The Dead Sea Scrolls Today*, 113: "Through their special techniques of interpretation the expositors of Qumran also derived from the biblical laws other laws and precepts that, they believed, lay hidden in the revealed words of the Torah . . . The series of legal texts at Qumran proves the importance of the rules derived from their exegesis of the Torah." For a more subtle and nuanced suggestion, that "the laws of the community were revealed (or "derived by inspired exegesis") *from* the Torah of Moses," see Fraade, "Interpretive Authority," 57, 66 n68.

22. Both texts even display the traditional pattern of the Mosaic Covenant evident

equated with the torah of Moses, and these texts use a number of terms that appear to be synonymous, such as "the torah," "the torah of Moses," "the books of the torah," the "laws/precepts of the Covenant," "the commandments of the torah," and "the commandments of God."

The Community Rule, however, does not refer to or cite any particular laws or teachings from "(the books of) the torah (of Moses)." The Damascus Rule does cite very brief passages in the "Exhortations" (26+), mostly from prophets, and far fewer in the "Statutes" (9), and of these only a few "statutes" reference a "saying" from (Leviticus or) Deuteronomy as a "prooftext." These few references hardly constitute the derivation of the rules and regulations of the community by means of "exegesis" of passages in (the books of) the Torah. The Covenant community(ies) that understood itself (themselves) as returning to the Covenant of Moses was rather formulating its (their) own "statutes and ordinances" for its obedience to the torah, including its community life, and not trying to obey the particular laws and ordinances from the "books" of the Torah/Pentateuch.[23] These rules and regulation are likely what is referred to in the "searching the justice-ruling" (*mishpat*) that accompanied the "recitation of the book" in nightly sessions (1QS 6:6–8).

The second recognition, closely related to recent investigation of scribal practice summarized above, is that the scribes and priests at Qumran were appropriating, indeed internalizing texts of torah individually and collectively. Like Judean scribes before them, the principal way that the scribes and priests at Qumran would have appropriated texts of torah would have been by repeated recitation so that the texts became written on the tablet of their heart (as discussed above). For earlier generations of scribes, a

---

in Exod 20; Josh 24; and Deuteronomy. In the Damascus Document the "exhortations" function as a new ("updated") declaration of deliverance by God, then the "statutes" provide the demands or covenantal commandments for the people/community. The Community Rule begins with the priests reciting "the favors of God manifested in His mighty deeds . . . to Israel" (1QS 1:11–12), then proceeds to the rule (*serekh*) for the members of the *yahad* and the justice-rules (*mishpatim*), including instructions for the organization of the community and its leadership (1QS 5–9). In both texts, the blessings and the curses appear prominently, now transformed into aspects of the new declaration of deliverance (1QS 2:1–19). This reinforces other indications in the texts that they are reflections of, even instructions for community rituals of renewal of the Covenant and the induction of new members.

23. One important effect of regular ritual recitation of authoritative texts would have been directly related to the appearance of what seem like "biblical" phrases, yet not what could be called "quotation" of particular passages in a stricter sense. Ritual recitation would have intensified the scribal-priestly participants' familiarity with the texts so that they were thoroughly imbued with the language of authoritative books. This and other ways in which scribes cultivated (learned, taught, recited) various authoritative texts of Torah would help explain why the language, for example, of Qumran's own Community Rule closely resembles "biblical" wording and style.

principal purpose and effect of their learning texts by recitation was the formation of a disciplined conservative character appropriate for service in the temple-state. As indicated in the passage quoted from the Community Rule above (1QS 6:6–8), the Qumran community evidently practiced a collective ritual recitation of torah that helped shape community as well as individual discipline.[24]

The oral "recitation of the book" (of torah) at these group meetings illustrates a way of appropriating scripture common in many societies and religious groups. Regular ritual recitation of revered texts is not only a common way of appropriating meaning that transcends the discursive level and works more at the affective level. Such recitation in groups also helps bind members together in common ritual action and deeper emotional appropriation of the sacred text. And it also helps "internalize the values and norms implicit in the text, even if they are not grasped in a cognitive, intellectualized way."[25]

The scribes and priests of the Qumran community were appropriating the torah not by interpretive study of texts, but by intense exposure to the torah/Covenant so that it would *inform* their community life and discipline.[26] Repeatedly in the Community Rule and Damascus Rule come exhortations to *keep the torah*, exhortation for *close observance*, not interpretation of torah. The "searching" and "digging" (CD 6:3–4) was about community discipline, about "walking" guided by "ordinances."[27] This deep appropriation of (the "book" of) covenantal torah through repeated recitation, moreover, helps explain why their formulations of the rules and regulations of their community seem to have repeated allusions to texts of torah. They had become deeply rooted in "biblical" idiom that appears repeatedly in their own language, judging from the texts produced in the community, such as the Community Rule (1QS).

---

24. On the likelihood that the "book" recited was a version of Deuteronomy, it is noteworthy that some of the manuscripts (ostensibly) of Deuteronomy found at Qumran were comprised of excerpts and were apparently "used for liturgical purposes," as noted by Ulrich, *Dead Sea Scrolls*, 26.

25. See further Graham, *Beyond the Written Word*, 114, 161.

26. Cf. Fraade, "Interpretive Authority," 52.

27. Fraade, "Interpretive Authority," 53.

The Laws/Customs and *Politeia* of the Judeans in the Accounts of Josephus

In several passages in his histories and *Life*, Josephus provides one principal set of sources for the role of the Pharisees in late second temple Judean history. But the voluminous works of Josephus are also the most important sources for the history of the Judeans in second-temple times in general and (perhaps) for the law(s) and customs in particular.

In the elite political-cultural climate of the Roman Empire toward the end of the first century CE, in the aftermath of the self-proclaimed glorious victory of the Romans over the revolt of the Judeans, Josephus produced his *Antiquities* of the Judean people. Two of the key interrelated issues were the relative antiquity of each of the peoples in the *oikumene* and the merits of each people's "constitution" (*politeia*), understood as their set of laws (*nomoi*). The history of the Greeks and their great lawgivers had long been prominent as the standard in this discussion. In producing his apologetic "archaeology" of the Judeans it was important for Josephus to present the antiquity and veracity of their *politeia* and *nomoi* as having been "written" in "books" by their great lawgiver Moses centuries before the great lawgivers of Greece. It was the constitution and laws of Moses enshrined in his "books" that the Judeans continued to observe. Accordingly, Josephus followed the authoritative "books" of the Judeans/Hebrews as his sources. The books of Exodus, Leviticus, Numbers, and Deuteronomy thus figure prominently in his accounts. The result is two lengthy accounts summarizing, first, the "constitution" and "laws" that correspond, first, to the great lawgiver Moses mediating the Covenant on Sinai and the ensuing revelation on the mountain (*Ant.* 3.84–321) and second, Moses' farewell speech in the book of Deuteronomy, which is covenantal in form and substance (*Ant.* 4.196–319).

In his account of the assembly of the people in which they received the Mosaic covenant (their "ordered constitution," *politeias kosmon*, *Ant.* 3.84), Josephus himself follows the traditional covenantal pattern, prefacing the pronouncement of the ten *logoi* ("words," commandments) with a summary of God's acts of deliverance (*Ant.* 3.86–87). After receiving the "ten words" of the covenant, the people are eager to hear (the) *nomoi* from God, which Moses subsequently established and later indicated how they should act in all circumstances (obviously a wide range of laws and customs). Josephus says he will come back to these, but leave the majority of the laws for another, special treatise (*Ant.* 3.93–94; mentioned elsewhere as the planned "On Customs and Causes," *Ant.*1.25; 4.198). Then, following the sequence of events in Exodus and what was surely central to the *politeia* of the Judeans, Josephus presents a long account of the tabernacle (based on Exod 25–38, drawing also on Leviticus), which was the sacred shrine that prefigured the temple in Jerusalem in Judean tradition.[28] As economic support for the elaborate furnishings and decor of the tabernacle Moses imposed a contribution of a half-shekel from every adult male (3.195).

Mentioning that Moses was committing the *politeia* and *nomoi* to writing (*Ant.* 3.213), Josephus proceeds into a lengthy summary of them (3.214–279), insisting that the Hebrews had never transgressed any of them (3.223). In this summary he surveys all sorts of laws, ranging from regulations concerning purifications and sacrifices and various offerings, including the choice portions devoted to the priests, to those concerning festivals such as Passover. Moses then walks through laws pertaining to issues such as adultery and priestly purity, and mentions laws for the people's life in Canaan such as the sabbatical fallow year and the Jubilee in which debts are cancelled and debtors set free (3.273–286). In the course of this survey, Josephus includes many references to laws in Leviticus and Numbers, and uses synonyms for *nomoi,* such as *nomima.* He also insists that what he is summarizing are laws in the *grammata* ("writings") of Moses, which signal both their veracity (truth) and their antiquity. In fact, some of the laws in this summary are not from any of the books of Moses or differ from laws there, such as those on debt, debt-slavery, and the jubilee year.

In *Antiquities* book 4, when Josephus has brought the people to the Jordan River, he constructs a farewell speech for Moses (based on Deut 31) in which he has Moses lay out another summary of the *politeia* and *nomoi*, which he exhorts them to follow and obey (4.180, 184). Moses presents them with the constitution and laws recorded in a book.

Josephus proceeds to summarize the constitution as laid out in Deuteronomy. It is not surprising that this wealthy priest who had become a client of the Flavian imperial house emphasized the importance of Judeans' obedience to the rulers who held authority over them (*Ant.* 4.184–186). "Let there be one holy city . . . and one temple" (4.200) indicates the centralization in "the place that God would choose" prescribed in Deuteronomy. There follow his paraphrases of the laws concerning pilgrimage festivals, the tithes to be given to the priests and Levites, and the grand ceremonial recitation of the laws every seven years by the High Priest.[29] Josephus adds here how he understands the laws to have functioned: the laws would be so engraved on their hearts and stored in their memory that the people would keep them. He has Moses declare that aristocracy, headed by a High Priest, is the best

---

28. He includes a lengthy description of how the dimensions and fixtures of the tabernacle and the high priest's garment and its decor symbolize key features of the cosmos and calendar as well as some aspects of the people (*Ant.* 3.99–187).

29. There is no solid evidence that this was practiced in late second temple times.

constitution, under God as the ultimate ruler and the laws which govern all actions (4.223–224). The long ensuing exposition of the laws (4.223–301) covers mainly laws in Deuteronomy plus others in Leviticus: the provision of gleaning by the destitute and other agricultural rules, tithes, marriage laws, prohibition of interest on loans, laws governing pledges, debt slaves and their release, the lex talionis, prompt payment of wages to laborers, etc.

Confirming that all these laws are demands of the Mosaic covenant, Josephus has Moses, at the end of his speech in the continuing assembly of the people, deliver the blessings and curses that serve as the sanctions on keeping the laws (4.302). Finally, "all these books" (books of Moses?) he consigned to the priests (along with the "ten words" deposited in the ark), with the clear implication that they were all laid up in the temple (303–304).

As he launched into his summary in *Antiquities* 4, Josephus insisted that "all is here written as he [Moses] left it; nothing has been added for embellishment . . . The one innovation is to classify the several subjects" (*Ant.* 4.196–197).[30] In the lengthy exposition that follows, however, he (again) included several laws and regulations that were not in the books of Moses (as we know them), but must have been from a wider scribal repertoire of laws and customs and standard practices in Judea (e.g., 4.212, 214, 219, 220, 227, 238).[31] Of course, it seems likely that Josephus assumed these laws and customs were in "(the books of) the laws of Moses." This self-proclaimed distinguished priest and others simply did not critically distinguish between the contents of the laws of Moses written on scrolls and ancestral customs and temple-state practices that were cultivated in scribal and priestly circles.[32] This fits with the variety of evidently synonymous terms that Josephus uses in his repeated references to and discussions of the Judean *nomos, nomoi, nomima, ethe,* and *patria* throughout the histories, the *Life,* and the treatise *Against Apion.* It also fits with what we are learning about scribal training and practice and the scrolls of the books of the Pentateuch that display different versions of those books all of which were still undergoing development, as well as the existence of alternative texts of torah. That is,

---

30. Thackeray's translation of "code of our laws" in 4.198 is an anachronistic projection. The Greek term *diataxis* refers to the basic "arrangement of our laws which pertain to our constitution."

31. In his critical survey Knight makes the fundamental point that "All of Israelite laws did not find their way into the biblical canon," in *Law, Power, and Justice,* 15.

32. Josephus and probably no one else except Sadducees distinguished much within "the law(s)" between what was in "the laws of Moses" that were written (and had various recensions) and other laws/rulings/etc. such as those promulgated for the people by the Pharisees or those included, e.g., in the Torah Scroll (but not included in the Pentateuch). So we need to be cautious about assuming fixed forms, including what may be implied in our concepts of "the Law," "Scripture," or "the laws of Moses."

scribes held a broader range of laws and custom in their memory along with already well-delineated texts of the laws in the books of Moses such that the former could influence the continuing development of the latter.

As he begins the exposition of the constitution and laws in *Antiquities* book 4, Josephus (again) also states explicitly that he is summarizing the laws that pertain to the constitution, while postponing coverage of what Moses "had left to us in common concerning our mutual relations" to his planned treatise on "Customs and Causes" (4.198; cf. 1.25; 3.93–94). This suggests that he made a distinction within the broader range of the *nomoi, nomima, ethe,* and *patria* of the Judeans between the laws and customs that pertained to the constitution of the Judean temple-state and those that applied to the common life of the Judean people and not specifically to the temple-state. Since we do not have his anticipated treatise on "Customs and Causes," however, such a distinction is not clear. The laws and customs he paraphrases in the summary of the laws in book 4, whether in one of the books of Moses or not, include several that seem to pertain to the common life of the people, and not to the functioning of the temple-state.

Josephus presents a much shorter summary of the laws in his polemical apologetic treatise *Against Apion* (2.190–219). As with the other summaries, he includes laws and stipulations that were not in the books of Moses, but evidently come from customs or accepted traditions understood as belonging to Mosaic law.

In the subsequent narrative of the history of the Judeans in his *War* as well as in the *Antiquities*, Josephus presents the law as having two purposes and effects, exclusive loyalty to God and justice or community among the people. Addressing a Hellenistic and Hellenistic Jewish audience Josephus presents these in the key Hellenistic terms of *eusebeia* and *dikaiosyne* or *koinonia*. Especially in the fields of biblical studies and Jewish history but also in classics, *eusebeia* is translated with "piety," a term with rather narrow religious connotations in today's culture. In his histories and autobiography, however, Josephus is presenting the *politeia* and *nomoi* of the Judeans as the Judeans' political system, inseparably political-religious. In ancient texts *eusebeia* meant *loyalty* as well as devotion to the gods or parents. Similarly, *dikaiosyne* meant not narrowly "righteousness" (as often translated in biblical studies), but *justice* in social-political life. Even more, *koinonia* pointed to the common good of a people. Josephus asserts repeatedly that the laws of the Judeans produced loyalty to God (e.g., *Ant.* 1.6; 10.50; 14.65; *Ag. Ap.* 2.145–146, 291, 293). Josephus also often pairs *eusebeia* and *dikaiosyne/koinonia*. The customs (*ethe*) of the Judeans are all concerned with loyalty and justice (*Ant.* 12.56; 16.42). The criteria by which a king might be judged good was that he keep loyalty to God and justice toward people (e.g., Jotham, in *Ant.* 9.236).

If we project behind Josephus' Hellenistic terms to the Judean people in Palestine centralized under the temple-state in Jerusalem, it seems evident that "loyalty" to God and "justice" or "community" among the people are the two sides of the Mosaic covenant, which was elaborated in covenantal laws and customs. Loyalty to God was what the first four "words" or commandments of the Covenant required, and justice or community among the people were what the other commandments required. Josephus repeatedly mentions that the recitation of the laws and customs meant the inscription of the laws on the people's memory so that they would obey them, thus producing loyalty to God and justice in the community.

For Josephus, the proud wealthy priest presenting the constitution and laws of the temple-state, of course, and surely for (most) scribes as well, loyalty to God was embodied in service of the temple and its priesthood and its festivals and tithes and offerings. This is evident in what he covers in his expositions of the laws and history. In the course of his historical accounts, however, Josephus offers other exemplars of loyalty and justice who evidently questioned loyalty to the temple. The primary oaths taken by the Essenes, says Josephus admiringly, were loyalty toward the Deity and justice toward people (*War* 2.139). But if the Essenes are to be linked with the priests and scribes who withdrew from Jerusalem to found a new exodus and renewed Covenant (community) in the wilderness, they rejected the incumbent Hasmonean high priest(s). They did this, moreover, precisely because of their commitment to loyalty and justice in adherence to the Covenant and its laws. Josephus also says that the popular prophet John the Baptist exhorted the people to act with justice toward one another and loyalty to God (*Ant.* 18.117). But John was leading a movement of renewal of the Covenant in his ritual of baptism that was not connected with the temple.[33]

In the fields of biblical studies and Jewish history, considerable emphasis is given to *interpretation* of the Torah, the law(s) of Moses. By contrast, like the authoritative texts that he is drawing on, however, Josephus repeatedly emphasizes *the keeping of* or *obedience to the laws and customs*, indeed *the keeping of the laws* akribos: *accurately/exactly/strictly*. A brief survey of some key passages lend a sense of how he understood the *strict* keeping of the laws. Those who are engaged in the *strict* observance of the laws will

---

33. Looking ahead to the Gospels' accounts of the scribes and Pharisees, it was not by accident that Jesus, spokesperson for ordinary people, and the scribes in Jerusalem were agreed that the two "greatest commandments" were intense love of God and love of neighbor (Mark 12:28–34). Or at least, that was the basic ideology of the *politeia* of the Judean scribes and the Judean/Israelite people.

prosper (*Ant.* 1.14). In the final assembly of the whole people that concludes Moses' historical lawgiving, he has them swear to observe the laws, showing themselves to be *accurate* accountants of the mind of God (who had given the covenantal laws; *Ant.* 4.309). Josephus claims that Moses was unusual among famous lawgivers in requiring that the people should assemble weekly to obtain a thorough and *accurate* knowledge of the law (*Ag. Ap.* 2.175). In this way they would practice the laws with all *accuracy* (2.149). The importance of accuracy in the transmission and keeping of the laws comes through in the prominence of *akribeia/akribos* in his discussion of the translation of the laws of the Judeans from their original Hebrew into Greek (where he is repeatedly adding the term into his source, the letter of Aristeas). In his scheme for the project Josephus has Ptolemy Philadelphus command the Judeans to select six prominent elders from each of the twelve tribes whose thorough knowledge of the laws will enable them to make an *accurate* translation of them (*Ant.* 12.48). The designated translators were supplied with everything they needed so that they could work ambitiously and painstakingly to make the translation *accurate* (*Ant.* 12.104; cf. further 12.35, 63, 95, 99).[34]

As might be expected from one proud of his prominent priestly lineage and role in the temple-state, Josephus explains in his exposition of the laws in *Against Apion* that the *politeia* of the Judeans places the administration of the highest affairs in the hands of the priests, headed by the High Priest, so that they will maintain *strict* superintendence of the law and of the pursuits of everyday life (*Ag. Ap.* 2.184–187). He boldly claims that because he was already so thoroughly knowledgeable as a priest at only fourteen years of age, chief priests and leading men of the city would come to him for *more precise* information about the laws (*nomima*; *Life* 9).

Were the Pharisees *Interpreters* of the Law(s)?

As discussed at the outset of this chapter, the standard picture of late second temple "Judaism" included the belief that the Pharisees were the principal or at least the most important "interpreters" of the Torah/Law. This conception of the Pharisees as interpreters of the law(s) has been based largely on early twentieth century translations of three key passages from Josephus that present them as known for their "accurate/precise/exact *interpretation*"

---

34. For a helpful juxtaposition of passages from Josephus exposition of Ptolemy's instructions and the account in Aristeas that he is using as his source, see Mason, *Flavius Josephus and the Pharisees*, 91–92.

of the laws. These translations[35] were made in keeping with the standard picture in an (usually) unexamined circularity. It is thus of considerable importance for understanding of Josephus' presentation of the Pharisees to examine these key passages more closely.

As noted above, Josephus, as a wealthy priest who had played a prominent role in Jerusalem in the 60s and was now presenting the history of the Judeans, stressed that their constitution placed the administration of the laws in the hands of the priests (like himself) who by lineage and learning had acquired accuracy/precision in the ancestral laws.

In the course of his historical accounts of Hasmonean and Roman-Herodian times, however, Josephus mentions other figures who were (recognized as being) precise/accurate in the laws. First, as Herod lay dying, two sages/teachers highly regarded as *accurate/expert* with regard to the ancestral laws/traditions (*akriboun ta patria*) urged their students to cut down the golden Roman eagle from above the gate of the temple, which was in violation of the covenantal commandments (*War* 1.648-650). Second, King Izates of Adiabene had received instruction in the ancestral traditions/laws of the Judeans from the Judean merchant Ananias, who was permissive about Izates' reluctance to become circumcised. But then another Judean, Eleazar, who had a reputation for *accuracy* in (with regard to) the ancestral traditions/laws (*peri ta patria dokon akribes*), insisted that he not merely read but actually carry out what the law commands (*Ant.* 20.38-45). Third, the High Priest Ananus son of Ananus, a follower of the Sadducees who (says Josephus) were more heartless than any of the other Judeans, accused James the brother of Jesus and others of violating the law and delivered them to be stoned (thus acting against the Roman policy that reserved capital punishment for the Roman governor). The residents of the city who were considered most fair-minded and *strict/accurate* in the laws (*peri tous nomous akribeis*), appealed Ananus' action to the newly appointed governor, Albinus, then on his way to take up his post, and to King Agrippa II, who proceeded to depose Ananus (*Ant.* 20.199-203). In all of these cases, accuracy in the laws involved *keeping* them, *acting* on what they command.

Despite these passages in which Josephus presents "accuracy/precision/expertise" in the laws to refer to *keeping* them, with no suggestion of "interpretation," when scholarly interpreters come to Josephus' passages on the Pharisees, they continue to read "interpreting" into the text (following the older translations).[36] These passages about the Pharisees, however, like

---

35. Translation of *War* in the Loeb Classical Library by H. St. John Thackeray in the 1920s and of *Antiquities* by Marcus and Feldman in the 1940s, and to an extent continued in the new translations by Mason et al.

36. E.g., Mason, *Flavius Josephus on the Pharisees*, 92.

those just discussed, refer to their accuracy/precision in (knowing-and-) *keeping* the laws, not in interpreting them.[37] In his *Life* (189–192), Josephus expresses high regard for Simon son of Gamaliel, of an illustrious Jerusalemite family and of the party of the Pharisees, who have a reputation of being different from others in their *accuracy* in the ancestral laws (*peri ta patria nomima . . . akribeia*). This was evidently a standard observation about the Pharisees that Josephus is repeating.

The passage that may have been susceptible of translation in terms of interpretation is one of Josephus' passages standardly understood as about "the Jewish sects" (*War* 2.162–164). He presents the Pharisees as those who have a reputation for *relating/reciting/expounding the laws with accuracy* (*met' akribeias dokountes exegeisthai ta nomima*). The term *exegeisthai* in Greek, however, did not mean "to interpret" (in the modern sense it has in biblical studies), but "telling/expounding/reciting". As we are slowly learning from recent research, this is what professional scribal teachers (such as Judas and Mattathias, mentioned just above) were preoccupied with: learning and teaching by repeated recitation (so that their students would internalize the laws and thus keep them).

Finally, what was the first passage in Josephus' works that mentions the Pharisees refers to their accuracy in keeping the laws, not interpreting them. His first presentation of the Pharisees proceeds as a comparison with their patroness, Alexandra Salome, the wife and successor to the brutal Alexander Jannaeus as Hasmonean ruler of the now expanded realm of the Jerusalem temple-state (*War* 1.107–111). Alexandra had a reputation for *loyalty* (to God). For she was *extremely strict* about the ancestral laws of the people (*akribou gar de malista tou ethnous nomous*) and would banish from the realm (or remove from office) any offenders against the sacred laws (*plemmelountas eis tous hierous nomous*). She was not "interpreting" but keeping and enforcing the sacred laws. Josephus then introduces the Pharisees in comparative terms. "Growing up into authority with her was a body of Judeans with the reputation of excelling others in greater loyalty (to God) and greater accuracy in presenting/reciting/expounding the laws (*tous nomous akribesteron afegeisthai*). More than others, evidently including Alexandra in the narrative, the Pharisees were accurate or strict regarding the laws. And this, suggests the continuing narrative, is what enabled them to become the real administrators of the whole realm, with power to banish and recall prominent figures who had violated the laws.

---

37. As stated in Aristeas 127, "For proper living consists in keeping the laws and this is achieved more by hearing than reading."

In addition to these key passages, Josephus has an explicit reference to the Pharisees as strict in keeping or adhering to the laws in his story of their scheming at the court of Herod: a group of Judean men priding itself on its strict adherence (*exakribosei*) to the ancestral way of life (*tou patriou*) and to observance of the laws. In the course of the following chapters it will be important to remind ourselves of these key passages in Josephus' histories in a critical examination of Josephus' accounts of the role of the Pharisees in the Judean temple-state in late second times.

This critical reading of Josephus' references to the Pharisees, Alexandra Salome, and others as accurate in knowledge and keeping of the laws/customs/ancestral traditions thus accords with what we are learning about (oral-written) scribal training and practice, as discussed in the previous chapter. From repeated oral recitation of texts scribes held the laws in their memory. In temple-state life, the laws, like the "books" that "contained" them, *were* their oral declamation and aural reception.[38] And the emphasis in the laws is to keep them.

---

38. Cf. Jaffee, *Torah in the Mouth*, 18.

4

The Political Prominence of the Pharisees at Mid-First Century CE

In exploring the history of the Pharisees' role in the Judean temple-state in Roman Palestine it makes sense to start at the end, with their prominence at the beginning of the Great Revolt. Josephus' description of their prominence in political affairs in this historical crisis should clear up some significant misunderstandings of the Pharisees.

The Pharisees have standardly been understood as the leading *sect* of Judaism in late second-temple times in the fields of Jewish history and New Testament studies. But nothing in the sources for the Pharisees suggests that they were a sect.

The early work of Jacob Neusner set rabbinics scholarship on a solid broader critical scholarly footing. His probing study of the rabbinic traditions of the Pharisees became the basis of subsequent investigation of the Pharisees, particularly of skepticism regarding the continuity between the Pharisees and the rabbis. In the prevailing vacuum of solidly critical work on the Pharisees, Neusner's more popular booklet *From Politics to Piety* (1973) became widely influential. He discerned clearly that the Pharisees were actively engaged in the politics of Judea under the Hasmoneans. The importance of that recognition was then blunted by his thesis that they withdrew from political affairs under Herod and became closely focused on eating their food in a state of priestly purity. In effect this reinforced the standard view that they were one of the sects of late second-temple Judaism. The sources for the Pharisees, however, do not indicate that the Pharisees ever withdrew from politics.

Scholarship in the English-speaking world had assumed that Josephus, who provides much of the source material, was himself a Pharisee. This led scholars to puzzle how Josephus, himself presumably a Pharisee, could have been so critical of the Pharisees at points in his accounts. A critical reexamination of a passage toward the beginning of Josephus' *Life*, however, indicates not that he was a Pharisee but that when he engaged in political life in Jerusalem, it operated according the views of the Pharisees.

That and other key passages in *Life* indicate that far from having withdrawn from politics, the Pharisees had only become more prominent in the attempt of the temple-state to control public affairs in Judea.

Josephus' Accounts of the Impending Revolt

It took the Romans a frustrating four years to finally crush the Great Revolt of the Judean and Galilean people. They not only devastated the countryside, slaughtering the people and burning their villages, but decimated the city of Jerusalem and destroyed the fortress-like temple where the people who fled their scorched-earth advances hoped to hold out against their overwhelming military machine. Sixty-some years earlier, ten years after the Romans had decisively suppressed the widespread revolt at the death of Herod in 4 BCE, the Romans had placed Judea (including Samaria and Idumea) under the control of the expanded high priestly aristocracy who headed the Jerusalem temple-state, under the watchful eye of a Roman governor. By contrast, after finally destroying the city and temple as well as decimating the countryside in 70 CE, the Romans did not restore the temple-state as the form of their indirect rule.

The high priestly families who headed the temple-state in Jerusalem evidently knew what Rome would do if they proved incapable of containing the revolt that erupted in the summer of 66. According to the wealthy priest and historian Flavius Josephus, the leading high priests and *the leading Pharisees* (*hoi protoi Pharisaioi*) formed a "council," whose principal purpose was to contain the revolt. Here Josephus, a participant in the events of the revolt from the outset, presents the leading Pharisees as already occupying a position in Jerusalem such that they worked side by side with the leading high priests to restore political order in the city and in Galilee as well as in the Judean countryside. This does not fit with the scholarly construction of the Pharisees as, variously, the most prominent "sect" of late-second temple Judaism and/or the leading interpreters of the torah. The labels of "sect" and "interpreters of the torah" hardly appear adequate, perhaps not even appropriate, to describe the position of "the leading

Pharisees" at the outbreak of the Great Revolt. From Josephus' accounts in both *War* and his *Life*, it appears that the Pharisees, especially "the leading Pharisees," had been involved in the administration, even the leadership, of the Jerusalem temple-state in the decades before the Great Revolt. Thus the best point at which to begin critical consideration of the position and role of the Pharisees would be at the end of the second temple period, and not in the historical circumstances in which they first make an appearance, for which only fragmentary and "circumstantial" evidence is available.

Flavius Josephus insists that the writing of history should rely on eyewitnesses, and that he himself was an eyewitness of the recent history of the Judeans just before and during the Great Revolt. In his earliest work, the *Jewish War*, he exaggerates his own role as the great Jewish general who is a worthy opponent of the Roman warlords Vespasian and his son Titus. The later *Life* in which he is defending himself against charges that he had been actively involved in the revolt against Rome, appears to be a more credible account of the early stages of the revolt. The beginning of the *Life,* moreover, is the source of the claim that Josephus himself was a Pharisee, which has played a key role in the reading and interpretation not only of his own works but of other sources for the Pharisees. Most important perhaps, the *Life* also happens to indicate the prominence of "the leading Pharisees" in the politics of the temple-state at the very end of its history.

Josephus' histories and *Life* are our principal sources for the origin, history, and political-economic-religious role of the Pharisees in the Judean temple-state. In older reconstructions of the Pharisees as one of the "philosophies" or "sects" of "Judaism," as noted in the Introduction, passages from Josephus would be compared and combined with text-fragments from the other two principal sets of sources, rabbinic texts and texts from the New Testament, without much critical evaluation. As noted in the Introduction, roughly fifty years ago scholars began evaluating each of the major sources (Josephus' histories, rabbinic texts, and New Testament texts) separately to discern what each set of sources said about the Pharisees before moving to historical reconstruction of the Pharisees.[1] A closely related move was assessing the perspective, agenda, and rhetoric of particular texts, such as Josephus' *Antiquities* or the Gospel of Matthew, as a basis or a critical step toward using their representations of the Pharisees in historical construction.

Also as noted in the Introduction above, the agenda of both Josephus' *War* and his *Antiquities* was to demonstrate and defend the nobility and antiquity of the Judean people in the aftermath of the Roman victory over

---

1. All profoundly influenced by the prolific early work of Jacob Neusner; see especially his early summary in the accessible textbook, *From Politics to Piety*.

the revolt of the Judeans in 70 CE. Imperial Rome celebrated its great military triumph in monuments and other forms of propaganda and Roman historians and poets did not spare criticism of "the Judeans." As he explains in the *Life* more explicitly than in the *War* Josephus, a wealthy Judean priest aspiring to a prominent role in Jerusalem affairs, joined the coalition of high priests, other wealthy elite, and leading Pharisees, in attempting to keep a lid on the revolt. They evidently were only too aware that if they could not restore public order in Judea, the Romans would seek an alternative to controlling the province through the client rule of the temple-state. Having formed the "council," a provisional high priestly government that included the leading Pharisees, they sent Josephus to Galilee with his own body guards and private forces to control that district. When the Roman forces swept through Galilee in their devastating reconquest in 67 CE, says Josephus, he surrendered to the Romans, lauded Vespasian as the fulfilment of his own and other "Jewish" prophesy, and accompanied the Roman troops in the completion of their re-conquest. Josephus was richly rewarded by the new emperor Vespasian, including the grant of a large estate to compensate him for his loss of land in the military devastation of Judea proper.

Not surprisingly he took the name *Flavius* Josephus and took up residence in the palatial compound of the Flavian emperors in Rome. His status as a member of the Roman imperial elite thus compounded his heritage as a Judean noble. He claimed descent from a wealthy priestly (but not high priestly) family descended from the Hasmonean dynasty that two centuries earlier had reestablished Judean independence in alliance with Rome. In his histories and *Life* his perspective, values, and attitude are elitist. He looks down on those of lesser status and absolutely despises ordinary people, Jerusalemites and villagers alike, particularly when they make trouble for their rulers in protests, popular movements, and the Great Revolt. While his agenda is to demonstrate the nobility and antiquity of the Judean people, his rhetoric is derived from the ethos of the imperial Roman elite. As Steve Mason, who has carefully investigated the influence of this ethos on Josephus' works explained, he lived and worked

> in a world of "doublespeak," dissonance, irony, and indirection in imperial Rome... [He] has his characters (including himself) say things that the audience knows to be either completely or substantially false. It is a world of unsettling and constant double games, where nothing is what it appears to be. In Josephus, as in Tacitus, we see vividly the "rhetoricized mentality" fostered by Greco-Roman education for elite males.[2]

2. Mason, "Pharisees in the Narratives of Josephus," 13; Mason references Rudich,

While his arrogant elitist perspective and attitude are usually abundantly clear, what he recounts and claims in his histories is not necessarily trustworthy. It is thus important to compare the different accounts of events and incidents in *War* with those in the *Antiquities* and *Life* and any and all of those works with other sources, if possible.

The Integral Role of the Leading Pharisees in the Temple-State During the Great Revolt

In his *Life* Josephus claims that, as commissioned by the "Jerusalem council," he was attempting to control "the Galileans" and some of the populace in Tiberias who were eager to revolt. In the *War* he had portrayed himself as a great general, organizing the fortification of Galilean towns in anticipation of the massive Roman reconquest everyone knew was coming. In the *War* he had also claimed that Justus of Tiberias was fomenting revolt. Justus had in turn accused Josephus of organizing revolt. *Life* is Josephus' self-defensive revision and "updating" of his role and actions, in the course of which he provides important information about the political prominence and role of the Pharisees in the Jerusalem temple-state in mid-first century CE and its effort to control the revolt. While we surely cannot trust his claims of his popularity and support among the Galileans, his accounts of the (motives and) actions of the leading high priests and leading Pharisees, with whom he was initially allied, appear more reliable (when critically evaluated).[3]

Josephus explains that when he returned from Rome in the summer of 66 he found revolt already well underway in Jerusalem (*Life* 17–19). Fearing that his vocal opposition to revolt brought him under suspicion, he sought asylum in the inner court of the temple. Once the people of the city had killed Menahem, the self-designated "messiah" of the *Sicarioi*, and driven out his followers who attempted to take over leadership at the outset of the revolt,

> I ventured out of the temple and again consorted with the high priests and the principal men of the Pharisees. We were deeply alarmed to see that the people of the city (*demos*) were armed and we were at a loss about what to do since we were powerless to check the rebels. In such obvious and imminent peril we professed to concur in their views, but counseled them to stand fast even if the enemy soldiers advanced, so that they should be given credit for taking up arms only in self-defense. We did

---

Dissidence and Literature under Nero; and Bartsch, *Actors in the Audience*.

3. Critically examined in Horsley, "Power Vacuum and Power Struggle."

these things hoping that before long [the Roman general and governor of Syria] Cestius would come up with a large force and quell the revolt. (*Life* 21–23, adapted from the Loeb and Mason translations)

Thus Josephus who was himself "consorting with" them indicates that (at least) the leading Pharisees were closely involved with the chief priestly heads of the temple-state in trying to control the revolt in the summer of 66.

Cestius did come up to Jerusalem but the Judean rebels defeated his forces and drove them out. "After the defeat of Cestius, the leading men (*hoi protoi*) in Jerusalem, observing that the brigands and rebels were well provided with arms, feared that, being without weapons themselves, they might be left at the mercy of their adversaries, as in fact eventually happened" (*Life* 28). The *protoi* of Jerusalem here evidently refers to the same coalition of "chief priests and leading Pharisees" with whom Josephus had been consorting earlier. Josephus' revised account then jumps to the situation in Galilee and his own supposedly heroic role:

> Being informed, moreover, that all of Galilee had not yet revolted from Rome, and that a portion of it was still tranquil, they dispatched me with two other priests, Joazar and Judas, men of excellent character, to induce the disaffected to lay down their arms ... (*Life* 29)

This sets the scene for the rest of his self-defensive narrative.

This representation of the panic of the ruling elite in Jerusalem, including the chief priests and leading Pharisees, collapses the complex sequence of events in Jerusalem in the summer of 66 CE that he had recounted in *War* 2. His own "consorting with the chief priests and the leading Pharisees" appears to correspond with the assembly of "'the powerful ones with the chief priests and the most distinguished Pharisees" to try to head off further revolt (in *War* 2.409–417). As the Roman governor Florus had imposed one outrageous attack after another on the people and even the elite, the social turmoil was more than the high priestly rulers could control. What is more, the tribute to Rome was in arrears, something the Romans viewed as tantamount to revolt. Desperate to head off rebellion or Roman attack, both the high priestly rulers and the counselors (did those include "leading Pharisees"?) dispersed into the villages to levy the tribute (which would likely have seemed like further humiliation for the villagers). The exasperated people of Jerusalem proclaimed a banishment from the city of king Agrippa (ruler of eastern Galilee and Gaulanitis), who had urged continuing submission to the Romans. The king then sent the (high priestly) rulers together with the magnates (of the city) to Florus to be delegated to collect the tribute from the (rest of) the countryside.

At this point, says Josephus,

> Eleazar, son of the High Priest Ananias, a very daring youth who held the position of the temple-captain (second-ranking to the High Priest and in charge of temple-operations), persuaded those who officiated in the temple services to accept no gift or sacrifice to be offered from a foreigner. This action laid the foundation of the war against the Romans. For the sacrifices offered on behalf of Rome and Caesar were thus rejected. (*War* 2.409)

In desperation, the high priests and leading Pharisees and magnates assembled to deliberate their next move. They called a city-wide assembly, stressing the danger of terminating the sacrifices for Caesar and Roma, insofar as such sacrifices were the key symbol of the loyalty of the Judeans to their imperial rulers. They also "produced priests experienced in the ancestral traditions (*ton patrion*) who declared that their ancestors had accepted the sacrifices of aliens. But none of the rebels would listen, and even the temple-ministers (*leitourgoi*) failed to come to their support" (*War* 2.417).[4]

To assess the credibility of Josephus' account here and understand the issue at stake may take a little "unpacking." He states explicitly that what Eleazar and the officiating priests had done was to cease accepting sacrifices in honor of (the divine) Caesar and Roma (the semi-deified imperial city). But in the ensuing account he obfuscates the issue by pretending that the issue was acceptance of sacrifices and gifts *from* foreigners. Their forefathers, they said, had adorned the sanctuary with gifts from foreigners and had never forbidden anyone from sacrificing. To now terminate such acceptance is absurd as a "pretext" (*prophasis*) for stopping the sacrifices for

---

4. Mason claims again and again in his survey of Josephus' accounts of the Pharisees that they had great popularity and "a massive public following" and "massive popular support." As he confidently asserts in *Flavius Josephus on the Pharisees*, 243, "That the Pharisees have a mass following is indicated throughout Josephus' writings." But this is a serious misreading of Josephus' accounts, one that seems to perpetuate what one finds in many earlier treatments. Josephus' accounts of the Pharisees under the Hasmoneans claims only that they were influential among the (mainly city) people, but not that they had the support or a "massive following" among them. Perhaps it is this misreading of Josephus' accounts of earlier periods that leads him to imagine that at the outbreak of the revolt in Jerusalem the high priests needed the leading Pharisees "to help calm the masses," something of which he finds hints, for example, in *War* 2.411 and *Life* 21. But neither before nor after the outbreak of the revolt do Josephus' accounts indicate that the leading Pharisees had any popular following; in fact, Josephus includes incidents that suggest the opposite, for example, in the sequence of this interaction in *War* 2.411–417.

Caesar and Roma (*War* 2.412–413). The high priests' and leading Pharisees' argument—or is it Josephus' obfuscation?—does not make sense. Josephus says explicitly or implicitly elsewhere (*Ag. Ap.* 2.77; *War* 2.197) that the Judeans financed the daily sacrifices for Rome. So "why does the stoppage of sacrifices *from* Gentiles entail the stoppage of those *for* Rome?"[5] Josephus himself must have known the argument was on shaky ground. The only cases he mentions of foreigners sacrificing in the Jerusalem temple are of Alexander the Great, Ptolemy III, Antiochus VII Sidetes, and Marcus Vipsanius Agrippa (*Ant.* 11.336; *Ag. Ap.* 2.48; *Ant.* 13.242–243; and *Ant.* 18.122, respectively). All of these are either emperors or high-ranking imperial officers, for whom temple priests presumably made an exception to the ban on aliens sacrificing (or being sacrificed to) in the temple.

If we review the *politeia* and the laws/customs of the Judeans that Josephus summarized so extensively in books 3 and 4 of *Antiquities*, the foundational covenantal commandments, particularly the first two, prohibited both payment of the tribute and sacrifices in honor of a divine figure (other than the God of Israel) such as Caesar or Roma. This will surface again (in chap. 7 below) when we discuss the Fourth Philosophy's campaign to refuse payment of the tribute to (the divine) Caesar because God was their only master. Josephus explained that the Fourth Philosophy, led by a scribal teacher and a Pharisee, agreed with the Pharisees on everything except their passionate commitment to freedom. The issue will surface again in the Pharisees' attempt to entrap Jesus over whether payment of the tribute is lawful in the Gospels (to be discussed in Vol. 2).

If, as Josephus mentions several times, the Pharisees were reputed to be accurate in their knowledge and keeping of the law, then they surely (would have) agreed with their fellow scribes in the Fourth Philosophy in principle about the tribute and with the temple-captain Eleazar about the sacrifices for Caesar. Eleazar and the officiating priests in the temple in the summer of 66 surely understood and acted on the implications of the commandments. But the Pharisees, who were in positions of responsibility in the service of the temple-state, were evidently "political realists" who knew the implications of not paying the tribute and not continuing the sacrifices to Caesar and Rome. Their political position and role required compromise of the covenantal principles. We might also give them the benefit of the doubt in relation to what may well have been their understanding of their role as mediators of Roman rule to make possible the continuation of a semblance of the people's life according to their ancestral laws.

---

5. Quoted from the critical treatment of this issue by D. R. Schwartz, "On Sacrifice by Gentiles in the Temple of Jerusalem," 113.

In the immediate situation of the incipient revolt in the summer of 66, however, the motivation may have been self-preservation by the leading Pharisees as well as the high priests (except for Eleazar). When the rebels refused to listen to their arguments, they quickly sought to exonerate themselves and salvage their own positions: they appealed to both Florus, the abusive Roman governor, and King Agrippa to send troops to crush the revolt (*War* 2.418).

Cestius Gallus came with troops; but he was driven out of Jerusalem. In comparison with accounts of the action taken by the *protoi* of Jerusalem following the defeat of Cestius in *Life* 28–29, Josephus' account in *War* 2.562–568 seems misleading and inconsistent, particularly with regard to how the "generals," including himself, came to be appointed. In the account in *War*—after many ranking chief priests and descendants of the Herodian royal family had fled the city—instead of the ruling elite of Jerusalem trying to protect themselves and control the revolt, he has those who defeated Cestius "bring such pro-Romans as remained over to their side, partly by force and partly by persuasion." Assembling in the temple, "they appointed additional generals to conduct the war." The ensuing list of generals, however, pointedly excludes earlier leaders of the revolt and includes high priests and other elite. In the subsequent narrative, moreover, Josephus explains just how, using his own (private?) soldiers, he (in effect) made hostages of local Galilean leaders to keep them under control. Josephus' representation in *Life* appears to be more honest, while self-serving and exculpatory, than his misleading account that he and certain high priests were heading rather than trying to control the revolt in *War* 2.

In *Life* 21–28, as in *War* 2, Josephus indicates that the leading or most distinguished Pharisees were working in coalition with the chief priests (and "the powerful ones"), evidently as some of the *protoi* of Jerusalem, first to prevent further revolt and then to try to control it, until they could buy time to negotiate with the Romans. Far from being a mere religious "sect" or having withdrawn from politics, they or at least the most prominent of them were centrally involved in political affairs, in the operation of the Jerusalem temple-state (which was also the local representative and face of the Roman imperial order in Judea). Their involvement, moreover, would not have been a sudden response to the crisis in 66 CE. If they were in close coalition with the chief priests as the revolt unfolded, they must have already been involved in the leadership of the temple-state, at least in the preceding decades.

This is more than confirmed by Josephus' narrative of what is evidently the central crisis of his time in Galilee: the "council" (*koinon*) of chief priests and (leading) Pharisees in Jerusalem sent a delegation to remove Josephus from his command (*Life* 189–335). In Josephus' maneuvering among and manipulation of various forces, factions, and leaders in Galilee his principal rival was John of Gischala. In *War* he had portrayed John as a local big-man turned brigand leader in Upper Galilee. In *Life* John appears to have been initially an ally of Josephus in a common aim of controlling revolt. But having good relations with leaders in the countryside, he became the principal rival of Josephus for influence in Tiberias and Tarichaeae. Evidently it was not a problem for Josephus to insist that John was a serious rival for the loyalty and control of the Galileans while also making grandiose claims of the Galileans' overwhelming and widespread loyalty to and even affection for himself. Josephus claims it was John who pressed his "old and intimate friend" Simon son of Gamaliel to lobby the council of chief priests and leading Pharisees in Jerusalem, particularly the leading high priests Ananus and Jesus, to relieve him of his command in Galilee.

At the beginning of his narrative about this Josephus cannot avoid acknowledging just how distinguished and respected Simon was in the Jerusalem temple-state: he was evidently a skilled statesman, experienced in the politics of Roman Palestine.

> This Simon was a native of Jerusalem, of a very illustrious family, and of the party of Pharisees, who are considered experts in [or: have a reputation of excelling over others in accuracy concerning] the ancestral laws. This man, full of intelligence and judgment, was capable of retrieving an unfortunate situation in affairs of state by himself. (*Life* 191–192)

"At that time," says Josephus, "he had differences from me"—which suggests that such had not always been the case. Josephus presents Simon first trying to persuade the high priests Ananus and Jesus and others of their faction, but many chief priests and others of eminence defended Josephus' ability as a general. So he has Simon then suggest that John's representatives bribe Ananus and his circle, which brought them around. Of course he does not mention other reasons the council may have had for deciding to remove Josephus from his command in Galilee.

Josephus' account of the council's plan for action indicates just how centrally involved the Pharisees were in the decisions and actions of the Jerusalem council.

> The scheme agreed upon was to send a delegation comprising persons of different classes of society but of equal standing in education. Two of them, Jonathan and Ananias, were of the (lay) people of the city (*hoi demotikoi*) and of the party of the Pharisees. The third, Joazar, was of a priestly family and also a

> Pharisee. Simon, the youngest, was descended from high priests. Their instructions were to approach the populace of Galileans and ascertain the reason for their friendship/loyalty toward me. If they attributed it to my being a native of Jerusalem, they were to reply that so were all four of them; if to my expert knowledge of the laws, they should reply that neither were they ignorant of the ancestral customs; if it was due to my priestly office, they were to answer that two of them were also priests. (*Life* 197–198)

This description of the council's scheme gives a good deal of information about the Pharisees and about the key factors that mattered to the Jerusalem aristocracy that understood themselves as the rightful rulers of the Judeans and Galileans. The Pharisees consisted of ordinary priests as well as non-priestly people of the city (*demotikoi*). The most important and distinctive feature of the Pharisees was their (reputation for) learning, particularly their accurate knowledge of the ancestral laws.

It seems doubtful that Josephus' description here accurately represents what would have been important to the Galileans. Rather it represents what was important to Josephus himself and other members of the Jerusalem aristocracy as features of the rulers of the temple-state: being natives of Jerusalem, accurate knowledge of (supposedly adherence to) the ancestral laws, and priestly (but especially high priestly) lineage. The Jerusalem council (*koinon*) was comprised of just such people, a coalition of high priests, led by Ananus and Jesus, and leading Pharisees, such as Simon son of Gamaliel, and other "powerful ones." Josephus never lists the "membership" of the council. Judging from his narrative here, however, the council headed by the high priests Ananus and Jesus either included or at least consulted other high priests and leading men (rulers/officers/powerful) of the people of Jerusalem in making an important decision (*Life* 194). It is unclear whether the three Pharisees and the High Priest in the four-member delegation were "members" of the council. But they were evidently heavily involved in its actions, such as the (attempted) implementation of its decision to remove Josephus.

A review of Josephus' accounts of several other important social-political conflicts and events in the deteriorating social order leading up to the eruption of the revolt may help us better appreciate the significance of the leading Pharisees' integral role in the Jerusalem council as the revolt began. Throughout the decades of their increasingly ineffective rule in Judea, the high priestly heads of the temple-state had not represented or defended the interest of the people. This should not be surprising since they owed their position of power and privilege to their Roman patrons, were subject to appointment and dismissal by the Roman governors, and collaborated with the Romans on occasions of conflict.⁶ The high priests' collaboration and complicity with the Romans, however, brought scribes trained for service in the temple-state, presumably including the Pharisees, into acute conflict between their loyalty to the covenantal constitution and laws of the Judean temple-state and their loyalty to their high priestly patrons' actions in violation of the covenantal laws. This is evident in some significant conflicts that Josephus recounts, even if he does not do so in explicitly covenantal terms.

The review of the training of scribes for service in the temple-state and the transformation of the Jerusalem temple-state into the Hellenistic *polis* of Antioch-in-Jerusalem in chapter 1 is a dramatic illustration of this conflict. This conflict led some scribal circles, notably the *maskilim* who evidently produced Dan 10–12 and the "Enoch"-scribes who produced the Animal Vision in 1 Enoch 85–90 to mount active resistance to the high priests whom they regarded as having abandoned the covenantal constitution of the Judean temple-state.

Josephus' accounts of some scribal groups' actions in the first-century CE appear to be later chapters in the same conflict between the high priestly heads of the temple-state and their scribal retainers.⁷ In 6 CE when the Romans reimposed payment of tribute to Caesar in connection with setting the high priests in charge of Judea, charged with responsibility of collecting the tribute, Josephus introduces the Fourth Philosophy, led by the scribal-teacher (*sophistes*) Judas of Gaulanitis/Gamla and the Pharisee Saddok (to be discussed more fully in chap. 7 below). In direct opposition to the high priests' and a challenge to Roman rule, they organized refusal to "render to Caesar," honored throughout the Empire as divine, insofar as they already had God as their master and ruler. It is not difficult to discern that refusal to "render to Caesar" was a violation of the first two covenantal commandments.⁸ Josephus says also that, except for their intense passion for freedom, the Fourth Philosophy agreed in everything with the Pharisees, who were known for their strict adherence to the laws. That the leading Pharisees remained in the service of the temple-state in collaboration with the high priestly rulers as high priestly figures became downright predatory on the people as well as complicit in Roman rule is a striking contrast with the Fourth Philosophy who agreed with them in principle and especially in contrast especially with the scribal "dagger men."

6. Documentation and critical discussion based mainly Josephus' accounts, in Horsley, "High Priests and the Politics of Roman Palestine"; and Goodman, *The Ruling Class of Judea*.

7. Critical examination of the many cases of scribal criticism or conflict with the imperial rulers and/or the client rulers in Judea in Horsley, *Revolt of the Scribes*.

8. *Ant.* 18.4–5, 23. See further Horsley, *Revolt of the Scribes*, 183–88.

On the other hand, another conflict mentioned by Josephus, in *Life* 64–69, suggests that the leading Pharisees were attempting to enforce the keeping of the covenantal laws from their position in the Jerusalem council while attempting to regain the temple-state's control over the revolt. Addressing "the principal men" of Tiberias, he claims that he had been "commissioned by the Jerusalem council to press for the demolition of the palace of Herod the Tetrarch which contained representations of animals, such a style being forbidden by the laws." Here we can readily suspect the influence of the leading Pharisees on the council with their reputation for strict adherence to the laws. The leading Pharisees in their role in the council of the Jerusalem temple-state would appear to be "political realists," maintaining their responsibility to enforce the covenantal laws while also compromising their principles in yielding to the high priests in their collection of the tribute in their attempt to regain the temple-state's control of the society.

Was Josephus Himself a Pharisee?

Nearly all research on and interpretation of the Pharisees has assumed that Josephus himself was a Pharisee, or at least claimed to be. "The foundational scholarship on Josephus and all of the major modern translations of his works have been done by critics who believed him to have been a Pharisee."[9] It then seemed difficult to understand how he could at several points portray them negatively and criticize their actions. This led to the search for, hypotheses about, and debates over the sources he drew upon in the accounts in *War* and *Antiquities* in order to account for the critical passages. More recently prominent has been the hypothesis that Josephus only claimed to have been a Pharisee in connection with certain passages in *Antiquities* in which he seemed to be arguing that the Pharisees were the key to controlling the Judean population. This was supposedly a political ploy to identify himself with the Pharisees as the Romans were considering who they might place in charge of Judean society in the aftermath of their destruction of the temple and temple-state.[10] All of these interpretations, both the standard older ones and the skeptical recent ones, were dependent on a brief passage toward the outset of *Life* (10–12).

As just noted, in the course of the narrative of events in Jerusalem and Galilee in his *Life* Josephus describes himself as having "consorted with the

---

9. Mason, *Flavius Josephus on the Pharisees*, 325.

10. This is argued strongly by Cohen, *Josephus in Galilee and Rome*, 144–51, 237–38, elaborating on the view of Neusner, "Josephus's Pharisees," 231, and their teacher Morton Smith, "Palestinian Judaism in the First Century."

leading Pharisees" along with the chief priests. Then he indicates personal acquaintance as well as close knowledge of the distinguished Pharisee Simon son of Gamaliel. Later in his narrative of the delegation's maneuvers to remove him from command in Galilee, he admits that they reminded him that they (two or more of them who were Pharisees) were his teachers as fellow natives of Jerusalem (*Life* 274). Then in his account of his attempted replacement as general in Galilee he claims that he is an expert in the ancestral laws, which is how he characterizes the Pharisees in key passages in three different works. Insofar as it was Pharisees who advocated and then implemented the (attempted) removal of Josephus, he has reason to compose a hostile account of their character and maneuvering in Galilee (which is very similar to his own maneuvering and manipulation throughout his months in Galilee). But there is a striking asymmetry in his account of the council's scheme to compose a delegation to remove him that is comprised of different statuses of Jerusalemites but equal standing in education. He says that they picked three Pharisees so that the delegation could (out-)match his knowledge of the ancestral laws. It is striking, however, that he does not say that they picked three Pharisees because he himself was a Pharisee.[11]

This would not have bothered, perhaps not even been noticed by, earlier readers of Josephus since they simply assumed that Josephus was a Pharisee or that he pretended to have been a Pharisee by the time he composed *Antiquities* and *Life*. Critical analysis of the various arguments made for his having been a Pharisee, however, shows that none are persuasive and that the view of Josephus as having been or having claimed to be a Pharisee is based narrowly on that brief passage early in *Life*, particularly on a single sentence in *Life* 12. It seems likely that the 1926 translation by Thackeray in the Loeb Classical Library has been the basis for many interpretations of Josephus himself having been a Pharisee: "Being now in my nineteenth year I began to govern my life by the rules of the Pharisees." It also seems likely the immediately preceding passage in *Life* 10 set up this reading of *Life* 12.

> At about the age of sixteen I determined to gain personal experience (*empeiria*) of the three schools among us [i.e. Judeans], ... of Pharisees, ... Sadducees, and Essenes. I thought that after a thorough investigation, I should be in a position to select the best. So I submitted myself to hard training and laborious exercises and passed through the three courses. (trans. Thackeray)[12]

---

11. Mason, *Flavius Josephus on the Pharisees*, 369, emphasizes this.

12. In an influential handbook, Attridge, comments, "The account, which has its parallels in other stories of philosophers' quests, serves to indicate that Josephus made an informed choice in opting for the Pharisees" ("Josephus and His Works," 18).

As Mason points out, however, the reading of *Life* 10–12 which has been the principal basis on which interpreters have concluded that Josephus was (or claimed to be) a Pharisee is problematic in several ways: it misses the logic of the paragraph; it does not fit the lengthy ensuing narrative; and it misunderstands the key clause in 12b.[13] After submitting to the hard training in the three schools he says he was not content with the experience thus gained. So he became a devoted disciple of the ascetic Bannus who was practicing frequent ablutions in the wilderness for purity sake. After "living with him for three years and, having satisfied my yearning (*epithumia*), I returned to the city" (*Life* 12a). Also, we must marvel that in the same span of three years between the ages of sixteen and nineteen, he had somehow undergone the rigorous training of the three courses of the Pharisees, Sadducees, and Essenes and also spent three years in the wilderness with Bannus.

Thackeray and many others have also missed the meaning of the next sentence in *Life* 12b which became the basis of the assumption that Josephus was a Pharisee. The Greek text of the key clause—*erxamen te politeuesthe te Pharisaion hairesei katakolouthon*—requires critical reading and translation. With one critical eye on the immediate narrative in Josephus' texts and the other on Liddell and Scott, the standard Greek-English lexicon,[14] Steve Mason carried out important word-studies in this and other passages on the Pharisees.[15] The controlling verb in the key sentence, *politeuesthe*, usually refers to taking part in political affairs, holding political office, or governing, in a wide range of Greek texts. The tiny number of "Jewish" or "Christian" text-fragments listed to attest "behave" or "deal with in private affairs," must have been influenced by modern Christian theologians who thought that such texts by definition referred to private religious life separated from political life. Once we consider the broader narrative contexts and the social-political contexts of 2 Macc 11:25; Acts 23:1; and Phil 1:27, it is clear that the term refers to political life in the Judean temple-state or in one of the assemblies Paul and coworkers catalyzed. While older German scholarship somehow understood that in this verb and sentence Josephus was referring to political life, Anglophone translators and interpreters "[took] the

---

13. Mason's critical analysis of this key passage in *Life* 10–12 in *Flavius Josephus on the Pharisees*, chap. 15, 342–56, appears to be decisive for further study of Josephus' histories as sources for the Pharisees. He made the same argument two years earlier (1989) in "Was Josephus a Pharisee? A Re-Examination of *Life* 10–12."

14. Liddell and Scott, *A Greek-English Lexicon*. Originally published in 1853, revised and expanded by Jones (1940) and then by McKenzie (1996)—with many updates and reprints over the past 150 years.

15. Mason, *Flavius Josephus on the Pharisees*, 347–53.

phrase *erxamen politeuesthe* as a conversion statement, with the sense that Josephus became a Pharisee."[16]

While the personal behavior reading would be a jarring break from the narrative, however, the political reading "I began to engage in public life" fits both the immediate narrative context and the overall narrative in *Life*. Josephus begins his autobiography by claiming an illustrious noble ancestry of descent from the Hasmoneans, with his father one of the most distinguished men in Jerusalem. His early education gave him the accurate knowledge of the ancestral laws requisite for active life in the politics of the temple-state; he claims that as a precocious youth of fourteen he gained wide appreciation from the chief priests and *protoi* of the city. He supposedly deepened that knowledge in his rigorous training among the Pharisees and other schools. Then after being satisfied from his religious quest with Bannus in the wilderness, he returned to the city (*polis*), and at age nineteen he began active participation in political life.

The continuing narrative then picks right up with his life in political affairs. At age twenty-six he was sent to Rome as an envoy to negotiate the release of some (fellow) priests who had been sent to render account to Caesar. Upon his return to Jerusalem he found the revolt well underway and, after taking refuge from the rebels' initial attacks on their rulers, swung into action with chief priests, leading Pharisees, and other prominent figures to limit the revolt and then to exert some control over it. In the course of the narrative of his maneuvering with the delegation of priests and Pharisees sent to remove him he twice more uses *politeuomai* in reference to how he had "governed" or conducted his public life in Galilee (*Life* 258–262, as Thackeray himself rendered the term). Thus the translation "I began to participate in political life" fits both the immediate and the overall narrative.

How he participated in public life in the Jerusalem temple-state is then indicated in the ensuing phrase, *tei Pharisaion hairesei katakolouthon*. Josephus usually uses *katakoloutheo* in reference to obeying or conforming to the commandments or laws or God's will. His other usage for following or emulating an example such as a person fits less well in *Life* 12b and the broader narrative context. The appropriate translation of the whole sentence would thus be something like, "I returned to the city. Being now in my nineteenth year, I began to participate in politics, following the school of the Pharisees."

To understand the substance of that last phrase, however, it is necessary to resort to another of Josephus' accounts of the Pharisees and the other schools, anticipating fuller discussion in subsequent chapters. Josephus'

16. Mason, *Flavius Josephus on the Pharisees*, 347–48.

account of the schools of the Judeans that is most discussed, partly because he also mentions, and compares and contrasts, "the fourth Philosophy," comes at the beginning of *Antiquities* book 18. After his harangue against "the intrusive Fourth Philosophy" he again discusses in sequence the Pharisees, the Sadducees, and the Essenes. In this his most favorable treatment of the Pharisees, he mentions their simple life with no concession to luxury and their respect and deference to their elders, as well as their views of fate and free will and rewards and punishment. He then says that on account of their views, "they are very influential among the city-people (*tois demois*), and all prayers and sacred rites happen to be done according to their prescriptions."[17] "The (people of the) cities attest the strength (*arete*) of their high ideals both in their way of living and in their discourse" (18.12–15; Greek text uncertain). The implication is that their influence guides not only "religious" rites (which were not separate from political life anyhow) but all affairs and operations of the temple-state.[18] In his brief discussion of the Sadducees, who are few but are men of the highest standing, he says that they accomplish practically nothing, "for whenever they assume a position of (high/ruling) office, they defer, albeit unwillingly and by necessity, to whatever the Pharisee dictates, since otherwise the populace would not tolerate them" (18.17).

It may not be clear from this discussion of the schools whether the affairs and operations of the Jerusalem temple-state were done according to the Pharisees' (supposedly) "accurate knowledge/application of the laws" already at the beginning of the first century. But these comments about the Pharisees and Sadducees and their respective relation to the populace and operations of the temple-state in his discussion of the schools help us understand why Josephus explains in his autobiographical narrative in *Life* 10–12 that when he returned to the city he "began to participate in politics *following the school of the Pharisees*."

In his letter to the Philippians, the apostle Paul has an autobiographical summary similar to that of Josephus in *Life* 2–12. Until recent decades—and continuing in some enclaves—standard Christian and Christian scholarly interpretation held that Saul/Paul was a Pharisee—just as nearly all interpreters of Josephus have believed that he was or later pretended to be a

---

17. In translating *exegesei* it is important not to project the modern practices of biblical interpretation or even the supposed rabbinic derivation of rulings from "interpretation" of some ruling in the Torah. An *exegetes* in the ancient world was an adviser of the rulers, in this case like the scribal advisers of the high priests, who had accurate knowledge of the laws and could interpret dreams and omens—the traditional role of scribes in the ancient Near East.

18. So also Mason, *Flavius Josephus on the Pharisees*, 353.

Pharisee. The Book of Acts has Paul asserting this himself in two passages in which he is attempting to save himself from entrapment by the temple authorities when he returns to Jerusalem (Acts 23:1–10; cf. 26:2–8).

In Phil 3:3–6, however, in a self-defensive statement similar to that of Josephus, he lays out his credentials as a bona fide Judean: circumcised on the eighth day, a member of the people of Israel, of the tribe of Benjamin, a Hebrew of Hebrews. Then in a series of clauses he lays out the principal aspects of his earlier public life (as Saul, mainly in Jerusalem): "as to the law/torah, a Pharisee, as to zeal, a persecutor of the *ekklesia* (i.e., the assembly of all Judeans), as to justice under the law, blameless." Like Josephus later, he does not say that he himself was a Pharisee. He refers to how he had been proceeding in his public life that was governed by the law: with regard to the law, he had operated according to the Pharisees' understanding and application (according to which Josephus claimed that the Jerusalem temple-state operated). Paul's autobiographical statement is further confirmation of the political reading of *Life* 10–12 that does not reduce the Pharisees and their application of the law to individual religious piety.

In the last clause of the key paragraph of Josephus' autobiographical narrative he adds that the school of the Pharisees "is similar to (resembles; *paraplesios*) that called the Stoics by the Greeks" (*Life* 12b). Contrary to some older interpreters, the comparison here is probably not primarily about similarity of doctrines between the Pharisees and Stoics. As is widely recognized about philosophies in Hellenistic-Roman culture, including political culture, in the first century, Stoicism had become dominant among them. The Alexandrian Jewish philosopher Philo's worldview, for example, is predominantly Platonic (Academic); but his many treatises are prime sources for Stoic teachings in the syncretistic philosophy of the day. Stoicism became particularly influential in political culture, most famously illustrated in the first century BCE by Cicero and in the first century CE by Seneca, who had considerable influence in Rome in the generation before Flavius Josephus. Almost certainly what Josephus is saying here is a further explanation of why in entering participation in political life he—like the Sadducees—had to defer to the views of the Pharisees who had a function in the Jerusalem temple-state similar to that of Stoicism among the political elite in Hellenistic cities of the empire.

The overall narrative of *Life*, like its opening paragraphs, in comparison with some of his other comments about the Pharisees, provide other indications that Josephus himself was not a Pharisee. In one of his accounts of the three principal "philosophies" of the Judeans, in contrast with some of his sharp criticisms, he comments that "the Pharisees simplify their standard of living, making no concession to luxury" (*Ant.* 18.12). In *Life*, as in his other works, however, he is clearly proud that he was a wealthy priest of distinguished ancestry, with a luxurious lifestyle supported by his extensive estates. From this wealth he could afford not only his personal bodyguards but his own private troops that enabled him to exercise "forceful suasion" with the Galileans and the leading men of Tiberias, as evident throughout his narrative in *Life*.

In stark contrast to the simplified standard of living he attributes to the Pharisees, moreover, Josephus reports several situations in which he extended his control of resources, admitting his own corruption, as when he took spoil that he sent to his family in Jerusalem (e.g., *Life* 81). We may wonder what exactly he had in mind when he says he intended to reserve the imperial grain stored in the villages of Upper Galilee "either for the Romans or for my own use" (*Life* 71–72). And he admits just how duplicitous he could be with suspicious villagers who had ambushed a caravan loaded with wealth that they viewed as extracted from their fellow villagers subjected to Herodian rulers of the area (*Life* 126–131). In contrast with his standard characterization of the Pharisees as known for their accurate adherence to the ancestral laws, Josephus frequently disregards or blatantly violates them. As the "general" charged with controlling the revolt in Galilee, Josephus is repeatedly manipulative, deceitful, and duplicitous.

It is thus evident that *Life* 10–12 cannot serve as a basis for imagining that Josephus himself was a Pharisee. This passage indicates, however, that in entering public life he was constrained to operate according to the influential application of the ancestral laws by the Pharisees that had come to prominence in the operations of the temple-state. It also helps to explain why the wealthy priest Josephus, who claimed that he also possessed a deep knowledge of the ancestral laws, would have been jealous of the influence of the Pharisees in the operation of the temple-state. And the focal narrative in *Life* of how the delegation consisting of three Pharisees and a High Priest that attempted to remove him in Galilee and the *koinon* of high priests and leading Pharisees who sent them explains how he would likely have been seriously resentful of the Pharisees' role and influence in the temple-state.

This critical rereading of key passages in Josephus' *Life*, particularly his account of the beginning of his entry into public life, challenges previous controlling assumptions in the scholarly fields of ancient Jewish history and New Testament studies. Josephus' historical works in general and his accounts of the Pharisees and other philosophies of the Judeans in particular are not focused on individuals' practice and personal behavior in "Judaism."

They are about the history of the Judean people focused mainly on their rulers but also on the *politeia* and laws according to which their collective life is governed. In the late "second-temple" period the focus is mainly on the Jerusalem temple-state and how its rulers relate to a succession of imperial regimes, particularly the Romans, on the one hand, and how it controls the people of the city and the people of the countryside, the vast majority of Judeans, on the other. The relatively few accounts about the Pharisees in Josephus' histories are not about "Pharisaic Judaism," as if it were a religion or the mainline of the religion of "Judaism." Rather they focus on the Pharisees' role and activities in the operations of the temple-state, mainly on their knowledge of the ancestral laws and their relations with the high priests (and/or kings). Like Ben Sira's self-description of the role of learned scribes in the early second century BCE, moreover, Josephus presents the Pharisees as those who have expertise in the ancestral traditions of the Judeans in the operations of the temple-state. In the decades before the outbreak of the Great Revolt, the Pharisees and their expertise in the laws and customs of the Judeans had become ever more prominent in the operations of the temple-state in Jerusalem.

5

The Pharisees under the Hasmoneans

Jewish history of the early second century BC is often simplified into three major phases: the Hellenizing Reform, the Maccabean Revolt and the purification of the recaptured temple, and the rise of the Hasmonean high priesthood. All three of what Josephus calls the Judean "philosophies," the Pharisees, the Sadducees, and the Essenes (now thought to be related in some way to the Qumran community) evidently emerged early in Hasmonean times. So it is important to appreciate the more complex steps in which the early Hasmoneans maneuvered between rival claimants to Seleucid rule and gained a degree of independence for the temple-state and for the extension of its rule to additional territory. Jonathan's crucial steps of gaining Seleucid recognition as High Priest and his re-establishing the temple-state appear to be the events that precipitated the emergence of the Pharisees as well as the Qumran community. These were different responses by surviving and/or emerging groups of scribes (and priests) to what had been developing in Jerusalem and Judea in relation to the vacuum of imperial power in the region.

Because they usually focus almost exclusively on political leaders engaged in wars, the sources (1 Maccabees and Josephus's *War* and *Antiquities*) pay little attention to the scribal(-priestly) circles who also played a role in key events. As noted in chap. 1, because of their role and stake in the temple-state, certain scribal circles were engaged in resistance to the Hellenizing Reform and the invasion of Antiochus Epiphanes even before the outbreak of the Maccabean Revolt. From their visionary histories we know of at least two scribal circles actively engaged in resistance, the *maskilim* and the "Enoch"-scribes, as discussed in chap. 1 above. Also, from 1 Maccabees we know of a less adamant resistance group of *hasidim*, who were ready to reach a truce once a High Priest with proper Aaronid lineage (Alcimus) was appointed (1 Macc 7:12-16). There were probably other circles of scribes who were more or less actively involved while also committed to conserving traditional Judean scribal culture. And some of the *maskilim* and "Enoch"-scribes may have survived the attacks by Antiochus Epiphanes and the Revolt. Similarly, there were surely priestly aristocrats other than the dominant reforming faction, who simply hunkered down through the Reform, the imperial military invasion, and the Maccabean Revolt. Some of these probably just "went with the flow" of events. Such scribal circles and priestly aristocrats as well as regular priests would have been personally and "professionally" concerned about the temple-state and had a stake in events as they unfolded after the capture and "cleansing" of the temple in 164 BCE. So it is important to keep their potential response in mind as we trace events in Judea.

The Rise of the Hasmoneans

For the rise of the Hasmonean dynasty of high priests there are three interrelated sources. 1 Maccabees narrates Mattathias' and Judas' leadership of the Maccabean Revolt and then the continuing struggle of the Judeans led by Judas' brothers Jonathan and Simon. The book is historical propaganda for the Hasmonean regime, particularly for Simon's high priesthood (see esp. 1 Macc 13-14). In the *War* and especially in the *Antiquities*, Josephus is dependent on 1 Maccabees. Josephus is thought to be particularly favorable to the Hasmonean dynasty insofar as he took pride in his Hasmonean lineage (*Life* 1-9).

After Judas had been killed in 164 BCE the aristocratic reform faction that had abandoned the ancestral way of life regained control of Jerusalem.[1] The Seleucid imperial officer Bacchides placed them in charge of the countryside (*chora*; 1 Macc 9:25). They proceeded to seize, torture, and

---

1. The following account draws on and parallels Horsley, "The Expansion of Hasmonean Rule in Idumea and Galilee," 137-39. A far more detailed study is Babota, *The Institution of the Hasmonean High Priesthood*, with four chapters and over a hundred pages on Jonathan's military maneuvers and high priesthood and one chapter on Simon. In chap. 4 he argues persuasively that Judas the Hammer was never formally declared High Priest (despite Josephus account, *Ant.* 12.414, 419, 434). He argues that Jonathan and Simon had already set up a Hellenistic-style high priesthood prior to the high priesthood of Hyrcanus and Jannaeus. In contrast with some earlier studies, Babota recognizes that the Judean high priests exercised civil (political) as well as religious power.

kill rebel leaders.[2] Reviving the revolt, Judas' brother Jonathan fled to the wilderness and resumed guerrilla warfare (again fighting on the sabbath, 1 Macc 9:28–33; *Ant.* 13.8). After fortifying a base in a village, Jonathan recruited a large force among those sympathetic in the *chora*, that is, peasant fighters (*Ant.* 13.26–28). After losing a battle, Bacchides became impatient with the reforming elite (presumably in Jerusalem) and agreed to a "friendship" (treaty) with Jonathan. With greater freedom of action, Jonathan then administered the affairs of the people from the town of Michmash (eight miles northwest of Jerusalem) for several years and purged "the wicked and godless" (13.32–34).

Then, taking advantage of the continuing conflict between rival Seleucid factions, Jonathan took control of Jerusalem. As the rival Seleucids outbid one another for his loyalty he gained appointment as High Priest, remission of the tribute to the Seleucid regime (*Ant.* 13.40–46), and control over more territory (13.49–57). As the narrative in 1 Maccabees indicates, by contrast with the confirmation of the previously hereditary high priesthood by the imperial regime, the Seleucid king Alexander now appointed Jonathan High Priest because of his military prowess: "We have heard that you are a mighty warrior and worthy to be our Friend" (10.18–21). Jonathan then expanded his control of the surrounding cities toward the coast, taking Joppa, Azotus, and Ascalon, and received additional territory to be colonized (13.99–102). Having gathered a much larger popular army from "all Judea" (13.121, 124), he won an important battle against one of the rival Seleucids and sent envoys to Rome to secure his position vis-à-vis the rival Seleucid pretenders (13.163). That is, already in the first generation, the Hasmoneans pursued an expansion of the territory and people they controlled. Opposition to Jonathan's rule in Judea had not ended, however. The only way he could maintain control of territory and people was by maneuvering between rival Seleucid factions, gaining recognition by the one or the other or both.

After Jonathan was captured, having unwisely relaxed his guard militarily, his brother Simon assumed the leadership, supposedly acclaimed by an assembly of the Jerusalem populace (*demos, plethos*) in the temple, to have authority (*prostasia*) over them in place of his brothers Judas and Jonathan (1 Macc 13:1–8; *Ant.* 13.197–201). Mindful of the importance of religious-political propaganda for the legitimation of the fledgling Hasmonean regime, Simon built for his father and brothers a great monument of polished white marble with high pillars, and porticoes and pyramids for

---

2. Josephus exclaims in hyperbole that their torture and murder of the leaders of the Revolt "was a greater calamity than any the Judeans had experienced since the return from Babylon" (*Ant.* 13.5).

each one as well (1 Macc 13:25-30; *Ant.* 13.210-212). Whether he was recognized by one of the rival Seleucids or not, Judean sources have him chosen High Priest by the populace (142-135 BCE). Simon managed to liberate the people (*laos*) from servitude to the Macedonians so that they no longer had to pay tribute. He also (again) subdued the nearby (enemy) cities of Gazara, Joppa, and Jamnia, and captured the citadel in Jerusalem by a siege. Calling the populace to an assembly (*ekklesia*), he persuaded them to raze it to the ground, leaving the temple as the sole prominent edifice in Jerusalem (*Ant.* 13.213-217). Josephus claims that the populace so honored Simon that they (or more likely he) dated public documents by the year of his rule as "benefactor and ethnarch of the Judeans" (13.214).

The Hasmonean propaganda in 1 Maccabees is far more elaborate and laudatory of Simon:

> In the third year of the great High Priest Simon in the assembly of the priests and the people and the rulers of the people (ethnos) and the elders of the countryside the following was proclaimed (and engraved on a bronze tablet): (after praising him for spending large amounts of his own resources and arming his soldiers and paying them wages and settling Judeans in cities toward the coast) the Judeans and their priests have resolved that Simon should be their leader and High Priest forever, until a trustworthy prophet should arise, and that he should be governor over them and that he should take charge of the sanctuary and appoint officials over its tasks and over the country and the weapons and the strongholds, and that he should take charge of the sanctuary, and that he should be obeyed by all ... and should be clothed in purple and wear gold. (1 Macc 14:27-43)[3]

It is not difficult to "read between the lines" and discern what all was coming together in Simon's consolidation of power. The proclamation of the "great assembly" probably formalized negotiations and compromises with rival leaders and their followers. That it was necessary to prohibit meetings without Simon or speaking against him points to such opposition that may

---

3. First Maccabees as a whole is usually seen as Hasmonean propaganda. S. Schwartz, "Israel and the Nations Roundabout," however, makes a convincing argument that passages such as the decree in 1 Macc 14:27-43 and other examples that are clearly Hasmonean propaganda are in tension with the Deuteronomic rhetoric against the Gentiles in the narrative of 1 Maccabees, that fits its praise of Judas and his brothers Jonathan and Simon as heroes, but "is at odds ... with the realities of Hasmonean politics under John Hyrcanus and his sons" (v. 29). Except for its "updating" to include reference to John Hyrcanus, 1 Maccabees must therefore date from before Hyrcanus mounted wars of expansion with his foreign mercenaries and his "annexing" of (superficially "Judaized") non-Judeans such as the Idumeans.

well have been continuing (14:41–45). Previous priestly aristocratic office holders (the *archontes tou ethnous*), different factions among the ordinary priests, and prominent 'elders from the countryside' had to be appeased.[4] Some of the opposition, such as the priestly-scribal faction that had withdrawn to Qumran, was not so easily placated.

After the Maccabean Revolt, the fundamental social structure evidently remained much the same as in the days of Ben Sira (discussed in chap. 1). Although the population had expanded, with the colonization of territory taken in battles or granted by the Seleucids (settling Judeans in cities toward the coast), the Judean peasants lived in villages scattered through the countryside, with the more powerful men prominent as "elders." Political-economic power was concentrated in Jerusalem, legitimated as a temple-state staffed by ordinary priests, but dominated by a priestly aristocracy (the *archontes tou ethnous*), with the whole headed by the High Priest.

As reestablished by the Hasmoneans, however, the Judean temple-state was significantly different from the previous temple-state in which the priestly aristocracy was subject to and dependent on the Persian and Ptolemaic and Seleucid imperial regimes. As imagined in the decree that empowered Simon as commander of the weapons and fortresses as well as High Priest, the Hasmonean temple-state was no longer subservient to imperial rule. Whereas the Zadokite high priesthood had held legitimacy as a lineage of hoary antiquity, however, the principal base of power of the nascent Hasmonean high priesthood was the Judean army, not an imperial regime. Drawing on the spoil that Jonathan and Simon had taken in their conquests over the previous decades ("spending large amounts of their own resources"), the latter had created a professional army ('arming his soldiers and paying them wages'). With this military base Simon could further consolidate his power by placing his own officers in crucial administrative and military positions, including commanders of the "strongholds." Jonathan and Simon were not just restoring the temple-state in Jerusalem. They were also establishing a militarized monarchic high priesthood more significant for its army and the expanded territory it ruled than for presiding over the rituals and festivals in the temple itself.

---

4. In a careful reading of the conflicting sources, Sievers, *The Hasmoneans and their Supporters*, explains that the rise of the Hasmoneans to the high priesthood succeeded by patching together an inherently unstable coalition of different groups. As noted above, Bobota, *The Institution of the Hasmonean High Priesthood*, focuses on how the Hasmonean high priesthood was "instituted," mainly under Jonathan, in great detail.

The Origin of the Three "Philosophies" of the Judeans

It is surely significant that Josephus interrupts his narrative of Jonathan's maneuvering among the declining "great powers" of the time (roughly from 161 to 143 BCE) for his first brief account of the three main "philosophies" or "ways of life" among the Judeans.

> Now at this time there were three schools (*haireseis*; "choices") among the Judeans, which held different views concerning human affairs; the first being the Pharisees, the second the Sadducees, and the third the Essenes. (*Ant.* 13.171–173)

In two much longer and more descriptive passages Josephus refers to "philosophizing among the Judeans" as taking three forms (*War* 2.119–166) and to the Judeans having "three philosophies of their ancestral traditions from the most ancient times" (*Ant.* 18.12–25).[5] Interpreters of the Pharisees and the others have tended not to investigate the understanding and practice of "philosophy" and the different schools of philosophy in elite cultural circles under the early Roman Empire.[6] Modern western academic philosophy has tended to be abstract reasoning and reflection on ethical and metaphysical issues. By contrast, philosophy (lit.: devotion to wisdom) in Josephus' historical context in elite urban circles of the Roman world meant the pursuit or practice of (interrelated) justice in political life and happiness in personal life.[7] It involved rigorous training and discipline and a personal commitment to the "toughening" of character in the practice of virtues such as courage and honor, an adaptability to hardships, and in some cases a simplicity of life. This was somewhat similar to scribal training in Judea as sketched in chap. 1 above, only in a very different political culture. In the early Roman imperial period, the aristocratic elite underwent rigorous training in philosophy, often including learning the teachings of the principal philosophical schools, to prepare for engaging in public life in Rome and other cities. As noted in the previous chapter, Josephus claimed to have

---

5. The Greek term *haireseis* had so often been used with reference to the different schools of philosophy that it was a virtual synonym for "philosophies."

6. The three "philosophies" have been discussed extensively as the "sects" of Judaism. Because "sects" and "sectarian" are often poorly defined and understood modern concepts anachronistically applied to Judean society under the temple-state, I am not seriously considering such concepts in this study. But see the appreciative discussion of Albert Baumgarten's *The Flourishing of Jewish Sects* in the Introduction, n24.

7. In an important step toward more appropriate understanding of Josephus' accounts of the Pharisees, Sadducees, and Essenes, Mason, *Flavius Josephus on the Pharisees*, chaps. 6 and 8, explained what "philosophy" and the "philosophies" meant and how they functioned in the elite political life of the Roman empire.

undergone similar "toughening" in the three schools of Judean philosophy as part of his preparation for engaging in the political life of the Jerusalem temple-state (*Life* 9–12).

If we consider the context of the lengthy history of the Judeans in the *Antiquities*, it is evident that Josephus understands and presents the Judean way of life, its *politeia* and ancestral laws, as a philosophy (*Ant.* 1.10–25). In accord with the purpose of philosophy, what Moses had received from God and mediated to the people were rules for prosperity (*eudaimonia*) and a well-ordered political life (*politeias kosmos*; *Ant.* 13.84). The synthetic constructs that have become standard in translation of Josephus' texts, such as "Jewish religion" for *ta ioudaion ethe* ("the customs of the Judeans," *Ant.* 20.38) or "Judaism" for *ta patria ton ioudaion* ("the ancestral traditions of the Judeans," *Ant.* 20.41) are reductionist and simply block recognition of his principal subject: the ethical-political ancestral laws/customs or *politeia* (way of life, or "constitution") of the Judeans, the observance of which brings a just political order and happiness. That there were three particular philosophies or schools among the Judeans means that particular groups had developed particular understandings and applications of the ancestral laws and way of life. Once we recognize that in Rome and other cities of the Empire, the political-cultural elite prepared for their leading roles in political life by undergoing training in one or more of the standard philosophies, then Josephus' placement of this brief reference to the philosophies of the Judeans (*Ant.* 13.171–173) makes good sense. The brief note about the three philosophies comes just at the point in the narrative where the Judean temple-state and the *politeia* of the Judeans, headed by the priestly aristocracy (as Moses had instructed) were being restored.

At this point in his narrative Josephus only briefly mentions their different views on the Greek philosophical issue of fate vs. free will that was a prominent *topos* that Roman or provincial elites would learn in their philosophical training. His placement of this reference to the three *haireseis* at this point in his narrative, however, suggests that some or perhaps all three of these understandings and practice of the Judean "way of life" emerged in response to Jonathan's (or at the latest Simon's) assumption of the high priesthood, presumed reestablishment of the temple-state, and consolidation of power in Judea (1 Macc 10:15—11:37; Josephus, *Ant.* 13.80–170).[8]

It may help to review the situation of the high priesthood and temple-state, including the priestly aristocrats, the regular priests, the other Jerusalemites, many of whom worked in support of temple-state functions, and the scribal circles who served as cultivators and guardians of Judean

---

8. Mason, *Flavius Josephus on the Pharisees*, 201.

tradition, particularly of the ancestral laws. Menelaus had maneuvered to be appointed High Priest for the purpose of abandoning the traditional way of life, the covenantal "constitution" of the temple-state, and the transformation of Jerusalem from a temple-state to the Hellenistic *polis* of Antioch. So there had, in effect, been no traditional high priesthood and temple-state since 170 BCE, except for the interlude of the Seleucid appointment of Alcimus as High Priest (164–161 BCE) in response to the Maccabean Revolt. This situation of no High Priest and no functioning temple-state would then have continued for another seven years while the "reforming" aristocrats were still (nominally) in control of Jerusalem and the countryside.

There may have been others of "high priestly" lineage still in Jerusalem, or in hiding or in exile. Among regular priests some, such as the Hasmoneans from Modein, were involved in and even leading the continuing revolt. Those who (had) lived in Jerusalem were either involved in revolt or at least not carrying out the traditional temple rituals. With temple-operations in abeyance, moreover, there was presumably no demand for the services of Jerusalem artisans whose work had previously been supported from temple/priestly revenues. Besides the *maskilim* and the "Enoch-scribes" who had rebelled (with some having been martyred), there would supposedly have been other scribal circles who were simply quiet, hoping to survive the conflict, but presumably continuing to cultivate the Judean scribal repertoire in which they had undergone rigorous training.

Once Jonathan had retaken Jerusalem and been appointed High Priest, we could reasonably surmise, some of the sacrifices, other rituals, and festivals would have been restored and some ordinary priests and some artisans would have resumed their functions in the operations of the temple. But Jonathan himself, from an ordinary priestly family, would have had limited acquaintance with temple procedures from only a few weeks a year of service in the temple many years before. From the beginning of the revolt until being appointed High Priest, moreover, he had been a leader of guerrilla warfare and then the principal leader of the continuing revolt, with increasing skill at maneuvering between rival imperial pretenders. Even after his appointment as High Priest, his principal activities were recruiting an army, obtaining armaments, and leading battles, as he gained power and territory with honors and wealth. Josephus comments that at certain points "he returned to Jerusalem," which indicates that he had been absent from Jerusalem much of the time, leading various defensive battles or preemptive attacks on nearby cities. The rival Seleucid imperial pretenders valued him mainly as a military ally. So Jonathan would have had little understanding of the procedures and principles of operating the temple-state and no service in the temple for fifteen-plus years. Also the more conservative tradition-minded chief priests, ordinary priests, scribal circles, and artisans would have viewed him as an illegitimate figure who had usurped the high priesthood by military and diplomatic maneuvering. The new high priesthood of Jonathan (and then of Simon), moreover, was no longer the head of a priestly aristocracy so much as a priestly monarchy whose power lay in the army.

Since the discovery of the Dead Sea Scrolls over seven decades ago we have a fourth set of sources for the Pharisees. A few of the Scrolls offer information directly on the historical origins of the Pharisees and of the Qumran community that produced many of these texts, a group variously identified or linked with the Essenes mentioned by Josephus. Archaeological analysis of the site where the Scrolls were discovered dated the origin of the community in mid-second century, just about the time that Jonathan and then his brother Simon had gained appointment to the high priesthood. The Damascus Document (CD) dates the beginning of the movement (that evidently bore some relation to Qumran) to the "age of wrath," 390 years after the conquest of Jerusalem by Nebuchadnezzar, king of Babylon, which would bring us roughly into the early second century, when the crisis of reform and resistance evolved in Jerusalem.[9]

The *pesharim* on several texts from the prophets found at Qumran are particularly helpful for historical reconstruction since they apply particular statements and names in the prophetic texts to particular groups and figures of recent or current history. The *pesher* on Hab 2:5–6 refers to

> the Wicked Priest [who] was called by the name of truth when he first arose. But when he ruled over Israel his heart became proud, and he forsook God and betrayed the precepts for the sake of riches. He robbed and amassed the riches of the men of violence who rebelled against God... and he took the wealth of the peoples... (1QpHab 8:4–13; cf. 9:5–12; 12:2–9)

This would fit Jonathan's move from leader of the people, in continuing to battle the reformers who controlled the temple, to "ruler of Israel" as the new High Priest. With his take-over of Jerusalem he began expropriating the wealth of the previously exploitative Hellenizing reformists and plundering and taking spoil from the nearby cities that he attacked.[10] Because of his persecution of "the righteous teacher" and the break-away covenantal community he would "be delivered into the hand of the violent of the

---

9. Vermes, *The Dead Sea Scrolls*, 58; his observations include that ancient Judean texts do not have an accurate reckoning of time, for example, of how long Persian domination had lasted.

10. Vermes, *Dead Sea Scrolls*, 60–62.

peoples" (4Q171 4:6–12). Indeed, Jonathan was eventually defeated, captured, and killed by Trypho, one of the usurpers and pretenders to the tottering Seleucid regime.

Other passages in the scrolls vilify the new High Priest for abandoning the proper way of running the temple cult and for persecuting their group of "the sons of Zadok." The "righteous teacher" (who is apparently a priest, and probably a Zadokite, as in 1QpHab 2:8; 4Q171; 4Q173) and his followers might well have been some of the priests and scribal associates who were displeased when the village priest and warrior Jonathan and his faction took over the high priesthood.[11] From the Community Rule and other texts, it is clear that the renewed covenant community organized in the wilderness of Qumran was extremely strict in its rigorous community discipline and rituals, following not "the literal letter of the law," but their own continuing collective "recitation of the "book" and "searching" of the *mishpat* (1QS 6:6–8).

Interrelated with the harangues against the Wicked Priest in the *pesharim* are polemics against "the seekers of smooth things," particularly in the *pesher* on the text of Nahum.[12] There is consensus among interpreters of the Scrolls that the phrase "seekers of smooth things" and the name "Ephraim" (one of the sons of Joseph and one of the tribes located just north of Judah) are code for the Pharisees. "The city of lies . . ." in Nah 3:1 is taken as a reference to "the city of Ephraim, those who seek smooth things during the last days, who walk in lies and falsehood." The seductress who sells peoples into ruin in Nah 3:4 "concerns those who lead Ephraim astray, who lead many astray through their false teaching, their lying tongue, and deceitful lips, (that is) kings, princes, priests, and people . . . Cities and families shall perish through their counsel . . ." (4Q169 2:7–10). The intervening sentences in Nah 3:1c–3 are taken as a reference to "the government of those who seek smooth things, from the midst of whose assembly the sword of the peoples shall never be wanting . . . A multitude of guilty corpses shall fall in their days . . . because of their guilty counsel" (4Q169 2:4–6). Accordingly, the reference to the destruction of Nineveh in Nah 3:7b is taken to concern "those who seek smooth things, whose council shall perish and whose congregation shall be dispersed. They shall lead the assembly astray no more, and the simple shall support their council no more" (4Q169 3:6–7).

This text states clearly that these "seekers of smooth things" are a group (assembly/congregation/council) who are currently leading rulers as well as the people astray by their false teaching and deceitful advice and are

---

11. Schiffman, *Reclaiming the Dead Sea Scrolls*, 87–95.

12. Critical detailed discussion of the *pesher* on Nahum, 4QpNah 4:3–6, in Schiffman, "Pharisees and Sadducees in *Pesher Nahum*." See also Horgan, *Pesharim*.

even participating in governance in Jerusalem. The Qumran community views them as utterly lacking in rigor in their understanding and advice of how the Judean temple-state should be governed. Given the prolonged crisis and conflict of the reform, imperial invasion, Maccabean Revolt, and continuing resistance, there were presumably many trained scribes, some of whom were probably also priests, still resident in Jerusalem or refugees in the countryside who were not insistent on Judean traditions such as high priestly lineage. Such "political realists" may well have welcomed the opportunity of participating in the restoration of the temple-state, its rituals, festivals, and governance of now expanded territory that Jonathan and his popular army had made possible. They were trained in temple-state and general Judean traditions and practices.

Jonathan, usurper of the high priesthood, would have needed their knowledge, advice, and whatever legitimating "authorization" they might provide. The very composition of 1 Maccabees—presenting the Revolt as an imitation of one Israelite/Judean tradition after another, and especially the ideology evident in its concluding declaration of Simon's high priesthood—indicates that considerable scribal knowledge and reflection had been devoted to the operation and legitimation of the Hasmonean high priesthood during the ten years of Jonathan's (often absentee) tenure and the first three years of Simon's. Josephus' account of John Hyrcanus' break with this "philosophy" (in *Ant.* 13.288–298, to be discussed below) indicates that the Pharisees had been his mentors and close advisers serving in the temple-state evidently from early in his high priesthood after he succeeded his father, Simon. It thus seems credible that the Pharisees had begun (as one of the Judean "philosophies") probably by the end of Jonathan's high priesthood—and had negotiated a role in the operations of the temple-state.

Sources for the origin of the Sadducees are virtually non-existent. It is difficult to find any clear allusions to them in any text from among the DSS.[13] That they were the party of the wealthy and had a following only among the wealthy could have been a development under Hyrcanus' long high priesthood as wealth piled up in Jerusalem, including in the Hasmonean family. There could have been wealthy (high) priestly families who survived the reform, revolt, continuing conflict between the renegade reformers and the popular forces led by Jonathan, and confinement in the citadel. Assuming they had not been among the reformers, they would have been a conservative party.[14]

---

13. Schiffman, "Pharisees and Sadducees in *Pesher Nahum*," 284–88, argues that 4QpNah 4:3–6 (on Nah 3:10–11) refers to them.

14. Some scholars, such as Schiffman, *Reclaiming the Dead Sea Scrolls*, 87–95, believe that the Zadokites who withdrew from Jerusalem to Qumran had split off from

Another text from the Dead Sea Scrolls sheds further light on the origins and relations of the three "philosophies" of the Judeans close to the time of their origins. 4QMMT ("Some Observances of the Law") is thought to have been a "letter" sent by a group at an early stage in its development into the break-away movement of priests and scribes that produced the Damascus Document (CD) and/or the Qumran Community Rule and the *pesharim*. It presents a list of over twenty of "our" teachings or preferred practices that should be carried out by the priests in the sacrifices and other rites in the temple in contrast with "their" practices. It has been observed that the teachings or practices presented in 4QMMT resemble the positions that the rabbis later attributed to the Sadducees, while the rabbis themselves agree with the contrary views held by the Pharisees.[15] On this basis it is thought that the group that produced 4QMMT is appealing to a ruler to change temple-procedures recently established by the Pharisees (back) to their preferred practices. This does not mean that the group that made the appeal were Sadducees. They were rather Zadokites who had previously split away from other Zadokites and, as suggested in CD 1:10, "for twenty years were like blind men groping for the way" before more decisively forming a break-away movement or community. 4QMMT thus provides another indication that the Pharisees had assumed positions of authority under the early Hasmoneans, Jonathan and Simon.[16]

John Hyrcanus' Expansion of Hasmonean Power— and Alienation of the People

In order to critically evaluate the accounts of John Hyrcanus in the histories of Josephus it is important, once again, to appreciate the wealthy Judean priest Flavius Josephus' perspective and agenda. As noted previously, Josephus boasted proudly of his illustrious priestly and royal Hasmonean lineage (*Ant.* 16.187; 20.266; *Life* 1–7). John Hyrcanus in particular was his hero, as suggested by his encomium at the end of his accounts of the illustrious High Priest (*War* 1.68–69; *Ant.* 13.299–300). It may seem to the modern reader with less elitist sympathies that Josephus is being overly candid

---

these Zadokites/Sadducees.

15. See further D. R. Schwartz, "MMT, Josephus, and the Pharisees," 72–73; J. M. Baumgarten, "Pharisaic-Sadducean Controversies About Purity and the Qumran Texts."

16. As D. R. Schwartz, "MMT, Josephus, and the Pharisees," 80, concludes, while MMT does not say anything about broader popular support for the Pharisees, it does show "that they were in the ruling coalition in the early Hasmonean period."

at a few points in these accounts. But success in gaining and using political power was all-important for ancient aristocratic or monarchic rulers in Hellenistic and Roman antiquity and the historians and poets who recounted their exploits.

Hyrcanus got his start by building on his father Simon's carefully-cultivated relations with the populace of Jerusalem. When his father, mother, and brothers were victims of an internal court coup by a brother- in-law, the populace (*plethos; demos*) welcomed him into the city, where he assumed the high priesthood, which the Hasmoneans thus successfully made hereditary in their own lineage (*War* 1.54–56; *Ant.* 13.228–230). Taking advantage of the Seleucid emperor Antiochus' unusual reverence for the divine, Hyrcanus negotiated for imperial reaffirmation of the restored Judean ancestral *politeia* (*Ant.* 13.245).

In *Antiquities* (13.249), expanding on his earlier narrative (*War* 1.61), Josephus recounts that Hyrcanus "opened the tomb of David, who surpassed all other kings in wealth, took out three thousand talents of silver, and became the first Judean ruler to hire foreign mercenaries." He first supplied auxiliary troops for Antiochus Sidetes' expedition against the Parthians. As soon as he heard of Antiochus' death, however, Hyrcanus launched wars of expansion to take control of cities in Syria, including the Nabatean city of Medaba (with considerable losses) and Shechem and Garizein in Samaria, and destroyed the temple there (*Ant.* 13.254–256). He then conquered the cities of Adora and Marisa in Idumea and after subduing all the Idumeans required them, if they wanted to remain in their countryside (*chora*), to become circumcised and to observe the laws of the Judeans (13.257–258).[17]

---

17. Josephus' claim that from that time the Idumeans made their way of life conform to that of the Judeans and thereafter continued to be Judeans has been claimed as a religious conversion of the Idumeans to Judaism. Conversion, however, is an anachronistic conceptualization that does not fit the ancient historical context, as I explained in *Galilee*, 42–45, with many references to secondary literature. For example, Kasher, *Jews, Idumeans, and Ancient Arabs*, chap. 3, takes some sources at face value, while dismissing others as propaganda. See further the critique of particular points by Shatzman, *The Armies of the Hasmoneans and Herod*, 58–59 n90. The "conversion" interpretation is contradicted by Josephus' subsequent indications that Idumeans, including elites who played prominent political roles in the Jerusalem regime, continued in a traditional Idumean way of life, including devotion to their god Cos. A more appropriate interpretation is that Hyrcanus forced a change of polity on the Idumeans, requiring them to submit to "the laws of the Judeans" (*Ant.* 13.257; cf. 15.254). That the Idumeans were subjugated by Hyrcanus is independently suggested by Jub. 36:1—38:14, esp. 38:1–14: under a "yoke of servitude" they were forced to "pay tribute." The requirement that the Idumeans, who already practiced circumcision, submit (again) to circumcision was a symbol of their submission to the wider social-political community centered in the Jerusalem temple and ruled by the Hasmonean high priesthood. Fuller discussion in Horsley, "The Expansion of Hasmonean Rule in Idumea and Galilee," 148–53; and a

Hyrcanus also sent envoys to secure an alliance with Rome (13.259-266). During a period of over a decade, says Josephus, while rivals to the declining Seleucid realm fought one another, Hyrcanus lived in peace. This offered him "the leisure to exploit Judea undisturbed, with the result that he amassed great resources" (*chremata*, i.e., more than just "money"; 13.273-274).[18]

Finally, toward the end of his reign, Hyrcanus and his sons attacked the city of Samaria, which was strongly fortified. After a year-long siege he finally took the city and utterly destroyed it (*Ant.* 13.281; in *War* 1.65 Josephus says that his sons also enslaved the inhabitants).[19] As if in conclusion of his account about (his hero) Hyrcanus, he asserts: "At this time the Judeans in Jerusalem and in the countryside were flourishing" (*Ant.* 13.284). Josephus concludes his narratives by glorifying Hyrcanus and his thirty-one year rule with admiring encomiums. "Now he was accounted by God worthy of three of the greatest honors: the rule of the people (*ethnos*), the high office of the high priesthood, and prophecy; for the deity was with him and enabled him to foresee and foretell the future" (*War* 1.68-69).

In both narratives, however, after recounting all of Hyrcanus' successful conquests of nearby cities and their territory and peoples, Josephus suddenly reports that the envy of the Judeans was aroused by "the successes" of Hyrcanus and his sons. More than envy must have been involved, however, because Josephus admits that "large numbers of them held meetings to oppose [Hyrcanus] and continued to agitate until the smoldering flames burst out into open war," after which he adds merely, 'but the rebels were defeated" (*War* 1.67-68; *Ant.* 13.288a). Did the glorious "successes" of the warrior High Priest Hyrcanus lead in the end to "rebellion"? In the course of his narratives of Hyrcanus' "successes," particularly in *Antiquities*, Josephus provides several indications of why the people of Jerusalem and Judeans in

---

further critical examination of the evidence on the subjection of the Idumeans and the Galileans in *Galilee: History, Politics, People*, 46-52. In an apparent reconsideration of his earlier interpretation, Cohen, in *The Beginnings of Jewishness*, suggests that the Idumeans retained their prior ethnicity and much of their religion and culture" (105, cf. 118).

18. This, of course, was the common practice of rulers and aristocracies, to extract just as much from their productive peasantry as possible without destroying their economic base.

19. Josephus immediately juxtaposes "an extraordinary story" about how "the deity" communicated with Hyrcanus. While he was alone in the temple burning incense, he heard a voice saying that his sons had just defeated the first Seleucid pretender who intervened to rescue Samaria, which he mentioned upon emerging from the temple; and it turned out to be true.

the countryside would have become hostile to him and eventually mounted serious opposition.[20]

In an inauspicious beginning of Hyrcanus' reign, Antiochus Sidetes invaded Judea, ravaged the *chora*, and shut up the new High Priest in the besieged city (*Ant.* 13.236–239). With provisions in the city dwindling, Hyrcanus retained only those people able to help fight and drove out the "useless" to wander around between the city walls and the enemy camps. When the festival of Tabernacles came around, however, the people within the city took pity and admitted them again (240–241). Hyrcanus gained the Seleucid reaffirmation of the restored Judean *politeia* only at the cost of paying tribute for control of Joppa and other nearby cities he had previously conquered plus surrendering hostages and five hundred talents of silver (245–248). Later, only a few years before the time that Josephus says the country was flourishing, much of the Judean *chora* had been ravaged by Egyptian troops trying to force Hyrcanus to lift the siege of Samaria (278).

It may also be pertinent to ask how the people understood the vast wealth deposited in the tomb of David, the great hero of yore who had established their independence and whose legends had become sacred by this time (e.g., as memorialized in the magnificent tomb). The ideology of a temple-state or monarchy in the ancient Near East was that the wealth accumulated in the temple or the royal palace was representative of the whole people and in some way belonged to the people. How would the people have felt about Hyrcanus' raiding that ancestral wealth for purposes of his own regime? Under Jonathan and Simon the power of the Hasmonean dynasty had rested on the support of the army that had been recruited from the people before being made professional by Simon. In taking the unprecedented step (for a Judean ruler) of hiring foreign mercenaries John Hyrcanus shifted the base of his power to a professional *foreign* army that he used to conquer nearby cities and peoples.

In ancient monarchies and temple-states it is often unclear how the people of the royal and/or sacred capital city and the villagers in the countryside view one another. The artisans and others in the cities have a stake in and are economically dependent on the royal and/or priestly regime. They often have little or no interaction with the peasantry in the countryside. In the Judean temple-state, however, many of the ordinary priests lived out in villages and came into the temple for their terms of service and at festival times. There was thus a network of communication between the *demos* of

---

20. Despite their prominence in Josephus' histories, S. Schwartz, *Imperialism and Jewish Society*, 36–40, generally avoids acknowledgment and discussion of the revolts of the Judeans against Hyrcanus and his son Alexander Jannaeus and their opposition by the Pharisees, including their hiring of and dependence on mercenaries.

Jerusalem and the villagers in the *chora*. At the beginning of the Hasmonean high priesthood under Jonathan and Simon, moreover, there was frequent contact, cooperation, and common cause between the populace of the city and people in the countryside. Thus, when Seleucid armies periodically ravaged the countryside of Judea early in Hyrcanus reign it seems likely that many Jerusalemites may well have been sympathetic and concerned.

Most onerous for the Judean villagers would have been the enormous costs of Hyrcanus prolonged wars of expansion, including the support of his mercenary troops, for which he had already raided the tomb of David. We can surmise that Hyrcanus could have managed some of the costs from the spoil taken from conquered cities and taxation of conquered peoples. Hyrcanus will have drawn considerable revenue from the royal estates that he or his predecessors had acquired from the weakening Seleucids, including the "king's mountain country," the three districts (*nomoi*) of Lydda, Aphairema, and Ramatayyim, the district of 'Eqron that had been ceded to Jonathan (1 Macc 10:89), and the royal lands in the Great Plain that had fallen under his control by the end of his conquests.[21]

Those new sources of revenue, however, would not have sufficed to cover the exorbitant cost of his conquests. Hyrcanus could have managed the extraordinary cost of his wars of expansion only by also taxing the long-settled villagers of Judea.[22] It is in this context that we should read Josephus' statement that the rival Seleucid factions' wars on each other gave Hyrcanus "leisure to exploit Judea undisturbed, resulting in a great stockpiling of resources." Josephus must mean that he now focused on how to intensify his exploitation of the Judean peasantry.[23] It would have evoked increasing resentment among the Judean peasants living close to subsistence when Hyrcanus had the leisure to more systematically organize sending his troops to the villages at harvest time to skim the regime's revenues from the top of the piles of grain on the threshing floors. This would have threatened their subsistence and forced them further into debilitating debt.

Ordinary priests who lived in villages and/or city-based priests who relied on tithes from Judean villagers struggling to subsist, as well as Pharisees and other scribes who may, like Ben Sira, have been sympathetic with the poor, moreover, might well have been concerned about Hyrcanus' more intensified and systematic exploitation of the Judean villagers. And the conquests were likely a drain on the Jerusalemites as well as on the villagers in

---

21. These are critically discussed by Applebaum, "The Hasmoneans."
22. Applebaum, "The Hasmoneans," 28–29.
23. Had Hyrcanus directly or indirectly learned from the Ptolemaic practices of systematically extracting as much as possible from the *chora* of Egypt?

the countryside. It would be hard to believe that either would have been "flourishing" as Hyrcanus was undertaking more and more conquests.

Finally, the Jerusalem populace and Judean people in general had in the previous generation just gone through the intense trauma of their own high priesthood having abandoned the traditional Judean way of life in order to transform Jerusalem into a Hellenistic *polis*, and then an invasive attack on the city and temple by Antiochus IV Epiphanes to enforce the "reform." It may have seemed like a reversion to that Hellenizing reform to have a new warrior High Priest now imitating the Hellenistic imperial practice of conquering other cities and their territories with mercenary troops.[24] Hyrcanus seems to have been building up an empire of his own in Palestine. And in this connection, we may note the tension, not to say conflict, between the stated ideal of a priestly aristocracy as the *politeia/ancestral laws* of the Judean people and Hyrcanus operating increasingly as a monarch. Josephus' encomium honors him as having been not only the High Priest but the ruler of the people. In his policy and practice, he seems to have been a local Hellenistic king "in all but name" (a phrase Josephus uses later).[25]

Hyrcanus and the Pharisees

By critically "reading between the lines" it thus becomes more understandable when at the end of his narratives about Hyrcanus' high priesthood Josephus announces abruptly that "large numbers of Judeans held meetings to oppose him and continued to agitate until the smoldering flames burst out into open war." In his fuller account in *Antiquities*, moreover, this is the point in the narrative at which Josephus recounts a story about the close cooperation between Hyrcanus and the Pharisees and then the High Priest's break with them. This is one of the most important and informative of Josephus' accounts about the Pharisees.

> The envy of the Judeans was aroused against him . . . Especially hostile to him were the Pharisees, one of the schools of thought among the Judeans, as we have explained above. So strong is their influence among the populace that even when they speak

---

24. On the other hand, Hyrcanus' (and his sons') actions as Hellenistic kings may have "integrated" them with neighboring regimes, as discussed by Erich Gruen, *Heritage and Hellenism*.

25. Schaefer, *History of the Jews in Antiquity*, 70, reaches a similar conclusion. S. Schwartz, "Israel and the Nations Roundabout," 33, characterizes John Hyrcanus as "a petty late Hellenistic monarch who gave all his sons Macedonian dynastic names and was protected by foreign mercenaries."

against a king and against a High Priest they are immediately believed. (*Ant.* 13.288)

Now Hyrcanus was also a disciple of theirs, and he was greatly loved by them. And he invited them to a feast and entertained them hospitably. When he saw how delighted they were, he started telling them that they knew he wished to be [a] just [ruler] and to do all things so as to please God and them (for the Pharisees pursue a certain way of life [*hoi gar Pharisaioi philosophousin*]); nevertheless, he requested that if they noticed him doing anything wrong and veering from the path of justice, they were to lead him back and restore him to it. But they attested to his consummate virtue and he was pleased by their compliments.

However, one of the guests, named Eleazar, who was malicious by nature and took pleasure in dissension, said, "Since you have asked to know the truth, if you want to be just, then relinquish the high priesthood and be content with ruling the people (*to archein tou laou*). When Hyrcanus asked him the reason why he should relinquish the high priesthood he replied, "because we hear from the elders that your mother was a captive in the reign of Antiochus Epiphanes." But the story was false, and Hyrcanus became furious with the man and the Pharisees were all very indignant.

Then someone from the school (*hairesis*) of the Sadducees, who espouse a policy (way of life) opposed to that of the Pharisees, a certain Jonathan, who was among the most intimate friends [advisers/confidants] of Hyrcanus, began to say that Eleazar had uttered his slanders in agreement with the collective opinion of all the Pharisees. And this would become clear to him, Jonathan said, if he asked them what punishment was appropriate for what had been said.

When Hyrcanus asked the Pharisees what they considered a worthy punishment. . . they proposed lashes and chains; for it did not seem right to punish someone with death on account of verbal abuse and, in any case, the Pharisees are naturally merciful in the matter of punishments. At this response, Hyrcanus became very angry and assumed that the man had slandered him with their approval.

Jonathan exacerbated his anger greatly and achieved the following result: he induced him to join the Sadducean party and to abandon the Pharisees, and to abrogate the regulations that they had established for the people (of Jerusalem; *ta katastasthenta nomima to demo*) and to punish those who observed them. This is the reason, then, that hatred developed among the populace (*tou plethous*) toward him and his sons. (*Ant.* 13.289–296)

Now I want to explain here that the Pharisees passed on to the (city-)people (*paredosan to demo*) certain ordinances (*nomima*) from a succession of ancestors (*ek pateron diadoches*), which are not written down in the laws of Moses. For this reason the group (*genos*) of the Sadduccees dismisses these [regulations], saying that it is necessary to keep regulations (*nomima*) that are written, but not to observe those from the tradition of the ancestors (*ta ek paradoseos ton pateron*). Also concerning these issues the two parties came to have conflicts and major differences, the Sadducees persuading only the wealthy but with no following among the people, while the populace (*to plethos*) is an ally of the Pharisees.[26] (*Ant.* 13.297–298; trans. adapted from Mason and from Loeb)

It is clear from a critical reading that the story Josephus recounts does not fit his framing (*Ant.* 13.288b).[27] Immediately after attributing the Judeans' opposition to Hyrcanus to the people's envy aroused by his "successes," he adds that the Pharisees were especially hostile to him. But the story in 289–296 does not indicate any such hostility. Indeed just the opposite: the Pharisees love Hyrcanus and praise his virtue (289–290). They are indignant when Eleazar speaks against him (292). Josephus claims in the framing (288b) that when the Pharisees speak against a king or High Priest they are immediately believed. But the story gives no hint of the Pharisees speaking against a king or High Priest. In the story, the provocateurs are Eleazar, with no indication that he was a Pharisee or spoke for them, and Jonathan the Sadducee. It is Hyrcanus who takes the initiative against the Pharisees. He not only makes a break with them, his former mentors, but completely removes them from their previous function in his regime of promulgating ordinances for the people, with penalties for anyone who continues to observe them, and installs the Sadducees in their place. The framing sentence at the end of the story, that the hatred of the populace grew out of Hyrcanus sacking the Pharisees (296), is not grounded in the story or the previous narrative. Josephus is here anticipating his subsequent account about how Alexander Jannaeus viewed the Pharisees, as will become more evident below.

---

26. Not "the Pharisees have the support of the masses," vs. Thackeray and Mason.
27. So also Mason, *Flavius Josephus on the Pharisees*, 218–29.

That the story (in *Ant.* 13.289–296) does not fit the narrative framing and does not arise from the preceding narrative is clear from a comparison with a very similar story in much later rabbinic texts told about Hyrcanus' son, Alexander Jannaeus. The similarity suggests that Josephus has inserted here a traditional legend pertaining to the Pharisees' relations with Hasmonean kings.[28]

> It is taught: The story is told that Yannai [Jannaeus] the King went to Kohalit in the wilderness and conquered there sixty towns. When he returned, he rejoiced greatly, and invited all the sages of Israel.
>
> He said to them, "Our forefathers would eat salt fish when they were engaged in the building of the holy house. Let us also eat salt fish as a memorial to our forefathers." So they brought up salt fish on golden tables. And they ate.
>
> There was there a certain scoffer. Evil-hearted and empty-headed, and Eleazar ben Poirah said to Yannai the King, "O King Yannai, the hearts of the Pharisees are [set] against you."
>
> "What shall I do?"
>
> "Test them by the plate that is between your eyes [the high priest's medallion]." He tested them by the plate that was between his eyes.
>
> There was a certain sage, and Judah b. Gedidiah was his name. Judah b. Gedidiah said to Yannai the King, "O King Yannai, Let suffice for you the crown of sovereignty [kingship]. Leave the crown of the [high] priesthood for the seed of Aaron." For people said that his [Yannai's] mother had been taken captive in Modin [and was therefore suspected of having been raped]. The charge was investigated and not found [sustained]. The sages of Israel departed in anger.
>
> Eleazar b. Poirah then said to Yannai the king, "O King Yannai, That is the law (not here specified, as the punishment inflicted on Judah) even for the ordinary folk in Israel. But you are King and high priest—should that be your law too?"
>
> "What should I do?"
>
> "If you take my advice, you will trample them down."
>
> "But what will become of the Torah?"
>
> "Lo. It is rolled up and lying in the corner. Whoever wants to learn, let him come and learn."

---

28. For a wide-ranging exploration of such legends and their use, see Noam, *Shifting Images of the Hasmoneans*. Chapter 3 suggests that behind these parallel versions of the story is a lost fragment of a Pharisaic work.

The evil blossomed through Eleazar b. Poirah. All the sages of Israel [= the Pharisees] were killed. The world was desolate until Simeon b. Shetah came and restored the Torah to its place. (b. Qiddushin 66a)[29]

Since the basis of the challenge to the Hasmonean ruler, that the mother had been a captive in war-time, is more likely for Hyrcanus' mother than for Jannai's, it seems somewhat more likely that it did originally pertain to Hyrcanus. The opposition between the Pharisees and the Hasmonean rulers became much worse. Josephus has unnamed opponents of Alexander Jannaeus charge that he was descended from captives and therefore unfit to hold the high priestly office and officiate at sacrifices (*Ant.* 13.373), paralleling the rabbinic legend. In any case, since the Hasmonean ruler's power in Judea itself was rooted in his occupying the office of high priesthood, the challenge to the legitimacy of the ruler, who had to be born of a chaste mother, threatened to undermine his rule.

From this critical reading and comparison, it seems clear that the story that Josephus inserted in his account ran from *Ant.* 13.289 until the last two sentences of 296, where he adds his own framing again and gives his own version of the Pharisees' *nomima* as "from the ancestors/fathers." Josephus expressed his own view, critical of the Pharisees, in the framing of a traditional Judean story, at the beginning and end, and in his further comment about the differences between them and the Sadducees in terms of their influence.[30]

The story he has inserted without more fully editing it to fit the framing provides a description of the Pharisees' previously close relation with Hyrcanus and their earlier role in the temple-state under his high priesthood. The story, moreover, offers a more traditional Judean understanding of the ancestral covenantal *politeia* (constitution/way of life), evidently advocated by the Pharisees. This can be detected from key terms in the account of Hyrcanus' close relationship with the Pharisees as their "disciple." In his historical accounts, Josephus almost always uses the term *dikaios* in reference to justice in the Hellenistic cultural usage and the term *hodos* in the literal sense. In this story (*Ant.* 13.289–290), however, these terms are different from his usual usage. Here *dikaios* is more like the Hebrew term *tsedek* ("just") in the Judean covenantal sense of ("pleasing God" by) observing the law. *Hodos*, "the way," a metaphor for following in the covenantal

---

29. Translation from Neusner, *From Politics to Piety*, 59–60.
30. So also Mason, *Flavius Josephus on the Pharisees*, 227–30.

way of the torah, is specified as "the just way" or "the way of justice" (as in the LXX).³¹

From this story Josephus tells of Hyrcanus and the Pharisees, it is possible to discern important aspects of their previous relationship with him and of their role in the temple-state earlier in his reign.³² During the time they were in favor with him, they had evidently been far more than simply advisers or mere custodians of Judean cultural and legal traditions but were vested with considerable political authority. As discussed in chap. 1 above, in Judean scribal tradition, judging from the ideology articulated by Ben Sira, the high priesthood had authority over Judean torah, but seems to have delegated it to the learned scribes (sages) who served in the temple-state. Judging from Josephus' comment after the end of the story, John Hyrcanus (or a Hasmonean predecessor?) had included the Pharisees' *nomima* in the authoritative laws of the temple-state, to be obeyed by the people. This is indicated in Hyrcanus break with the Pharisees when he "abrogates" or "rescinds" (*katalusai*) the *nomima* which the Pharisees had established for the city-people (*demos*), that is for public life in Jerusalem (which was centered in the operations of the temple). This is indicated again in the subsequent account that Alexandra Salome "restored/re-established" (*apokatestesen*) the Pharisees' legal traditions, apparently as state law. The authority of the High Priest, moreover, appears to have "enforced" the Pharisees' regulations/laws, as implied by Hyrcanus doing the opposite when he rescinded them. This also is paralleled later in Josephus' narrative when Alexandra "commanded the people to obey them as having authority" (*peitharchein*). Correspondingly, when Hyrcanus had replaced the Pharisees with the Sadducees, the power of the state was used against their influence, as he "punished those who observed [the rulings] of the Pharisees." The Pharisees thus had apparently exercised legal authority under Hyrcanus (and perhaps already under his predecessors?).³³

---

31. See further Mason, *Flavius Josephus on the Pharisees*, 219–21.

32. As he explains, such analysis is not included in Mason's agenda in *Flavius Josephus on the Pharisees*.

33. The story that Josephus recounts in *Ant.* 13.289–296 does not explicitly indicate what aspects of life under the temple-state the Pharisees' *nomima* covered. But the narrative sequence in the story in which Hyrcanus rescinding the *nomima* follows the information that the Pharisees were merciful in punishments suggests that the Pharisees *nomima* may have included (although not primarily concerned with) matters of disobedience and punishment. This aspect of the traditional story is also an indication of Hyrcanus' reason for breaking with the Pharisees: they were a restraint on his treatment of the people. The rabbinic story in b. Qiddushin cited above, however, suggests that with the departure of the Pharisees/sages, the high priest/king (and the temple-state) was left without access to the Torah that depended on their knowledge, the scroll

When they had been in favor with Hyrcanus the Pharisees also appear to have wielded considerable influence (on him), and not just in "establishing rulings for the people." This is indicated in the story's portrayal of the close relationship between the Pharisees and Hyrcanus. For a ruler such as Hyrcanus to be a "disciple" of the proponents of a "philosophy" ("school of thought/way of life") in the Hellenistic world, and for his philosophical mentors to "love him," meant that they were his close advisers and that he was following the political policy they espoused. This is exactly what the story suggests in Hyrcanus' statement to the Pharisees at the banquet scene (*Ant*. 13.289–290). Changing policy and changing advisers were two aspects of the same political change in Hyrcanus' break with the Pharisees and shift to the Sadducees (296).

A noted above, the story portrays the initiative in the break as coming from Hyrcanus as influenced by Jonathan, of the school of the Sadducees, who have views different from the Pharisees. He had become a very close "friend," that is, high-ranking adviser of the High Priest. This also suggests that Jonathan had already enjoyed a long-standing relationship with Hyrcanus. And it suggests that Hyrcanus' break with the Pharisees had come earlier in his reign, not at the very end, where Josephus locates the story in his narrative. There must have been reasons why Hyrcanus had become discontent with the Pharisees as his "friends." The story obscures any such reasons in attributing the break to Jonathan's manipulation of Hyrcanus after the outburst of the brazen Eleazar.

Yet the story may offer a hint in the comment that the Pharisees were lenient in the matter of punishment, particularly as the story and Josephus' framing are followed immediately by the brief note about Hyrcanus' suppression of the rebellion of the Judeans. As already noted, while Josephus pointedly includes reports of the High Priests Jonathan and Simon calling assemblies of the populace for consultation and consent, he mentions no such consultation by Hyrcanus. After his robbery of the tomb of David and his unprecedented hiring of foreign mercenaries, it seems that Hyrcanus came to rely on his professional army to accomplish his expansion of territory and power, with little or no concern for whether he had the support of the people. Hyrcanus may well have come to feel constrained by the Pharisees' emphasis on adhering to the covenantal "way of justice" in obedience to the laws. The story's statement that Hyrcanus punished those who (still) observed the Pharisees *nomima* suggests that, having shaken off the restraining influence of the Pharisees, he may have become seriously repressive in treatment of the people following his break with the Pharisees.

---

lying rolled up in the corner being not much use without them.

Correspondingly, there would have been reasons why the Pharisees, as well as the people of Jerusalem, came to oppose Hyrcanus.[34] Josephus says specifically that his and his sons' "successes," evidently referring to their conquests, were what led the people to resistance. The Pharisees, like the populace of Jerusalem, may also have been concerned, and perhaps objected to Hyrcanus' continuing conquests with his army of foreign mercenaries. Once Hyrcanus had "unfriended" the Pharisees, their economic support probably disappeared, and they may well have spoken publicly against a High Priest who operated as a warrior king. They may also have been concerned about some of the other actions of Hyrcanus that had built up opposition among the people: his treatment of the "useless" people while under siege, his raiding of what may have been understood as common ancestral wealth laid up in David's tomb, the unprecedented hiring of foreign mercenaries, a Hellenistic imperial, not an ancestral Judean practice, and his centralization of power and lack of concern about the people. And, more generally, if the Pharisees had undergone the rigorous training in the standard traditional scribal curriculum (the torah of the Most High, the prophecies, and different kinds of wisdom), their understanding of how the temple-state should rule would hardly have included the expansionist imperial military practices of Hyrcanus.

Finally, the fuller context of the Pharisees under the John Hyrcanus, along with the implications of recent research into Judean scribal practices, may lead to more appropriate understanding of Josephus' brief account that has been the basis of the standard view of the "oral" and the "written" Torah/Law. Josephus presents the Sadducees as one of the three principal "philosophies" of the Judeans and, like the Pharisees, focused on the *nomima* important in the operation of the temple-state. Also he indicates that, like the Pharisees, they were familiar with both the *nomima* that were written in the laws of Moses and with other *nomima* that were from a succession or a tradition (*paradosis*) of the ancestors. From recent studies of scribal training and practice, as discussed in chap. 2 above, it is clear that Judean laws and traditions were learned through repeated recitation, so that they were "written" in the memory of those with scribal training. Accordingly, functionally all torah/law would have been oral-memorial, accessed in memory, and not by consulting unwieldy scrolls.

Extended collections of teachings/laws, however, stood written in "the laws of Moses," having special numinous authority because they were

---

34. An earlier treatment that (while at points somewhat speculative) takes seriously the political and economic aspects of Hyrcanus conquests of nearby people and territory, and his conflict with the Pharisees, is that of Abraham Schalit, "Domestic Politics and Political Institutions," 269–77.

written, while an even larger repertoire of laws/teachings (and other traditions) were also cultivated in Judean scribal circles. According to Josephus" brief account, the Sadducees held that it was necessary to observe the regulations written in the laws of Moses, but not the regulations the Pharisees had passed on to the people from the tradition of the ancestors. By implication, the Pharisees held it necessary to observe these as well. From various texts found among the Dead Sea Scrolls it is clear that the Qumran community held that the collective recitation-and-hearing of the "book" of torah and (oral-aural) searching of the *mishpat(im)* was instrumental to their communal discipline (that is the hearing-and-keeping of a wide repertoire of laws/teachings, including the book of torah).

From the context of Josephus' brief account against the background of what we know from texts of torah from second-temple times it may be possible to discern a bit about what these respective *nomima* were about. A review of the contents of the books of Deuteronomy and (particularly) of Leviticus in chapter 3 indicated that the focus was on priestly practice in the temple. The multiple scrolls of 4QMMT found at Qumran that many scholars suggest was indicative of the principal concerns of the group that established the renewed covenantal community plead the importance of their priestly practices in the temple in contrast to the corrupt practices they oppose. In his account of their difference on the *nomima* Josephus says that the Sadducees have the confidence of the wealthy, which was the priestly aristocracy, but no trust among the city-people (*to demotikon*), while the Pharisees have the populace as their allies. The Sadducees' claim that only the priestly practices as specified in the written laws of Moses, such as in Leviticus, need be observed—but not what was covered in the continuing development of regulations pushed by the Pharisees—would have left welcome leeway for Hyrcanus in his economic exploitation of the Judean villagers and his military conquests of the Samaritans and Idumeans. Correspondingly, the *nomima* of the Pharisees derived from ancestral tradition (the earlier authorization of which Hyrcanus rescinded) must have restricted his operations in certain ways. As will become evident in the next sections, that the Pharisees later sought to bring the military officers of Hyrcanus' son Alexander Jannaeus to justice once Alexandra Salome had restored the authorization of their *nomima* suggests that they pertained to social-political relations beyond priestly practices in the temple.

Alexander Jannaeus' Conflict with the People—and the Pharisees

In transition to the accounts of his two elder sons, Aristobulus and Alexander Jannaeus, Josephus says that Hyrcanus (supposedly) predicted that they would not remain masters of political affairs (*Ant.* 13.300). Although Hyrcanus had left the realm to his wife, Aristobulus seized power and imprisoned his mother and brothers. He became the first Judean ruler since the Babylonian captivity to declare himself "king," with the title "Philhellene," as he transformed the rule into a "kingdom," recounts the disapproving Josephus (*War* 1.70; *Ant.* 13.301). In a brief and unclear concluding account of his one-year rule, Josephus says that he took control of a good part of the Itureans' territory (*chora*) and forced the inhabitants, if they wished to remain in the *chora*, to be circumcised and to live in accordance with the laws of the Judeans (*Ant.* 13.301, 318–319). He thus extended Hasmonean control as far as upper Galilee.[35]

Upon Aristobulus' death, his wife Salina (Salome) appointed Alexander Jannaeus as king (no mention of "high priest" as well), and evidently also married him. He resumed conquests where his father and brother left off, beginning with Ptolemais and the remaining cities on the coast not yet controlled by the Hasmonean regime. But he suffered serious reverses when Ptolemy Lathyrus' forces swept into his territory and ravaged areas of Judea and its villages. At the cost of several reverses he managed to expand his conquests of coastal cities and others in Coele-Syria (*War* 1.85–87; *Ant.* 13.320–347, 356–371).

Before long into his reign, says Josephus, "his own people revolted against him—for the people (*ethnos*) arose against him—at the celebration of the festival [of tabernacles] and, as he stood beside the altar and was about to sacrifice, they pelted him with citrons" (*War* 1.88).[36] Then Josephus cites a partial parallel to the story about Hyrcanus that the later version in the rabbinic text (b. Qiddushin 66a) told about King Yannai: "they added that he was descended from captives and was unfit to hold office [as high priest] and to sacrifice" (*Ant.* 13.372). Enraged at this, "he killed six thousand of them" ... and blocked people's access to himself in the temple with a

---

35. Because it has serious implications for both Jewish and Christian understanding of and claims about "Judaism," interpretation of archaeological finds, and present-day political claims to the control of Galilee, Josephus' brief account, parallel to his account of Hyrcanus' conquest of the Idumeans, has been the subject of considerable dispute among historians. It will be important to review this issue in Vol. 2.

36. Schäfer, *History of the Jews in Antiquity*, 75, has the people "supposedly incited by the Pharisees." But this is an inference by modern scholars. Neither in *War* nor in *Antiquities* does Josephus suggest this. Rather Josephus presents the Pharisees merely as having influence among the people whom they relate to as an ally.

wooden barrier (373). "He also maintained foreign mercenaries of Pisidians and Cilicians" (374). After he fell into an ambush fighting the Arabs and "the people (*ethnos*)" attacked him, he made war on his people and within six years slew no fewer than fifty thousand Judeans.[37] When he sought a truce and asked what they wanted of him, says Josephus, they all cried out, "to die!" (376).

The conflict then escalated into a full-scale civil war. The people invited help from Demetrius Akairos, who came with an army to confront Alexander with over six thousand mercenaries and twenty thousand Judeans who supported him (*War* 1.92–95; *Ant*.13.377–378; as usual, Josephus exaggerates the numbers). Having lost the battle badly, Alexander fled to the mountains, but out of pity six thousand Judeans deserted to his side, and Demetrius withdrew.

> The remainder of the populace (*plethos*), however, continued to wage war with Alexander until, after killing a very large number of them, he drove the rest into Bemeselis (Bethoma). Upon subduing this city, he brought them up to Jerusalem as prisoners. So furious was he that his savagery went to the length of impiety.[38] He had eight hundred of his captives crucified in the midst of the city and their wives and children butchered before their eyes, while he looked on, drinking, with his concubines reclining beside him. Such was the consternation of the people (*demos*) that on the following night eight thousand fled completely beyond Judea. (*War* 1.96–98//*Ant*. 13.379–380)

Curiously, following his later account in *Antiquities*, Josephus offers excuses for Alexander, saying that he had suffered such great hardships in his wars against his people and was almost in danger of losing his kingdom and had suffered countless other insulting acts from them (*Ant*. 13.381–382). As a result of his excessive cruelty, however, he was called "The Thracian" (383); the Thracians had a reputation for ferocity and savagery.

Alexander then continued his wars of expansion, finally finishing the conquest of cities on the coast and fortresses inland, such as Gamala. "Having spent three whole years in the field (83–80 BCE) he returned to his own country where the Judeans welcomed him eagerly because of his

---

37. Josephus' numbers are serious exaggerations, evoking the suggestion that we divide by as much as ten.

38. A more appropriate translation would be "disloyalty (to God)," that is, for not observing the covenantal law according to which the High Priest heading the temple-state supposedly operated.

successes" (*Ant.* 13.394).³⁹ Considering the account of severe conflict Josephus is concluding, this seems an ironic contrast to the way he concluded his narrative of Hyrcanus (that he and his sons provoked a revolt, *War* 1.67; cf. *Ant.* 13.288, 299). Josephus follows the statement about the Judeans' eager welcome with a list of all of the cities of Syria, Idumea, and Phoenicia that "the Judeans" held by the end of Hyrcanus' and his son's conquests (*Ant.* 13.395–397).⁴⁰

In *Antiquities* (but not in *War*), he adds a long transitional "deathbed" exhortation by Jannaeus to his wife, Alexandra. He advised her that

> she should yield a certain amount of authority (*exousia*) to the Pharisees, (and) they would dispose the people (*ethnos*) favorably toward her. They had such influence with the Judeans that they could injure those whom they hated and help those to whom they were friendly; for they had considerable trust among the populace (*plethos*) even when they spoke harshly of someone out of envy. He himself, he said, had come into conflict with the people (*ethnos*) because these men had been badly treated by him . . . "They have suffered many injuries from me." (13.401–404)

Interpreters of Josephus have debated whether the Pharisees were involved in the opposition to Alexander Jannaeus, especially whether "the eight hundred" he crucified were Pharisees or at least included Pharisees. Josephus never mentions the Pharisees in the parallel accounts in *War* and *Antiquities*. But there are two clear indications that they were involved and that those crucified included Pharisees. One is Alexander's mentioning twice in his deathbed advice to his wife (composed of course by Josephus) that they had been badly injured by him. Even clearer is the *pesher* on Nah 2:11–12.

> This concerns Demetrius king of Greece who sought, on the counsel of those who seek smooth things, to enter Jerusalem . . .
> *The lion chokes prey for its lionesses* (2:12) . . . This concerns the

---

39. Shortly thereafter in the account, Alexandra Salome states a more obvious assessment that accords more with the preceding narrative of Alexander's rule: "you know how hostile the nation feels toward you" (*Ant.* 13.399).

40. *Ant.* 13.394 and the immediately following sentence in 13.395 provide illustration of the different ways the term "Judeans/Jews" can be used: in 13.394 "the Judeans" evidently refers mainly to the inhabitants of Jerusalem, although in context they would appear to have been the only Judeans left after Alexander had slaughtered thousands of them. In 395, "the Judeans" refer to the rulers of the Judeans, that is Hyrcanus, Aristobulus, and Alexander and their mercenary army, who had conquered all of these cities and territories and peoples.

furious young lion [who executes revenge] on those who seek smooth things and hangs men alive, . . . [a thing never done] formerly in Israel. Because of a man hanged alive on [the] tree, He proclaims, "*Behold I am against [you, says the Lord of Hosts]*"] (4QpNah = 4Q169 1:3–8)

This is a clear reference to King Yannai having crucified what Josephus says were the eight hundred who had continued to fight against him. These texts do not supply evidence of whether the Pharisees were involved from the beginning of the resistance to and battles against Alexander. But the *pesher* Nahum indicates that they were involved in the appeal to Demetrius for assistance against their High Priest and "king" and were among those who continued to fight against Alexander after Demetrius withdrew. They were at least among the victims of "the furious young lion's" revenge, but it seems doubtful that there were as many as eight hundred Pharisees at this time. If there were any Pharisees still alive after the gruesome mass crucifixion, as is presupposed in Alexander's advice to his wife, they were probably among those who fled into exile.

Thus, it appears that the Pharisees were involved in the resistance to and fighting against Alexander. But they would have been relatively few among the large number of the populace of the city who fought against him and the thousands that he and his mercenaries killed. Josephus' suggestion (voiced by Alexander Jannaeus) that it was his mistreatment of the Pharisees that caused his conflict with the people is part of his anti-Pharisee polemic seen elsewhere in his narrative and is not credible historically. His own accounts have the popular opposition to the Hasmoneans having started under Hyrcanus and then having escalated under the arrogant and repressive Alexander. Josephus' defense of Alexander's gruesome mass crucifixion as partly justified because of the opposition he suffered may be the most blatantly uncomfortable passage in his apology for the excesses of Hasmonean rule that had become so tyrannical.

If we know a little about Judean tradition and history in the previous centuries it is not difficult to discern the reasons for the people's and the Pharisees' intensifying opposition to the Hasmonean regime during the reigns of Hyrcanus and then Alexander Jannaeus.[41] The following interrelated factors lie more or less on the surface or just under the facade of Josephus' narratives.

One was simply the Hasmoneans' consolidation of power, first in their assumption of the high priesthood by deft political maneuvering, but then

---

41. On the political-economic practices of Alexander Jannaeus, see Schalit, "Domestic Politics and Political Institutions," 277–84.

Hyrcanus' behaving more like a monarch and his sons transforming the polity into a monarchy. The "Maccabean" brothers came to power as popular leaders of a coalition of ordinary priests, scribes, and peasants against the "reforming" high priests who had attained power by manipulation of and collaboration with the Seleucid imperial regime. The Maccabean war was a prolonged struggle in which the Hasmonean leaders from an ordinary priestly family fought in alliance with these other Judean constituencies. But Jonathan and Simon, from a village priestly family, made themselves High Priests through their skillful maneuvering with rival Seleucid pretenders. That was precisely what the Maccabees and their allies had fought against, that is, ambitious Judean strongmen gaining power over temple and people by special arrangements with the imperial regime (authorities) that violated tradition and (potentially) worked to the people's detriment. As noted above, Jonathan and Simon depended for their power and support primarily on a people's army that they had recruited. Hyrcanus took what was for the history of the temple-state the unprecedented step of hiring foreign mercenaries, and Alexander Jannaeus, if not Hyrcanus himself, used these to suppress resistance among the people. The frustrated people made their concerns known in resistance and rebellion.

Second, the Hasmoneans also quickly broadened the scope of the High Priest's power. As long as the Jerusalem high priesthood was sponsored by the empire, in effect constituting a subdivision of the imperial administration, the power of the Jerusalem rulers was checked by imperial constraints, their prerogatives confined to administration of the temple-state limited to the tiny territory of Judea. However, with the demise of imperial power, and Hasmoneans moving to fill the void, they emerged with considerable imperial power themselves.

In the second and third generations of their rule, the Hasmoneans made two dramatic moves. They expanded their rule far beyond the tiny area of Judea to include the Great Plain and Galilee as well as Samaria and Idumea. And both of Hyrcanus' sons were so bold as to assume the imperial title of "king" in addition to that of "High Priest." Opposition to this consolidation of power and its imperial symbolization as kingship persisted throughout the Hasmonean period. This is evident somewhat later in the delegation that appealed to the Roman warlord Pompey, as the Hasmonean ruling house became divided against itself, that "the people" (*ethnos*) did not want to be ruled by a king, the ancestral tradition being rule by the priests.[42]

---

42. It may seem puzzling on the surface that in both the story about Hyrcanus and the Pharisees and in rabbinic memory of Yannai and the sages, "Eleazar" claims that since they lack legitimacy as high priests (that is, uncertain paternity insofar as their mothers had been captives of the Seleucids) they should be content to be only

Third, the objection to the "successes" of Hyrcanus and his sons also suggests that the Pharisees and others also opposed their military conquests of surrounding areas and peoples. The almost continuous warfare, through several decades, would have meant a considerable economic and manpower drain on the people. The economic burden placed on the Judean people would only have increased under Alexander Jannaeus, as he mounted continuing conquests of Hellenistic cities that surrounded the areas and peoples already conquered by Hyrcanus.[43] The burden would have offset whatever pride may have accompanied the new international prominence of Judea. Jannaeus, moreover, had turned his military against his own people when they resisted.

Fourth, the later Hasmoneans' transformation of their regime in the direction of a Hellenistic kingdom must have seemed to utterly contradict the traditional Judean way of life, or *politeia*, that their ancestors had been fighting for in the Maccabean Revolt. Although we can no longer view that revolt only or even primarily in the simplistic and anachronistic terms of an essentialist "Judaism" against an essentialist "Hellenism," conflict between traditional Judean/Israelite and Hellenistic cultural-religious and social-political forms were involved. Under the later Hasmoneans, however, Greek became the dominant language at court, the Cilician and Pisidian mercenaries were presumably Greek speaking, and Aristobulus even took the title Philhellene, indicating his political-cultural loyalty. Alexander Jannaeus was basically a conquering king imitating the practices of the Seleucids as he asserted Hasmonean control of Syria-Palestine-Phoenicia in the vacuum of power left by the declining Seleucid empire. So a cultural divide between the Hasmonean regime and both the people and the Pharisees compounded the widening political-economic conflict between rulers and ruled.

Josephus does not even mention a factor of the Hasmoneans' expansion of the territory and peoples they ruled, that is the corresponding expansion

---

rulers of the people. Eleazar's charge, however, is also an indirect challenge to their being "king" in/over Judea insofar as their being high priests was the basis of political-religious power. Without that a 'king' would have no authority. This story in Josephus and parallel rabbinic memory have long been discussed by scholars in terms focused on whether ancient Judean tradition allows a combination or insists on a separation of (Hellenistic-style) political authority and (traditional Judean) religiously-based authority. See the incisive review by D. R. Schwartz, "On Pharisaic Opposition to the Hasmonean Monarchy." In second temple Judea the high priesthood was inseparably the traditional political as well as religious authority/ruler (as in the decree of the Judeans that invested Simon explicitly as High Priest *and ruler* in 1 Macc 14:27–43). Adding the title "king" was, in the Hellenistic imperial context, the Hasmonean High Priests' claim to also being imperial rulers over the other areas and cities they had conquered with their mercenaries.

43. Applebaum, "The Hasmoneans," esp. 27–29, draws out the implications clearly.

and other changes in the temple-city of Jerusalem. As extensive archaeological explorations have shown, Persian and early Hellenistic Jerusalem had been the capital of a tiny insignificant province. Under the Hasmoneans the city was expanded onto the Western Hill, with corresponding construction of the city walls. 1 Maccabees refers to both Jonathan and Simon as having ordered the building of the city walls (10:10-11; 13:10). The construction of walls around what became the Upper City was probably done under Hyrcanus (1 Macc 16:23-24) and especially Jannaeus.[44] The expansion of the temple-city into a major capital from which other peoples as well as Judeans were ruled may have been disturbing to tradition-minded Jerusalemites.

With both the people of Jerusalem and the Pharisees having been opposed to and then fighting in some kind of alliance against Alexander we should consider their relative positions in the temple-state and in relation to each other. As already noted just above, Alexander's assertion in his supposed death-bed advice to Alexandra that he had come into conflict with the people (*ethnos*) because he had mistreated the Pharisees was, according to Mason, part of Josephus' polemic against them for supposedly weakening the Hasmonean dynasty. Josephus' account of Alexander's advice to Alexandra and his account of Hyrcanus' break with the Pharisees are two of only three passages in which he mentions explicitly their relation with the people (*Ant.* 13.288, 298, 401). A comparison with the third (*Ant.* 18.15) is instructive. In the latter, in one of his presentations of the Pharisees as a "philosophy," he says that "they happen to be credible among the people (of the city)" (*kai di' auta tois te demois pithanotatoi tygchanousin* . . .), which is connected directly with their views on matters such as fate and freewill, rewards and punishment. He further explains that prayers and sacred rites are performed according to their rulings.[45] Their credibility with the people and their influence on ritual matters in the latter passage is far removed from the rough and tumble of political conflict and civil strife of the earlier account.

In the two passages about their conflict with the Hasmoneans, their "credibility" or "influence" with "the populace" (*malista gar pisteuesthai para to plethei*) is portrayed as a serious threat to the regime. Loose and misleading translation and interpretation of these passages have been the basis of serious misunderstanding of the Pharisees' relation with the people. This has led previous generations of interpreters to make sweeping claims and generalizations about the Pharisees having been popular with or having

---

44. Avigad, *Discovering Jerusalem*, 71-75.

45. Josephus here may well be minimizing the Pharisees' authority by reducing it to rituals.

the support of the people. So it is important to note critically what Josephus is *not* saying in these passage in order to then discern critically what he is saying.

For decades, misleading translations and interpretations of Josephus' accounts have resulted in misunderstanding of the Pharisees' relations with the people of Jerusalem, precisely as portrayed by the wealthy Jerusalemite priest who identifies with the high priestly rulers. The problem is evidently rooted in the vague sense that biblical scholars and Jewish historians have had about the structure and dynamics of Judean society headed by the temple-state. As noted in the Introduction, the controlling synthetic theological construct of Judaism has tended simply to block discernment of the political-economic-religious structure of the temple-state presupposed and portrayed in Josephus' histories and other texts. Josephus indicates explicitly and repeatedly that the priestly aristocracy prior to the Hasmoneans, then the Hasmoneans, and then Herod *ruled* and economically exploited the city of Jerusalem as well as the villages in the *chora*. Josephus is fairly clear most of the time also that the high priestly rulers and kings dealt mainly with the "Jerusalemites" or the *demos* or *plethos* of the city. And when he mentions the *ethnos* he is thinking primarily of the people of Jerusalem, although he is fairly clear about the differences between the city and its people and the villages (*komai*) in the *chora*. Of course, as a wealthy priest of distinguished ancestry, he looks down his nose at ordinary city-people, views them with suspicion, and detests them when they make trouble for the rulers.

Once we discern more critically the political-economic-religious structure and dynamics of Judean society centered in the temple-state that Josephus presupposes and portrays, however, it is no longer justifiable to be vague or inconsistent in translation. Translations such as those in the Loeb Classical Library and scholars who follow and even embellish them have made the *demos* or *plethos,* which are interchangeable synonyms for the people or populace of Jerusalem, into "the masses" or "the mob" or "the rabble."[46] The population of Jerusalem in mid-second century BCE was not large enough to have been "the masses." As seen in the summary of Josephus' accounts above, Jonathan and Simon summoned the populace to assemblies in the temple for consultation on major projects for which they needed the people's support. Had the populace suddenly become "the masses/rabble" when Hyrcanus no longer called assemblies and they began opposing the

---

46. In the Loeb translation of *Ant.* 13.288, 296, 298, 402, Marcus has made "the populace" (*to plethos*) into the "masses." Following widespread scholarly practice, Mason perpetuates the misleading translation in *Flavius Josephus on the Pharisees,* 298; and has "masses" and "rabble" in the later summary of the book in "Pharisees in the Narratives of Josephus," 29, 34, 48.

incessant conquests of expansion? Throughout his works, it is fairly clear that Josephus despises the populace of Jerusalem—if only somewhat less than he despises the villagers in the countryside. But at least he is clear about the *demos* or *plethos* of Jerusalem in distinction from the villagers in the *chora*, using more precise terms that modern translators whose own elitist bias appears in their transformation of the populace into "the masses."

The difference and relations of the Pharisees and the people of Jerusalem was clear from the story that Josephus tells at the end of his account in *Ant.* 13.288–298 that he frames with the sudden announcement that "the Judeans were aroused against Hyrcanus by his successes; and particularly hostile were the Pharisees, one of the schools of the Judeans." The story explains that under Hyrcanus the Pharisees had been close advisers of (their "disciple") Hyrcanus and indicated that he had been backing and enforcing the regulations from the traditions of the ancestors they promulgated for the people, presumably because they possessed the knowledge of Judean tradition, polity, and the ancestral laws that were needed in the operation of the temple-state. They had been involved at a high level in the politics of the temple-state.

When Hyrcanus broke with the party of the Pharisees, he switched to the party of the Sadducees. Josephus adds a comment that is often loosely translated and misinterpreted: concerning the *nomima* of the Pharisees and evidently the ancestral laws in general, the two parties came to have serious differences, "the Sadducees having the confidence of the wealthy only, but having no following among the city people (*to demotikon*), while the Pharisees have the populace (*to plethos*) as an ally (*summachon*)" (*Ant.* 13.298). In this and related passages in Josephus' accounts about the Hasmoneans, *demos/demotikon* and *plethos* are synonyms. Josephus does *not* say here, as in the translation by Marcus in the Loeb Classical Library, that "the Pharisees have the support of the masses." In his framing of the story, he says that the Pharisees have such influence with the populace that they are believed even when they speak against a king or High Priest. But he does *not* say that the Pharisees are "popular" or that "they have massive public following" or that they were able to win massive popular support for their ordinances."[47]

---

47. In making such assertions Mason, *Flavius Josephus on the Pharisees*, 224, 243, 245, seems to be following Marcus' translation in the Loeb Library. In his later summary of the book, in "Pharisees in the Narratives of Josephus," the Pharisees' (supposed) popularity and massive support has become "enormous" (61)." The lay movement of the Pharisees" has become "immensely popular" (53) so that "the Pharisees and their program hold complete sway over the masses and therefore over political life" (52). It is not clear what justifies this exaggeration. The claim that "the Pharisees' popularity keeps them near the center of power" (44) certainly does not fit Josephus' accounts of their being dismissed by Hyrcanus or their situation under the long reigns of the

In connection with the people's opposition to Hyrcanus Josephus does say in his framing of the story that the Pharisees have *influence* (not popularity or support) with the populace. But neither Josephus nor the story he recounts addresses the question of whether the Pharisees had gained "massive public support for their regulations," much less had a "massive popular following."

Alexandra Salome and the Pharisees

Josephus presents closely parallel accounts in his two histories that reveal his or his source's disdain both for Alexandra Salome, a woman who presumed to become a ruler, and for the Pharisees whom she restored to positions of authority in the temple-state. Josephus' account in *War* is (initially) less cynical and critical of both queen and Pharisees than the account in *Antiquities*.

> Alexander left the kingdom to his wife Alexandra, being convinced that the Judeans would submit to her because of her utter lack of his brutality and because she had won the affection of the populace (*demos*) by her opposition to his crimes . . . This frail woman ruled the state thanks to her reputation for *eusebeia* (loyalty to God). For she was especially exact in her observance of the ancestral traditions of the people (*ethnos*) and would expel from governing those who violated the sacred laws. She appointed her elder son, Hyrcanus, as High Priest and confined the younger, Aristobulus, to private life because he was impulsive (hotheaded).
>
> Growing up around her [Alexandra] into authority (*exousia*) were the Pharisees, a body of Judeans evidently more loyal to God (*eusebesteron*) and more exact in their exposition of the laws than others [Judeans]. To them, being herself intensely religious, she listened with too great a deference; while they, gradually taking advantage of the ingenuous woman, became at length the administrators of everything (*dioiketai ton holon*), at liberty to banish and to recall, to loose and to bind whomever they wished. Thus, the enjoyments of royal authority were theirs; its expenses and burdens fell to Alexandra. She proved able to administer the larger affairs, doubling her army by recruiting and collecting a considerable body of foreign mercenaries, so that she strengthened her own people (*ethnos*) and was a formidable foe to foreign potentates. But if she ruled the others (the Judeans), the Pharisees ruled her.

---

repressive Alexander Jannaeus and Herod.

> Thus, they put to death Diogenes, one of the notable figures (*tina ton episemon*) who had been a friend of Alexander, accusing him of having advised the king to crucify his eight hundred victims. They further urged Alexandra to make away with the others who had instigated Alexander to punish those men; and as she from superstitious motives always gave way, they proceeded to kill whomsoever they would. The prominent figures (*hoi dokountes*) who were thus imperiled sought refuge with Aristobulus, who persuaded his mother to spare their lives in consideration of their rank but to expel them from the city if not convinced of their innocence. (*War* 1.107–114).[48]

Josephus begins his account in *War* by portraying Alexandra as an ideal Judean and ideal monarch. Besides having opposed her husband's crimes (brutal slaughter of the people) she had a reputation for the combination of loyalty (to God) and strict observance of the ancestral traditions, even to the point of excluding from her government those who did not observe the ancestral traditions. The interrelated loyalty to God and observance of the ancestral laws are what Josephus later elaborated in the early books of the *Antiquities* (somewhat in Hellenistic cultural terms) as the traditional covenantal *politeia* of the Judeans.[49] This same combination appears in a wide variety of Judean texts as the Mosaic covenant, including the commandments of exclusive loyalty to God and of justice in social-economic relations). In some texts this appears simplified into the two commandments of intensive love of God and love of neighbor and is developed into the "two-ways" teaching in wisdom texts and the Dead Sea Scrolls. Moreover, says Josephus, the Pharisees who were growing up around Alexandra into

---

48. In translation of Josephus' Greek account, Thackeray, followed by Mason, represent Diogenes and the others who advised Alexander to crucify the eight hundred as "distinguished" and as "the most eminent citizens" and Mason adds that the Pharisees were killing them "on false charges" (111). The meaning and connotations of terms, however, must be determined from the broader narrative context. It is apparent from Josephus' account of Alexander's killing of thousands of his subjects who opposed him, and particularly the crucifixion of the eight hundred, that he does not approve of this slaughter and cruelty. Even in his equivocation in *Ant.* 13.381–383, Josephus calls Alexander's actions "excessive cruelty." (Mason, *Flavius Josephus on the Pharisees*, 83, does not mention the eight-hundred Alexander crucified in his summary of the literary "context.") Thus, the term *episemoi* in the account of Alexandra and the Pharisees hardly carries the positive sense of "distinguished," but rather the negative sense of "notorious" or at least the more neutral "notable," which leaves why they were notable vague. Also, the text does not imply that these figures were members of the *demos*, hence not "citizens" and not "eminent" but "prominent" in the sense that high-ranking military officers would have been prominent figures around the city.

49. As discussed in chap. 3 above.

authority (*exousia*) were even more loyal to God and more exact in exposition of the laws. But she, being overly pious toward (or: devoted to) the divine, and they, taking advantage of this, became the administrators of all (domestic) affairs. Here Josephus uses *dioiketai*, a standard term referring to (non-military) administrators appointed by and under the authority of ruler(s).

As usual, Josephus' main concern is about the continuation of Hasmonean military power. And in this regard Alexandra proved to be an able administrator in larger affairs, with a sufficiently formidable army, including a large body of foreign mercenaries, to intimidate other rulers in the area. It would appear to be out of this concern that Josephus clearly does not approve of Alexandra having allowed the Pharisees to prosecute (and seek execution of) those advisers of Alexander who advised him to crucify the eight hundred of his active opponents. If we read critically for what evidently underlies Josephus' account at key points we can discern a delicate "balance of power" between the Pharisees and Aristobulus, as both sides tried to influence Alexandra on how to handle those high-ranking officers. The Pharisees are seeking justice in the execution of those officers. After the Pharisees succeeded in getting some of them executed, however, Aristobulus persuaded his mother simply to expel these prominent figures from Jerusalem and allow them to "disperse" about the country. In the account in *War* Josephus withholds information on what this meant and we are left to learn later in the narrative that they came to control the military fortresses and were instrumental in enabling Aristobulus to seize power.

The account in *Antiquities* is more cynical and critical, especially of Alexandra but also of the Pharisees. Josephus also includes information that was missing in *War* that serves as a kind of "back-story" to the earlier account. At the beginning of his *Antiquities* account of Alexander Jannaeus (*Ant*. 13.320–322) Josephus portrayed the queen, whom he had denigrated as "this little woman" in *War*, as savvy and skillful in political maneuvering. When her first husband, the *Philhellene* king Aristobulus, died after only a year's reign, she released his brothers from prison and appointed Jannaeus as king, and also evidently married him. Josephus suggests that she may have thought that he "knew his place;" since his superstitious father Hyrcanus had sent him far away to be brought up in Galilee he would have had little or no experience in the operations of the regime and political relations with the already restive Jerusalem *demos*. But after he immediately took over the kingdom and killed a brother he suspected, Alexandra presumably lived through twenty-seven years of his open warfare with and brutality to the people.

In *Antiquities* Josephus makes Alexander Jannaeus a calculating politician who at the end of his reign recognizes that the best way to salvage the Hasmonean dynasty would be reconciliation with the Pharisees. Alexandra is savvy enough to take his advice. She negotiated with the Pharisees and brought them back into positions of authority in the regime. In return for her delegating (internal) affairs of state to them and making them her "friends," that is, trusted intimate advisers, they attempted to reconcile the people to the regime, propagandizing among the populace with speeches that Alexander had not been so bad after all. In this turn of affairs, suddenly

> the woman was loved by the populace because she was thought to disapprove of the crimes committed by her husband. Alexandra then appointed [her elder son] Hyrcanus as High Priest and entrusted the Pharisees to do everything,[50] and also commanded the people to obey them as authorities (*peitharchein*). And whatever regulations (*nomima*) the Pharisees introduced in accordance with the ancestral tradition (*nomima... kata ten patroan paradosin*) had been abolished by her father-in-law, Hyrcanus, these she again established (*apokatestesen*). And so, while she had the title of sovereign (*to onoma tes basileias*), the Pharisees had the power (*ten dynamin*). For they even recalled exiles and freed prisoners, and differed in no way from rulers (*despoton*).[51] The woman, moreover, took measures for the security of the kingdom, both recruiting a large force of mercenaries and doubling her own army so that she struck terror into the surrounding rulers and received hostages from them. The whole country was quiet except for the Pharisees; for they worked on the queen and tried to persuade her to kill those who had urged Alexander to slaughter the eight hundred. They themselves killed one of them, named Diogenes, and after him others, . . . until the officers (*dynatoi*, powerful ones) came to the palace and with them Aristobulus, . . . who made it plain that he would not leave his mother any power at all . . .

Josephus then constructs for these officers a tear-jerking complaint that they had been loyal to their ruler, who had bestowed great honors upon them, a promise to be loyal to the regime, and a threat that they might become mercenaries for Aretas and other monarchs.

> But if she was going to favor the Pharisees, next best for them was for her to station each of them in one of the garrisons . . .

50. "Permitted the Pharisees to do as they liked in all matters" is too "permissive."
51. Thackeray's "absolute rulers" is an exaggeration.

And so the queen, not knowing what to do consistent with her dignity, entrusted to them the guarding of the fortresses, except for Hyrcania, Alexandreion, and Machaerus, where her most valuable possessions were. (*Ant.* 13.408–414, 417)[52]

According to the account in *Antiquities*, the plan to save the dynasty from further opposition or rebellion of the *demos* by bringing the Pharisees back into the regime worked. Presumably the people, who had risen against Alexander and then experienced such brutality from the king-High Priest and his military officers, would have been at least somewhat mollified by the Pharisees' efforts to bring the officers to justice. Or at least the plan worked for nearly a decade, until Aristobulus, with the aid of his father's military officers, seized power, touching off an escalating war between rival Hasmonean factions. At least, Josephus mentions no further opposition by the people under Alexandra. As in the account in *War*, the result under Alexandra was a balance of power in the regime between the Pharisees that she restored to authority, on the one hand, and Aristobulus, now "a man of action" instead of a "hothead," and his father's senior military officers, on the other. Alexandra herself was in command of her own army and mercenaries, while Hyrcanus as High Priest was a non-factor politically.

The Pharisees were entrusted with domestic social-political affairs. Of special significance, evidently, for the subsequent history of the temple-state as well as the needed pacification of the realm, was Alexandra's restoration of the regulations (*nomima*) of the Pharisees according to the ancestral tradition (*kata ten patroan paradosin*). She gave these as well as the Pharisees official sanction by commanding the people to obey them as authorities (*peitharchein*). Now again having authority in the temple-state after the serious rebellions and heavy repression at the end of Hyrcanus reign and throughout that of the tyrant Alexander Jannaeus, the Pharisees recalled those who had been exiled and released the political prisoners.

Josephus' caustic comment that in these matters the Pharisees differed in no way from rulers (*despoton*), however, is a polemical exaggeration. As in the *War* account, so in the *Antiquities* Josephus portrays the situation under Alexandra as a balance of power between the Pharisees and the professional military built up under John Hyrcanus and coming to tyrannical heights under "the Thracian," Alexander.[53] The Pharisees were evidently

---

52. Adapted from Mason's translation, *Flavius Josephus on the Pharisees*, 253.

53. Mason, *Flavius Josephus on the Pharisees*, 251, finds that Alexandra "has given absolute power to the Pharisees" and has little left for the two sons. Josephus' account reads otherwise. She has already appointed the elder son Hyrcanus as High Priest and he later had the elders of the Judeans around him (*Ant.* 13.428–429); and the Pharisees can only compete with her other son Aristobulus to "persuade" Alexandra, who allows

seeking at least some justice for the worst of Alexander's brutalities. Lacking the power themselves, they had to try to persuade Alexandra to take decisive action to clip the wings of the senior military officers still in the city. But despite Alexandra building up her own military, Alexander's officers and especially her son Aristobulus were still forces with some persuasive power of their own, including the threat of offering their services to rival monarchs. While knowing that she could not trust them in the fortresses where her own valuable possessions were stored, all she could do to perhaps reduce the threat they posed to her rule was to "disperse" them to guarding the other fortresses. This, of course, left them in prime position to support Aristobulus when he finally moved to seize power.

While Josephus admits that both Alexandra and the Pharisees were capable administrators, he passes a strongly negative judgment, particularly on the queen, at the end of his account in *Antiquities* (13.430–432). His misogyny is palpable and idealization of military power unrelenting. Indeed, "she was a woman who showed none of the weakness of her sex; she showed by her deeds the ability to carry out her plans." But she was nevertheless responsible for the demise of the Hasmonean dynasty because of her desire for power that was unbecoming of a woman, "and because she expressed the same opinions as did (or "lent the weight of her authority to") those who were hostile to her dynasty" (presumably the Pharisees?). In the end, says Josephus, she squandered the power that her dynasty had acquired in the face of the greatest dangers and difficulties. Josephus had earlier declared that she had no excuse for continuing to rule when her sons were in the prime of life, meaning Aristobulus, the "man of action" (13.416–417). Josephus' earlier and subsequent narratives, however, suggest rather that the principal cause of the demise of the dynasty were the tyranny of her husband Alexander Jannaeus and the ambitious seizure of power by her son Aristobulus. Thus, his last sentence in *Antiquities* book 13 seems ironic. Nevertheless, "she had kept the people (*to ethnos*) at peace."

The Pharisees under the Hasmoneans

Whatever anti-Pharisee polemic he weaves into his historical narrative(s), Josephus presents the Pharisees as well-placed advisers and administrators of John Hyrcanus and then of Alexandra Salome. The Hellenizing reform and the Maccabean Revolt had constituted a highly significant break in the continuity of the temple-state and its ideology. The Hasmonean high priests who then restored the temple-state as the form of their rule in Judea were, in

---

the officers and advisers of Alexander to guard the fortresses.

terms of Judean tradition, illegitimate "upstarts" of lowborn priestly origins, not from high-priestly lineage. That means they also lacked the knowledge and experience of priestly aristocrats. Moreover, they had been away from the temple in Jerusalem for well over a decade as guerrilla fighters and then as leaders of battles against Seleucid imperial control of Judea. After Jonathan maneuvered to gain recognition as the new High Priest from a weakened Seleucid regime, some Zadokites and their scribal associates withdrew from Jerusalem in protest against the "Wicked Priest," whom they charged with persecuting their leader. But Jonathan was able to consolidate his power as High Priest by further military maneuvering, despite his lack of the requisite aristocratic lineage.

To operate the temple-state Jonathan and his successors needed those with the training and knowledge of Judean temple-state traditions and laws, as well as whatever semblance of legitimacy they might bring to the regime. Those scribes who at some point under Jonathan and/or Simon and/or Hyrcanus came into the service of the temple-state and were the "friends" of Hyrcanus early in his reign must have been from among those with such training. Only such learned scribes would have been able to serve Hyrcanus with, and teach him, ordinances from the tradition of the ancestors that he authorized and enforced as laws of the temple-state. In the context of Judean history, they were in a political-religious position and role similar to the learned scribes (or sages) in earlier generations, as represented by Ben Sira in his instructional speeches. In terms of the historical sociology of agrarian societies, they were the intellectual-legal retainers of the Hasmonean temple-state. That they served as advisers and administrators of the upstart Hasmonean priests is confirmed by the polemics of key Qumran texts. Some of the dedicated traditionalist Zadokite priests and scribes, who had withdrawn from the Jerusalem temple-state in protest, rejected them as lax on keeping the traditions strictly, seeking "smooth things" in their advising the Wicked Priest.

As he consolidated his power and wealth, conquering Idumea and Samaria with mercenary troops, Hyrcanus broke with the Pharisees and installed the Sadducees as advisers. They were evidently more conservative traditionalists with scribal training. Their acceptance of only the laws of Moses that were written meant that they avoided other traditions and teachings (torah) that probably placed more limitations on the power of the high priests. When Hyrcanus broke with the Pharisees, however, he did not expel them from Jerusalem. Perhaps in the balance of different interests of the people in Jerusalem it was tradition to have different scribal circles resident in the city (as had been the case in the early second century under the Oniads). As Josephus explained, while the Sadducees were the party of the wealthy priestly aristocrats, the Pharisees had (much of) the populace of the city as their "allies." When the people began to revolt against Hyrcanus and the revolt expanded, exacerbated by Alexander's brutal measures of suppression, the Pharisees evidently joined their "allies"—and were among those crucified or exiled. In this conflict between the Hasmoneans and the Pharisees, who made common cause with the people, the Pharisees were repeating the course of action taken a few generations earlier by the *maskilim* and the "Enoch-"scribes in their resistance to and struggle against the "reforming" priestly aristocrats who were pursuing Hellenistic imperial political polity and practice. The Pharisees were evidently acting in rejection of the Hasmonean wars to expand their power with the aid of mercenary troops, in alliance with the people's revolt—but not as the leaders of the people.

When offered the opportunity, however, they once again served as the advisers and administrators of the temple-state under Alexandra. Their agenda included checking the power of Alexander's military officers and his power-hungry son, Aristobulus. They attempted to bring the military officers to justice for their brutal suppression of the rebels, who probably included some of their fellow Pharisees. But far from having unfettered power in domestic affairs, contrary to Josephus' rhetorical flourishes, they worked in a balance of power with Aristobulus and those military officers who were allowed to occupy the fortresses around the country.

The historical accounts of Josephus indicate that the Pharisees served as temple-state advisers under the High Priest John Hyrcanus (and perhaps under his predecessors) and then again as administrators of domestic affairs in the temple-state under Alexandra. It seems highly likely that as a result their regulations (*nomima*) from the tradition of the ancestors, established as state law under Hyrcanus and again under Alexandra, became part of the laws and traditions of the Jerusalem temple-state.[54] And the Pharisees themselves continued to be active, in some capacity, in the temple-state city of Jerusalem, to be discussed in the next chapters.

---

54. Schaefer, *History of the Jews in Antiquity*, 71, suggests that the Pharisees "attempted to put the ideal of the religious *and* political realization of the Torah into concrete political effect." While overly idealistic, this formulation of the Pharisees' program under the Hasmoneans at least discerns the political aspect. But like other scholars, Schaefer is still thinking in terms of the synthetic construct of Judaism and the standard concept of the Torah, terms that can now be recognized as overly simple historically. Josephus, the source on which Schaefer relies has a more complex portrayal: he has the Pharisees applying more broadly regulations (*nomima*) derived from the tradition of the ancestors, which were more inclusive than what Josephus calls the written laws of Moses that the Sadducees accept as authoritative. See the discussion of this broader, more inclusive conception of the *politeia* and laws of the Judeans in chapters 2–3 above.

6

The Pharisees under Roman and Herod's Rule

For the period of the Roman conquest through Herod's conquest and rule, Josephus offers only brief accounts of individual figures named as Pharisees and a few incidents of the Pharisees' and other scribes' relations with Herod. If these brief accounts and few incidents are understood in broader historical contexts, however, important information can be detected about the Pharisees' continuing participation in the politics of Roman Judea.

In imposing the young military strongman Herod as King of the Judeans, the Romans added another layer of client rule on the territories previously conquered and controlled by the Judean temple-state. Herod retained, expanded, and transformed the temple and the high priestly aristocracy as instruments of his and Roman imperial rule. Compared with their exercise of considerable authority under Alexandra as the scribal "retainers" of the temple-state, the Pharisees under Herod's rule thus, in effect, found themselves in a more complex constellation of political interaction in the governance of "greater" Judea. Yet by no means did they withdraw from political affairs. Instead, we find them engaged in politics, particularly with regard to Herod's rise to power and his later autocratic measures. They even managed to gain influence in the royal court. Also, other scribal figures and circles were active under Herod's rule. The overall political structure and political dynamics in Palestine, moreover, had undergone a decades-long series of severe conflicts topped by the Roman conquest and reconquests and the regional effects of the empire-wide civil war between rival Roman warlords.

It is thus of special importance to gain at least an elementary sense of the historical context in which the Pharisees and other scribal circles were operating. And since the wealthy Judean historian Josephus provides our principal sources for the period, it is important to investigate how he portrays the multiple interrelated conflicts, between rival Hasmonean factions, rival Roman warlords, and factions among the Jerusalem populace, including particularly the concerns of the *protoi* of the Judeans. In his earlier account in *War* Josephus presents a positive picture of Herod focused primarily on his relations with the Romans and his many extensive benefactions to Caesar and cities of the Roman imperial world, with little coverage of the impact on his subjects. Josephus' later account in *Antiquities* is much more critical of Herod, including how in so many ways he took actions and mounted so many projects that were contrary to the ancestral laws and basic way of life or constitution (*politeia*) of the Judeans, and then took severe repressive measures against the people when they protested. The later account is also more candid about Herod's utterly calculating brutality in dealing with his wives, sons, any possible rivals, and any protestors.

Most important, because they are often overlooked or downplayed, are Josephus' accounts (a) of the severe violence and destruction unleashed by the continuing and repeated Roman conquest, (b) of how intensively the Judeans struggled against the prospect that the Romans would subject them to the rule of the young military strong-man Herod, (c) of how intensively Herod exploited his subjects economically, and (d) of how intensively the Judeans and other subjects in adjacent areas resented and resisted Herod's rule in violation of the ancestral laws, customs, and general way of life (*politeia*).

Hasmonean Civil War, Roman Intervention, and the Relentless Rise of Herod

As Josephus signaled what was coming under Alexandra, her ambitious younger son Aristobulus seized power with the support of his father's military officers who already controlled the fortresses. Particularly important for subsequent developments, however, the wealthy Idumean Antipater, whose father had been appointed military governor of Idumea by Alexander and Alexandra, maneuvered his way into a position of power, with the support of the most influential Judeans, and operated under the ostensible authority of the High Priest Hyrcanus II (*Ant.* 14.8–20). In crucial battles Antipater and Hyrcanus had the support of the city-people (*demos*). Both the Antipater (Hyrcanus) side and the Aristobulus side turned to the Roman warlord

Pompey, then steadily taking control of Syria-Palestine, with lavish gifts (of the wealth stored up in temple or palace or fortresses). Josephus mentions that while Pompey heard the case of (prominent figures representing) the Judeans and their rival would-be Hasmonean rulers, Hyrcanus and Aristobulus, "the people (*to ethnos*) were against them both and asked not to be ruled by a king, saying it was their ancestral custom to obey as authorities the priests of the God who was venerated by them" (*Ant.* 14.41–45).[1]

After Aristobulus and his forces moved into active resistance to the Roman take-over and occupied the (well-fortified) temple, the Hyrcanus faction delivered the city and palace to Pompey, who besieged the temple. When it was finally taken (in the summer of 63), the Roman and other forces burst into the temple and slaughtered the Judeans there, including priests who continued to offer sacrifices. Some were slain by Judeans of the opposing faction (*Ant.* 14.58–71; *War* 1.128–151).[2]

In both of his parallel accounts, Josephus expressed horror about the calamity of Pompey and his staff having penetrated into the inner sanctuary. Such entry was unlawful for anyone but the High Priest; the inner sanctuary had never before been seen by any other Judean, much less foreigners. There Pompey and his soldiers beheld the golden table and the sacred lampstand and the libation vessels and a great quantity of spices and a treasury of two thousand talents. But Pompey touched none of these. He ordered the temple servants to cleanse the temple and offer the customary sacrifice to God. And he restored the high priesthood to Hyrcanus, particularly because he had prevented Judeans of the countryside (*chora*) from fighting on Aristobulus' side. Pompey subjected Jerusalem and the *chora* to the payment of tribute. He also confined the people to earlier boundaries and restored the cities that (mainly) Alexander Jannaeus had conquered to their former inhabitants, subject to Roman rule (*Ant.* 14.71–76; *War* 1.152–157).

In *Antiquities* Josephus also pronounces judgment on the historical outcome, from the perspective of a wealthy Judean priest of distinguished lineage:

---

1. Although Josephus' account gives no indication, there is credible speculation that the "people's" delegation represented or was influenced by the Pharisees, whom Alexandra Salome had restored as "administrators" of the temple-state, nearly a decade before. Cf. the earlier account in Diodorus Siculus 40.2, on which see Stern, *Greek and Latin Authors on Jews and Judaism*, 1.185–87. See also Hengel and Deines, "E. P. Sanders' 'Common Judaism,'" 53.

2. In his usual exaggeration, Josephus says 12,000 Judeans were slain. Even if we (again) move the decimal point one place to the left, 1200 is still a huge number to have been killed.

> For this misfortune which befell Jerusalem Hyrcanus and Aristobulus were responsible, because of their dissention. For we lost our freedom (*eleutheria*) and became subject to the Romans, and the territory which we had gained by our arms and taken from the Syrians we were compelled to give back to them, and in addition the Romans exacted of us in a short space of time more than ten thousand talents; and the royal power, which had formerly been bestowed on those who were high priests by birth became the privilege of commoners.[3] (*Ant.* 14.77–78)

So the demise of the Hasmoneans was not due solely to a woman's (Alexandra's) supposed lust for power and the Pharisees who were seeking justice for the eight hundred whom Alexander Jannaeus had crucified (as Josephus had claimed earlier in his narrative). The wealthy Jerusalem priest and loyal Flavian, moreover, claims for the Judeans generally the conquests of their (then unprecedented) "kings" and their mercenaries which, he had said, many or most of the Jerusalemites had actively opposed at the time. And he indicates clearly that he is not (or no longer) a fan of the upstart military strong man who, although only a commoner, was appointed king of the Judeans by the Romans.

Successive Roman warlords imposed new arrangements in Palestine. Gabinius transformed the monarchy (of Hyrcanus) into five districts each headed by a council, that is, an aristocracy again (*Ant.* 14.91). Ten years after Pompey had left untouched the wealth in the temple, the warlord Crassus stripped away all the gold and talents to help fund his campaign against the Parthians (105–110). Josephus explains all that wealth as the accumulation of gifts from diaspora Judean communities around the empire, which probably did provide a supplement to what was extracted from the Judeans in tithes and offerings and other revenues. Says Josephus, "there is no public money [among us] except that which is God's" (113). After Crassus' disastrous invasion of Parthia, Cassius took command in Syria and enslaved thousands in (the area of) Tarichaeae (119–120).

Meanwhile, Aristobulus (and his sons) and Antipater (the power behind Hyrcanus II) became mixed up in the empire-wide Roman civil war. Antipater wisely deserted to the side of Julius Caesar, who confirmed Hyrcanus II as High Priest and appointed Antipater as viceroy of all Judea (that is, all the territories that the temple-state still ruled), who in turn used his new authority to warn the people about any unrest (14.127–157).

---

3. The irony of this last statement is palpable: the wealthy Judean priest and historian who boasted of his descent from the Hasmoneans, a common priestly family that had usurped the high priesthood, complains about the debasement of the high office in another revolt, two centuries later.

Antipater appointed his son Phasael as military governor of Jerusalem and his younger son Herod as military governor of Galilee. Herod proceeded to kill Hezekiah and his large troop of brigands operating on the frontier of Syria, which brought him into favor with Sextus Caesar, governor of Syria. But as the Judeans-in-office (*en telei*; i.e., high-ranking priests in the temple-state) observed Antipater's and his sons' growing power and wealth and Hyrcanus' wealth, they became hostile. The *protoi* of the Judeans in the account in *Ant.* 14.158–180—surely more likely historically than the "malicious persons at court" in *War* 1.209—began to fear that Herod had designs on becoming a tyrant.[4] Protesting to Hyrcanus that Antipater and his sons had become the real rulers, they insisted that Herod be brought to trial for killing Hezekiah and his men "in violation of our law, which forbids us to kill someone, even if wicked, unless he has first been condemned by the council" (*Ant.* 14.158–167).[5] Hyrcanus' anger was further kindled by the mothers of the men whom Herod had murdered, for every day in the temple they pleaded that Herod be brought to judgment in the council for what he had done. After Hyrcanus summoned Herod to trial, however, Sextus, governor of Syria, warned him to acquit Herod of the charge (*Ant.* 14.163–170).

This is the context in which Josephus first mentions a certain Samaias, later identified as a Pharisee (a "disciple of the Pharisee Pollion," to whom the speech is attributed, *Ant.* 15.3–4), who was also evidently a member of the council. Herod, appearing for trial surrounded by his soldiers, overawed them all, and none of those who had denounced him before dared to accuse him further. Josephus thus stages a speech by Samaias, "a man of justice (*dikaios*), and for that reason superior to fear." In the speech placed in his mouth by Josephus, he arose and said:

> "Councilors and King: I do not myself know of, nor do I suppose that you can name anyone who, when summoned before us for

---

4. The much more pro-Herod account of this important incident, told from Herod's viewpoint, speaks of "malicious persons at court" urging Hyrcanus to bring Herod to trial (*War* 1.203–212). The more balanced account of Herod in *Antiquities* (14.158–180) appears to be closer to what were likely the dynamics of politics (including certain details) in the interaction between Roman officials, Hyrcanus and Antipater, and "those in office" or the *protoi* of the Judeans who operated the temple-state.

5. Much of the older secondary literature on Jewish history (often as the historical context of Jesus) refers to *The Sanhedrin* as if it were a standing institution in the temple-state with certain membership. Josephus' principal references to "the council" are to the trial of the young Herod and the trial of James, brother of Jesus, in mid-first century CE (*Ant.* 14.167–180; 20.200–202), as well as a reference to "the council" (also called a *koinon*) in Jerusalem during the early days of the Great Revolt (*Life* 62). The first two references are evidently to an *ad hoc* judicial council convened by the High Priest (Hyrcanus II and later Ananus), and not a standing institution with a set membership.

trial, has ever presented such an appearance. For no matter who it was that came before this council for trial, he showed himself humble and assumed the manner of one who is fearful and seeks mercy from us by letting his hair grow and wearing a black garment. But this fine fellow Herod, who is accused of murder and has been summoned on no less grave a charge than this, stands here clothed in purple, with his hair carefully arranged and with his soldiers around him, in order to kill us if we condemn him, as the law prescribes, and to save himself by outraging justice. But it is not Herod whom I should blame for this or for putting his own interests above the law, but you and the king, for giving him such great license. But know well that God is great, and this man, whom you now wish to release for Hyrcanus' sake, will one day punish you and the king as well." (*Ant.* 14.172–174)

And, sure enough, Josephus comments, "when Herod received the kingship, he killed Hyrcanus and all the members of the council except Samaias" (*Ant.* 14.175). Herod held Samaias in honor, however, because of his justice (*dikaiosyne*) and because when Herod later besieged the city, Samaias advised the people to admit him, since because of their sins they would not be able to escape him (176). Despite their lack of courage in the trial, members of the council insisted that Herod be executed, but Hyrcanus postponed the trial and advised Herod to flee, knowing that he might well march on Jerusalem to seize power, particularly after Sextus Caesar appointed him military governor of Coele-Syria in return for a substantial bribe (177–184).

Samaias' speech to the council and Hyrcanus is primarily a sharp admonition and warning to execute justice according to the ancestral laws of the Judeans. But it is also a prediction of future events that will happen as a result of their paralysis in taking action. Josephus' phrasing makes Samaias' warning sound similar to prophecies of earlier ("classical") prophets, with a direct reference to God as the source of the prediction and the introduction of the prophecy with the warning "know well . . ." (*Ant.* 14.174). This suggests that Samaias stands in the tradition of well-trained scribes who, as Ben Sira laid out (Sir 38:32—39:1), had learned "prophecies" as well as "the torah of the Most High" so that, understanding the decisions of courts, they are prepared to speak in the council among the rulers. So whether we attribute the framing of the prophecy to Josephus' own knowledge of the form of "classical" prophecies or to the collective memory about Samaias on which he draws, this prophecy resembles those familiar to scribes from their rigorous learning of the Judean cultural repertoire, and not the "predictions" or application of dreams by seers contemporary with Josephus.

From Josephus' account(s) of this incident a number of the conflictual dynamics in the politics of the temple-state in the context of Roman Palestine are evident. First, as military conflicts, battles back and forth between rival Hasmonean pretenders and Roman warlords, disrupted both Jerusalem (and other cities) and the countryside, destroying or commandeering crops and killing villagers, the area was far from being under control of its competing rulers. Epidemic banditry, as along the Syrian frontier, is often a barometer of political-economic chaos and crisis.[6] The Romans' principal concern was control, for which they looked to military strongmen such as Herod. One of the immediately ensuing events offers an illustration of the Romans' application of raw power in exploitation of the people and brutal punishment. When Cassius took control in Syria after his and Brutus' assassination of Julius Caesar, he imposed a special levy of tribute on the people "beyond their ability to pay," (to the value of) seven-hundred talents of silver from greater Judea (*War* 1.218–222; *Ant.* 14.272–276). Herod raised the hundred talents quota from Galilee, thereby appeasing Cassius and becoming one of his "friends." Comments Josephus: "For he thought it prudent to court the Romans and secure their goodwill at the expense of others" (*Ant.* 14.274). Four district towns in northwest Judea, on the other hand, perhaps not having been "strong-armed" so severely, being slower to produce, brought down the Roman warlord's direct punishment. The people were sold as slaves (275).

Second, Antipater and his sons had become masters at manipulating the situation and particularly the Roman warlords to gain power and wealth themselves as they sought control of affairs under the thin veneer of legitimacy that Hyrcanus provided as the hereditary High Priest (and king). But meanwhile both the city-people (*demos/plethos*) and "the Judeans in office" or the *protoi* of the Judeans, who were probably the ranking high-priestly office holders, were political players in the shifting fortunes of the temple-state. At this time they were of sufficient importance for the operation of the temple-state that Hyrcanus would convene a "council" (*synedrion*) for deliberation and advice on important cases of violation of the ancestral laws. It may be that Antipater and Hyrcanus had been using the council as a way of "governing" the temple-state and city in the fluid historical situation. But tensions and contradictions in the situation were growing into increasing conflicts between the High Priest Hyrcanus and the *demos* and the *protoi* over the increasing power of Antipater and his sons, particularly the arrogant and impetuous young Herod.

6. Discussed in Horsley with Hanson, *Bandits, Prophets, and Messiahs*, 52–63, and the fuller references and discussion in Horsley, "Josephus and Bandits"; and Horsley, "Ancient Judean Banditry."

Finally, at least one important and bold Pharisee who was devoted to justice according to the ancestral laws of the Judeans was a member of the council. This might lead to a surmise that the Pharisees, and their *nomima* according to the ancestral tradition, having been restored to authority by Alexandra, who had appointed Hyrcanus High Priest, continued at some level of authority under the high priesthood of Hyrcanus, which was confirmed and backed by the Romans. Josephus may not find this important to mention, or he may not want to mention it. But it is surely historically significant that he mentions Samaias in an important role in the temple-state at this key juncture in Herod's relentless rise to power.

In Josephus' continuing narrative of Herod's rise to power it is striking how persistently and intensively the Judeans attempted to head off the possibility that Herod would become ruler over them. When Cassius left Syria, the *demos* took up arms against Herod's brother Phasael, who had previously been appointed military governor of Jerusalem (*Ant.* 14.294). After Cassius was defeated at Philippi by Antony and Octavian, "the officers of the Judeans" came to Antony in Bithynia to protest that, while Hyrcanus ostensibly held sovereignty, Herod and Phasael had all the power. But Herod was held in great honor by Antony, whom he had liberally bribed (*War* 1.242; *Ant.* 14.302–304). Then when Antony came to Syria, "a hundred of the most influential Judeans" came to accuse Herod and his men. But when Hyrcanus backed Herod, who had recently arranged to marry his (grand-)daughter, Antony appointed Herod and Phasael tetrarchs (presumably under Hyrcanus as ethnarch) and entrusted to them the government of the Judeans. He also imprisoned fifteen of their opponents, intending to execute them (*War* 1.243–245; *Ant.* 14.324–326). This action only intensified agitation in Jerusalem. Knowing full well what Antony's response might be, a large embassy went to Antony at Tyre. Having already been heavily bribed by Herod and Phasael, Antony ordered the envoys punished. After they refused Herod's advice to disburse, the Romans rushed upon them with their daggers, killing and wounding many. Then when the *demos* cried out against Herod, an enraged Antony killed those whom he had taken prisoner (*War* 1.245–246; *Ant.* 14.327–329).

Even though Herod and his brother were now the actual rulers, with the facade of Hyrcanus as High Priest no longer providing much legitimacy, the Judeans continued to resist. Many flocked to Antigonus, the son of Aristobulus about to stage an invasion with the support of the Parthians. In Jerusalem an expanding number battled for control of the city. An enraged Herod turned his arms against the people (*demos*). At Pentecost large crowds from the countryside, some in arms, joined the struggle. Herod killed large numbers of the combined forces in opposition. When Herod finally recognized that he should flee with his mercenaries and family and seek fuller support from Rome, he was further harassed by the Judeans as well as the Parthians (*War* 1.250–265; *Ant.*14.334–364). While the Parthians brought Antigonus back to Judea, the Roman Senate declared that Herod should be king in greater Judea with a view to the war against the Parthians (*War* 1.282–285; *Ant.*14.384–389).

But Herod now needed to conquer the territories and subjects over which the Roman Senate had declared him to be the king. This became a prolonged process in which people were slaughtered and the land devastated, particularly in Galilee, Judea, and Jerusalem itself. Even with the massive forces he recruited and the supplementary forces the Romans provided, it took three years for Herod to finally subdue his subjects, who stubbornly resisted. He had, for example, to conduct three successive campaigns in Galilee to subdue the Galileans' persistent resistance. In his final and most crucial conquest in 37 BCE, he laid siege to Jerusalem with massive forces and the Roman general Sossius as co-commander. The account in *Antiquities* presents the struggle of the entire people (*ethnos*) of the Judeans in resistance to their subjugation by the Roman-backed Herod.[7] In addition to the wholesale massacre that took place when Herod's and the Roman armies took the city by storm, Herod took vengeance on those who had opposed his rule in a continuing purge (*War* 1.347–358; *Ant.* 14.470–486).

What Josephus does not tell in narrative sequence he does mention later following his statement that after he gained control in Jerusalem Herod displayed special favor to those who had been on his side when he was still a commoner and purged those who had opposed him (*Ant.* 15.2). He had already recounted the dramatic scene in which Samaias had courageously called for Herod's execution for murder. Now he states, curiously,

> Especially honored by him were Pollion the Pharisee and his disciple Samaias. For during the siege of Jerusalem these men had advised the citizens (*politai*) to admit Herod (into the city), and for this they received recompense (i.e., of not being punished). This same Pollion, when Herod was on trial for his life, had reproachfully told Hyrcanus and the judges that if Herod's life were spared, he would (one day) persecute them all. (*Ant.* 15.3–4)

It should be carefully noted that Josephus does *not* say that Pollion and Samaias were among those "rewarded" for having been on Herod's side

---

7. Minimizing the situation merely as "Herod arriving to assume his royal position" (Mason, *Flavius Josephus on the Pharisees*, 262) illustrates the importance of attending to the broader context in Josephus narrative in *Antiquities*.

earlier.[8] What the prophetic speech at the young Herod's trial had clearly been about was a warning to Hyrcanus and the council that Herod was hungry for power and would someday take revenge if they did not condemn him for violation of the ancestral laws in murdering the men in Galilee. Josephus is not clear about just who delivered that speech. But he does make reference to two well-known Pharisees involved in the events of Herod's rise to power. In the first, they insisted on the observance of the ancestral laws. They were dedicated to the enforcement of them even on the powerful (lest they expand their power), and they were fearless enough to push for justice even when it might cost them their lives. Both stories that Josephus knows and partially recounts, moreover, indicate the Pharisees were engaged in public affairs, at the center of the politics of the temple-state, and were "political realists." Midst an all-out struggle of the people for their freedom from tyrannical rule, they evidently knew that Herod's conquest was inevitable if he were acquitted for violation of the laws of the Judeans. And an integral component of their "accurate" knowledge (and application) of the ancestral (Mosaic covenantal) tradition (laws) was that God would exact punishment for failure to apply the laws, in this case, the failure to maintain justice in the case of Herod's murders.

Some speculation may be in order about Herod's motives in holding these two Pharisees in honor despite their opposition to him. He probably had his own version of what Pollion and Samaias were doing in advising the people to admit him to the city. As recounted in Josephus' continuing narrative, Herod retained the temple-state as a subsidiary instrument of his own rule. He needed this traditional Judean institutional form as a buffer and facade for his own rule which, as a Roman imposition by military conquest, had no legitimacy in Judean tradition. But having risen to power as an ambitious military strong-man of Idumean origin, he knew nothing about the operations of the temple-state. He surely knew of the Pharisees' reputation for accurate knowledge of the laws of the Judeans and the recent history of their role under Alexandra in keeping the temple-state functioning and avoiding continuation of the recurrent rebellion of the people under Alexander Jannaeus.

---

8. Cf. Mason, *Flavius Josephus on the Pharisees*, 262. Earlier studies of the Pharisees commonly identified Pollio with Abtalion, who with Shemaiah appears in the chain of tradition in m. Avot 1, from whom Hillel and Shammai had received torah.

The Pharisees Under Herod's Rule

The Pharisees' Role in Resistance to Herod's Violations of Traditional Judean Laws/Customs

In *Antiquities* Josephus quotes Strabo to the effect that the Judeans continued to hate Herod (perhaps even more so after his devastating conquest and purge), many remaining loyal to Antigonus. "Not even under torture would they submit to proclaiming him king" (*Ant.* 15.5–10). After Octavian defeated Antony at Actium, claiming victory in the great conflict between Roman warlords (31 BCE), Herod took the obvious course of switching his loyalty to "Caesar." He did this with skillful diplomatic maneuvering, although in the *Antiquities* (15.194–217) Josephus finds Herod's lavish gifts (bribes) to have been a bit stingy by the prevailing standards of imperial politics. He was nevertheless handsomely rewarded by (Augustus) Caesar, not only with confirmation of his kingship, but with a gift of a four-hundred man bodyguard of Gauls and the addition of more territories to his rule and economic base (Trachonitis, Batanaea, Auranitis; *War* 1.393–400). What Herod valued most was that "In Caesar's affection he stood next after (Octavian's closest "friend") Agrippa and in Agrippa's next after Caesar." This is a boastful exaggeration in retrospect; but one can easily believe that Herod quickly became Caesar's favorite client-king—because of the unsparing benefactions and honors he now lavished on Caesar himself, the imperial family, and many Greek cities of the Empire.

War presents these with blatant glorification of Herod: "He advanced to the utmost prosperity (*eudaimonia*); his noble spirit rose to greater heights, and his lofty ambition was mainly directed to works of devotion (*eusebeia*)" (*War* 1.400). He mounted a massive restoration of the temple with incalculable expenditure, "its magnificence never surpassed" (401). He restored the Jerusalem fortress in a palace-like style at a lavish cost, named after his earlier patron Antony. As his own palace he constructed two spacious and beautiful buildings that were more impressive than the temple, named for Caesar and Agrippa. He commemorated Caesar with even greater munificence with the construction of the whole new city of Sebaste (=Augustus) in Samaria with a massive temple dedicated to Caesar at its center. He built another temple to Caesar of white marble in Paneion near the headwaters of the Jordan. "In short, one can mention no suitable spot within his realm which he left destitute of some mark of homage to Caesar." Then, after filling his own territory with temples, he let the memorials of his esteem overflow into the province and erected in numerous cities monuments to Caesar" (402–407). Along the way there was the elaborately and magnificently constructed port-city of Caesarea with its temples and statues to Caesar, memorials to his relatives and fortress-palaces for himself (408–421). In addition, there were his lavish benefactions to many cities of the Empire, and his endowment of the Olympic Games (422–428).[9]

In *Antiquities*, however, Josephus presents a critical perspective and account of all such projects and accomplishments by Herod. Most of Herod's hugely expensive and massive building projects and his overly generous benefactions to Greek cities were in violation and subversion of the ancestral customs and laws of the Judeans. When his subjects objected or even dared to protest, moreover, Herod clamped down with severe measures of repression and further violation of the laws.

After Herod, in his paranoia, had killed any potential rival and any figure of royal or high priestly (Hasmonean) ancestry who might claim loyalty of traditionalists among the people (as opposed to his own common origins),

> there was no one of high rank to stand in the way of his unlawful actions. On account of this, Herod went still further in departing from the ancestral customs and through foreign practices he gradually corrupted the ancient way of life, which had hitherto been inviolable. As a result of this we suffered considerable harm at a later time as well, because those things were neglected which had formerly induced loyalty (to God, and presumably the temple-state) among the crowds (*ochloi*). (*Ant.* 15.266–267)

Josephus proceeds to reel off one foreign public institution and practice after another, some in Jerusalem itself: games in honor of Caesar, a theater and amphitheater in Jerusalem, lavish but against Judean customs. All around the theater were inscriptions concerning Caesar and trophies of the subject peoples which he had won in war, all of pure gold and silver. Particularly troublesome were gladiatorial contests, including throwing men to beasts for the entertainment of other people, and trophies with images surrounded by weapons in the amphitheater (*Ant.* 15.268–276). As Josephus "explains"

---

9. To support the extraordinary expenses of his lavish court, his extensive building projects in Palestine, his beneficence to cities of the Empire, and his lavish gifts to Caesar and the imperial family Herod did exploit his subjects in Judea and other areas as much possible without destroying this segment of his economic base. Tax collection was carried out with the usual brutal methods. But Herod also had at his disposal perhaps the majority of the most fertile land in the royal domains inherited from the Hasmoneans, which had already been royal land under the Ptolemies and Seleucids (as noted in the previous chapter). Herod also confiscated the holdings of his enemies (e.g., *Ant.* 15.5; 18.305, 307). Emilio Gabba, provides a concise sketch of "The Finances of King Herod," but underplays the economic burden laid on his Judean and other subjects.

later in his narrative, "because of the flattering attention that (Herod) gave to Caesar and the most influential Romans, he was forced to depart from the customs (of the Judeans) and to alter many of their regulations" (15.328).

Some people, convinced that the violation of the ancestral traditions would result in costly punishment thought it their sacred duty to oppose, at whatever risk, the forcible imposition of practices that would undermine their *politeia* (way of life/constitution) by Herod who had become the enemy of the whole people (*ethnos*). They were acting to defend "the communal customs" (*hoi koinoi ethoi*) that all people "have the duty either to preserve or to die for." Thus ten of the citizens (*politai*) planned to stage an assassination in the theater. But one of Herod's spies discovered the plot and they were tortured and killed. In response, the informer was identified, cut limb from limb, and thrown to the dogs. This was witnessed by many citizens, but none informed Herod's "authorities." So after having some women tortured, Herod punished entire families of those who killed the informer (15.280–290).

Recognizing the people's steadfast loyalty (*pistis*) to their laws,[10] and that such disturbances followed all of the objectionable events he staged, Herod took further steps to secure his position and launched repressive measures aimed at heading off open rebellion (*Ant.* 15.291). This was the purpose of several of his massive building projects, including his palace and the strong fortress of Antonia next to the temple. Building the city of Sebaste was a third rampart against the entire people (*laos*), in which he settled those who had fought as his allies. The new city of Caesarea was yet another fortress against (not "for") the people (*ethnos*). And in the fertile Great Plain at Gaba he established a military colony of his picked cavalrymen. He placed garrisons throughout the land against disturbances by the people when the slightest incitement was given. And he stationed spies among the people to keep them from starting trouble (15.292–298). Also, the measures he took to mitigate a famine during a severe drought to keep his economic base at least viable also bought him a modicum of good will among the multitude (*oxloi*) (299–316). As his prosperity returned, he built a more luxurious palace in the upper city and maneuvered to marry again, to the most beautiful young woman of the time, the daughter of a priest from Alexandria. To set this up he appointed her father as High Priest, after sacking the incumbent. "For he had no qualms about living for his own

---

10. In the fields of New Testament studies and ancient Jewish history in which *pistis/fides* is standardly translated as "faith" (and the verbal forms as "believe," with their modern connotations of individual religious belief), it is important to note that in the Roman world *pistis/fides* usually had the clear political sense of "loyalty," particularly to the Roman (imperial) state or a particular Roman ruler, especially the (divine) Caesar.

pleasure." And this is when he built Herodion, another luxurious fortress, to enhance his security as well as to commemorate his own reign (318–325).

In addition to these measures of security against any nascent revolt, says Josephus, Herod "kept his subjects submissive in two ways, namely by fear, since he was inexorable in punishment, and by showing himself generous when a crisis arose" (*Ant.* 15.326). He remitted a third of the taxes (in 20 BCE) under the pretext of letting the people recover from a period of insufficient crops, but really in order to get back their goodwill. For they resented his actions that "seemed to them to mean the dissolution of their devotion to God (*eusebeia*) and the disappearance of their customs. And these matters were discussed by all of them, for they were always being provoked and disturbed" (15.365). Herod, however, imposed repressive measures to take away any opportunity for agitation.

This is the context for Josephus's next reference to the Pharisees:

> Neither any meeting of those in the city (*synodos tois pros peri ten polin*) was permitted nor any association by walking or being together (*koinonia*), and all their movements were observed. Those caught were punished severely, and many were taken, either openly or secretly, to the fortress of Hyrcania and there put to death. Both in the city and on the open roads there were men who spied on those who met together. Those who obstinately refused to go along with his practices he persecuted in all kinds of ways. As for the rest of the populace, he demanded that they submit to taking an oath of loyalty (*pistis*), and he compelled them to make a sworn declaration that they would maintain a favorable attitude to his rule. Now most of the people yielded to his demand out of complaisance or fear, but those who showed some spirit and objected to compulsion he got rid of by every possible means. He also tried to persuade Pollion the Pharisee and Samaias and most of their associates to take the oath, but they would not agree, yet they were not punished as were the others who refused, for they were shown consideration on Pollion's account. (*Ant.* 15.366–370)

Josephus here mentions a larger group of Pharisees associated with Pollion and Samaias, and the Pharisees in general, who clearly opposed Herod's rule. It is important to discern what Josephus' account here does *not* say and what it does say. First, it should be noted that insofar as loyalty oaths are coercive measures, Herod's imposition would only have checked overt disloyalty but would not have "ensured the loyalty" of his subjects,[11] so

---

11. Cf. Mason, *Flavius Josephus on the Pharisees*, 263. On the basis of a wide range of particular cases, it can safely be said that loyalty oaths do not ensure loyalty of peoples

that only the Pharisees and certain other intransigent people still opposed his rule. His narrative in *Antiquities* has portrayed the city-people (*demos*, etc.) generally as resentful and disloyal from the beginning of Herod's rise and throughout his rule, particularly as he systematically undermined their ancestral *politeia* and laws. The repressive measures were aimed at preventing agitation by the people. Second, Josephus does not say that the Pharisees had acquired a position of influence with Herod.[12] It was speculated above that Herod may have found it useful in his rule to retain them as advisers in the temple-state. But it would be virtually impossible to find any suggestion in Josephus' long narrative of Herod's rule in *Antiquities* that they somehow acquired a position of influence on him. Third, Josephus does not suggest here that Herod favored the Pharisees.[13] He says only that Herod did not punish them and that this was because he (still) honored Pollion and/or Samaias, that is, ostensibly for having advised the people of Jerusalem to admit him to the city (as in *Ant.* 14.175–176 and 15.3–4).

Judging from this account of Herod's requirement of a loyalty oath understood in broader narrative (and likely historical) context, the Pharisees continued in their opposition to Herod's rule. They were not unusual among the Judeans, however, in their opposition. Judging from the narrative context, the overwhelming reason for the opposition to Herod was his abuse and subversion of the ancestral way of life (laws/customs/constitution) of the Judeans. Like Samaias (or was it Pollion? or both?) in the council decades earlier, they had the courage to resist despite Herod's efforts to intimidate, which were now much more intense and systematic. Nor were they alone in having this commitment to defending the traditional laws and customs, for others did also, and paid the price.

Again we may speculate on the various reasons Herod may have had, besides his ostensibly still honoring Pollion, for not punishing the Pharisees. But the immediately following account of why the Essenes were also excused from the loyalty oath is suggestive (*Ant.* 15.371–379). Josephus explains this as due to the prediction by

> a certain man of the Essenes named Menahem, whose virtue was attested in his whole conduct of life and especially in his having from God a foreknowledge of things to come. This man had (once) observed Herod, then still a boy, going to his teacher, and greeted him as "king of the Judeans." Herod, who thought that the man either did not know who he was or was teasing

---

to their rulers.

12. Cf. Mason, *Flavius Josephus on the Pharisees*, 263.
13. Cf. Mason, *Flavius Josephus on the Pharisees*, 263.

him, reminded him that he was only a commoner (*idiotes*). Menahem, however, gently smiled and slapped him on the backside, saying, "Nevertheless, you will be king, and you will rule the realm happily, for you have been found worthy of this by God. And you shall remember the blows given by Menahem, so that they, too, may be for you a symbol of how one's fortune can change. For the best attitude for you to take would be to love justice (*dikaiosune*) and devotion toward God (*eusebeia*) and mildness toward your citizens.[14] But I know that you will not be such a person, since I understand the whole situation. You will be singled out for such good fortune as no other man has had, and you will enjoy eternal glory, but you will forget devotion (to God) and justice. This, however, cannot escape the notice of God and, at the close of your life, His wrath will show that He is mindful of these things." (*Ant.* 15.373-376)

Later when Herod came to power as king, he sent for Menahem, seeking his further prediction of just how long he would remain in power, a concern typical of rulers. Josephus adds that "from that time on he continued to hold all Essenes in honor, explaining further that many such men have been deemed worthy of knowledge of divine things because of their virtue (378-379). Because Josephus' accounts of the Essenes as one of the "philosophies of the Judeans" and their apparent similarities with the Qumran community evident in the Dead Sea Scrolls we tend to think of the Essenes/Qumranites as withdrawn, not just from the Jerusalem temple-state but from political affairs generally. But in the cases of the Essene seers Menahem and the earlier Judas and the later Simon (*Ant.* 13.331; 17.346-347), they were making predictions about events that drew the attention of the rulers and the people. In his earlier account of Judas, an Essene seer who had never been known to speak falsely in his predictions, he was giving instruction in foretelling things to come in or in front of the temple.

These stories of Pollion (and/or Samaias) the Pharisee and Menahem the Essene have parallel predictions. On the one hand, Herod would become king. On the other hand, he had already flouted or would violate and undermine the ancestral laws of the Judeans (focused on loyalty to God and justice in the society, that is, the Mosaic covenantal laws and customs). Herod might well have been angry at their indictment of his rule. But typical of powerful ancient rulers, he valued their ability of prediction. He would again resort to seers to address his insecurities, as will be discussed later. Also like other ancient rulers, perhaps especially those like Herod with little

---

14. Note the standard Josephan language for the ancestral *politeia* and laws of the Judeans.

legitimacy of their own, he knew that he needed those deeply trained in Judean (scribal) tradition and experienced in the affairs of the temple, that is, principally the Pharisees, for the operation of the state.

Implications of Herod's Massive Rebuilding of the Temple

It is at this point in Antiquities that Josephus recounts Herod's massive rebuilding of the temple in Jerusalem. As Josephus says, Herod believed that this would be his most notable achievement and would assure his eternal remembrance. And indeed Herod's temple became one of the wonders of the Roman imperial world. As noted above, Herod had made the temple and high priesthood into instruments of his rule. His massive rebuilding of the temple, moreover, also dramatically transformed its function. The temple had started as the political-economic-religious center of collective life in the tiny area of Judea, subject to a succession of imperial regimes. It was then transformed to the institutional basis in Judea of the Hasmoneans as rulers of the Samaritans, Idumeans, Galileans, and other areas and cities in Palestine. Herod more dramatically transformed it into the symbolic political-economic center of world-wide Jewry, which became a sub-set of the Roman imperial order.[15]

Prior to the Hellenizing reform in the early second-century BCE the relatively small city of Jerusalem was dominated by the temple, the high priestly aristocracy being the ruling political-economic-religious elite (subject to and gathering revenue for the imperial regime). As the Hasmonean high priests/kings, now effectively free of imperial control, established their own mini-empire by military conquests, they expanded the city onto the Western hill. There the Hasmoneans built their palace and surrounded the expanded city with defensive walls. They also built a large fortress at the northwest corner of the temple. These developments changed Jerusalem into a city with two (or perhaps we should say three) foci: the expanding city dominated by the royal/high priestly palace on the Western Hill and the temple to the East, which was not integrated into the life of the city but separated by the massive Tyropean Valley in between. The Hasmoneans were the ruling political-economic-religious elite of both city and temple. Visually, architecturally, and politically the Baris fortress was a third institution that dominated the temple. Under Herod this bi- or tri-focal city was expanded further, and his massive reconstruction of the temple enhanced its spectacular appearance and function, while not integrating it any further into the life

---

15. Gabba, "The Finances of King Herod," 166, among others, comments on Herod's political aims in massively rebuilding the temple.

of the city. The expanded high priestly aristocracy held semi-independent authority over temple operations, while building their mansions in the Upper City opposite the temple, while Herod and his court ruled the city and, indirectly, the temple. At the time of Ben Sira, the temple-state dominated the economy of Judea. With the Hasmoneans' extension of the territories they ruled, they dominated the economy, although the temple remained central in certain ways. Under Herod, with his massive building programs and munificence to the imperial family and beneficence to many Hellenistic cities, the temple remained central to the economy of Judea proper while a subordinate factor to the Herodian economy.[16]

Herod's massive rebuilding of the temple was related to his (earlier) expansion of the high priestly aristocracy that included appointing figures of high priestly lineage from the Babylonian and Egyptian diaspora communities. Josephus mentions unrelated reasons for Herod's appointment of particular figures, his own creatures who would be beholden to him. Early in his reign he moved to get rid of remaining Hasmonean descendants. Before and again after appointing the youthful and handsome Hasmonean Aristobulus as High Priest (who drowned "accidentally,") Herod appointed Hananel (37 and again in 35–30 BCE) from a high priestly family in Babylon (*Ant.* 15.22–56). Because he desired marriage with the beautiful daughter of Simon son of Boethus from Alexandria he appointed Simon (25–24 BCE; *Ant.* 15.320). He thus forged closer ties between the priestly elite of both the large Babylonian and the Alexandrian diaspora communities and the Jerusalem temple and its high priestly aristocracy. Thereafter, and continuing into the first century CE, the high priestly aristocracy was expanded to four (large) families, from which Herod and later the Roman governors made appointments to the high priesthood. The high priestly families were thus interconnected with the priestly elite of the diaspora but as remote as the Hasmoneans had been from the people of Jerusalem and Judean (and Galilean) villagers.

The rebuilt temple itself was an impressive engineering feat and architecturally impressive in the extreme, its immense size accented by the elevation of its base and especially its three-columned, Roman-style colonnade on the south. It became a tourist attraction for people who could afford to travel, particularly for diaspora Judeans living in cities of the eastern Empire, but also from Mesopotamia. One of Augustus' favorite client kings, Herod was a major player in imperial politics. The rebuilt temple considerably enhanced Herod's fame in the Empire. Herod knew what he was doing.

---

16. On the vast sums that were built up in the temple treasury, despite Herod's rebuilding's drainage on its resources, see the discussion in Vol. 2, chap. 2.

It is no coincidence that the cities of the eastern Empire on which Herod lavished beneficence, gifts of buildings and colonnades, also had substantial diaspora Judean communities.[17]

The expanding influx of diaspora Judeans making pilgrimage to Jerusalem and Herod's temple in the last decades of his rule and on into the first century CE can be seen in the opening narrative of the book of Acts. Some, perhaps many devout diaspora Judeans who had come from around the Empire and beyond and were living in Jerusalem joined the earliest Jesus movement: The list includes Judeans from Parthia, Medea, Elam, and Mesopotamia; from Cappadocia, Pontus, and Asia; from Phrygia and Pamphylia; from Egypt and Cyrene; from Crete and Arabia; and from Rome itself (Acts 2:5–11). These diaspora Judeans had evidently come to the Jerusalem temple as pilgrims and then remained living in the city. In his massive rebuilding of the temple in Jerusalem, Herod posed as the patron of world-wide Jewry and symbolically integrated diaspora Judeans living in the Empire into the Roman imperial world, as a subset of the overall empire.

If we then attend to Josephus' description of the architectural structure of Herod's temple in comparison with available evidence for the pre-Herod (Hasmonean) temple it is evident that Herod had dramatically transformed the temple's function. Prior to Herod's rebuilding of the temple it had basically two courts, one in which all purified Judeans (Israelites) could assemble, the other for priests only, who would then officiate at the altar of the inner sanctuary. According to Josephus' first-hand descriptions (*Ant.* 15.380–419; *War* 5.184–247) Herod's temple had three courtyards. The innermost structure, narrow but of great height, contained the holy of holies (which only the High Priest entered once a year) and the holy place/chamber (*naos*) approached by steps on a wider porch, accessible only to priests. Surrounding the holy place was the court of the priests, containing places for the slaughter of sacrificial animals and the altar on which offerings were placed. Just beyond the court of the priests was the court of (purified) Israelite men (where they could hand their offerings to the priests). Beyond the court of Israelite men was a more spacious courtyard open to all Judeans/Israelites, the "court of the women." This was an innovation in Herod's temple. Surrounding this court where all purified Judeans could gather was a barrier, a balustrade with warning messages that non-Judeans/Israelites dare not enter. Beyond the barricade was the extremely spacious outer "court of the Gentiles" in which any and all could enter. And here

---

17. A point made by Gabba, "The Finances of King Herod," 164 and 166, among others.

is Herod's more significant innovation.[18] Herod's temple allowed diaspora Judeans who had not been purified and Gentiles to enter the temple court inside the perimeter colonnades, where they could observe what was happening inside the barrier.[19]

The court of the Gentiles was thus hardly exclusionary, but the opposite. The major innovation of Herod's temple, aside from its remarkably bold size, domineering colonnades, and other architectural features, was the inclusion of diaspora Judeans of questionable purity and of foreigners inside the perimeter enclosures.

We must wonder what the Pharisees' attitude was to this innovation. I am arguing that their commitment, their agenda through thick and thin of their service, or exclusion, under Hasmoneans and then Herod, was attempting to guide the operations of the temple-state according to the traditional covenantal "constitution," with some mitigation of the worst abuses by their rulers and a modicum of justice for the people. As Josephus reports, they refused an oath of allegiance to Herod or to Herod and Caesar. But as political realists they recognized that active resistance to Herod and the Romans would have been futile, and evidently adjusted to compromising the covenantal "constitution" by which the temple-state was supposed to rule the people. Herod's temple open to all comers may have been just one more feature of Herod's rule to which they adjusted. We can speculate that the Pharisees would have been involved in the increasing concern of the temple and priesthood to maintain the ritual purity of the priests who served in the temple and of the Judeans who entered the court of the Israelites to bring their offerings and sacrifices to the priests who served at the altar. We can imagine that Herod's rebuilt temple with its court of the Gentiles allowed inside the perimeter colonnades and walls would have raised concerns to protect the sanctity of the temple services in devotion to the Most High.[20]

---

18. Might Herod have consulted an assembly or court for his innovations? Later evidence from the Mishnah suggests as much: m. Sanhedrin 1:5 and m. Shebu'ot 2:2 refer to additions to the courts of the temple or additions to the space of temple courts requiring decision by the court of seventy-one or by the king, a prophet, urim and thummim, and a Sanhedrin of twenty-one.

19. The description of the ideal future Temple Scroll (11QT), which was probably composed before Herod's reign (Wise, *Critical Study of Temple Scroll*), portrays an arrangement of three courtyards, the outer third of which is a huge space for "daughters" and "strangers" (proselytes?). But this is outside the temple walls, not inside the porticoes and walls, as in Herod's temple.

20. See, for example, Josephus inclusion of restrictions about presence and participation in his long description of Herod's temple, *War* 5.227–229.

The Pharisees and Herod's Domestic Troubles

While the majority of Josephus' narrative about Herod in *War* is devoted to his domestic troubles, which are all blamed on Fortune/Fate (1.431–646), much of the account in *Antiquities* as well is devoted to them. Herod became increasingly suspicious about perceived threats to his autocratic rule from his nine wives and many children and their spouses, many of whom he ordered killed. For much of his reign his son Antipater was able to manipulate his father and situations that arose toward his own advancement as the successor. His manipulations came to a climax as his aging father declined and management of affairs fell increasingly to him. He had been cultivating Herod's brother Pheroras and enmeshed him with a circle of women at court, comprised of Pheroras' wife and her mother and sister, who seemed to be hostile to the king, as reported to Herod by his sister. It is not surprising to find the Pharisees had become active in and around the royal court, since that is where the power was, Herod often naming new occupants of the high priesthood of the temple-state according to his own perceived advantage and desire. And not surprisingly the Pharisees were implicated in a series of events at court.

> There was a group (*morion*) of Judean men that prided itself greatly on its extremely precise adherence to the ancestral heritage, claiming [to observe] laws with which the deity is pleased; by them the female faction [at court] was directed. Called Pharisees, these men were entirely capable of issuing predictions for the king's benefit, and yet, evidently, they rose up to combat and injure [him]. At least when the whole Judean people affirmed by an oath that it would be loyal to Caesar and the king's rule, these men, over six thousand in number, refused to take this oath, and when the king punished them with a fine, Pheroras' wife paid the fine for them." (*Ant.* 17.41–42)[21]

> In return for her friendliness they foretold—for they were believed to have foreknowledge of things through God's appearance to them—that by God's decree Herod's rule would be taken from him, both from himself and his descendants, and the kingdom would fall to her and Pheroras and to any children that they might have . . . The king put to death those of the Pharisees who were most responsible and the eunuch Bagoas and a certain Karos, who was outstanding among his contemporaries for his surpassing beauty and was a darling of the king. He also killed

21. Translation of the first sentence of this uncertain text adapted from Mason, *Flavius Josephus on the Pharisees*, 263, with discussion of terms, 264–67.

all those of his household who approved of what the Pharisee said. (*Ant.* 17.43–45; cf. *War* 1.571)

Josephus seems to be introducing the Pharisees to the audience again—"There was a group of Judean men ... called Pharisees"—but his identification of them is familiar: "priding themselves on accurate adherence to the ancestral tradition and claiming to observe the laws by which the deity is pleased."[22] The number of the Pharisees Josephus gives here, six thousand, is an exaggeration as usual. It seems historically more imaginable that there would have been six-hundred at most and probably fewer. The territory controlled by the temple-state and then Herod had been expanded considerably. But Josephus gives no indication that the Pharisees were ever delegated to deal with affairs in the conquered or annexed areas, which might have required an expansion of their number. Their base was in the capital temple-city where they served as advisers in the temple-state and sought influence in the royal court.

This oath of loyalty is evidently a different one from the oath the Pharisees refused earlier. Occurring at different points in Josephus' narrative, the oaths were separated by many years in Herod's reign. The circumstances and the results of the incidents recounted were different. The second oath included loyalty to Caesar as well as to that of Herod. This oath would have been all the more objectionable to the Pharisees and any Judeans concerned with observance of the ancestral laws. Indeed, the first two covenantal commandments required exclusive loyalty to God, including no "bowing down" to another "master and lord" such as Caesar, whom Herod as well as cities throughout the Empire had been honoring as divine in temples, shrines, and statues. The insistence on exclusive loyalty to God as their ruler, to the exclusion of loyalty to other (esp. human) rulers, by Pharisees and other scribal circles is about to be illustrated in both of Josephus' narratives of

---

22. Of all the passages on the Pharisees in Josephus' histories, this one is most commonly deemed to be from a source, most likely Nicolaus of Damascus, Herod's court historian. See, for example, D. R. Schwartz, "Josephus and Nicolaus on the Pharisees," 10; A. I. Baumgarten, "Rivkin and Neusner," 119 ("a nasty piece of anti-Pharisaic propaganda ... probably from ... Nicolaus of Damascus"); "The Name of the Pharisees," 414–15. Mason devotes six pages to detailed counterarguments, 274–80. It should also be noted that in his "Context" section on *Ant.* 17.41–45, Mason includes several twists and inaccuracies in reading Josephus' accounts. For example, as noted above, he considerably softens Herod 's and Socius' siege of Jerusalem as "when Herod arrives to assume his royal position" (*Flavius Josephus on the Pharisees*, 262) and exaggerates Samaias' "advising" (*parenese*) to "exhorting" the *demos* to admit Herod to the city. Josephus' extensive coverage of the people's intense resistance to having Herod as their ruler in *Antiquities* books 14–17 should be included in consideration of the literary context of the Pharisees' stance toward Herod's rule in the *Antiquities*.

other scribal teachers and their students cutting down the golden Roman eagle Herod had erected over the gate of the temple. And it will be illustrated again in his account of the Fourth Philosophy.

The Pharisees' refusal of the loyalty oaths suggest that they were engaged in carefully calculated resistance to Herod. Their refusal was evidently integral to their resistance to what Josephus indicates was Herod's close collaboration with the Romans as their client ruler, implementing the Roman imperial order in Judea and the rest of his realm. The Pharisees' resistance to Herod's rule is only what we would expect from a group that had a reputation for and/or took pride in accurate observance of the ancestral laws centered on loyalty to God and social-economic justice for and among the Judean people. In the long preceding narrative in *Antiquities* Josephus has recounted the many actions and projects of Herod that were opposed by the Jerusalem people generally because they went against the ancestral customs and constituted changes in their ancestral *politeia* (way of life/constitution). The narrative does not suggest, however, that the opposition by the people was influenced by the Pharisees. Given Herod's repressive measures against opposition and cruel treatment of those who resisted, most of the populace would have complied with his demand of the oaths. Some others, in addition to the Pharisees, did refuse, and suffered the consequences.

In this sequence of events, in contrast with the Pharisees' first refusal of an oath of loyalty, Herod did not refrain from punishing them.[23] Initially the punishment was only a fine, which Pheroras' wife paid for them. When he learned of their prophecy against his kingdom, ostensibly involving court intrigue, however, Herod took more severe action, killing the Pharisees involved and anyone who approved of what they said. In any case, since the Pharisees had consistently opposed Herod's rule, it is highly credible that they were involved in court intrigue as a route to effective opposition, given the "police state" he had by then set up. In critically evaluating this account, it is important to remember that Josephus cannot be trusted not to have invented or embellished a story that portrayed the Pharisees in a bad light as scheming behind the scenes against Herod, particularly with juicy tidbits that made Herod and ambitious members of the extended royal family also look bad. Nevertheless, given contemporary parallels of "prophetic" predictions, including Josephus' claims about his own precocious gifts,[24] this account has considerable credibility.

---

23. This suggests that Pheroras' wife had a serious interest in the Pharisees' views or role in the temple-state and/or Herod's administration. See the suggestive article of Tal Ilan, "Pheroras' Wife: A Pharisee Woman."

24. Discussed by in Blenkinsopp, "Prophecy and Priesthood in Josephus"; and van Unnik, *Flavius Josephus als historischer Schriftsteller*, esp. 42–54; and Mason, *Flavius*

In the story that Josephus recounts here the Pharisees, drawing on their knowledge of the future, are delivering prophecies in opposition to Herod in the inner circle of court intrigue. He mentions that "they were believed to have foreknowledge through manifestations by God." It is not clear whether this comes through visions, as in the stories in Dan 7, 8, and 10-11 and the Animal Vision in 1 Enoch 85-90, or through hearing "the word of God," as in the prophecies of Isaiah or Jeremiah. The subject of the prophecy, that "by the decree of God" the rule of a king and his dynasty would be terminated and the kingdom pass to others, was central for prophets, from Ahijah and Elijah and Micaiah ben Imlah to Jeremiah. A related prophecy mentioned in Josephus' account (*Ant.* 17.45) evidently foretold one "who would be appointed (from) above with the title of king" whose powers would include special rewards for a eunuch. The passive participle "be appointed (from) above" (*epikatastathesomenos*) indicates this king would be designated by God. The powers this king would have suggests a familiarity with a prophecy that we know as a late inclusion in the book of Isaiah (at Isa 56:1-5), calling on people to "maintain justice" and promising God's deliverance that would include that "eunuchs who keep [God's] covenant . . ." would be given "a name better than sons and daughters."

Much more than Samaias' prediction about what Herod would do to the council members and the High Priest Hyrcanus, these prophecies make these Pharisees sound like the successors of the learned scribes who had undergone training for service (of the high priestly councils and rulers) in the temple-state, as portrayed by Ben Sira (see again chap. 2). They were trained not only in the adherence to and application of the ancestral laws/torah of the Most High but also in knowledge of the prophecies of the Judean scribal repertoire. What is implicit in this story about the Pharisees Josephus makes explicit toward the end of his principal account of the Essenes (*War* 2.120-161): "there are some among them who claim foreknowledge of things to come, being versed from their early years in sacred books and various forms of purifications and the sayings of the prophets." On the basis of his priestly lineage, Josephus claims just such powers of prediction for himself that is also rooted in his knowledge of the earlier prophets, although his own prediction focuses more on divination and the application of dreams (*War* 3.350-354).

The prophecies of the Pharisees thus seem more like prophecies of the "classical" prophets of the eighth-seventh centuries rather than the predictions by contemporary "seers" (including *manteis*) such as the Essenes Judas and Simon and Josephus himself. Seers' divination and application

---

Josephus on the Pharisees, 267-71.

of dreams or earlier prophecies were of great importance to rulers such as Herod (and probably Vespasian). After his dream about ten thick ears of grain being eaten by oxen Archelaus, Herod's son and successor as ruler of Judea, sent for the *manteis* skilled in application of dreams, who could not agree. Then the Essene Simon, who by then knew he needed to ask for a guarantee of safety, predicted that the dream portended a foreboding change in Archelaus' situation (*Ant.* 17.345–348). The prophecies of the Pharisees, or Josephus' portrayal of them, seem grounded in knowledge of the earlier prophets in form, content, and motifs. Such knowledge was integral to scribal training, as known from Ben Sira.

If the story included the prediction that the kingdom would fall to Pheroras and his wife as Josephus presents it has any veracity, then the Pharisees appear to have been pandering to Pheroras' wife in return for her favor and payment of their fine. The second prophecy cannot be dismissed as simply a far-fetched creation by Herod's jealous sister Salome, who was embellishing reports of the court intrigue she passed on to her brother, insofar as Herod executed Bagoas, one of his court eunuchs who had been "carried away" by the prophecy. And the Pharisees most responsible presumably for the court intrigue as well as the prophecies were executed, along with those who approved and Herod's darling lover Karos. Yet although Josephus says that Herod executed those "who were most to blame," he does not give any indication that the rest suddenly fled into exile, as had several thousand opponents of Alexander Jannaeus, sensing that they too were now in danger.

As for the prophecies themselves, by Josephus' measure they probably seemed "false." For the Pharisees, however, if informed by "classical" prophecies in Judean tradition, prophecy may have been more a matter of God's justice than of predictions that proved true or false. Like many of the populace of Jerusalem they had been opposed to Herod's rule from the outset in the context of his systemic violation and undermining of the ancestral Judean way of life and laws. Now they were resorting to court intrigue to get at him. The intrigue happened in the context of the insecure Herod's cruel execution of one son after another, so that he was gradually himself eliminating the possibility of founding a dynasty. The Pharisees could have discerned that Herod was serving as the instrument of his own divine punishment. They would presumably also have been convinced, like the Essene seer Menahem, that God would someday deliver judgment on Herod himself. This was soon imminent in his increasingly painful and excruciating multiple illnesses toward the end of his reign.

These accounts of the delicately balanced conflictual relations between the Pharisees and Herod indicate clearly that the Pharisees had not withdrawn from politics at all under Herod, as some scholars supposed in recent decades. The Pharisees, or at least particular ones who were in prominent positions as members of or advisers to the high priestly council, opposed him from the start for his audacious violation of the ancestral laws of the Judeans. As can be discerned from Josephus' accounts, they insisted that the council and Hyrcanus convict and execute him for murder, and in their political realism warned that the brash and ambitious young Herod would become their tyrannical ruler. After the Romans had designated him as king of the Judeans and, with the aid of Roman legions, Herod was besieging Jerusalem, the Pharisees Pollion and Samaias, in their political realism, advised the people to admit him to the city. According to Josephus, Herod later excused the Pharisees from taking his loyalty oath because Pollion had given this advice. They, however, continued to oppose him while struggling for influence on his regime, including by infiltrating the royal court. Their principal concern and reputation evidently continued to be cultivation, practice, and application of the ancestral laws. But prophecies were also included in their repertoire as they attempted to influence the internal politics of the Herodian regime as well as the temple-state that he was using as an instrument of his rule.

We may suspect that Herod had other reasons for exempting them from the repressive measures he imposed to keep the populace in check. It seems that the Pharisees were important in the functioning of the temple-state that Herod needed as a buffer between his regime as a Roman client king and favorite of Caesar and the Judean populace still committed to the traditional Judean "way of life." Such a hypothesis would fit Herod's toleration of the Pharisees' opposition politics as well as Alexander Jannaeus' recommendation to his queen that allowing the Pharisees to exercise some authority in the functions of the temple-state was necessary for the continuing rule of the Hasmonean dynasty to which the Judean people had by and large become opposed.

Demonstration against Herod's and Roman Rule by Other Scribal Teachers-and-Students

Not long after the Pharisees and others became involved in the prophecies against him, Herod's illnesses became steadily worse. This is the point at which Josephus narrates, in both historical accounts, a major protest against Herod's blatant violations of the ancestral traditions by yet another group of scribal teachers and their disciples: the cutting down of the golden Roman eagle from above the great gate of the temple.

In the city there were two scholar-teachers (*sophistai*) especially recognized for accurate knowledge of the ancestral traditions (*malista dokountes akribouv ta patria*) who thus had the highest esteem of the whole people (*ethnei*), Judas son of Sepphoraeus and Matthias son of Margalus. Many youth attended their expositions (expoundings) of the laws and day after day they drew together quite an army of men in their prime . . . Hearing (that the king was dying) these scholar-teachers (suggested) it was a fitting time to pull down the structures that the king had erected in defiance of the ancestral laws (*para tous patrious nomous*), . . . (in particular) the golden eagle that the king had erected over the great gate (of the temple) . . . telling them . . . it (would be) a noble deed to die for the ancestral law (*huper tou patriou nomou*) . . . At midday, when numbers of people were perambulating the temple, (the young men) let themselves down from the roof by stout cords and began chopping off the golden eagle. . . . (After) the king's (military) officer, with a large force, . . . arrested about forty of the young men and brought them to the king, . . . he asked them "Who ordered you to do (this)?" "The ancestral law!" (they replied). (*War* 1.648–650)

Having given up hope of recovering, [Herod] became quite savage . . . , believing that . . . the people (*to ethnos*) took pleasure in his misfortunes, especially when certain men who were favorites among the city-people (*demotikoteron*) rose up against him. Judas son of Sariphaeus and Matthias son of Margalothus were the most learned of the Judeans and unrivalled expounders of the ancestral laws (*exegetai ton patrion nomon*), men especially dear to the people because they trained the youth . . . They told the youth that they should pull down all the works built by the king in violation of the ancestral law (*para ton nomon ton patrion*) and thus obtain from the laws the reward of their efforts of loyalty to God (*eusebeia*). Indeed it was because of his audacity in making these things in disregard of the law, they said, that all the misfortunes had happened to him, in particular his illness. For Herod had set about doing certain things that were contrary to the law and for these Judas and Matthias and their followers had reproached him . . . For the king had erected over the great gate of the temple, at great cost, . . . a great golden eagle, although the law forbids (this) . . . So the scholar-teachers (*sophistai*) ordered that the eagle be cut down (saying that those who court danger for a noble cause would win fame and glory. . . .). When a rumor reached them that the king had died, . . . the youth went up and pulled down the eagle and cut it up before the many people who were gathered in the temple. The (military) officer of the king, ... with a large force ... fell upon the crowd (*ochlos*), ... seized forty of the young men, who had courageously awaited his attack while the rest of the people fled, and also captured Judas and Matthias ... When they (were brought to) the king ... they declared that "we have come to the aid of a cause entrusted to us by God because he thought us worthy, and of deep concern to us who obey the law . . . It is of less importance to observe your decrees than the laws that Moses wrote as God prompted and taught him, and left behind. And with pleasure we will endure death ... because of our loyalty (or devotion) to God. (*Ant.* 17.148–160)

In *War* Josephus introduces these two teachers in exactly the same terms he uses several times as his principal characterization of the Pharisees, as recognized for accuracy in the laws. In *Antiquities* he introduces them similarly as unrivalled expounders of the ancestral laws. Yet this does not justify the conclusion that he is suggesting that they were Pharisees. Josephus' accounts present Judas and Matthias as prominent teachers and respected expounders of the ancestral laws, learned scribes/sages who were not Pharisees. He emphasizes that they played a prominent role in the training of young men, although Josephus may be exaggerating in his scene of large numbers of youth attending daily sessions in which they expounded the laws in public. From Josephus' accounts, they clearly had a faithful following of students who were committed to the ancestral laws and *politeia*. They thus appear to have been learned scribes/sages, thoroughly knowledgeable in the torah (and other Judean traditions), who also functioned in the training of proteges, scribes-in-training, as in Ben Sira's portrayal of scribes/sages.[25] Some such learned scribes served as representatives of the temple-state, and a few occupied high-ranking positions alongside priestly aristocrats, as represented in the Gospels' narratives of events in Jerusalem. Others had become dissidents, similar to the "Enoch" scribes before them, criticizing and even opposing the rulers, in this case Herod. And their students were personally devoted to their teachers who, for them, embodied the torah they were teaching, as finally exemplified in their leadership in this bold action.

According to Josephus' longer account in *Antiquities*, Judas and Matthias and their circle had previously criticized Herod for his actions contrary to the law (*Ant.* 17.151). Emboldened by reports of the Herod's

---

25. While Josephus' accounts do not mention the Pharisees' role in the training of proteges, this is implied in their deep regard for the tradition of their ancestors and in their accurate knowledge and application of the laws.

declining health, the scholars suggested to their students that this was the opportune time to "pull down all the works built by the king in violation of the ancestral law" (150). The golden Roman eagle Herod had erected was a prime example of the many imperial symbols he had displayed in public places, keeping the people constantly aware of their subjugation to Rome. Its position over the great gate of the temple would have been particularly outrageous to the priests, learned scribes, and the people of Jerusalem. This symbol of Roman domination was precisely what the laws against images in application of the second commandment prohibited.

The scholars' students could not have been bolder or more flagrant in carrying out their symbolic demonstration of opposition to Roman imperial rule as well as defiance of Herod. The great gate was a prominent location in the massive new temple-complex that Herod was constructing. Contrary to what Josephus suggests in *Antiquities,* the operation clearly involved considerable organization and discipline on the part of the large number of demonstrators involved, given Herod's usually tight security measures. When the king's officer hastened to the scene with military force, the student demonstrators, along with their teachers, calmly awaited capture while the crowd fled (*Ant.* 17.157).

Josephus' portrayals of the confrontation between the furious king and the scholars and their students resembles encounters between martyrs and the tyrants who are torturing and killing them in martyrological stories of previous generations of Judeans, such as 2 Macc 7.[26] Josephus' accounts locate Judas and Matthias and their students in this tradition of being ready to die for persisting in their commitment to the ancestral laws. Of course, we cannot know the extent to which Josephus' accounts reflect their motives. But like other Hellenistic historians Josephus was constructing speeches that would offer the gist of what historical figures would have said in a certain situation. Some of Josephus' phrases, on the other hand, such as "winning eternal fame and glory" and "death for a noble cause" (17.152–154), are adaptation of Hellenistic ideals.

Judas and Matthias, however, may be moving a significant step beyond the motive of resistance articulated in earlier Judean texts. Assessment of this possibility, of course, depends on both how much stock we put in Josephus' accounts and on whether, in extant texts, we possess an adequate articulation of the motives of other circles of learned scribes.[27] According to Josephus Judas and Matthias say, "we have come to the aid of a cause

26. Nickelsburg, *Resurrection, Immortality, and Eternal Life,* 42; further discussion in Horsley, *Revolt of the Scribes,* 181.

27. See the discussion of other, earlier dissident scribal circles who opposed and/or resisted imperial and/or high priestly rule in Horsley, *Revolt of the Scribes.*

entrusted to us by God . . . and of deep concern to us who obey the law" (*Ant.* 17.158-159). They would appear to be taking action out of a sense of having been commissioned by God. Their action itself was not simply a persistence in obeying the ancestral laws in the face of repressive action but taking deliberate organized action against Herod's imposition of the intolerable Roman imperial order of life onto the Judean people.

The now bed-ridden Herod had them bound and sent to Jericho, where he summoned the (presumably high priestly) officers of the Judeans to assemble in the amphitheater. He recounted how he had rebuilt the temple and adorned it with dedicatory offerings and hoped to have left a great memorial of himself; then he began shouting about how the scholars and their students had horribly insulted him in cutting down the Roman eagle (17.161-163). The assembled officers insisted that this had been done without their consent and called for punishment. Herod took the occasion, however, to depose the High Priest Matthias as partly to blame and appointed his wife's brother Joazar. Then he had the scholars and their disciples burned alive. "On that same night there was an eclipse of the moon" (164-167). Clearly Josephus mentions this as a bad omen and proceeds to explain that Herod's worsening illness was God's just punishment for his lawless actions. "It was said by the men of God (*hoi theiazontoi*) and those with special wisdom on such matters[28] that all this was the penalty that God was exacting of the king for his great 'impiety'" (disloyalty to God; 170-171).

According to Josephus' accounts, Herod knew how ardently the Judeans prayed for his death, because they had been eager to revolt and to show their contempt for his projects. So he devised a plan to ensure that there would nevertheless be mourning at his death. The most notable Judeans from the whole people (*ethnos*) were to be shut up in the hippodrome. At his death the soldiers posted around them who would remain unaware were to be ordered to kill them. He also gave orders to do away with one member of each household of the people, although they had done nothing wrong. This would give him the satisfaction that at his death there would be widespread mourning (17.174-181). Josephus concludes, in his account of Herod in *Antiquities*, that although he was greatly favored by fortune (*tyche*), "he was cruel to all alike and was contemptuous of justice (17.191).

While we cannot know if the scholars hoped to provoke a more general resistance to Herod's rule with their bold destruction of the Roman eagle, this was the effect of their defiance of Herod and their ensuing martyrdom, When Herod finally died shortly afterward (in 4 BCE), their brutal

28. Here is yet another indication of prominent sages with scribal training active in Jerusalem, whether they were Pharisees and/or others serving in the temples-state or more independent figures.

execution quickly became the rallying cry of the people of Jerusalem in demanding from his son and presumed successor Archelaus a reduction of taxes, the freeing of political prisoners, and the ouster of oppressive Herodian officials.

> [There began] a lamentation over the fate of those whom Herod had punished for cutting down the golden eagle from the gate of the temple . . . mourning . . . in honor of the unfortunate men who had in defense of the ancestral laws and the temple perished on the pyre. These men ought, they clamored, to be avenged by the punishment of Herod's favorites, and the first step would be the deposition of the High Priest whom he had appointed. (*War* 2.2–5)

When Archelaus responded with military repression, the protest intensified and escalated into widespread revolts in the countryside in Galilee and the TransJordan as well as Judea. These popular revolts took the distinctively Israelite form of movements of villagers who acclaimed their respective leaders as "kings," according to Josephus accounts (*War* 2.565; *Ant.* 17.260–285). This suggests they were patterned after the "messiahing" of the young David to lead the people against the invasion by the Philistines centuries previously (as known from 2 Sam 2:1–4; 5:1–4).[29] Although the bold demonstration and then martyrdom of the Jerusalem sages and their students may have touched off these regional revolts, Josephus gives no indication that any Pharisees were involved in them. The Roman retaliation and reconquest was systematic and brutal, terrorizing the people in destruction of villages, slaughter or enslavement of the people, and crucifixion of those suspected to have been leaders. But these movements were able to maintain a semblance of independence from Roman and high priestly rule for months and, in the case in Judea, for as long as three years, before the Romans could finally take more complete control.

Conclusion

This critical survey of Josephus' accounts of the rule of Herod and of his brief accounts of the Pharisees under that rule indicates that they were playing a delicate double game as political realists. They had evidently become integral to the operation of the temple-state from the reign of Alexandra Salome on through the chaos of Roman conquest and double-level conflict

---

29. Critical investigation in Horsley, "Popular Messianic Movements." Fuller discussion of these movements and their distinctive form in Vol. 2.

between rival rulers, both Hasmonean and Roman. As a central institution in his rule, Herod maintained and massively expanded the temple and high priestly aristocracy. It seems likely that the Pharisees were important in the operations of the temple-state, despite or perhaps because of the changes he was making. Recognizing that Herod's power backed by Rome was overwhelming, they advised others of prominence in Jerusalem, such as priests, to submit to his rule.

But they also resisted Herod's tyrannical rule. While others cowered and caved in, they were able to refuse to sign oaths of loyalty to his rule (and that of Rome), and not be executed like others were. They managed to infiltrate the court, perhaps by working on prominent women such as Herod's brother's wife. There they drew on their traditional scribal knowledge (and practice) of prophecy to scheme against him, which did result in some executions. The bold action of cutting down the golden Roman eagle from over the gate of the temple, moreover, indicated that other scribal circles besides the Pharisees, while biding their time, were deeply concerned about Herod's systematic flouting of Judean laws and traditions of which they were the cultivators, custodians, and perhaps embodiment, and were ready to take opportunities of public demonstration of resistance.

Appendix:
Scribal Opposition to the Hasmoneans and Herod in the Psalms of Solomon

Yet another scribal group active apparently at the time of Herod is attested in the Psalms of Solomon, a collection of eighteen psalms produced evidently in the mid-to-late-first century BCE. Composed originally in Hebrew, they are extant in Greek and Syriac translations.[30] While it is now doubted these psalms were produced by the Pharisees,[31] previous interpreters' instincts were right to associate the psalms with such a circle of scribes. The psalms are oriented to Jerusalem and the temple, where the high priests presided and scribes served as advisers in the temple-state (see especially Pss. Sol. 1, 2, 8, 11, 17). As those who cultivated the cultural traditions of Judea, the composers of the psalms were well prepared to ponder "the judgments of God since the creation of heaven and earth" in an attempt to justify God's acts of judgment in events of their own time (8:7).[32] They accuse others of "deceitfully quoting the law" (4:8), evidently assuming that they themselves are the experts. Scribes would presumably have been the only people in Judean society who possessed astronomical knowledge, to which psalm 18 appeals at the end. Like the earlier Jerusalem scribe Ben Sira they were satisfied with "a moderate sufficiency, for 'the Lord's blessing' comes to those satisfied with righteousness" (5:16–17).[33]

As suggested by this "beatitude", moreover, these psalms give expression to a kind of personal pietism of those who understand themselves as the faithful righteous at the center of the people of Israel. Those who love the Lord "live in the righteousness of his commandments, in the law, which he has commanded for our life" (14:1–2). The life of the righteous is penitential, since the Lord is good to those "who endure discipline," as in "the law of the eternal covenant" (10:1–4). This devotion to God and acceptance of whatever comes as the Lord's discipline appears to be closely related to the persecution about which several of these psalms complain (e.g., Pss. Sol.

---

30. On introductory matters such as language and dating, see Nickelsburg, *Jewish Literature between the Bible and the Mishnah*, 238–47.

31. The classic statement is by Ryle and James, *Psalmoi Solomontos*. On more recent scholarship, see Trafton, "The Psalms of Solomon in Recent Research."

32. The psalms are also full of language drawn from or alluding to passages in the prophets and psalms, which the scribes, along with the priests, learned and recited as part of the Judean cultural repertoire of which they were the professional guardians.

33. The discussion here draws on the more extensive treatment of the Psalms of Solomon in Horsley, *Revolt of the Scribes*, chap. 8.

12). But nothing in the Psalms of Solomon suggests that they were used by or addressed to a community of the "devout" separate from the rest of the people of Jerusalem and Judea (that is, a "sect").[34] The devout (scribes) may well have gathered for meetings, but we should not jump to conclusions from the line about "those who love the assemblies of the devout" (17:16). The parallel lines in psalm 10:5–8 that set "the assembly of the people" and "the assemblies of Israel" and "the house of Israel" as synonyms indicate that these phrases refer to Israel generally, with orientation to the people of Jerusalem.[35]

"The council of the devout" (4:1), on the other hand, seems to refer to a governing council of the temple-state, judging from the context.[36] The psalmist asks rhetorically, "Why are you sitting in the council of the devout, you profaner, . . . provoking the God of Israel by lawbreaking?!" This is evidently a reference to the Hasmonean Aristobulus, who carried out a military coup, displacing his older brother Hyrcanus as High Priest and king a short time after the death of Alexandra Salome, as discussed above. Some of those who produced these psalms, seeing themselves as (leaders of) the devout, were evidently members or advisers of this council who now condemn the usurping Hasmonean. The producers of the Psalms of Solomon thus appear to have been a group of scribes in Jerusalem, devoted to the laws and other traditions of Israel. They were attempting to explain the judgment of God in recent affairs of the temple-state.

Judging from the historical references in several of the Psalms of Solomon, the principal issue these scribes were dealing with, in their struggles to justify the judgments of God, was the Roman conquest of Jerusalem.[37]

---

34. Characterization of the community behind the psalms is the major concern of Atkinson, *I Cried to the Lord*. See especially his "Conclusion," where he argues for a "sectarian community, meeting in their own synagogues [buildings] in Jerusalem" (214, 218). His argument, however, is not convincing.

35. Although *yahad* may have been more often used in reference to the whole "assembly" of Israel/the people, it was sometimes almost interchangeable with *edah*, smaller or local "assemblies." In Greek translation, moreover, for example in the LXX, the terms *ekklesia* and *synagoge* were used somewhat interchangeably. While there were "prayer-houses" in diaspora communities, there is little or no evidence prior to late antiquity for "synagogues" as buildings in Judea or in Jerusalem. Fuller discussion of *synagogai* in Galilee as village assemblies in Horsley, *Galilee*, chap. 10.

36. This would be a reference to such a temple-state council convened by and advising the High Priest (Hyrcanus), near contemporary to the story about the Pharisee Samaias' speech in the council that Josephus knows and relates in *Ant*. 14.172–174 (discussed above). As noted above, however, such a council does not appear to have been a long-standing institution of the temple-state with a set membership, as imagined in older treatments of "Judaism."

37. Werline, "The *Psalms of Solomon* and the Ideology of Rule," offers a very

This is the concern particularly of psalms 2, 8, 17, and the opening psalm, which was evidently composed as an introduction to the whole collection.

The description of imperial wealth, glory, arrogance, and lawlessness in 1:4–8 surely pertains to the Romans. The Roman warlord Pompey "profaned the sanctuary of the Lord" (in 63 BCE), as had Antiochus Epiphanes before him (in 168–167 BCE). But extending their wealth and glory "to the ends of the earth" (etc.) fits the imperial reality as well as ideology of the Romans, not that of the Seleucids. The charge that "their lawless actions surpassed the nations before them" fits Roman actions in Judea from Pompey to Herod.

Psalms of Solomon 2 gives a reason why Pompey had breached the walls with a battering ram and then trampled the sanctuary in the temple: "the sons of Jerusalem" had "defiled the sanctuary of the Lord" and committed further lawless actions (vv. 1–14). Thus the peoples' (i.e., the Romans') trampling of Jerusalem is the just judgment of God on the wicked actions of the sinners, that is the Hasmoneans (vv. 15–21). Horrified at the vicious rage of the imperial attack, the psalm implores that Jerusalem has suffered enough, and appeals to God to punish the invaders (vv. 22–25).[38] The psalmist thus takes great satisfaction when "God showed me his insolence, pierced on the mountains of Egypt," where "the arrogant dragon" Pompey had finally been killed (vv. 25–26).

Despite the horror at the vicious rage of Pompey and the Romans, however, Psalms of Solomon 2 in effect blames the Hasmoneans for the Roman conquest of Jerusalem and trampling of the temple. This was the just judgment of God on "the sons of Jerusalem" for their sinful actions (vv. 3–10, 11–14, 15–21).[39] The most sustained charge is that they had turned Jerusalem into a "prostitute, . . . available to all" (11:14). Given the long tradition of such sexual promiscuity as a metaphor for compromises with foreign, often imperial, rulers and their gods and culture, these lines appear to be indicting the Hasmonean rulers of Jerusalem for having transformed the temple-state into a Hellenistic kingdom, with a lavish lifestyle at court and mercenary troops. Judging from the punishments mentioned, "the sons of Jerusalem" appear to refer primarily to Aristobulus, his family, and supporters. That "the sons and daughters" were taken "into harsh captivity, their

---

suggestive analysis and interpretation of the "ideology of rule" in psalms 1, 2, 8, and 17.

38. The reference to "the arrogant dragon" (25) compares Pompey to King Nebuchadrezzar who had "devoured" Jerusalem like a monster in the Babylonian destruction of the city and the temple centuries earlier that was prominent, indeed formative in the historical awareness of Judean culture (Jer 51:34; cf. Ezek 29:3; 32:2).

39. Regev, "How Did the Temple Mount Fall to Pompey?," argues that the partisans of Aristobulus in the siege of Jerusalem in 63 BCE were Sadducees.

neck in a seal, a spectacle among the nations" (2:6) accords particularly well with Josephus' accounts that Pompey carried off Aristobulus and his sons and daughters as prisoners to be displayed in his triumphal procession in Rome (*War* 1.157; *Ant.* 14.79).[40] One suspects that the "defilement of the sanctuary and profaning of the offerings" may refer more generally to the Hasmonean actions as high priests and kings reaching back at least as far as Alexander Jannaeus. Among the known acts of the Hasmoneans high priests, only Jannaeus' crucifixion of his opponents and slaughter of their wives and children before their eyes would seem to qualify for the description that "no one on earth had done what they did" (2:9).

Psalms of Solomon 8:14–22 presents a fairly detailed description of Pompey's attack on Jerusalem and the temple. This is God's punitive judgment evidently on the sins of the priests presiding in the temple (8:6–13). That "the leaders of the country met him with joy" (v. 16) must refer to the partisans of Hyrcanus II having admitted him to the city, whereupon he "captured the fortified towers and the wall of Jerusalem" (v. 19), as in both accounts by Josephus (*War* 1.142-151; *Ant.* 14.57-70). The psalmist is horrified at the violence between factions in Jerusalem, including that "everyone wise in counsel" had their blood "poured out like dirty water" (v. 20). That the Roman destruction and slaughter were God's judgment was difficult to accept, and one of the concerns of the psalm is to review the historical judgments of God to "prove God right" in his judgments (v. 7).

The specific set of sins by the priests who presided over the operations of the temple that have brought God's judgment upon the city include adultery, stealing from the sanctuary of God, walking on the place of sacrifice with uncleanness, defiling the sacrifices as if they were common meat (10–12).[41] Maintenance of the laws pertaining to the temple was important to scribes trained to apply them as well as to the priests who performed the sacrifices. The use and abuse of those resources (such as those intended for the poor, orphans, and widows) was yet another concern of scribes, as we know from the instructional speeches of Ben Sira and the Epistle of Enoch

40. Pss. Sol. 2:6 also stands parallel to the interpretation of Nah 3:10 in 1QpNah 4:2-4, where "Manasseh" is a code word for the Sadducees and (closely allied with) Aristobulus, "whose reign over Isr[ael] will be brought down [. . .] his wives, his children, and his infants will go into captivity. His warriors and his honored ones [will perish] by the sword."

41. These are the same general areas of sinning (the three "nets of Belial") with which the Damascus Document, now also known from Qumran manuscripts, charges the illegitimate Hasmonean priests: "fornication," "riches," and "the profanation of the temple" (CD 4:15-17). See the extensive, although not always apt, discussion of texts from the Dead Sea Scrolls on charges such as sexual impurity among ruling priests, with many references to scholarly literature, in Atkinson, *I Cried to the Lord*, 66-83.

(1 Enoch 92–104). Since scribal circles had no real power to prevent abuses, it is not surprising that they developed standard charges against the incumbents, in this case the Hasmoneans who had drawn wide opposition among the people as well as by scribal circles such as the Pharisees.

Psalms of Solomon 17 expresses sharp condemnation of the Hasmoneans, who were illegitimate usurpers who "despoiled the throne of David" (vv. 5–6). Again as in psalms 2 and 8, the overthrow of the Hasmoneans is God's own work, working through "a man alien to our race" (v. 7). While it may have been unclear how to understand the reference to God "uprooting their descendants from the earth" and "hunting down their descendants" (vv. 7, 9) the "man alien to our race," who "rose up against them," however, must be Herod, whose father Antipater was Idumean, not Judean. Like Pompey before him, Herod also laid siege to and conquered Jerusalem (Josephus, *Ant.* 14.468–491). And it was Herod who, according to Josephus' accounts, "hunted down their descendants" (v. 9) and executed the last of the Hasmoneans (*Ant.* 14.487–491; 15.5–10, 164–178).[42]

Parts of the extensive description of how "the lawless one laid waste our land, so that no one inhabited it" (Pss. Sol. 17:11–20, esp. vv. 11–13) would fit Pompey's actions in the initial Roman conquest. Most of the acts of desolation of Jerusalem and the Judeans mentioned in vv. 11–20, however, better describe Herod's conquest of his subjects with the aid of Roman troops and his tyrannical rule of Judea, as known primarily from the Antiquities of Josephus. After being appointed "king of the Judeans" by the Roman Senate, Herod literally "laid waste the land" and "massacred young and old" (Pss. Sol. 11; cf. *Ant.* 14.479–480, 482–486) in his three-year conquest of the people and on several occasions during his reign. As recounted above, moreover, Herod ruled with an iron fist, imposing repressive measures to control the people and to stifle dissent. At several points people would have become "refugees in the wilderness to save their lives" (Pss. Sol. 17:17). Drought ("springs were stopped," v. 19) and famine occurred during Herod's siege of Jerusalem and later during his reign (*Ant.* 14.475; 15.299–304). Under Herod, finally, "the king was [indeed] a criminal" (v. 20) in the minds of the people generally and certainly among scribal circles.

The focus on an "anointed king, son of David (17:21–44), moreover, seems more likely a response that would have emerged during or after Herod's tyrannical reign as "king of the Judeans" than after the later Hasmoneans who had added the title king to that of High Priest. Apart from the few passing references in the Qumran texts produced by a utopian

---

42. So also Atkinson, "On the Herodian Origin of Militant Davidic Messianism at Qumran," 441–44, with discussion of text and references to pertinent scholarly treatment.

community that had withdrawn into the wilderness, there is a paucity of Judean texts that express any interest in an "anointed king," a "messiah." Psalms of Solomon 17 (along with the brief reference in Pss. Sol. 18) is about the only text from late second-temple Judea to offer an extended passage on a "messiah."[43] As noted above, the complaint made against the rival Hasmonean pretenders, according to Josephus, was that they had arrogantly and against tradition claimed to be kings in addition to high priests. Herod was appointed "King of the Judeans" by the Romans, and then reduced the high priesthood to relative insignificance in comparison with his power. All of these considerations suggest it is most likely that Pss. Sol. 17 originated in response to Herod's kingship rather than the Hasmoneans.

The Psalms of Solomon are deeply rooted in a Deuteronomic view of societal life and history. What happened in people's lives depended on their adherence to the covenantal law, and God would judge on the basis of obedience or disobedience. The scribes who composed these psalms, moreover, believed that God's judgment, however delayed in particular circumstances, was active in current events. One of their own responsibilities as devout scribes, was to justify God's judgment in current events, interpretation based on their review of God's previous acts of judgment (Pss. Sol. 8:7). Thus, despite the horrific violence and slaughter involved, the Roman conquest of Jerusalem was God's judgment on the wicked Hasmoneans kings for their many sins. Herod, the Romans' client king, continued the divine punishment of the Hasmoneans but also was a criminal in the violence and suffering he visited upon the people. In their pious devotion to God, the composers of the psalms stress submission to the discipline of God. They appear to have been politically quietist. The Psalms of Solomon offer no hint at any action this circle of learned scribes may have taken. But the psalms they composed and presumably sang indicate that they condemned the Hasmonean kings/high priests, the destructive conquest by the Romans, and the tyrannical rule of Herod.

---

43. Psalm of Solomon 17 was the prime proof-text for the older Christian construct of the "Jewish expectation" of a "militant messiah." Since the 1960s there has been extensive critical discussion of the limited evidence for expectations of one or more "anointed" figures in Jewish texts. The Christian construct of a "militant messiah" who will lead a violent rebellion, however, is still perpetuated, for example, by Atkinson, "On the Herodian Origin of Militant Davidic Messianism"; and Atkinson, *I Cried to the Lord*, 139-44.

7

The Pharisees and Other Scribal Groups under the High Priests and Roman Governors

The Romans crushed the widespread popular revolts after the death of Herod with their usual brutal destruction of villages, killing or enslaving the people, and crucifying those they suspected of being agitators. They then confirmed Herod's son Archelaus as ruler of Judea, Samaria, and Idumea. Galilee and Perea were placed under the rule of another son, Herod Antipas, hence were no longer under Jerusalem rule.

Josephus gives "short shrift" to the reign of Archelaus, who continued the repressive rule of his father, having unleashed the military on the protesting people after Herod died (*Ant.* 17.206–218). After the Romans appointed him as Tetrarch, he treated not only the Judeans but also the Samaritans with brutality (*War* 2.111). After ten years the Romans deposed him and imposed more direct Roman rule through the high priestly families at the head of the temple-state under the oversight of a Roman governor based in Caesarea. They also re-imposed payment of tribute to Caesar. The re-imposition of the tribute, which the Romans charged the high priests with collecting, became the occasion for resistance by another scribal group closely related to the Pharisees.

Scribal-Led Resistance to the Roman Tribute: The Fourth Philosophy

Both Josephus' attempts to deny that Judeans generally were resistant to Roman rule, on the one hand, and to explain that some scribal circles as well as the people became engaged in acts of resistance, on the other, are exemplified in his accounts of the Fourth Philosophy. These accounts in narrative context also indicate how, as direct Roman rule was imposed on Judea through the high priesthood under Roman governors, at least some scribal resistance moved from acts of symbolic protest, however bold, to active resistance.

In his account in *War*, before jumping to events under Pontius Pilate, Josephus presents as the only event worth narrating, the immediate resistance to payment of the tribute.

> A certain Galilean man named Judas urged his countrymen to revolt (*apostatis*), reproaching them as cowards for consenting to pay tribute to the Romans and tolerating mortal masters after having God as their ruler. This man was a scholar (*sophistes*) who founded a school of his own that had nothing in common with the others. (*War* 2.118)

Josephus then immediately presents his major account of the three forms of philosophy among the Judeans that supposedly illustrates that last claim.

In his later account in *Antiquities* he is more careful and precise in particulars. Although the Judeans were shocked to hear of the Roman assessment of how much they could extract from the yearly harvest, they gradually consented, yielding to the arguments of the High Priest Joazar son of Boethus.

> But Judas, a Gaulanite man from the city named Gamala, in league with the Pharisee Saddok, pressed hard for resistance (*apostasis*). They said that [the Roman] tax-assessment amounted to slavery, pure and simple, and urged the people (*to ethnos*) to claim their freedom (*eleutheria*). If successful, they argued, the Judeans would have paved the way for prosperity (*to eudaimon*); if they were defeated in their quest, they would at least have honor and glory for their high ideals. Furthermore, the deity would eagerly join in promoting the success of their plans, especially if they did not shrink from the slaughter that might come upon them. The populace when they heard their appeals responded gladly and the daring scheme made real headway. (*Ant.* 18.4-6)[1]

---

1. Translation adapted from that of John S. Hanson, in Horsley with Hanson,

In the last sentence quoted Josephus begins his well-known harangue against this "intrusive Fourth Philosophy" and "innovation" in the ancestral traditions. In a blistering polemic he blames Judas and Saddok and their "philosophy" for events that happened several decades later, such shocking incidents as raids by hordes of brigands and the assassination of figures of the highest standing (priestly aristocrats and Herodians) and eventually the civil strife of the Great Revolt (*Ant* 18.6–10). What Josephus' polemic against Judas and Saddok does indicate is that by mid-first century resistance had become bolder and banditry and other political-economic disorder epidemic. But the social and political turmoil was not necessarily inspired by the Fourth Philosophy.

Judas and Saddok and the Fourth Philosophy have persistently been misunderstood as advocating revolt against Roman rule,[2] even by interpreters who recognize that they were not the founders of "the Zealots," the supposed revolutionary party in first-century Judea. It may help to clear up several misreadings of Josephus' and other accounts in preparation for a closer consideration of what Josephus does and does not say about the Fourth Philosophy, including in his polemic.

First, in *Antiquities* Josephus does not say that they advocated, much less engaged in, armed revolt. In fact, at the end of his account he blames the Great Revolt of 66–70 CE on the last Roman governor. Second, in construction of the synthetic concept of "the Zealots" scholars used to assume that Judas, one of the leaders of the Fourth Philosophy, was identical with Judas, the son of the brigand chieftain Hezekiah. The latter was acclaimed as "king" by his followers who rose in revolt in the area around Sepphoris in Galilee after Herod died in 4 BCE. The Judas from Gamala, an administrative and military town in Gaulanitis, east of Galilee, was a "scholar-teacher" (*sophistes*) who was active in Judea, not Galilee, in 6 CE as leader of the Fourth Philosophy. Third, that Judas from Gamala in Gaulanitis may have

---

Bandits, Prophets, and Messiahs, 191–92. In note "b" to his translation of *Ant.* 18.5, Louis Feldman (in the Loeb edition) indicates that he takes Josephus' following polemic at face value. But doing so is what misled earlier generations of readers and interpreters of Josephus' histories to the synthetic construction of "the Zealots" as a party that advocated armed revolt against the Romans from its supposed founding by Judas of Gamala in 6 CE to the outbreak of the Great Revolt in 66. The series of my articles in the late 1970s and early 1980s (now collected in *Politics, Conflict, and Movements*) attempted to lay to rest this utterly misleading scholarly construct that blocked recognition of the diversity of popular and scribal movements against the high priestly and Roman rulers of the Judeans and Galileans, the articles giving the research and discussion behind the chapters on those movements in *Bandits, Prophets, and Messiahs*.

2. This section builds on, but shifts the perspective and makes corrections in my previous treatments of the Fourth Philosophy in Horsley with Hanson, *Bandits, Prophets, and Messiahs*, 190–99; and Horsley, *Jesus and the Spiral*, 77–89.

been father or more likely grandfather of Menahem who led insurrectionary activity briefly in Jerusalem in 66 does not mean that he also was a messianic pretender or advocated revolt in different circumstances sixty years earlier.[3] Fourth, some translations of both Josephus' and the book of Acts' (5:37) accounts of Judas have apparently been influenced by the modern scholarly construct of "the Zealots," which in turn further reinforced the misunderstanding of the Fourth Philosophy.[4]

After he describes the Essenes, Sadducees, and Pharisees, ostensibly to show how the Fourth Philosophy was innovative and intrusive, Josephus continues in a way that seems almost appreciative of their steadfast commitment to the ancestral law and their courage in its defense.

> Judas the Galilean established himself as the leader of the fourth of the philosophies. They agree with the views of the Pharisees in everything except their unconquerable passion for freedom, since they take God as their only ruler and master (*hegemon kai despotes*). They shrug off submitting to unusual forms of death and stand firm in the face of torture of relatives and friends, all for refusing to call any man master (*despotes*) . . . The folly that ensued (in 66 CE) began to afflict the people (*to ethnos*) after Gessius Florus, who was governor, had by his overbearing and lawless actions provoked a desperate rebellion against the Romans. (*Ant.* 18.23–25)

It is surely significant that Josephus calls this the "Fourth" Philosophy and associates it with the others. Here and elsewhere he refers to Judas as a "scholar-teacher" (*sophistes*), like the revered Judas and Matthias ten years earlier, who inspired their students to pull down the Roman eagle. Here he identifies Saddok explicitly as a Pharisee and says the members of the Fourth Philosophy agree with the views of the Pharisees in everything, except for their passion for freedom. They must have been closely associated with the Pharisees, perhaps an activist spinoff of that long-established party. Judas and Saddok and their followers, like the Pharisees, were [thus] certainly actively involved in political affairs. But they were not a long-established "faction" among scribal circles like the Sadducees and Pharisees. They would appear to have been a smaller association of learned scribal teachers who

3. On Menahem, the Sicarii, and their relationship to Judas and the Fourth Philosophy, see Horsley, "Menahem in Jerusalem."

4. The term *apostasis* and its variants in both Josephus' and Acts' account, for example, was used a great deal more ambiguously and vaguely than the modern English term "rebellion" or "revolt." The NRSV translation (of Acts 5:37) that Judas "got people to follow him" is a good deal less ominous and more appropriate than the New English Bible's "induced some people to revolt under his leadership."

came together specifically in response to the imposition of direct Roman rule and the tribute-assessment in 6 CE.

Their most distinctive feature, says Josephus, was "their unconquerable passion for freedom." A passion for "freedom" (*eleutheria*) was not distinctive to Judas and his circle or to the Pharisees, but widespread in Judean society. Judeans annually celebrating their ancestors' liberation from subjugation in Egypt in the Passover festival kept up their focus on (their lost) freedom, particularly in circumstances of continuing domination by the Romans (*War* 2.223–227; *Ant.* 20.105–106). Distinctive to Judas, Saddok, and their followers, however, was their drive to act on the ideal in organizing collective resistance to the tribute.

The Fourth Philosophy's "unconquerable passion for freedom" was directly related to their conviction that God was "their sole ruler and master" (*monon hegemona kai despoten*, *Ant.* 18.23). Again this is hardly distinctive to them or to the Pharisees with whom they agreed in all things. This was the standard Judean "confession of faith" (see Deut 6:4–9; cf. Mark 12:29–30), that is, their exclusive loyalty to God that stands behind Josephus' summary of the *politeia* of the Judeans in the terms *eusebeia* and *dikaoisyne* (e.g., in *Ant.* 1–4). Josephus himself explains that the Judean constitution given by Moses was a "theocracy" that placed "all sovereignty and authority in the hands of God" (*Ag. Ap.* 2.164–165) and that the God-given "laws" were their "masters" (*despotas*) and God their true "ruler" (*hegemon*; *Ant.* 4.223). The phrase "*only* ruler and master" appears to allude to the first commandment of the Mosaic Covenant, that demands exclusive loyalty to God in a social-political sense inseparable from the religious. Judas and his circle's application of it to the Roman tribute indicates that they also took seriously the economic demands of the second commandment, the prohibition of bowing down and serving another "ruler and master" with the produce of one's labor (cf. *War* 2.118). This is the clear implication of their insistence that the tribute amounted to slavery, that is, service of a "ruler and master" other than or in addition to the God of Israel.

Thus in terms familiar from Josephus' accounts of the Pharisees, the activists of the Fourth Philosophy were "exact"—not only in their knowledge of the ancestral laws, but in their practice as well. For they were unwilling to compromise the first two commandments of the Mosaic covenant, in contrast, apparently, with the Pharisees who did not follow Saddok's lead. Already having God as their ruler and master, they insisted that Judeans could not then be "bowing down and serving" a human ruler and master by yielding up tribute to Caesar (honored throughout the Empire, including in Herod's realm, as "the son of God"). With regard to God as sole ruler the Fourth Philosophy was hardly innovative and "intrusive. In terms of the seriousness with which they took the conviction politically and economically, however, they went beyond compromises made by most Pharisees and the Sadducees.

Judas' and Saddok's sense that God would be helping or concurring in their action sounds like an "activist" variation on the Pharisees' belief that, in Josephus' Hellenistic terms of fate and free will, "to act rightly or otherwise rests, indeed, for the most part with men, but that in each action Fate cooperates" (*War* 2.163). This is evidently the simplistic Greek philosophical attempt at stating the more subtle Pharisaic (or perhaps more general Judean scribal) understanding of a certain synergism between God's and people's actions, God taking action through human action and interaction. Israelite tradition was rich in stories of God effecting liberation through the action of the people. The formative example in Judean/Israelite tradition was that God led the people out of hard bondage in Egypt, but only when the people finally fled, following Moses' lead.

Judas, Saddok, and company differed from the Pharisees in being ready to stand firm in their observance of the covenantal demands of God; they were no longer willing to compromise what Josephus terms the *eusebeia*, or exclusive loyalty to God required by the first and second commandment. But rather than preparing to engage in violent revolt, they were prepared to suffer violent repression, even the torture and death of themselves, relatives, and friends. They evidently understood that the Romans viewed failure to render up the tribute as tantamount to revolt, and would take severe repressive action to enforce their subjection. Cassius' enslavement of the residents of Emmaus and three other district towns for failure to raise an extraordinary levy of tribute in timely fashion would still have been alive in their memory (*War* 1.220–222; *Ant.* 14.271–276). In their readiness to face death for disciplined persistence in their exclusive loyalty to their divine Lord and master the Fourth Philosophy again stood in a scribal tradition. When imperial rule under Antiochus Epiphanes had become unacceptably intrusive and overbearing, learned scribes such as the *maskilim* had resisted and faced torture and martyrdom at the hands of the rulers they refused to obey (Dan 11:30–35).

What was distinctive about the Fourth Philosophy in comparison with both the Pharisees with whom they agreed and earlier circles of scribes who also engaged in resistance was their organization of wider resistance. They preached and planned an organized action of non-violent non-cooperation with the assessment for the tribute. Just before coming to Judas and Saddok, Josephus explains that the Romans' reimposition of the assessment for the tribute shocked the Judeans in general, but they were persuaded by the High Priest Joazar not to pursue their opposition (*Ant.* 18.2–3). What Judas and

Saddok did that was "intrusive" and perhaps unprecedented was to urge others to refuse to participate, i.e., to refuse payment of the tribute. And since "Judas persuaded not a few Judeans to refuse to enroll themselves" for the tribute (*War* 7.253), the plan of collective refusal made serious progress (*Ant.* 18.6). It is not clear what it meant that the High Priest Joazar, who had persuaded the people not to take action (18.3), was overpowered by the people, so that Quirinius deposed him and appointed Ananus son of Sethi (18.26). In any case, Josephus gives no further information, suggesting that the resistance to the tribute did not spread widely enough to evoke violent retaliation by Romans.

Josephus' Comparison of the Pharisees with the Other Philosophies

It seems clear that Josephus juxtaposed his major accounts of the three principal "philosophies" of the Judeans at least partly in order to provide a contrast with Judas and the Fourth Philosophy as an utterly alien or at least intrusive view. At the very end of his earlier account of the three principal schools of the philosophy of the Judeans (*War* 2.119–166), devoted almost entirely to his admiring description of the Essenes, he briefly contrasted the Pharisees, the leading school/party, with the Sadducees on only a few main points.[5] As in other accounts of the Pharisees he introduced them as recognized for expounding the laws with accuracy. The Pharisees, while holding that to act justly or otherwise rests mostly with people, maintain that Fate/God controls everything; and that souls are imperishable, but only the soul of a good person passes into another body. By contrast, the Sadducees (the second group) remove God from even the sight of evil and maintain that people have free choice of good or evil and dismiss ideas of persistence of the soul after death and of penalties and rewards. The Pharisees are affectionate with each other and cultivate harmony in the community. By contrast, the Sadducees are boorish in behavior and rude to their peers (2.162–166). In the account in *Antiquities,* Josephus seems to admit other positive aspects of the Pharisees whom he had sharply criticized for the effects of their practice in earlier narratives.

> The Pharisees simplify their standard of living, making no concession to luxury. They follow the guidance of that which their

---

5. Thus particular aspects of his characterizations of the Pharisees, Sadducees, and/or Essenes are not intended as contrasts to the Fourth Philosophy. In both the accounts, in *War* and *Antiquities,* Josephus presents the Pharisees explicitly in contrast with the Sadducees. Cf. Mason, *Josephus on the Pharisees*, 301.

teaching has selected and transmitted as good, attaching the chief importance to the observance of those commandments which it has seen fit to dictate to them. They show deference to their elders, nor do they contradict their proposals. Though they postulate that everything is brought about by fate, still they do not deprive the human will of the pursuit of what is in man's power, since it was God's good pleasure that there should be a fusion and that the will of man with his virtue and vice should be admitted to the council-chamber of fate. They believe that souls have power to survive death and that there are rewards and punishments under the earth for those who have led lives of virtue or vice: eternal imprisonment is the lot of wicked souls, while the good should receive an easy passage to a new life. (*Ant.* 18.12–14)

On account of these (views) they happen to be most influential among the city-peoples (*tois demois pithanotatoi tugchanousin*). Of prayers and sacred rites, [whatever] is considered divine happens to be conducted according to their application (or exposition). This much of their influence (*arete*)[6] the cities have demonstrated (attested), in both manner of life and discourse, by their adherence to the way that prevails over all. (*Ant.* 18.15)[7]

The Sadducees hold that the soul perishes along with the body. They own no observance of any sort apart from the laws (*ton nomon*). In fact they reckon it as a virtue to dispute with the teachers of the path of wisdom. There are but few people to whom this doctrine (*ho logos*) has been made known, but these are men of the highest standing. They accomplish practically nothing, however. For whenever they assume some office,[8] though they submit unwillingly and perforce, yet submit they do to the formulas of the Pharisee, since otherwise the populaces (*plethesin*) would not tolerate them. (*Ant.* 18.16–17)

Taken in the context of Josephus' overall histories of late-second temple Judea this is a highly telling account, particularly for reconstruction of the position and role of the Pharisees in the temple-state under Roman governors in the first century CE. Earlier in his narratives Josephus

---

6. For the translation of *arete* here as "strength" or "influence," see the discussion in Mason, *Josephus*, 302–4.

7. Translation adapted from Mason, *Flavius Josephus on the Pharisees*, 305.

8. As Goodblatt, "The Place of the Pharisees in First Century Judaism," 25, explains, this refers to an office that is political as well as religious, that is, an office in the temple-state.

was sharply critical of the political role played by the Pharisees under Alexandra Salome in the decline of the Hasmonean dynasty. And he may well have been trying to avoid mentioning the Pharisees in his accounts of political-religious affairs under Herod and under the Roman governors. Here in *Antiquities*, however, he not only presents a more positive portrayal of the Pharisees. More important, he acknowledges that they had become and remained central in the operation of the temple-state by the time that Rome attempted to control Judea through the weakened and unpopular high priestly aristocracy.

In his brief contrast of the Pharisees with the Sadducees at the same point in his earlier account (*War* 2.162–166) he had already admitted that they were "the leading school/faction" (*hairesis*) and that they were affectionate with each other and cultivated harmonious relations with the community (*eis to koinon homonoia*), in contrast with the boorish Sadducees.[9] These collective qualities of the scribal faction that had actively resisted Alexander Jannaeus and been restored to authority by Alexandra would have been a welcome relief to the people of Jerusalem. These collective qualities of the restored scribal retainers of the temple-state would also have helped stabilize public affairs at least temporarily before the self-destructive conflict between the rival Hasmonean pretenders and the Roman conquest. Assuming that the Pharisees continued in their restored role in the temple-state that Herod retained to serve his own rule and then massively rebuilt, these same qualities would have helped maintain at least minimal stability in relations between temple-state and people that Herod' innovations in the rebuilt temple would have placed under further strain (discussed in the previous chapter).

The parallel account in the later *Antiquities* further expands the positive presentation. Now the leading faction of the Pharisees also displays one of the key qualities of a Greek philosophy: they simplify their lifestyle, with no pursuit of an easy life of luxury—an utter contrast with the arrogant wealthy and boorish Sadducees. Josephus' next few sentences are hopelessly

---

9. Mason, *Flavius Josephus on the Pharisees*, 174–75, uses nuanced differences between Josephus portrayals of the Pharisees and the Essenes as a way of diminishing what might appear as positive representation of the Pharisees, whom he wants to distance from Josephus himself. To discount Josephus' mentioning that the Pharisees cultivated harmony with the people, he claims that Josephus devoted "two paragraphs" to a discussion of the Essenes' *homonoia*, 175. Josephus says, however, that the Essenes' "community of goods" (*to koinonikon*), not their non-economic social "harmony," is remarkable at the beginning of a list of topics that includes also oil, officers, possessions in common, dress, and no buying and selling (*War* 2.122–127). The Pharisees' *homonoia* is evidently with the community of other Judeans generally (but mainly Jerusalemites), while the Essenes' *koinonia* is within the separated community itself.

abstract and convoluted and impossible to translate or understand adequately. From the story that he recounted about John Hyrcanus' break with them, we can discern that one of the reasons the Pharisees were recognized for accuracy in knowledge of the ancestral laws is that they honored the teaching of their ancestors. The most important new information Josephus offers in this account is that the Pharisees are "most influential" among the people (of Jerusalem). To illustrate this influence, he mentions specifically that the prayers and other rites in the temple are carried out according to the exposition of the Pharisees. Then he appears to broaden their influence to public affairs generally: the cities attest their influence by adhering to the Pharisees' way in both manner of life and discourse.

Josephus further supports his new information about the Pharisees' influence in his ensuing comments about the Sadducees. Despite their being men of the highest standing (wealthy and high born), when they assume some office in the temple-state they must, however unwillingly, submit to what the Pharisees say, or the people would not tolerate them. As noted above in chapter 4, Josephus statement in *Life* 12 further confirms his generalization about the Pharisees' having become central authorities in the operations of the temple-state: when he entered public life he had to adhere to the Pharisees' prescriptions of how temple-state affairs were conducted. This decisive influence of the Pharisees in the operations of the temple-state should not be misconstrued as the people's support of the Pharisees. Their influence was coming from the top down, not from popular support up to the priestly aristocracy who still headed the temple-state.[10] The Pharisees exerted this influence not because they had the support of the people but because, having regained authority in the temple-state under Alexandra, they may have consolidated their authority under Hyrcanus II and then under Herod, even though, or perhaps because, they resisted his undermining of the ancestral laws while continuing their role its operation.

Finally, Josephus' framing of this discussion of the three traditional "philosophies" of the Judeans with his account of the Fourth Philosophy at the end as well as the beginning offers what appears as new information

10. Again, the conceptualization in terms of "Judaism" blocks recognition of the political-economic-religious structure and operations of the temple-state (cf. Mason, *Flavius Josephus on the Pharisees*, 202271, 301, 305). It was headed by the priestly aristocracy centered in the high priesthood, who were advised and assisted by a cadre of learned scribes/sages, with the ordinary priests carrying out the temple-rituals, including the sacrifices. The Pharisees' or the Sadducees' authority (not "power," cf. Mason, 206) was derivative of and dependent on being in favor with the High Priest and the dominant faction in the priestly aristocracy. At times the Pharisees may have made common cause with (some of) the people who were their allies, as when they resisted and joined the revolt against Alexander Jannaeus.

about the Pharisees. His statement that, except for their unconquerable passion for freedom, Judas and company agreed in all other respects with the views of the Pharisees suggests that the Pharisees also held that Judeans owed exclusive loyalty to God, as demanded in the first two commandments. In their position of authority as the retainers of the temple-state at the head of Judean society, however, their agenda was to guide the operation of the temple-state that provided a buffer between Roman domination and the continuation of the Judean way of life (*politeia*). The Saducees were the party of the wealthy and well-born, and unacceptable to the people. The dissident scribes and priests who, in their uncompromising commitment to their own understanding of the laws of the Judeans, which included uncompromising opposition to the domination of the Romans (the *Kittim*), had long since withdrawn to their own covenantal community(ies) at Qumran and elsewhere. The Pharisees, who might be characterized as political realists, evidently hoped to enable the Judeans to continue their traditional way of life (*politeia*, the laws) as much as possible while compromising certain aspects in view of the overwhelming military power of the Romans. That "the leading Pharisees" were active members of the "council" (*koinon*) in Jerusalem that attempted to hold the lid on the revolt in 66–67 CE, as discussed in chapter 4, indicates that the Pharisees must have sustained this agenda for six decades.

Scribal Circles behind the Updated Testament of Moses and the Parables of Enoch

Scribal circles or groups other than the Pharisees, Sadducees, and Essenes continued to operate in Judea under the rule of the Romans and their high priestly and Herodian client rulers.

The "updating" of the Testament of Moses in what we know as chaps. 6–7 and the section of 1 Enoch known as the Parables of Enoch are both dated by specialists to the early first century CE. Through a careful reading of these texts, which are presumably scribal compositions, we can discern dissident scribal circles that evidently opposed high priestly as well as Roman rule. From the breadth of the allusions in these texts, their scribal composers are reacting to the Roman conquest and to Herodian rule, like the students of the distinguished sages Judas and Mattathias who cut down the Roman eagle from the gate of the temple and the scribal circle that composed the Psalms of Solomon. They also have allusions to circumstances of domination and exploitation in the early first century CE, suggesting continuity of these groups over at least two generations. That the Parables of Enoch are attributed to the archaic scribe and that the text was included with other "Enoch" texts in 1 Enoch suggest that there may have been some continuity with the circle of "Enoch"-scribes of the third and second centuries BCE.

Chapters 6–7 of the Testament of Moses continue the review of rulers of the Judeans.[11] The first new rulers, the Hasmonean "kings," are bluntly rejected as illegitimate rulers of the temple-state. "They will be *called* priests of the Most High God [but are not]. They will perform great impiety in the Holy of Holies" (T. Mos. 6:1). Herod was even more illegitimate and downright brutal.

> A wanton king, not of priestly family . . . rash and perverse . . . He will shatter their leaders with the sword, and he will (exterminate them) in secret places so that no one will know where their bodies are. He will kill both old and young, showing mercy to none. Then fear of him will be heaped upon them in their land, and for thirty-four years he will impose judgments upon them as did the Egyptians . . . (T. Mos. 6:2–6)

The focus of the additions to the Testament of Moses on how Herod treated the elite, with no attention to his exploitation of the people, indicates a viewpoint of scribes who were oriented toward the operations of the rulers whom they served or from whom they had become alienated.

"The powerful king of the West who will subdue them" after Herod's death is clearly the Roman general Varus. He led the Roman reconquest that suppressed the widespread popular revolts that had erupted in the countryside following Herod's death. The brief account of Varus' reconquest (in T. Mos. 6:8–9), "taking away captives" and "crucifying" many, matches Josephus' longer accounts (*War* 2.49–50, 68, 75; *Ant.* 17.254–264, 289, 295). That insertion of chapters 6–7, including the reconquest by Varus, precedes (now) Antiochus Epiphanes' invasion of Jerusalem and the statement that he would "crucify" people in chap. 8 suggests that the composers saw Varus' reconquest as a repetition of Antiochus' attack, updated with a reference to Varus' brutality.

The short statement that Herod "would beget heirs who would reign after him for shorter periods of time" (T. Mos. 6:7)—both Antipas and Philip ruled longer than their father's thirty-four years—suggests a perspective from around the time the Romans deposed Archelaus and installed the high priests as rulers of Judea, under the oversight of a Roman governor. The supposed warning, "Do not touch me, lest you pollute me in the position I

---

11. This review of the "updating" of the Testament of Moses is dependent on my earlier discussion in Horsley, *Revolt of the Scribes*, 160–64.

occupy," indicates that the "destructive and godless men" were priests in the highest positions, who represented themselves as "righteous," probably by virtue of their ancestry and office (7:1-3). The charge that the "destructive men" love "gluttonous feasts," and "winings and dinings" (7:4, 8) suggests that the ruling high priestly families were already engaged in lavish living. The charge that they were "consuming the foods of the (poor)" and thus "committing criminal deeds" suggests that they were already engaged in the predatory practices that Josephus describes in later decades (*Ant.* 20.181, 206-207).

In the Book of Parables, as in the Book of Watchers, the antediluvian sage/scribe Enoch again steps into the role of prophet. In three "oracles" (cf. Num 23:7, 18; 24:3, 15, 21, 23, 29) he speaks "the words of the Holy One" that he claims are unprecedented revelation of wisdom (1 Enoch 37:2-5). The wisdom that "Enoch" "sees" is mostly astronomical and meteorological. Building on the tradition of prophetic audition of judgments in the heavenly court of "Yahweh of hosts," most of what he "sees" consists of scenarios of judgment in the heavenly court of "the Lord of the spirits." "Enoch" speaks three "parables" (oracles). The first two parables (1 Enoch 38-44; 45-57) focus on the judgment of "the kings and powerful." The third parable (1 Enoch 58-63 [+69:26-29?]) purportedly concerns the destiny of the righteous and chosen but devotes more attention to the judgment of "the kings and powerful." The Parables are dated to the early first century CE on the basis of the reference to the Parthians and Medes (56:5-7), who invaded Syria-Palestine in 40 BCE.[12]

Divine judgment on imperial rulers dominates the Parables from the beginning to the end.[13] It is clear from the extensive representations of judgment that the Parables focus on imperial domination and oppression of the subjected people by "the kings and powerful" (see, e.g., the extensive trial with which the third parable climaxes in 62:1—63:12). Particularly

12. The following discussion of the Parables of Enoch is dependent on my earlier discussion in Horsley, *Revolt of the Scribes*, 164-175, which in turn is dependent on the magisterial scholarship on Enoch texts by George W. E. Nickelsburg in many articles and books. His translation is available in Nickelsburg and VanderKam, *1 Enoch: A New Translation*, 50-95; Nickelsburg's updated introduction to the Parables is included in *Jewish Literature between the Bible and the Mishnah*, 248-56. In contrast to the "Enoch" texts from the late third and early second centuries, no copy of the Parables was found among the Dead Sea Scrolls. The text of the Parables is available only in Ethiopic, but the original language was probably Aramaic, as with the earlier Enoch texts.

13. Collins, *Apocalyptic Imagination*, 145-46, finds that "the major focus of the Similitudes is on the destiny of 'the righteous and the chosen,'" but must then note that the descriptions of their opponents ("the kings and the powerful") are "more frequent." It is the oppression of the righteous by the kings and the powerful, however, that has raised the issue of the destiny of both and drives Enoch's visions of the judgment.

noteworthy is the highly positive valuation of the earth. This view of reality is almost the diametric opposite of standard older generalizations about "apocalyptic" texts; the Parables articulate no stark heaven vs. earth dualism or "cosmic catastrophe." The result of the judgment is the end of imperial domination, which thus makes possible a good life on a renewed earth (see, e.g., 45:4–5).

Recognition of the highly positive valuation of life on earth under the direct rule of God may enable us to appreciate the Parables' sharp condemnation of imperial rule. The life God intended for the people to have on the earth has been made impossible by "the kings and powerful." This is articulated in the opening oracle that introduces the whole series of parables (38:1–4). "The sinners" who have possessed the land are "the kings and powerful ones;" the imperial rulers are represented as those who take over or trample or possess the (dry) land, the earth (see also 56:6; 62:1, 3, 6, 9; 63:1). Since land worked by peasants and laborers was the sole base of wealth in ancient agrarian societies, it was also the only basis on which rulers could build up empires. Insofar as the reference to "the Parthians and Medes" (56:5–7) who invaded Syria in 40 BCE is the basis of dating the Parables of Enoch to the early first century, "the kings and the powerful" clearly refer to the Romans and their empire.

It seems highly likely that "the kings and the powerful" include the Herodian kings and the high priestly aristocracy in Jerusalem, particularly since the Romans controlled their empire in the East through just such client rulers. The very face of Roman imperial rule in Judea in the first century CE was the high priestly aristocracy that headed the temple-state, along with the Herodian kings, who exercised control directly or indirectly. Other, contemporary Judean texts produced by scribal circles (e.g., the Psalms of Solomon) condemn incumbents of the high priesthood and Herodian kings for their oppressive rule and collaboration with the Romans. The "Wisdom-myth" that otherwise appears to be an intrusive interpolation into the first parable (42:1–2) would make sense in this connection. Ben Sira had claimed that heavenly Wisdom had been given dominion in the Jerusalem temple-state.[14] The statement in "Enoch's" first parable that Wisdom did not find a resting place among humans, hence withdrew to heaven, appears to be a diametrically opposite statement, in effect denying the legitimacy of the temple-state under its current incumbents.

Immediately following the vision of the military power of the kings and powerful in the third parable comes a vision of their economic exploitation of subject peoples.

---

14. See the discussion in Horsley, *Scribes, Visionaries*, 146–47.

> There my eyes saw a deep valley, and its mouth was open;
> And all who dwell on the dry land . . . will bring it gifts and tribute;
> But that valley will not be full.
> And everything that (the righteous) labor over, the sinners lawlessly
>   devour. (53:1–2)

The imperial rulers have an insatiable appetite for the produce of subject peoples that they expropriate in taxes, tithes, and obligatory gifts from client kings such as Herod. Rendering tribute to Caesar, however, was a direct violation of Israel's covenant with God, as in the organized resistance of the Fourth Philosophy just discussed. Accordingly, Enoch also saw "the angels of punishment . . . preparing all the instruments of Satan . . . for the kings and powerful of this earth, . . . [so that] the righteous will rest from the oppression of the sinners" (53:3–7). According to the traditional pattern, the imperial-scale punishment will fit the imperial-scale crime: "they brought the kings and the mighty and threw them into that deep valley" (54:2) where, in their insatiable appetite for wealth and luxury, they had devoured the goods of subject peoples.

More specific to the situation in Judea in the first parable, the Roman "kings and powerful" had "*persecuted the houses of his congregation*" (46:8). Enoch's vision elaborates on this in the next stanza.

> In those days the prayer of the righteous had arisen, . . .
> The holy ones . . . were uniting with one voice. . .
> interceding . . . in behalf of the blood of the righteous that had
>   been shed.
> . . . and the blood of the righteous had been required before the
>   Lord of spirits. (47:1–4)

The kings' persecution and shedding of the blood of the righteous may be closely related to the sinners' oppression of the righteous mentioned later in the second parable (53:7) and "the iniquity" that the kings had done "to his children and his chosen ones" for which retribution is exacted in the long trial scene in the third parable (62:11). In its context the "oppression of the righteous" appears to refer to economic exploitation of the Judean people generally. As indicated in the earlier instructional speeches of Ben Sira and the earlier Epistle of Enoch, scribal circles were concerned about the economic exploitation of the people generally by their rulers, including the wealthy and powerful Judean aristocracy in charge of the temple-state.[15] Similarly the kings' "iniquity to his children and his chosen ones" seems to

---

15. Discussed in Horsley, *Scribes, Visionaries*, 69, 139–40, 166–72.

have general reference to the people as a whole exploited and oppressed by the Romans (and their client rulers).

It is more difficult to discern whether "the houses of his congregation" that had been persecuted is a reference to the Judean people generally, repeatedly conquered with brutal violence by Roman armies (e.g., in 63 BCE and again in 4 BCE), or to the circles of ("Enoch" and other) scribes and teachers who had resisted Roman imperial rule in some way. Perhaps both.

However we read "the houses of his congregation," the parables portray a close relationship between "the chosen ones" and "the holy ones" and other heavenly forces. Already in the first vision of the first parable, "Enoch" sees the dwellings and resting places of the righteous with those of the holy ones and other heavenly messengers (angels; 39:4–5; cf. 41:2).

Even more striking is that "all the righteous and chosen will be mighty before him like fiery lights" (39:7) and, in the third parable, that "the righteous will be in the light of the sun (58:3).

These images are closely similar to the representation of the vindication of the martyred *maskilim* in Daniel (12:3) and the oppressed righteous in the Epistle of Enoch (104:1–6). The latter "will shine like the luminaries of heaven, . . . shine and appear, for the portals of heaven will be opened for you . . . You will be the companions of the host of heaven." Both the *maskilim* and the earlier Enoch scribes saw a close relationship between the scribes as recipients of heavenly wisdom and the glorious features of heavenly beings. The scribal and priestly community at Qumran spoke of the close communication back and forth between the heavenly world and the people in their community. The scribes who produced the Parables of Enoch evidently thought of the new life made possible by the end of empire in terms of life on earth under an open heaven, and eating with the righteous directly under the Lord of spirits (62:14).

The Gospel Stories' Portrayals of the Pharisees and Scribes

The Gospel stories, one of the four principal sets of sources for the Pharisees, focus on the mission of Jesus in opposition to and by the high priestly heads of the temple-state in the early 30s CE. They developed in movements of Jesus-loyalists that emerged from that mission, building on collective memories of Jesus' interaction with villagers in Galilee and beyond, with scribes and Pharisees, and finally with the high priests (and scribes and/or elders) and the Roman governor in Jerusalem. While still developing they reached roughly the forms in which we know them thirty to sixty years later. The Gospel stories will be the principal set of sources for the Pharisees' conflict with Jesus and his mission in Volume II. But they are also important sources for their portrayal of the Pharisees and scribes and their position and role in the Jerusalem temple-state in the decades prior to the Great Revolt and the Roman destruction of Jerusalem and the temple. The Gospel stories each have distinctive twists and episodes. Yet their portrayal of the Pharisees (and scribes and "lawyers") are relatively consistent. Perhaps more striking is that despite having an utterly different perspective on and attitude toward the Pharisees from those of Josephus—they present a "view from below"—their portrayals bear a fundamental resemblance to that in the accounts of Josephus.[16]

Both the Markan and Matthean Gospel stories present the Pharisees along with the scribes as "coming down from Jerusalem" to keep Jesus and his disciples under surveillance. Both stories have the Pharisees plotting to destroy Jesus (Mark 3:1–6; Matt 12:9–13). These stories also present the Pharisees and scribes as pressing the people to "devote" some of their land or its produce to support of the temple (Mark 7:1–13; Matt 15:1–9). Both stories represent the Pharisees (and scribes) as authoritative experts on the laws and customs such as keeping the sabbath, purity practices, and divorce. Most tellingly for their role in the temple-state, in Jesus' confrontation with the rulers after he pronounces God's condemnation of the high priests (and Pharisees) for exploitation of the people, (some of) the Pharisees are sent to entrap Jesus on the issue of whether it is lawful to pay the tribute (Mark 12:13–17; Matt 22:15–22). As the representatives of the temple-state, they are thus keepers of the Roman imperial order represented in Judea by the temple-state, in which the high priests were charged with the collection of the tribute to Caesar.

The Lukan Gospel story similarly has the Pharisees keeping Jesus under surveillance. Then, like the Matthean story, it includes a series of woes against the Pharisees and scribes/lawyers for the harmful effects of their role as representatives of the temple-state.

The Gospel of John presents the Pharisees as most closely associated with the high priests as the rulers of Judea. In several passages in the middle of the story the Pharisees in tandem with the high priests are synonymous with "the Judeans" who form and control the Jerusalem temple-state (e.g., John 7:32–48). In the climax of the story at a Passover festival the Pharisees work together with the high priests in the ruling council to deliberate how Jesus' can be stopped before he generates too large a following of loyalists

---

16. The Gospels' "view from below" becomes vitriolic at points, and it will be important to discuss that critically in the chapters of Vol. 2.

(John 11:45–48). In John the Pharisees have the authority to expel someone from the assembly of the people (John 12:42).

The portrayal of the Pharisees (and scribes) in the Gospel stories thus parallels that in Josephus' works for the decades before the destruction of the temple. They are representatives of the Jerusalem temple-state, experts in the laws and traditions of the Judeans. Whereas Josephus has the Pharisees collaborating with the high priests in trying to restore political order in the crisis of the Great Revolt, however, the Gospel stories represent the Pharisees and scribes as attempting to maintain social order in circumstances that have not yet moved into such a crisis.

The principal way in which at least the Markan story and the Matthean story differ from Josephus and the Gospel of John is in portraying the (scribes and) Pharisees as active in Galilee, confronting Jesus in village contexts. Mark, followed by Matthew (and perhaps by Luke) has them active in Galilee, at some considerable distance from their base in Jerusalem. During the lifetime of Jesus and for most of the next few decades before the Great Revolt, however, Galilee was not under the rule and jurisdiction of the high priests in Jerusalem. Yet except for their presence in Galilee the Markan and Matthean portrayal of the Pharisees as representatives of the temple-state is a striking parallel to Josephus' portrayal of them in 66–67 CE.

The Increasingly Repressive and Exploitative Context Created by the Roman Governors and the High Priests

That the Pharisees simplified their standard of living, making no concession to luxury (according to *Ant.* 18.12) was a remarkable contrast to the Sadducees. The Pharisees' modest lifestyle was even more of a contrast to the priestly aristocracy that the Romans placed in control of Judea, under the oversight of a Roman governor, following the experiment with Archelaus. After Herod's appointment of one of his favorites after another, the ruling priestly aristocracy consisted of four principal families. The Roman governors had the power to appoint and dismiss men from these families to the office of High Priest, although for a time Agrippa II held this power. This meant frequent changes subject to the whims of the governors and political maneuvering between the high priests and successive governors. It has been suggested that when a particular incumbent lasted for more than months or a few years, he must have been collaborating closely with the governor(s), as in the case of Caiaphas and Pontius Pilate. Presumably the high priests maneuvered among themselves for which figures held other offices, such as that of the temple-captain.

The Romans expected the high priests to control the populace as well as collect the tribute. The Roman governors made it difficult to do this by often flouting Judean traditions and ancestral customs, evoking popular protests and then sending out their military to suppress those protests or popular resistance movements in the countryside. The high priests themselves, concerned to protect their position by collaboration with the Romans, contributed to the decline in social order in two major ways. First, in Josephus' accounts, while the people protested the outrageous actions of the Roman governors, the high priests did not; nor did they protect or defend their Judean subjects from the abuses and retaliatory actions of the Romans. Second, they intensified their exploitation of villagers without concern for the effects on the society and the people's opposition to the central ruling institutions of the temple and high priesthood and Roman rule generally. Josephus gives several indications of both of these in his historical accounts.[17]

The greatest crisis by far for the Judeans was the emperor Gaius' (37–41) petulant order to Petronius, Legate of Syria, to lead a huge expedition of Roman legions and auxiliary troops to Jerusalem to install a statue of himself in the temple (*War* 2.184–203; *Ant*. 18.261–309). His orders were to kill those who might resist and reduce the whole people to slavery. As was the usual Roman practice, Petronius and his forces invaded from the North coming first to Ptolemais and into Galilee. Tens of thousands of "Judeans"[18] came to Petronius at Ptolemais (with their wives and children) to plead that he not forcibly transgress and subvert their ancestral laws. Impressed, he went through Galilee with his friends and attendants to Tiberias, summoning the populace (*plethos*) and all persons of distinction (*gnorimoi*) there. Tens of thousands (again Josephus exaggerates) gathered in protest, insisting they would sooner die rather than violate their laws, and baring their throats. They sustained the protest for 40 (or 50) days, meanwhile leaving their fields unsown, though it was the time to plant the crops. That the fields remained unsown indicates that the protests included what was in effect a peasant strike. That mainly Herodian officials from Tiberias were involved

17. Fuller documentation and discussion in Horsley, "High Priests and The Politics of Roman Palestine;" and more recently in Horsley, *Jesus and the Politics of Roman Palestine*, 28–36.

18. Through most of his long narrative of this crisis, Josephus refers to the protesters as "Judeans." It is not clear whether he is simply using the term from the viewpoint of the Romans and the Empire at large as a reference to those who were (previously) subject to the Judean temple-state or Herod (the crisis provoked by Gaius order was widely known through the Empire), who would have been people from Galilee in this case. It seems highly unlikely that he is referring to people from the territory of Judea proper who may have traveled north to meet Petronius or to Judeans living in cities such as Sepphoris or Tiberias, perhaps descendants of officers of Antipas.

and concerned about the ominous implications, indicates that the strike was by Galilean peasants under the rule of Agrippa. The protestors would have been fully aware that the only counterthreat they had was to deny Caesar the tribute he claimed as the divine ruler (in violation of the covenantal commandments), though at the cost of their own starvation or slaughter.

In *War* (2.200-202) Josephus says that Petronius himself realized that, with the land remaining unsown, there would be no tribute forthcoming from Galilee; so he should write to Gaius to call off the expedition that would end only with the destruction of the country and people. In *Antiquities* (18.273-278) Josephus has the highest ranking Herodian officials of King Agrippa's regime, together with the *protoi* of Tiberias, pressure Petronius to recognize that since the land remained unsown there would be no crops from which the tribute could be paid (not to mention their own revenue derived), but instead "a harvest of banditry" (from the mass of desperate hungry peasants). Agrippa himself was lobbying Gaius directly to call off the expedition. Through his long narratives of this crisis, however, Josephus makes no mention of involvement by the high priestly heads of the temple in which the statue of Caesar was to be installed. The crisis, which would likely have led to widespread revolt already in 39 CE (rather than 66 CE) subsided only with the (timely) assassination of Gaius.

When, in Josephus' narrative, the high priestly aristocracy in Judea did become involved, it was to try to restrain the people's protests or other reactions. When some pilgrims from Galilee to a festival in Jerusalem were killed by some Samaritans, the *protoi* of the Galileans appealed to Cumanus to take action, but he had been bribed not to do so (see the more detailed account in *Ant*. 20.122-124). The Galileans then appealed to the populace (of Jerusalem) to "assert their liberty." "Those in authority" in Jerusalem (i.e., the high priestly officers) tried to mollify them and offered to induce Cumanus finally to take action, but evidently had no influence with him. The populace, appealed for help from the brigand leader Eleazar ben Dinai, and sacked some villages of the Samaritans. Cumanus now took action, attacking the Judeans with his infantry and a squadron of Sebasteians. Those who by rank and birth were the *protoi* of the Jerusalemites then, with great sacerdotal drama, prevailed on the populace not to provoke military retaliation by the Romans against the temple. What they were really concerned about was exactly what happened: that the Romans would hold the priestly aristocracy responsible for not maintaining social-political order. The High Priest Ananias, the temple-captain Ananus, and others were sent to Rome to render account of their actions to the emperor Claudius (20.125-131). They were losing their case until Agrippa the Younger intervened through the wife of the emperor (135).

Meanwhile, the high priestly families were busy expanding their wealth. Archaeological excavations have found that they were constructing ever more luxurious mansions in Jerusalem[19] and steadily expanding estates in Judea northwest of the temple-city. This would have been accomplished by manipulating peasants into spiraling debt and then taking control of their land and forcing them to become dependent tenants who worked the fields that had previously been theirs. The wealthy priest Josephus, who himself controlled lands, includes incidents of how, by mid-century, the high priests had become downright predatory on the people they ruled as well as the ordinary priests whose temple-service they commanded. In a passage the text of which seems confused and confusing its seems that high priestly figures were preying on one another as well as other prominent figures and on the ordinary priests.

> Each of the factions collected and led a band of the most reckless ruffians, and when they clashed pelted one another with stones ... It was as if there was no one with authority in the city, so that they acted with utter license. Such was the shamelessness and audacity that possessed the high priests that they sent their servants to the threshing floors to take the tithes that were due to the (ordinary) priests, so that the poorer priests starved to death. (*Ant.* 20.180–181)

In what is either a duplicate passage or a continuation of the high priests' violence against priests and peasants a few years later, the former High Priest Ananias is depicted as buying the good will of the *politai* of the city and courting the governor Albinus (62–64 CE) and the current High Priest (Jesus son of Damnaeus). Moreover,

> Ananias had servants who were utter goons who, conspiring with the most reckless men, went to the threshing floors and forcibly took the tithes of the (ordinary) priests and beat those who refused to yield them up. The (other?) high priests were doing the same thing as his (Ananias') servants and no one could

---

19. In a summary description of these mansions based on archaeological explorations, Avigad, *Discovering Jerusalem*, 82–83, comments that "inner courtyards lent them the character of luxury villas ... [They were] ornamented with frescoes, stuccowork, and mosaic floors, and were equipped with complex bathing facilities, as well as containing the luxury goods and artistic objects which signify a high standard of living. This [was] where the noble families of Jerusalem lived, with the High Priest at their head. Here they built their homes in accordance with the dominant fashion of the Hellenistic-Roman period." Nevertheless, "the finds indicate that the laws of ritual purity were strictly kept, as were the injunctions against statues and images."

stop them. Thus the priests who previously were fed by the tithes now starved to death. (*Ant.* 20.205–207)

This high priestly abuse of the ordinary priests and peasants in such self-aggrandizing manipulations and blatant violence is confirmed by memories still alive in a later rabbinic text.

> Woe unto me because of the house of Baithos;
> woe unto me because of their lances!
> Woe unto me because of the house of Hanan (Ananus); . . .
> Woe unto me because of the house of Ishmael b. Phiabi,
> woe unto me because of their fists.
> For they are high priests and their sons are treasurers
> and their sons-in-law are temple overseers,
> And their servants beat the people with clubs! (b. Pesahim 57a)

Josephus' narratives thus offer particular aspects and episodes of how the Roman imperial *dis*order was expanding in Judea in the decades before the eruption of the Great Revolt, due to the provocations of the Roman governors and the failures and predatory actions of the high priestly heads of the temple-state and prominent Herodian figures.[20] Such is the historical context for his account of figures who may have been Pharisees and his accounts of a group of dissidents with scribal background who turned to terrorist tactics.

Other Actions by Pharisees (?) or Scribes under the Roman Governors and High Priests

As noted already in chapter 4, Josephus indicates that operations of the temple-state proceeded according to the Pharisees' most accurate knowledge (or application) of the ancestral laws of the Judeans. He also indicates that the leading Pharisees were consorting with the high priests and other prominent figures in Jerusalem and joined with them in the *koinon* in Jerusalem that attempted to control the revolt in 66 CE. These accounts thus indicate

---

20. Several other powerful and wealthy figures joined in the general predatory exploitation of the people, in seeming competition to outdo one another in their outrageous actions. Agrippa II, who at this time held the power to appoint the High Priest, was exploiting his own realm to gain the resources he needed to rebuild Caesarea Philippi and to lavish benefactions on Beirut (*Ant.* 20.211–212). He replaced one figure named Jesus with another, and they both hired gangs of goons who extended their rivalry for power in Jerusalem. The High Priest Ananias bribed other prominent figures, and the Herodians Costobar and Saul had gangs of goons that plundered the property of weaker figures.

that, while he rarely mentions them in his narrative of events in Judea under the Roman governors, the Pharisees must have continued to serve as advisers in the operations of the temple-state in the decades in which the actions and inactions of the high priestly rulers, exacerbated by the provocations of the Roman governors, steadily undermined any authority they had left. By the outbreak of the Great Revolt in 66 CE, they had effectively lost control both of the city people and of the Judean villagers. In his accounts of these decades of increasing social turbulence, Josephus does not mention the Pharisees by name. But he does make a few references to particular figures and scribal groups who evidently resisted the high priestly rulers of the declining temple-state. Some of these may well have been Pharisees.

Gamaliel

Josephus evidently cannot help representing Simeon son of Gamaliel as a distinguished adviser and representative of the temple-state who became prominent in the Jerusalem *koinon* in 66 (as discussed briefly in chapter 4). While Josephus makes no mention of his father, the Book of Acts not only identifies Gamaliel as a Pharisee but portrays him as having a prominent role in the Jerusalem council (somewhat reminiscent of Josephus' portrayal of Samaias). The high priests and Sadducees are eager to deal severely with the apostles leading the community of Jesus-loyalists that is expanding in Jerusalem. Gamaliel calmly advises them to simply wait to see how the movement develops or disappears. He points to the rapid demise of both the scribal movement led by Judas and the popular prophetic movement led by Theudas—failing to mention that the Romans had militarily suppressed the latter (Acts 5:33–39).[21] That Josephus knew about Gamaliel is indicated in his account of his son Simeon. Yet presumably he purposely omits mentioning him in his narrative of events in *Antiquities*, for whatever reason. Again, it is worth noting from the fragments of Josephus' accounts that Simeon is another case of a son or "son" following in his father-teacher's footsteps, devoted to the teaching of his scribal father.

James and Simon, Sons of Judas of Gamala

About Tiberius Alexander as governor (46–48 CE) Josephus reports in *War* (2.220) that he kept the people at peace by abstaining from all interference

---

21. Of course, we cannot jump directly from the portrayal in Acts to any historical reconstruction of Gamaliel's role in the temple-state more generally.

with their customs. In *Antiquities* (20.102) the one incident Josephus mentions is that he crucified James and Simon, the sons (*hoi paideis*) of Judas of Galilee who had urged the people to revolt against the Romans when Quirinius was taking the census in Judea. Josephus identified Judas as a scholar-teacher (*sophistes*), and usually fathers gave their sons the rigorous training to follow in their footsteps (the best known examples would probably be the one just mentioned of Gamaliel I followed by his son Simeon followed by his son Gamaliel II). Of course, some fledgling scribes were the students, not the descendants, of established learned scribes/sages and they too were identified as "sons." In any case, the James and Simon crucified by Tiberius Alexander here were probably also scholars-teachers like their "father" Judas who had urged resistance to the tribute forty years earlier. That the governor crucified them, a Roman form of execution especially for recalcitrant slaves and rebellious provincials, strongly suggests that they were at least suspected of some form of resistance against Roman rule.

The *Sicarioi*

The group known as the *Sicarioi* (mentioned briefly in chapter 4 above) may have sprung from the same scribal "lineage" of resistance to Roman and high priestly rule.[22] Their name came from the weapons they used: "daggers resembling the scimitars of the Persians in size, but curved and more like the weapons called *sicae* by the Romans" (*Ant.* 20.186). Josephus' accounts clearly indicate just how new and distinctive this group was when it emerged in the 50s. The governor Felix had just captured and crucified large numbers of brigands and of common people convicted of complicity with them.

> When they [the social bandits] had been cleared from the countryside (*chora*), a different type of "bandit" sprang up in Jerusalem, known as the *sicarioi*, who murdered people in broad daylight in the heart of the city. Mixing with the crowds especially during the festivals, they would stab their opponents with the short daggers concealed under their garments. Then when the victims fell, the murderers simply melted into the outraged crowds, undetected because of the naturalness of their presence. The first to be assassinated was Jonathan the High Priest, and after him many were murdered daily. (*War* 2.254–256)[23]

---

22. The following discussions draws on, but has different emphases from, the fuller exploration in Horsley, 'The *Sicarii*: Ancient Jewish Terrorists."

23. The parallel passage in *Ant.* 20.160–166 offers a different twist on the account in *War*. The High Priest Jonathan, who had been a close collaborator with the Romans,

It was standard in both the fields of Jewish history and New Testament studies to lump these "dagger men" together with the scribal Fourth Philosophy nearly fifty years earlier, the peasants-turned-brigands, and various popular movements in early Roman times under the synthetic scholarly construct of "the Zealots." But Josephus could not be clearer that they were "a different form (*eidos*) of bandits" and operated in Jerusalem, not the countryside. Bandits lived by robbing the wealthy who had possessions or, in the case of Judean bandits, Roman baggage trains, then fled to mountain hideouts, their whereabouts protected by the peasants familiar with them. The "dagger men," on the other hand, operated in the very heart of Jerusalem in clandestine manner, especially at festival times. There may have been some continuity of leadership from Judas, the *sophistes* who helped found the Fourth Philosophy, his two "sons" (*paides*) crucified forty years later, and Menahem, a key leader of the *Sicarioi* in the summer of 66 whom Josephus also calls a *sophistes* (*War* 2.445). It seems that Josephus' accounts offer clear clues that they were a scribal or scribally-led group based in Jerusalem, perhaps even focused on the role of the temple (festivals) and high priests.

In Josephus' accounts the *Sicarioi* employed three closely related tactics. Primary was selective symbolic assassinations. In other times and places of similar political circumstances, terrorist groups have carried out assassinations for their "demonstration effect." Judging from the passages in *War*, the *Sicarioi* began their campaign with the assassination of the former High Priest Jonathan, a key symbol for the Judean people, but far from a positive one insofar as he was known to have collaborated closely in Roman rule as well as to have exploited the people. Judging from comparative studies of assassination, they may have hoped that the assassinations would have reverberated among both the high priestly rulers and among the people. For the high priestly aristocracy, these would likely have been intended as punishment for their collaboration and exploitation and a warning about continuation in the future—and a demonstration of their vulnerability and

---

urged the emperor to send Felix to Judea as governor to succeed Cumanus—perhaps when he was taken to Rome to be interrogated about the conflict with the Samaritans. Once in Judea, Felix was aggressive in arresting and crucifying not just brigands but people in general as well. Jonathan, fearing that he would incur the hostility of the people, now urged Felix to improve his administration of affairs. An annoyed Felix bribed Jonathan's trusted friend Doras to invite "brigands" to kill him, following which ensues the story of the "dagger men's" assassinations of Jonathan and others. It is quite conceivable that the tactics of the *Sicarioi* were mixed up in the intrigue and in-fighting between leading high priestly figures, other wealthy power-brokers, and the Roman governors. As indicated in his later account of the kidnappings in *Antiquities* (20.208–210), the assassinations by the *Sicarioi* were not just something Josephus portrayed specially for *War*.

of the inability of the Romans to protect them. The hoped-for effect on the people would have been somewhat the same, but from the opposite viewpoint. Josephus reports that the assassinations had the desired "demonstration effect," at least on the high priests.

> The fear of attack was worse than the crimes themselves, just as in war one expects death at any moment. Men watched their enemies from a distance, and not even approaching friends were trusted. Yet even when their suspicions were aroused and they were on their guard, they fell, so suddenly did the conspirators strike and skillfully avoid detection. (*War* 2.257)

The second, related tactic was extension of assassinations into the countryside where the estates of the pro-Roman Judean rulers were located. "Splitting up into armed groups they ranged into the countryside and killed the powerful rich (*hoi dynatoi*), looted their houses, and set fire to the villages" [in the land they controlled] (*War* 2.265). To the peasants in other villages, these attacks may have had the effect of lessening the fear of the powerful rich and frightening them about cooperation with their pro-Roman creditors and/or forcing them to choose sides.

The *Sicarioi* employed a related third tactic typical of terrorist groups elsewhere: kidnapping an important person in order to extort the release of some of their own members who had been taken prisoner. At the time of the festival under the governor Albinus (62–64 CE),

> the *Sicarioi* sneaked into the city by night and kidnapped the (scribal) secretary of (the temple-captain Eleazar, son of) the High Priest Ananias and spirited him away in bonds. They then sent to Ananias and said they would release the (scribal) secretary to him if he would persuade Albinus to release ten of their number who had been taken prisoner. Having no option, Ananias successfully persuaded Albinus to make the exchange. But this was just the beginning. In various ways the "brigands" managed to kidnap some (other) members of Ananias' household and held them until exchanged for some of their own *Sicarioi*. (*Ant.* 20.208–210)

In all of their actions recounted by Josephus, the *Sicarioi* were highly discriminating, directing their attacks against the powerful wealthy heads of the temple-state and not the Roman governors.

These terrorist tactics of the group are suggestive for their broader strategy of resistance. From their direct experience of several decades of Roman (mis)rule, it was painfully evident that even scribal servants of the priestly aristocracy that ruled Judea no longer had influence on affairs.

There was no possibility of influencing the Roman governors. To stay in favor with the Romans, the high priests simply went along or collaborated closely, regardless of the effect on the people of the city or the villagers in the *chora*. Meanwhile, prominent high priestly figures were escalating their exploitation of the villagers, forcing many into tenancy. Some scribal groups must have concluded that with all channels of influence and protest closed to them, in order to be loyal to the covenantal commandments and protect the ancestral way of life (*politeia*) of the Judeans, it was necessary to attack the high priests who were the proximate representatives of and collaborators in Roman (mis)rule. As in other times and places where colonial or imperial rule and its local representatives have closed off virtually all channels for people to voice their opposition to oppression, abuse, and indignities, especially intellectuals acutely aware of their situation have resorted to terrorist assassinations.

The *Sicarioi* evidently continued to agitate through the 60s CE and then joined and even attempted to take the leadership when wider revolt erupted in Jerusalem in the summer of 66. Their role in the revolt, however, was brief and limited, contrary to some previous claims. The revolt was already well underway when some *Sicarioi*, along with some feebler folk, slipped into the temple during the feast of wood-carrying. They were then recruited by the rebels who had already laid siege to the high priests and the (other) *dynatoi* in the upper city (*War* 2.422–425). They were thus involved in setting fire to the royal palaces and the mansion of the High Priest Ananias and the archives that housed the records of debts (426–427). But these actions were not initiated or implemented only by the *Sicarioi*. Large numbers of the city populace and perhaps ordinary priests as well would have been eager to join these attacks.

It was not the *Sicarioi*, moreover, who captured the fortress of Masada from the Roman garrison there (*War* 2.408). Among the rebel groups already active in the summer of 66 some of the most ardent stormed Masada by stealth, killed the Roman garrison and set up one of their own (408). Only later did Menahem and other *Sicarioi* arm themselves from Herod's old armory at the fortress (433–444). Furthermore, Menahem, perhaps the grandson of Judas of Gamala, was not the principal leader of the revolt, and evidently not even of all of the *Sicarioi*. Other *Sicarioi* were already active in Jerusalem before Menahem entered at the head of another band. Josephus does not give him any prominence, in contrast with other leaders such as Simon bar Giora or Eleazar the temple-captain. The most distinctive thing about his brief leadership was his posturing as the messianic king, a stance unprecedented in the Fourth Philosophy and the *Sicarioi*.[24]

The aggressive role of the *Sicarioi* in the revolt was brief, since the other insurgents quickly turned against them. The temple-captain Eleazar's forces and the rest of the *demos* attacked the *sophistes* and his followers in the temple and put them to flight. Menahem was discovered hiding in the lower city, tortured, and killed. Some escaped to Masada, captured the fortress from the garrison there, and proceeded to sit out the rest of the revolt, occasionally raiding the surrounding countryside to obtain food. When the Roman forces finally got around to besieging Masada as part of their "mopping up" operations in 73 CE, the *Sicarii* offered no active resistance, finally committing mass suicide (*War* 7.320–401). But this was hardly "the Zealots' last stand."[25]

The point to be recognized from Josephus' coverage of the *Sicarioi*, particularly their attempt to take leadership of the revolt, is that as an apparently scribal group they had no base of support among the city people, much less in the countryside. Their earlier terrorist tactics, moreover, would have alienated other scribal groups, not drawn sympathy. By contrast, the strategy of the Pharisees was to continue to influence the operations of the temple-state as mediators of high priestly (and Roman) rule, perhaps hoping to mitigate its worst effects.

Those Accurate in Observance of the Laws Who Objected to Ananus' Execution of James

Josephus includes a suggestive account of an event just before the outbreak of the Great Revolt that some have thought must be referring to Pharisees. If they were not Pharisees, then here is a scribal circle that was still attempting to exert influence on the high priesthood and its relations with the Roman governors. While Albinus was on his way to Judea to replace the recently deceased Festus as governor (62 CE), King Agrippa had deposed Joseph as High Priest and replaced him with Ananus son of Ananus.

> He was rash in his temper and unusually daring, and he followed the school of the Sadducees, who are indeed more savage about court punishments than all other Judeans, as I have already explained [13.294] . . . He convened the judges of the

24. See further the critical examination of Josephus' accounts in historical context in "Menahem in Jerusalem."

25. The political propaganda of "the Zealots' last stand" was built on an unhistorical synthetic construct.

council (*synedrion*) and brought before them the brother of Jesus who was called messiah, named James, and certain others. He accused them of breaking the law and delivered them up to be stoned. Those of the inhabitants considered the most fair-minded and strict in observance of the law were offended at this. They therefore secretly sent to King Agrippa urging him to order Ananus to desist from any further such actions, for he had not even been correct in his first step.[26] Some of them even went to meet Albinus, who was on his way from Alexandria, and informed him that Ananus had no authority to convene the council without his consent. Convinced by what they said Albinus angrily wrote to Ananus threatening to take vengeance on him. And King Agrippa, on account of [Ananus' action] deposed him from the high priesthood which he had held for three months and replaced him with Jesus son of Damnaeus. (*Ant.* 20.199–203)

Josephus' representation of the inhabitants of the city most "strict in (observance/application of) the law," which is very similar to how he characterizes the Pharisees in three different passages is what suggests that they may have been Pharisees. Of course he also uses a similar phrase about the two scholar-teachers who inspired their students to cut down the golden Roman eagle, and there is insufficient evidence to determine whether these other Jerusalemites strict in observance of the law were Pharisees. There appear to be more clues, however, in Josephus' account here toward the end of *Antiquities*. The High Priest Ananus had replaced the Pharisees with the Sadducees as his principal advisers; the displaced Pharisees would have had reason to protest and resist Ananus' action in execution of James. That "the inhabitants considered the most fair-minded and strict in observance of the law" are disturbed at the severity of the execution of James and the others by stoning recommended by a council composed mainly of (or dominated by) Sadducees presents an opposition between the two groups that Josephus often makes. In particular, the story that Josephus had repeated in his account of John Hyrcanus' break with the Pharisees in favor of the Sadducees includes just this contrast between the moderation of the one and the savagery of the other in punishments (*Ant.* 13.294). That these "inhabitants of the city considered the most fair-minded" presumed that they had the standing to appeal to Agrippa (who at that point had the power to depose and appoint the High Priest) and to travel to meet Albinus indicates that they had an important role and authority in the politics of the Jerusalem

---

26. That is, of convening the council without Albinus' consent, mentioned just below.

temple-state that would have been recognized by both the King and the Roman governor.

These accounts of Gamaliel, the sons of Judas of Gamala, and those considered the most fair minded and strict in observance of the law indicate that Pharisees continued active in political affairs in the Jerusalem temple-state. Not only that, but they had evidently become ever more prominent in the operations of the temple-state. And this would appear to have been related to the high priestly heads of the temple, having become ever more predatory on the people, losing control of public order. In his historical narratives in *War* and *Antiquities* Josephus is evidently trying to partially obscure the identity of Pharisees and the ever more prominent role they were playing as the Roman imperial order in Jerusalem was falling apart. But his hints of their identity provide indications of what he is forced to admit in his defense of his own role in the Great Revolt, that "the leading Pharisees" had gained influential roles in the temple-state in close collaboration with leading high priests before the outbreak of the revolt.

The continuing "political realism" and attempts by Pharisees to mitigate the effects of the abuses of the people by both high priests such as Ananus son of Ananus and Roman governors such as Festus stands in stark contrast with the resort to terrorist tactics by that other circle of scribes, the *Sicarioi*. Frustrated that the high priestly rulers had abandoned the traditional Judean *politeia* and ancestral laws in their violent raids on the people and collaboration in Roman rule, the *Sicaroi* sought to force the situation with assassinations of the most prominent high priestly figures and seizing hostages to extort release of their colleagues who had been caught, tactics that led to further break-down of the social-political order. By contrast, the Pharisees attempted, on the one hand, to restrain high priestly rulers' punitive repressive measures that would only exacerbate the social disorder and, on the other hand, to facilitate the Roman imperial order in Judea via in a new Roman governor and a Herodian ruler who could more effectively restrain an arrogant High Priest.

8

The Pharisees and the Politics of Roman Palestine

Understanding of the Pharisees can be considerably enhanced by more complex consideration of the sources, by fuller attention to the complexities of the historical context(s), and by considering the implications of new lines of recent research into ancient communications media.

The limited sources from the early second-temple period such as the book of Nehemiah indicate that under Persian imperial rule the tiny area of *Yehud* became ruled by a temple-state headed by a High Priest at the head of a priestly aristocracy, subject to the Persian imperial regime. This institutional form that ruled the Judean people has been obscured in the academic fields of ancient Jewish studies and biblical studies by the controlling construct of Judaism. Religious and political-economic affairs were inseparable in the Judean temple-state under imperial rule. The priests who performed sacrifices and other ceremonies were supported by animals and crops supplied by the peasant villagers they ruled. The priestly aristocracy, under the enforced supervision of Persian governors such as Nehemiah, also extracted produce for the tribute required by the imperial regime. As also indicated in Nehemiah (e.g., 5:1–13), structural conflict between the rulers and the ruled was built into the political-economic-religious institution of the temple-state under imperial rule. The institution proved to be unstable as the successive empires continued to maintain the temple-state as their form of rule in Judea.

A more complete and careful reading of the instructional speeches of the Jerusalem scribe Yeshua ben Sira collected in the book of Sirach finds a description and several supporting clues of the political-economic-religious structure of the Judean temple-state. He offers additional indications of the dominant conflict between the ruling high priests and the people, both Jerusalemites and the vast majority of Judeans who worked the land. Particularly important for better understanding of the Pharisees and other scribal groups in subsequent generations is the first-hand description of the position and role of learned scribes who devoted their lives to learning the torah of the Most High and prophecies and various forms of wisdom in order to serve in the councils of the priestly aristocracy. Ben Sira's instructional speeches indicate that he and other scribes trained for service in the temple-state did not *interpret* particular laws that they quoted in fixed form, but rather strove to dutifully expound and *keep* the covenant and its commandments (presumably adaptations of the Mosaic tradition). He exemplifies how in their position as intellectual-legal retainers of the high priestly rulers, the scribes' role is advice, assistance, and on occasion glorification of the high priests who preside in temple affairs and ceremonies. Yet he also warns his proteges to watch their words in their contacts with priestly aristocrats and admonishes them to mitigate the worst effects of high priests' exploitation of the people.

Several lines of recent research into ancient communications media, if brought together, can illuminate the importance of the learned scribes as the cultivators of the culture of the Judean temple-state. In Judean society as in all ancient societies oral communication was dominant, with literacy being limited in Judea to the scribes who served as advisers of the high priests in the temple-state. In their rigorous training scribes learned torah (teaching/law), prophecies, and wisdom in general and already defined "texts" by oral recitation, so that the tradition in general and texts in particular became "written on the tablet of their heart," that is "inscribed" in their memory. Learned scribes (sages) cultivated the extensive repertoire of torah, prophecies, and wisdom in their individual and collective memory. In contrast to writing in modern print-culture, written texts in antiquity were not necessarily intended for reading or consultation. Texts inscribed on scrolls or monuments were "monumental," intended to impress and awe the people, who could not have read them. Some, probably including scrolls of torah, were numinous sacred objects, like the "constitutional" text inscribed on a scroll that Ezra held aloft and the people worshipped (in Neh 8:1–8).

Recent studies of such scribal training helps us understand what text-critics have found in close examination of the manuscripts found among the Dead Sea Scrolls of what later became the "biblical" books of the Torah (Pentateuch) and Prophets: there were multiple versions of each book and all those versions were still developing. So it seems that in late second temple times there was not yet a standardized text of what only much later could be called Scripture. With literacy confined to scribal circles, ordinary people could not have been reading scrolls. So the written texts of books of the Torah and Prophets used by modern scholars, which are based on much later (medieval) manuscripts, are not direct sources for what Judeans in general knew and practiced. By discerning how ancient Judean scribes may have adapted Israelite tradition (laws, customs, prophecies, etc.), however, some material in books the Torah and the Prophets offer indirect sources for the Israelite popular tradition in which life in village communities were rooted.

The "books" of (proto-)Deuteronomy and (proto-)Leviticus, however, which legitimated and applied to temple-state operations, were known, and evidently continued to be cultivated, in scribal circles. A survey of Josephus' systematic exposition of the laws indicates the laws/customs/ancestral traditions of the Judeans included some that were not included in the defined texts that were later included in the Hebrew Bible. It seems clear that scribal circles, whether in service of the temple-state or dissidents, were cultivating a wider and deeper repertoire of laws, customs, and traditions than those contained in already defined texts that were being inscribed on scrolls.

Especially significant are Ben Sira's indications that the learned scribes serving in the temple-state had developed a sense of their own authority directly from the Most High, distinct from their authority delegated from their high priestly patrons. This set up a potential conflict between the authority of the scribal tradition of which they were the professional guardians and that of their high priestly patrons, who were themselves subject to the imperial overlords and the imperial cultural forms.

This is the conflict into which the learned scribes or sages came when the dominant faction of the ruling high priestly aristocracy carried out the Hellenizing reform, in effect abandoning the traditional covenantal "constitution" (or way of life) of the Judean temple-state for the dominant Hellenistic political culture of the *polis* in the 170s BCE. The book of Daniel (7–12) and the Animal Vision in 1 Enoch (85–90) provide vivid visions of Hellenistic imperial rule that had become invasively predatory on the Judeans and indications that the scribal circles of the *maskilim* and "Enoch"-scribes mounted active resistance to their "reforming" high priestly patrons who had abandoned the covenant. The ensuing invasion by the Seleucid emperor Antiochus Epiphanes to enforce the "reform" and the eruption of guerilla warfare led by the Hasmonean family of ordinary priests that fought the imperial armies to a stand-off meant, in effect, a multi-year hiatus in which rule of the temple-state was in abeyance.

In the vacuum of imperial power created by the demise of the Seleucid regime that split into rival factions, Judas "the hammer's" brother

Jonathan maneuvered to be recognized by rival Seleucids as the new High Priest and restored the temple-state as the form of his rule. Jonathan and his brother and successor as High Priest, Simon, however, not only lacked legitimacy, coming from a family of ordinary priests and not from a high priestly lineage (Zadokite or Aaronid) of hoary antiquity. As rural priests who had been leading guerrilla warfare for more than a decade, moreover, they lacked experience in the operation of the temple-state in Jerusalem. They would have needed scribes trained the laws, traditions, and practices of the temple-state that would have helped legitimate the restoration under upstart new high priests. It thus cannot be by accident that Jonathan's maneuver to become the new High Priest is the context in which Josephus first mentions the three principal "philosophies" of the Judeans, the Pharisees, the Sadducees, and the Essenes. From the Dead Sea Scrolls is it evident that the Essenes are closely related to the Qumran community, which sharply rejected the "Wicked Priest," illustrating the legitimacy problem of the upstart Hasmonean High Priests. Soon after their apparent origin, the Pharisees appear as the advisers of Simon's son John Hyrcanus, before the Sadducees maneuver to replace them as advisers of Hyrcanus, in Josephus' narrative in *Antiquities.*

The histories of Josephus, of course, are the principal sources for the Pharisees and Sadducees and other scribal groups active in late second-temple times. It is thus of great importance to recognize what Josephus' histories are about to understand his almost incidental mentions of the Pharisees, Sadducees, and other scribal groups in the changing historical contexts of Hasmonean rule, then Herodian and high priestly rule under the overarching Roman imperial rule. That is, Josephus' histories are primarily about the rulers of the Judean temple-state in their relations with the imperial rulers. Josephus' incidental references to Pharisees and scribal groups can be appropriately understood only in the contexts of the temple-state and their position and role, as they may have been impacted by the political relations between the rulers of the temple-state and their imperial overlords.

Chapters 4 through 7 above have attempted to discern the history of the Pharisees and other scribal groups through a critical examination of Josephus' accounts and related sources in literary and historical contexts.

The Pharisees evidently enjoyed considerable influence in the temple-state under the early Hasmoneans, perhaps already under Jonathan and Simon and certainly in the reign of John Hyrcanus. If we trust the superficially edited legendary story Josephus repeats, they were the "friends" of Hyrcanus, that is, his intimate advisers. He had authorized their *nomima*, derived from ancestral traditions but not included in the written laws of Moses, as official state law. Here is an early indication of how they came to have the reputation of having exact/expert knowledge and application of the laws. The laws they cultivated, moreover, included not only those already also written in the "books" of Moses, but a wider range of laws, customs, practices that scribal groups had been cultivating. The Pharisees and perhaps other scribal groups understood these as having the special authority of having been from the ancestors, perhaps meaning that they had been cultivated by previous generations of scribes serving in the temple-state. That Hyrcanus had been their student (according to the story cited by Josephus) suggests that the Pharisees had been teaching him a range of laws, customs, and traditional practices. That Hyrcanus had authorized the Pharisees' laws derived from the ancestors as official laws of the temple-state suggests that they pertained to the operations of the temple-state.

That the Pharisees had promulgated these or handed them down to the *demos*, one of the standard terms used to indicate the "city-people" of Jerusalem, suggests that they pertained, at least partly, to "civil" interactions as well as perhaps conduct of temple procedures. That Josephus specifies "to the city-people" may indicate that scribal concern in cultivating the laws and customs, and perhaps the concern of the temple-state, pertained mainly to the people of temple-city of Jerusalem, with little or no concern for the surrounding village communities that were semi-self-governing. This is confirmed by Josephus' description of their return to favor under Alexandra Salome. In any case, it seems that central to their role in the temple-state was cultivation and application of the customs, laws, and traditions of the Judean temple-state.

As Hyrcanus then conquered the adjoining Samaria and Idumea with the mercenary army he had hired (with the immense treasure taken from the tomb of David), he became increasingly remote from the Jerusalem populace. As he consolidated his rule over Judea, he intensified his exploitation of the villagers to amass great wealth. At some point he took the initiative in breaking with the Pharisees and rescinded the ancestral laws (*nomima*) they had passed on to the people as laws of the temple-state. He turned instead to the wealthy Sadducees as advisers. Their recognition of only the written laws of Moses as authoritative would have given him greater leeway to rule without the Pharisees' additional regulations. We may surmise that the Pharisees had questioned his hiring of mercenaries and military conquests of neighboring peoples, as well as the intensified exploitation of the people, seemingly in imitation of Hellenistic imperial rulers. By the end of his reign, the people had begun to resist, but Hyrcanus suppressed their resistance.

The precedent of territorial expansion having been established, his son Aristobulus continued the expansion in a take-over of Galilee and claimed explicitly that he was king as well as High Priest. In a long reign another son,

Alexander Jannaeus, retaining the title of king and relying even more on mercenary forces, took another major step in expansion by conquering the Hellenistic cities around the now vastly expanded territory controlled by the Jerusalem temple-state. The people of Judea mounted widespread and sustained revolt. The extent of the revolt (the numbers greatly exaggerated by Josephus) suggests that villagers as well as Jerusalemites were involved. Although Josephus does not identify their participation, references in some Qumran texts suggest that the Pharisees themselves, who no longer had authority in the operations of the temple-state, also joined in active opposition at some point in coalition with the populace. Jannaeus, brutal and vicious in his military suppression of the opposition, crucified a large number of rebels, who may well have included (some of the) Pharisees, after which others fled into exile.

In his few short accounts of the Pharisees under the Hasmoneans, Josephus says that they had influence on the people. Contrary to previous claims, however, he does not say that they were popular among the people or that they had the support of the people or that the people's support of or opposition to the Hasmonean rulers was determined or led by the Pharisees. It is clear from his accounts that whatever authority the Pharisees or their laws enjoyed derived from the high priestly rulers. Under Hyrcanus they and their ancestral laws were authorized by Hyrcanus early in his reign. After Hyrcanus broke with the Pharisees later in his reign, they evidently became active in resistance, even revolt, against the blatantly expansionist and repressive Alexander Jannaeus. As Josephus must admit, Jannaeus was vicious and brutal in the extreme in his crucifixion of a number of those who had fought against him, including many Pharisees, as survivors fled into exile.

Whether or not at Jannaeus' recommendation, his wife and successor Alexandra Salome restored the Pharisees and their ancestral *nomima* to authority in the operations of the temple-state. That the Pharisees were ready to come back into service in the temple-state after the crucifixion or exile of many of their number attests their commitment to its functioning as the central ruling political-economic-religious institution in the now greatly expanded territory it ruled. Josephus disapproves of Alexandra's having given them considerable authority in the conduct of domestic Judean affairs. His report that they worked to mollify the people's anger at Jannaeus to ease Alexandra's ascendancy suggests that a compromise of their own resentment and principles was the price of returning to positions of authority. His statement that the Pharisees became the administrators of domestic affairs, however, seem credible, while his bitter complaint that they became "the real rulers of the state" under Alexandra is an exaggeration. He expresses outrage in particular that they pushed for justice in the punishment of Jannaeus' military officers who had advised (and assisted) him in the crucifixion of his opponents.

The rest of his account, however, indicates that the Pharisees were only one of the major forces in the operations of the Jerusalem temple-state under Alexandra. They would have been dependent on Alexandra's approval or consent in whatever actions they took to bring those officers to justice. One gains the sense that once restored to positions of authority so that they were administering domestic affairs, with Alexandra having commanded the people to obey their *nomima,* they gained sufficient role and reputation in the temple-state so as to survive through the political chaos of the next decades. That chaos started when, before many years had passed, Alexandra's impetuous younger son Aristobulus and those officers of Alexander who had control of many of the fortresses around Judea staged a take-over of Judea and, at least temporarily, the temple-state.

The Pharisees' patience and persistence would have been seriously tested in the next decades of the Roman conquest, the Hasmonean and Roman civil wars, and the recurrent conflicts of Herod's rise to power. The Roman conquest was seriously destructive and divisive. The Romans restored Hyrcanus II to the high priesthood; his rule became a façade for the Idumean Antipater to mediate and manipulate Rome's rule through the temple-state. This arrangement evidently enabled the Pharisees to continue to exert influence on the operations of the temple. At least one Pharisee, Samaias, or was it Pollion, or both, was a member of the council that Hyrcanus convened to try Herod, Antipater's son and military governor in Galilee, for the murder of some Galileans. When Hyrcanus and other prominent Jerusalemites in the council were intimidated by the arrogant young military strong-man, Samaias (or Pollion) was bold enough to warn them that if they did not convict Herod then, he would eventually kill them all when he rose to power. When Herod moved to take control of Jerusalem as the king of the Judeans appointed by the Romans, Samaias and Pollion, continuing in their political realism, advised that he be admitted to the city.

But this was not an indication that they supported him. Like the people of the city in general, Pollion and Samaias and other Pharisees continued to oppose, even resist Herod, although Josephus offers no information about particular actions of Herod that the Pharisees objected to. They refused to take an oath of loyalty to his rule and later also refused an oath both to Herod and to Caesar. Yet while Herod punished others who refused his loyalty oaths, he did not punish the Pharisees, evidently out of appreciation of their role in admitting him to the city he had besieged. Only when some of the Pharisees conspired against him with women in the royal court did he execute those involved. Otherwise, considering how severely he suppressed other dissenters, he was remarkably lenient to the Pharisees despite their opposition. Why? Considering that Herod was trying to use the temple-state as an instrument of his own rule that otherwise was almost systematically undermining the ancestral *politeia* of the Judeans, it seems likely that he knew he needed them to influence its operations in accordance with the laws.

Judging from their refusal of the second loyalty oath, to Caesar as well as to Herod, it seems likely that the Pharisees' opposition was to his rule more generally, which was a model of loyalty to Caesar and aggressively embodied Roman imperial rule in the Hellenistic world. Josephus presents the scholar-teachers who inspired their students to cut down the golden Roman eagle, symbol of the subordination of Judea and its temple to Rome, as similar to the Pharisees in their reputation for accuracy in (knowledge and application of) the ancestral laws. He also claims that the Fourth Philosophy who advocated refusal to pay the tribute to Caesar agreed with the Pharisees' position on all fronts. The close similarities of these other two scribal groups to the Pharisees suggests that the Pharisees persistently opposed Herod because his actions were undermining the most basic commandments of the covenant, the very center of the *politeia* of the Judeans that they were personally committed to cultivate and obey.

The Pharisees opposed Herod's rule, however, while also evidently maneuvering to maintain their influence in the operations of the temple-state. Josephus does not provide any direct statement to this effect. But we can deduce this from the combination of his account of the Pharisees and the Sadducees in *Ant.* 18.12–17 and autobiographical account at the beginning of *Life*. In his most positive general account of the Pharisees at the beginning of *Antiquities* book 18, Josephus suggests that procedures in the temple and temple-state were done according to the views of the Pharisees. He states, moreover, that even the prominent but crude Sadducees serving in some office must, however unwillingly, adhere to the rules or procedures established by the Pharisees. At least by sometime during the increasing social unrest under the high priestly aristocracy and Roman governors operations of the temple-state were done increasingly according to the views of the Pharisees.

One suspects that with leading high priestly figures more interested in advancing their own fortunes in collaboration with the Romans than in operating the temple-state, the Pharisees moved into the political vacuum of domestic affairs, effecting their own application of the laws and customs on which they were the acknowledged experts. That this was the situation in the 60s CE is confirmed by Josephus admission that in entering public life in Jerusalem he had to pursue politics in accordance with the views of the Pharisees. It seems apparent that, dedicated to maintaining the operations of the Jerusalem temple-state under what they knew was the overwhelming military power of Rome, they sought to mitigate the abuses by both high priestly figures and Roman governors. In order to maintain at least a modicum of the traditional Judean way of life under the temple-state, they ironically mediated as well as moderated Roman imperial rule in Judea.

The Pharisees, of course, were not the only group with scribal training for service in the Jerusalem temple-state. As discussed in chapter 1, as the crisis of the Hellenizing reform developed, there were evidently several different circles of scribes. As noted above, at least two of these, the *maskilim* who produced Dan 10–12 and the "Enoch"-scribes who produced the Animal Vision in 1 Enoch 85–90 mounted active opposition to the dominant faction of the priestly aristocracy that had abandoned the covenantal "constitution" of the Judean temple-state.

As noted briefly above, as the Hasmonean Jonathan maneuvered between rival factions of Seleucids to become the High Priest of a reestablished temple-state, a sizeable group of traditionalist scribes and priests withdrew to the wilderness to establish a rigorous covenantal *yahad* of the true Israel at Qumran. As the Pharisees were securing a certain level of authority under the Hasmoneans, the far more traditionalist circle of scribes, the Sadducees, emerged to rival them. John Hyrcanus replaced the Pharisees with the Sadducees as his advisers; they were probably more useful to him and his successors as they consolidated their power in Judea and launched extensive conquests. Despite, or perhaps because of their expanded military power, however, the Hasmonean high priests-kings could not secure a modus vivendi with the populace of Jerusalem and the villagers in the countryside—without the more flexible application of the Judean laws and customs cultivated by the Pharisees.

Josephus' historical accounts indicate that, at least toward the end of Herod's reign, other scribes/sages were still active in Jerusalem, although not apparently involved in the operation of the temple-state, much less active in Herod's court. The circle of scribes who produced the Psalms of Solomon opposed Herod's rule as well as the Hasmoneans, but evidently kept a relatively low profile. Like the Pharisees, presumably, the scholar-teachers Mattathias and Judas were engaged in cultivating and teaching their students the covenantal laws and customs of the Judeans. Evidently, they had not attempted to subvert Herod's constructions and practices that went against the laws until he appeared to be dying. But then they took the bold action of cutting down the golden Roman eagle from the gate of Herod's temple—and were martyred for their defiance. By comparison the

Pharisees, who continued to work inside the temple-state now subordinated to Herod's rule, took a stand against him only on the matter of the loyalty oath, except insofar as they attempted to subvert through court intrigue and only then by prophecy that would possibly provoke agitation in the Herodian inner circle.

Most interesting in terms of the relationship between the Pharisees and other scribal groups is what Josephus labels the Fourth Philosophy, which organized refusal to pay the tribute to Caesar. Josephus states that they agreed in all things with the Pharisees except for their intense passion for freedom—and willingness to suffer the consequences of resistance. This suggests that not only Saddok, the co-founder of the group, but others as well, were Pharisees and that the Pharisees' shared the view that Roman rule over the Judeans was against the Judean covenantal constitution and that payment of the tribute was against the covenantal commandments, since the Judeans had God as their ruler and master. The Pharisees, however, had compromised their ideals in order to serve in the temple-state where they might mediate between the illegitimate rule of Rome and their compromised patrons, the high priests, and the Judean populace.

As high priestly and Roman rule became ever more predatory and exploitative toward mid-first century, however, while the more adamant dissident scholar-scribes known as the *Sicarioi* resorted to surreptitious violence in their frustration, the Pharisees continued in their role as legal retainers integral to the operations of the temple-state. From Josephus' accounts it is clear that while leading high priestly figures had become downright predatory on the people, at least "the leading Pharisees" had secured a prominent role in the temple-state's operations by the outbreak of the Great Revolt.

In both of his accounts of events in Jerusalem in the summer of 66 CE, says Josephus as a direct participant in the events, at the eruption of the revolt in Jerusalem in the summer of 66 CE, "the leading Pharisees" joined with the high priests who still remained in the city in a fortified hideout from the rebelling people of Jerusalem. When they dared come out of hiding, the leading Pharisees were integral members in the high-priestly-led council in Jerusalem that attempted to keep a lid on the revolt until they could negotiate with the Romans, presumably for a restoration of their rule. But the leading Pharisees and high priests in the Jerusalem *koinon* could not control the revolt carried out mainly by large coalitions of villagers who converged on Jerusalem and its temple as the principal fortified place where they could take refuge from the Roman onslaught. With their overwhelming military might the Romans brutally suppressed the Great Revolt and destroyed the temple-state along with Jerusalem and the temple.

For most of the two hundred years prior to the Roman destruction of the temple the Pharisees had served as the legal-intellectual retainers in the Judean temple-state, advising the high priestly rulers and cultivating and applying the laws, customs, and traditions of the Judeans. They evidently were personally and collectively committed to the *politeia,* the torah (teachings/laws/customs) or covenantal "way of life," that the temple-state supposedly embodied and observed. When the Hasmoneans consolidated their power and seriously compromised or seemingly abandoned the covenantal constitution, the Pharisees resisted, even joined the popular revolt.

After they were restored to their position and role, they continued in service of the temple-state through a period of political chaos, including the Roman conquest. When the Romans installed Herod as King, they submitted to his rule as political realists who understood that it would be impossible to revolt against the overwhelming military power of Rome. Yet when Herod systematically violated the laws of the covenantal constitution in effectively integrating his realm into the Roman imperial order, they found ways to resist his rule.

When the Romans then installed the high priestly aristocracy under Roman governors, the Pharisees, again as political realists, sought to continue as the legal retainers of the temple-state. They sought to mitigate the worst effects on the people as leading high priestly figures became predatory on their own people and Roman governors became increasingly provocative. By the time of the Great Revolt they had become prominent in the temple-state, and the leading Pharisees joined the high priests is attempting to control the Great Revolt. By then, however, the priestly aristocracy had lost all legitimacy and control of the society. The history of the Pharisees ended with the Roman destruction of the Jerusalem temple-state.

Bibliography

Applebaum, Shimon. "The Hasmoneans—Logistics, Taxation, and the Constitution." In *Judaea in Hellenistic and Roman Times: Historical and Archaeological Essays*, 9–29. Studies in Judaism in Late Antiquity 40. Leiden: Brill, 1989.
Assmann, Jan. "Kulturelle und Literarische Texte." In *Ancient Egyptian Literature: History and Forms*, edited by Antonio Loprieno, 60–82. Probleme der Ägyptologie 10. Leiden: Brill, 1996.
Atkinson, Kenneth. *I Cried to the Lord: A Study of the Psalms of Solomon's Historical Background and Social Setting*. Journal for the Study of Judaism Supplements 84. Leiden: Brill, 2004.
———. "On the Herodian Origin of Militant Davidic Messianism at Qumran: New Light from *Psalm of Solomon* 17." *Journal of Biblical Literature* 118 (1999) 435–60.
Attridge, Harold W. "Josephus and His Works." In *Jewish Writings of the Second Temple Period: Apocrypha, Pseudepigrapha, Qumran Sectarian Writings, Philo, Josephus*, edited by Michael E. Stone, 2:185–232. Compendia rerum Iudaicarum ad Novum Testamentum II/2. Philadelphia: Fortress, 1984.
Avigad, Nahman. *Discovering Jerusalem*. Nashville: Nelson, 1983.
Babota, Vasile. *The Institution of the Hasmonean High Priesthood*. Journal for the Study of Judaism Supplements 165. Leiden: Brill, 2014.
Bartsch, Shadi. *Actors in the Audience: Theatricality and Doublespeak from Nero to Hadrian*. Revealing Antiquity. Cambridge: Harvard University Press, 1994.
Baumgarten, Albert I. *The Flourishing of Jewish Sects in the Maccabean Era*. Journal for the Study of Judaism Supplements 55. Leiden: Brill, 1997.
———. "The Name of the Pharisees." *Journal of Biblical Literature* 102 (1983)411–28.
———. "Rivkin and Neusner on the Pharisees." In *Law and Religious Communities in the Roman Period: The Debate over Torah and Nomos in Post-Biblical Judaism and Early Christianity*, edited by Peter Richardson and Stephen Westerholm, 109–26. Studies in Christianity and Judaism 4. Waterloo, ON: Wilfrid Laurier University Press, 1991.
Baumgarten, J. M. "The Pharisaic-Sadducean Controversies about Purity and the Qumran Texts." *Journal of Jewish Studies* 31 (1980) 157–70.
———. "The Unwritten Law in the Pre-Written Period." *Journal for the Study of Judaism* 3 (1972) 7–29.
Beard, Mary et al. *Literacy in the Roman World*. JRASup 3. Ann Arbor: Journal of Roman Archaeology, 1991.

Bickerman, Elias. *From Ezra to the Last of the Maccabees: Foundations of Post-Biblical Judaism*. New York: Schocken, 1962. (Reprint of two essays from 1947 and 1949)

———. *The God of the Maccabees: Studies on the Meaning and Origin of the Maccabean Revolt*. Translated by Horst R. Moehring. Studies in Judaism in Late Antiquity 32. Leiden: Brill, 1979. (German original 1937)

Blenkinsopp, Joseph. "Interpretation and the Tendency to Sectarianism: An Aspect of Second Temple History." In *Jewish and Christian Self-Definition*, vol. 2, edited by E. P. Sanders, 1–26 + 299–310. Philadelphia: Fortress, 1981.

———. *The Pentateuch: An Introduction to the First Five Books of the Bible*. Anchor Bible Reference Library. New York: Doubleday, 1992.

———. "Prophecy and Priesthood in Josephus." *Journal of Jewish Studies* 25 (1974) 239–62.

Botha, Pieter J. J. "Graeco-Roman Literacy as Setting for New Testament Writings." *Noetestamentica* 26 (1992) 201–22.

Bottero, Jean, "Le Code de Hammur-abi." In *Annali della Scuola Normale Superiore di Pisa clase di littere filosofia* 12.3 (1982) 409–44.

Bowman, Alan K., and Greg Woolf, eds. *Literacy and Power in the Ancient World*. Cambridge: Cambridge University Press, 1994.

Boyarin, Daniel. *Judaism: The Genealogy of a Modern Notion*. Key Words in Jewish Studies 9. New Brunswick, NJ: Rutgers University Press, 2019.

———. "Place Reading: Ancient Israel and Medieval Europe." In *The Ethnography of Reading*, edited by Jonathan Boyarin, 10–37. Berkeley: University of California Press, 1993.

Broshi, Magen. "The Role of the Temple in the Herodian Economy." *Journal of Jewish Studies* 38 (1987) 31–37.

Camp, Claudia V. "Understanding a Patriarchy: Women in Second Century Jerusalem through the Eyes of Ben Sira." In *"Women Like This": New Perspectives on Jewish Women in the Greco-Roman World*, edited by Amy-Jill Levine, 1–39. Early Judaism and Its Literature 1. Atlanta: Scholars, 1991.

Carr, David M. *Writing on the Tablet of the Heart: Origins of Scripture and Literature*. Oxford: Oxford University Press, 2005.

Carruthers, Mary J. *The Book of Memory: A Study of Memory in Medieval Culture*. 2nd ed. Cambridge Studies in Medieval Literature 70. Cambridge: Cambridge University Press, 2008.

Clanchy, M. T. *From Memory to Written Record: England 1066–1307*. Cambridge: Harvard University Press, 1979. (2nd ed., 1993.)

Cohen, Shaye J. D. *The Beginnings of Jewishness: Boundaries, Varieties, and Uncertainties*. Berkeley: University of California Press, 1999.

———. *From the Maccabees to the Mishnah*. Library of Early Christianity 7. Philadelphia: Westminster Press, 1987. (3rd ed., 2014.)

———. *Josephus in Galilee and Rome: His Vita and Development as a Historian*. Columbia Studies in the Classical Tradition 8. Leiden: Brill, 1979.

Collins, John J. *The Apocalyptic Imagination*. New York: Crossroad, 1984.

———. *Jewish Wisdom in the Hellenistic Age*. Louisville: Westminster John Knox, 1997.

———. "Wisdom, Apocalypticism, and Generic Compatibility." In *In Search of Wisdom: Essays in Memory of John G. Gammie*, edited by Leo G. Perdue et al., 165–86. Louisville: Westminster John Knox, 1993.

Cribiore, Raffaella. *Gymnastics of the Mind: Greek Education in Hellenistic and Roman Egypt*. Princeton: Princeton University Press, 2001.
DiLella, Alexander A. "Wisdom of Ben Sira." In *The Anchor Bible Dictionary*, edited by David Noel Freedman, 6:939–94. New York: Doubleday, 1992.
Finkelstein, Jacob. "Ammisaduqa's Edict and the Babylonian Lawcodes." *Journal of Cuneiform Studies* 15 (1961) 19–104.
Fitzmyer, Joseph A. "The Languages of Palestine in the First Century A.D." *Catholic Biblical Quarterly* 32 (1970) 501–31.
Foley, John Miles. *How to Read an Oral Poem*. Urbana: University of Illinois Press, 2002.
Fraade, Steven D. "Interpretive Authority in the Studying Community at Qumran." *Journal of Jewish Studies* 44 (1993) 46–69.
Gabba, Emilio. "The Finances of King Herod." In *Greece and Rome in Eretz Israel*, edited by Aryeh Kasher et al., 160–68. Jerusalem: Israel Exploration Society, 1990.
Gamble, Harry Y. *Books and Readers in the Early Church: A History of Early Christian Texts*. New Haven: Yale University Press, 1995.
Goodblatt, D. "The Place of the Pharisees in First Century Judaism: The State of the Debate." *Journal for the Study of Judaism* 20 (1989) 12–30.
Goodman, Martin. *The Ruling Class of Judea: The Origins of the Jewish Revolt Against Rome A.D. 66–70*. Cambridge: Cambridge University Press, 1987.
Grabbe, Lester L. "The Law of Moses in the Ezra Tradition: More Virtual Than Real?" In *Persia and Torah: The Theory of Imperial Authorization of the Pentateuch*, edited by James W. Watts, 91–113. Symposium Series 17. Atlanta: SBL, 2001.
Graham, William A. *Beyond the Written Word: Oral Aspects of Scripture in the History of Religion*. Cambridge: Cambridge University Press, 1987.
Green, William Scott. "Writing with Scripture: The Rabbinic Uses of the Hebrew Bible." In *Writing with Scripture: The Authority and Uses of the Hebrew Bible in the Torah of Formative Judaism*, edited by Jacob Neusner, 7–23. Minneapolis: Fortress, 1989.
Gruen, Erich. *Heritage and Hellenism: The Reinvention of Jewish Tradition*. Hellenistic Culture and Society 30. Berkeley: University of California Press, 1998.
Harris, William V. *Ancient Literacy*. Cambridge: Harvard University Press, 1989.
Hengel, Martin. *Judaism and Hellenism: Studies in Their Encounter in Palestine during the Early Hellenistic Period*. 2 vols. Translated by John Bowden. 1974. Reprint, Eugene, OR: Wipf & Stock, 2003.
Hengel, Martin, and Roland Deines. "E. P. Sanders' 'Common Judaism,' Jesus, and the Pharisees." *Journal of Theological Studies* 46 (1995) 1–70.
Hezser, Catherine. *Jewish Literacy in Roman Palestine*. Texts and Studies in Ancient Judaism 81. Tübingen: Mohr Siebeck, 2001.
———. *The Social Structure of the Rabbinic Movement*. Texts and Studies in Ancient Judaism 66. Tübingen: Mohr Siebeck, 1997.
Himmelfarb, Martha. "Elias Bickerman on Judaism and Hellenism." In *The Jewish Past Revisited: Reflections on Modern Jewish Historians*, edited by David N. Myers and David B. Ruderman, 199–211. New Haven: Yale University Press, 1998.
Horgan, Maurya P. *Pesharim: Qumran Interpretation of Biblical Books*. Catholic Biblical Quarterly Monograph Series 8. Washington, DC: Catholic Biblical Association, 1979.
Horsley, Richard A. "Ancient Judean Banditry." In Horsley, *Politics, Conflict, and Movements in First-Century Palestine*, edited by K. C. Hanson, 58–81. Eugene, OR: Cascade Books, 2023. (Orig. pub. 1981)

———. "Contesting Authority: Popular vs. Scribal Tradition in Continuing Performance." In *Text and Tradition in Performance and Writing*, 99–122. Biblical Performance Criticism Series 9. Eugene, OR: Cascade Books, 2013.

———. *Covenant Economics: A Biblical Vision of Justice for All*. Louisville: Westminster John Knox, 2009.

———. *Empowering the People: Jesus, Healing, and Exorcism*. Eugene, OR: Cascade Books, 2021.

———. "The Expansion of Hasmonean Rule in Idumea and Galilee: Toward a Historical Sociology." In *Second Temple Studies III: Studies in Politics, Class, and Material Culture*, edited by Philip R. Davies and John M. Halligan, 134–65. Journal for the Study of the Old Testament Supplements 340. London: Sheffield Academic, 2002. Republished in Horsley, *The Galileans under Jerusalem and Roman Rule*, edited by K. C. Hanson, 27–60. Eugene, OR: Cascade Books, 2024.

———. *The Galileans under Jerusalem and Roman Rule*. Edited by K. C. Hanson. Eugene, OR: Cascade Books, 2024.

———. *Galilee: History, Politics, People*. Valley Forge, PA: Trinity, 1995.

———. *Hearing the Whole Story: The Politics of Plot in Mark's Gospel*. Louisville: Westminster John Knox, 2001.

———. "High Priests and the Politics of Roman Palestine: A Contextual Analysis of the Evidence in Josephus." *Journal for the Study of Judaism* 17 (1986) 23–55. Republished in Horsley, *Politics, Conflict, and Movements in First-Century Palestine*, edited by K. C. Hanson, 1–29. Eugene, OR: Cascade Books, 2023.

———. *Jesus and the Politics of Roman Palestine*. Revised with a new Preface. Center and Library for the Bible and Social Justice Series. Eugene, OR: Cascade Books, 2021.

———. *Jesus and the Spiral of Violence: Popular Jewish Resistance in Roman Palestine*. 1987. Reprint, Minneapolis: Fortress, 1993.

———. "Josephus and the Bandits." In *Politics, Conflict, and Movements in First-Century Palestine*, edited by K. C. Hanson, 33–57. Eugene, OR: Cascade Books, 2023. (Orig. pub. 1979).

———. "The Languages of the Kingdom: From Aramaic to Greek and Galilee to Syria." In *Text and Tradition in Performance and Writing*, 198–219. Biblical Per-formance Criticism Series 9. Eugene, OR: Cascade Books, 2013.

———. "Menahem in Jerusalem: A Brief Messianic Episode among the Sicarii—not 'Zealot Messianism.'" *Novum Testamentum* 27 (1985) 334–48. Republished in Horsley, *Politics, Conflict, and Movements in First-Century Palestine*, edited by K. C. Hanson, 192–204. Eugene, OR: Cascade Books, 2023.

———. "The Origins of the Hebrew Scriptures under Imperial Rule: Numinous Writing and Ceremonial Performance." In *Text and Tradition in Performance and Writing*, 31–52. Biblical Performance Criticism Series 9. Eugene, OR: Cascade Books, 2013.

———. *The Pharisees and the Temple-State of Judea*. Eugene, OR: Cascade Books, 2022.

———. *Politics, Conflict, and Movements in First-Century Palestine*. Edited by K. C. Hanson. Eugene, OR: Cascade Books, 2023.

———. "Popular Prophetic Movements at the Time of Jesus: Their Principal Features and Social Origins." *Journal for the Study of the New Testament* 26 (1986) 3–27. Republished in Horsley, *Politics, Conflict, and Movements in First-Century Palestine*, edited by K. C. Hanson, 142–63.. Eugene, OR: Cascade Books, 2023.

———. "The Power Vacuum and Power Struggle in 66–67 C.E." In *The First Jewish Revolt: Archaeology, History, and Ideology*, edited by Andrea M. Berlin and J. Andrew Overman, 87–109. London: Routledge, 2002. Republished in Horsley, *The Galileans under Jerusalem and Roman Rule*, edited by K. C. Hanson, 101–26. Eugene, OR: Cascade Books, 2024.

———. *The Prophet Jesus and the Renewal of Israel: Moving beyond a Diversionary Debate*. Grand Rapids: Eerdmans, 2012.

———. *Revolt of the Scribes: Resistance and Apocalyptic Origins*. Minneapolis: Fortress, 2010.

———. *Scribes, Visionaries, and the Politics of Second-Temple Judea*. Louisville: Westminster John Knox, 2007.

———. "The *Sicarii*: Ancient Jewish Terrorists." *Journal of Religion* 59 (1979) 159–92. Republished in Horsley *Politics, Conflict, and Movements in First-Century Palestine*, edited by K. C. Hanson, 167–91. Eugene, OR: Cascade Books, 2023.

———. *Text and Tradition in Performance and Writing*. Biblical Performance Criticism Series 9. Eugene, OR: Cascade Books, 2013.

Horsley, Richard A., with John S. Hanson. *Bandits, Prophets, and Messiahs: Popular Movements in the Time of Jesus*. New Voices in Biblical Studies. Minneapolis: Winston, 1985.

Horsley, Richard A., and Tom Thatcher. *John, Jesus, and the Renewal of Israel*. Grand Rapids: Eerdmans, 2013.

Horsley, Richard A., and Patrick A. Tiller. *After Apocalyptic and Wisdom: Rethinking Texts in Context*. Eugene, OR: Cascade Books, 2012.

———. "Ben Sira and the Sociology of the Second Temple." In *Second Temple Studies III: Studies in Politics, Class, and Material Culture*, eds. Philip R. Davies and John M. Halligan, 74–107. Journal for the Study of the Old Testament Supplements 340. Sheffield: Sheffield Academic, 2002. Reprinted in Horsley and Tiller, *After Apocalyptic and Wisdom: Rethinking Texts in Context*, 19–55. Eugene, OR: Cascade Books, 2012.

Ilan, Tal. "Pheroras' Wife: A Pharisee Woman." In *Gender and Second-Temple Judaism*, edited by Kathy Ehrensperger and Shayna Sheinfeld, 185–96. Lanham, MD: Lexington/Fortress Academic, 2020.

Jaffee, Martin S. *Torah in the Mouth: Writing and Oral Tradition in Palestinian Judaism, 200 BCE–400 CE*. Oxford: Oxford University Press, 2001.

Kasher, Aryeh. *Jews, Idumaeans, and Ancient Arabs: Relations of the Jews in Eretz-Israel with the Nations of the Frontier and the Desert During the Hellenistic and Roman Era (332 BCE—70 CE)*. Texts and Studies in Ancient Judaism 18. Tübingen: Mohr Siebeck, 1988.

Kautsky, John H. *The Politics of Aristocratic Empires*. Chapel Hill: University of North Carolina Press, 1982.

Kelber, Werner H. *Imprints, Voiceprints, and Footprints of Memory: Collected Essays of Werner H. Kelber*. Resources for Biblical Study 74. Atlanta: SBL, 2013.

———. "Jesus and Tradition: Words in Time, Words in Space." In *Imprints, Voiceprints, and Footprints of Memory: Collected Essays of Werner H. Kelber*. Resources for Biblical Study 74. Atlanta: SBL, 2013.

———. *Mark's Story of Jesus*. Philadelphia: Fortress, 1979.

Knight, Douglas A. *Law, Power, and Justice in Ancient Israel*. Library of Ancient Israel. Louisville: Westminster John Knox, 2011.

Lenski, Gerhard E. *Power and Privilege: A Theory of Social Stratification*. New York: McGraw, 1966. (2nd ed., Chapel Hill: University of North Carolina Press, 1984.)

Levine, Lee I. *The Rabbinic Class of Roman Palestine in Late Antiquity*. New York: Jewish Theological Seminary of America, 1989.

Liddell, H. G., and Robert Scott, Henry Scott Jones, and Roderick McKenzie. *A Greek-English Lexicon*. Oxford: Clarendon, 1996. Original publication, 1853.

Lieberman, Saul. *Hellenism in Jewish Palestine*. 2nd ed. Texts and Studies of the Jewish Theological Seminary of America 18. New York: Jewish Theological Seminary of America, 1962.

Machinist, Peter. "Assyrians on Assyria in the First Millennium B.C." In *Anfänge politischen Denkens in der Antike: Die nahöstlichen Kulturen und die Griechen*, edited by Kurt A. Raaflaub and Elisabeth Müller-Luckner, 77–104. Munich: Oldenbourg, 1993.

Mason, Steve. *Flavius Josephus on the Pharisees: A Composition-Critical Study*. Studia Post-Biblica 39. Leiden: Brill, 1991.

———. *Josephus, Judea, and Christian Origins: Methods and Categories*. Peabody, MA: Hendrickson, 2009.

———. "Josephus's Pharisees: The Narratives." In *Quest for the Historical Pharisees*, edited by Jacob Neusner and Bruce Chilton, 3–40. Waco: Baylor University Press, 2007.

———. "Pharisees in Josephus: Narratives and Philosophy." In *Josephus, Judea, and Christian Origins: Methods and Categories*. Peabody, MA: Hendrickson, 2009.

———. "Was Josephus a Pharisee? A Re-Examination of *Life* 10–12." *Journal of Jewish Studies* 40 (1989) 31–45.

McBride, S. Dean. "Polity of the Covenant People: The Book of Deuteronomy." *Interpretation* 41 (1987) 229–44.

Miller, Shem. *Dead Sea Media: Orality, Textuality, and Memory in the Scrolls from the Judean Desert*. Studies on the Texts of the Desert of Judah 129. Leiden: Brill, 2019.

Mroczek, Eva. "Thinking Digitally About the Dead Sea Scrolls: Book History Before and Beyond the Book." *Book History* 14 (2011) 241–69.

Najman, Hindy. *Seconding Sinai: The Development of Mosaic Discourse in Second Temple Judaism*. Journal for the Study of Judaism Supplements 77. Leiden: Brill, 2003.

Neusner, Jacob. *From Politics to Piety: The Emergence of Pharisaic Judaism*. 1973. Reprint, Eugene, OR: Wipf & Stock, 2003.

———. "Josephus's Pharisees." In *Ex orbe religionum: Studia Geo Widengren*, 224–44. Studies in the History of Religions 21. Leiden: Brill, 1972. Reprinted in *Josephus, Judaism, and Christianity*, edited by Louis H. Feldman and Gohei Hata, 274–92. Detroit: Wayne State University Press, 1987.

———. *Rabbinic Traditions about the Pharisees before 70*. 3 vols. 1971. Reprint, Eugene, OR: Wipf & Stock, 2005.

Nickelsburg, George W. E. *1 Enoch 1: A Commentary on the Book of 1 Enoch, chapters 1–36, 81–108*. Hermeneia. Minneapolis: Fortress, 2001.

———. *Jewish Literature between the Bible and the Mishnah*. 2nd ed. Minneapolis: Fortress, 2005.

———. *Resurrection, Immortality, and Eternal Life in Intertestamental Judaism*. Harvard Theological Studies 26. Cambridge: Harvard University Press, 1972.

Nickelsburg, George W. E., and James C. VanderKam. *1 Enoch: A New Translation. Based on the Hermeneia Commentary*. Minneapolis: Fortress, 2004.

Niditch, Susan. *Oral World and Written Word: Ancient Israelite Literature*. Library of Ancient Israel. Louisville: Westminster John Knox, 1996.

Noam, Vered. *Shifting Images of the Hasmoneans: Second Temple Legends and Their Reception in Josephus and Rabbinic Literature*. Translated by Dena Ordan. Oxford: Oxford University Press, 2018.

Pedersén, Olaf. *Archives and Libraries in the City of Assur: A Survey of the Material from the German Excavations*. Studia Semitica Upsaliensia 6, 8. Uppsala: Almquist & Wiksell, 1986.

Poirier, John C. "The Linguistic Situation in Jewish Palestine in Late Antiquity." *Journal of Greco-Roman Christianity and Judaism* 4 (2007) 55–134.

Popović, Mladen. "Reading, Writing, and Memorizing Together: Reading Culture in Ancient Judaism and the Dead Sea Scrolls in a Mediterranean Context." *Dead Sea Discoveries* 24 (2017) 447–70.

Portier-Young, Anathea. *Apocalypse Against Empire: Theologies of Resistance in Early Judaism*. Grand Rapids: Eerdmans, 2011.

Redford, Donald B. "Scribe and Speaker." In *Writings and Speech in Israelite and Ancient Near Eastern Prophecy*, edited by Ehud Ben Zvi and Michael H. Floyd, 145–218. Symposium Series 10. Atlanta: SBL, 2000.

Regev, Eyal. "How Did the Temple Mount Fall to Pompey?" *Journal of Jewish Studies* 48 (1997) 276–89.

Rudich, Vasily. *Dissidence and Literature under Nero: The Price of Rhetoricization*. London: Routledge, 1997.

Ryle, H. E., and M. R. James. *Psalmoi Solomontos: Psalms of the Pharisees, Commonly Called the Psalms of Solomon*. Cambridge: Cambridge University Press, 1891.

Saldarini, Anthony J. "Johanan ben Zakkai's Escape from Jerusalem: Origin and Development of a Rabbinic Story." *Journal for the Study of Judaism* 6 (1975) 189–220.

———. *Matthew's Christian-Jewish Community*. Chicago Studies in the History of Judaism. Chicago: University of Chicago Press, 1994.

Schäfer, Peter. "Die Flucht Johanan b. Zakkais aus Jerusalem und der *Gründung* des 'Lehrhauses.'" In *Aufstieg und Niedergang der roemischen Welt* II.19.2, edited by W. Hase und H. Temporini, 43–101. Berlin: de Gruyter, 1979.

———. *The History of the Jews in Antiquity: The Jews of Palestine from Alexander the Great to the Arab Conquest*. Luxembourg: Harwood, 1983/1995.

Schalit, Abraham. "Domestic Politics and Political Institutions." In *The Hellenistic Age: Political History of Jewish Palestine from 332 B.C.E. to 67 B.C.E.*, edited by Abraham Schalit, 255–97. The World History of the Jewish People 1/6. New Brunswick, NJ: Rutgers University Press, 1972.

Schaper, Joachim. "The Jerusalem Temple as an Instrument of the Achaemenid Fiscal Administration." *Vetus Testamentum* 45 (1995) 528–39.

Schatzman, Israel. *The Armies of the Hasmonaeans and Herod: From Hellenistic to Roman Frameworks*. Texts and Studies in Ancient Judaism 25. Tübingen: Mohr Siebeck, 1991.

Schiffman, Lawrence H. "Pharisees and Sadducees in *Pesher Nahum*." In *Minḥah le-Naḥum: Biblical and Other Studies Presented to Nahum M. Sarna in Honour of His 70th Birthday*, edited by Marc Brettler and Michael Fishbane, 272–90. Journal for the Study of the Old Testament Supplements 154. Sheffield: Sheffield Academic, 1992.

———. *Reclaiming the Dead Sea Scrolls: The History of Judaism, the Background of Christianity, the Lost Library of Qumran*. Philadelphia: Jewish Publication Society, 1994. Reprint, Anchor Bible Reference Library. New York: Doubleday, 1995.

Schwartz, Daniel R. "Josephus and Nicolaus on the Pharisees." *Journal for the Study of Judaism* 14 (1983) 158–71.

———. "MMT, Josephus, and the Pharisees." In *Reading 4QMMT*, edited by John Kampen and Moshe J. Bernstein, 67–69. Symposium Series 2. Atlanta: SBL, 1996.

———. "On Pharisaic Opposition to the Hasmonean Monarchy." In *Studies in the Jewish Background of Christianity*, 44–56. Tübingen: Mohr Siebeck, 1992.

———. "On Sacrifice by Gentiles in the Temple of Jerusalem." In *Studies in the Jewish Background of Christianity*, 102–16. Wissenschaftliche Untersuchungen zum Neuen Testament 60. Tübingen: Mohr Siebeck, 1992.

Schwartz, Seth. *Imperialism and Jewish Society, 200 B.C.E.–640 C.E.* Jews, Christians, and Muslims from the Ancient to the Modern World. Princeton: Princeton University Press, 2001.

———. "Israel and the Nations Roundabout: 1 Maccabees and the Hasmonean Expansion." *Journal of Jewish Studies* 42 (1991) 16–38.

———. "On the Autonomy of Judaea in the Fourth and Third Centuries B.C.E." *Journal of Jewish Studies* 45 (1994) 157–68.

Scott, James C. *Moral Economy of the Peasant: Rebellion and Resistance in Southeast Asia*. New Haven: Yale University Press, 1976.

———. "Protest and Profanation: Agrarian Revolt and the Little Tradition." *Theory and Society* 4 (1977) 1–38, 211–46.

———. *Weapons of the Weak: Everyday Forms of Peasant Resistance*. New Haven: Yale University Press, 1985.

Sievers, Joseph. *The Hasmoneans and Their Supporters: From Mattathias to the Death of John Hyrcanus I*. South Florida Studies in the History of Judaism 6. Atlanta: Scholars, 1990.

Smelick, Willem. "The Languages of Roman Palestine." In *The Oxford Handbook of Jewish Daily Life in Roman Palestine*, edited by Catherine Hezser, 122–41. Oxford Handbooks in Classics and Ancient History. Oxford: Oxford University Press, 2010.

Smith, Morton. "Palestinian Judaism in the First Century." In *Israel: Its Role in Civilization*, edited by Moshe Davis, 67–81. New York: Harper & Row, 1956.

Speyer, Wolfgang. *Die literarische Fälschung im heidnischen und christlichen Altertum: Ein Versuch ihrer Deutung*. Handbuch der Altertumswissenschaft 1/2. Munich: Beck, 1971.

Stern, Menahem. *Greek and Latin Authors on Jews and Judaism*. Edited with Introduction, translation, and commentary. 3 vols. Fontes ad res Judaicas spectantes. Jerusalem: Israel Academy of Sciences and Humanities, 1976–1984.

Street, Brian V. *Literacy in Theory and Practice*. Cambridge Studies in Oral and Literate Culture 9. Cambridge: Cambridge University Press, 1984.

Talmon, Shemaryahu. "The Emergence of Jewish Sectarianism in the Early Second Temple Period." In *Ancient Israelite Religion: Essays in Honor of Frank Moore Cross*, edited by Patrick D. Miller et al., 587–616. Philadelphia: Fortress, 1987.

Tcherikover, Victor A. *Hellenistic Civilization and the Jews*. Translated by S. Applebaum. 1959. Reprint, New York: Atheneum, 1977.

Thackeray, H. St. John. *Josephus: The Man and the Historian*. New York: Jewish Institute of Religion Press, 1929.
Theissen, Gerd. *The Sociology of Early Palestinian Christianity*. Translated by John Bowden. Philadelphia: Fortress Press, 1978.
Thomas, Rosalind. *Literacy and Orality in Ancient Greece*. Key Themes in Ancient History. Cambridge: Cambridge University Press, 1992.
———. "Literacy and the City-State in Archaic and Classical Greece." In *Literacy and Power in the Ancient World*, edited by Alan K. Bowman and Greg Woolf, 33–50. Cambridge: Cambridge University Press, 1994.
———. *Oral Tradition and Written Record in Classical Athens*. Cambridge Studies in Oral and Literate Culture 18. Cambridge: Cambridge University Press, 1989.
Toorn, Karel van der. "The Iconic Book: Analogies between the Babylonian Cult or Images and the Veneration of the Torah." In *The Image and the Book: Iconic Cults, Aniconism, and the Rise of Book Religion in Israel and the Ancient Near East*, edited by Karel van der Toorn, 229–56. Contributions to Biblical Exegesis and Theology 21. Leuven: Peeters, 1997.
———. *Scribal Culture and the Making of the Hebrew Bible*. Cambridge: Harvard University Press, 2007.
Trafton, Joseph L. "The Psalms of Solomon in Recent Research." *Journal for the Study of the Pseudepigrapha* 12 (1994) 3–19.
Ulrich, Eugene C. "The Bible in the Making: The Scriptures at Qumran," in *The Community of the Renewed Covenant: The Notre Dame Symposium on the Dead Sea Scrolls*, edited by Eugene Ulrich and James VanderKam, 77–93. Christianity and Judaism in Antiquity 10. Notre Dame, IN: University of Notre Dame Press, 1993.
———. *The Dead Sea Scrolls and the Origins of the Bible*. Studies in the Dead Sea Scrolls and Related Literature. Grand Rapids: Eerdmans, 1999.
Unnik, W. C. van. *Flavius Josephus als historische Schriftsteller*. Franz Delitzsch-Vorlesungen, n.F. 1972. Heidelberg: Schneider, 1978.
VanderKam, James C. *The Dead Sea Scrolls Today*. Grand Rapids: Eerdmans, 1994.
Vermes, Geza. *The Complete Dead Sea Scrolls in English*. New York: Penguin, 1997.
Watts, James W., ed. *Persia and Torah: The Theory of Imperial Authorization of the Pentateuch*. Symposium Series 17. Atlanta: SBL, 2001.
Weinfeld, Moshe. *The Place of the Law in the Religion of Ancient Israel*. Vetus Testamentum Supplements 100. Leiden: Brill, 2004.
Werline, Rodney A. "The *Psalms of Solomon* and the Ideology of Rule." In *Conflicted Boundaries in Wisdom and Apocalypticism*, edited by Benjamin G. Wright and Lawrence M. Wills, 69–88. Symposium Series 35. Atlanta: SBL, 2005.
Wise, Michael Owen. *A Critical Study of the Temple Scroll from Qumran Cave 11*. Studies in Ancient Oriental Civilization 49. Chicago: Oriental Institute of the University of Chicago, 1990.

Index of Ancient Documents

Hebrew Bible

Genesis
74

Exodus
72, 74–75, 97
19	74
20	81, 95
21–23	80, 87, 89
22:24	91
24:3–7	72
24:12	72
25–38	97
28:58–61	72
31:18	72
31:24–26	72
32:16	72

Leviticus
74–75, 83, 86–88, 91, 95, 97–99, 150, 238
1–16	86
4:3	86
4:22–26	86
17–26	86
18:24–30	88
19	86
21:10	86
25	80, 86–87, 89
26	86
27	86

Numbers
74–75, 97–98
21:18	54
23:7	218
23:18	218
24:3	218
24:15	218
24:21	218
24:23	218
24:29	218

Deuteronomy
72, 74–75, 81–87, 91–92, 95–99, 150, 205, 238
1–31	82
1–4	82
4:13	72
5	82
5:1–33	81
5:22	72
6–11	82
6:4–9	210
7:3–4	88
9:10	72
12–26	80–82, 89
12	83
15	87
15:1–10	91
20	92
24:1–4	71
27:1–8	83
27:3–8	72
28–29	82

Deuteronomy (continued)

28:58–61	70, 72
28:58	83
29:1	83
29:14–15	83
31–34	53
31	82, 98
31:9–13	83
31:9	83
31:24–26	70, 72
32	54, 82
32:43	54

Joshua

	72
8:30–35	72
8:31–32	72
8:32	72
24	81, 95
24:25–27	72
24:25–26	72

Judges

	54

1 Samuel

8:4–18	82

2 Samuel

2:1–4	198
5:1–4	198

1 Kings

20	46

2 Kings

	72
22–23	82
22:8—23:3	84
23:4–20	84
23:21–23	84
23:24–25	84
23:24	84

Ezra

	24, 26, 35, 40, 88–90
1:1–4	40
4:13	24
4:20	24
6:1–5	40
7:24	24
9:10–15	88
9:11–12	88
10:1–44	88

Nehemiah

	24, 26, 35, 72, 88–90
5:1–13	236
5:4	25
5:6–13	88
8	84, 91
8:1–8	237
8:4–5	84
8:6	84
8:13–18	85
9	41
9:36–37	41
10:29	89
10:30	88
10:32–39	24, 89
10:32	89
10:36–37	25
10:36	89
12:44–47	24
13:1	89
13:4–14	24
13:10	89
13:19–21	89

Proverbs

	38
3:3	4, 67
7:3	67

Isaiah

	68, 191
13	54

26:19	50	3:1c–3	135
40	46	3:4	135
56:1–5	191	3:10	203

Jeremiah

Habakkuk

	68, 191	2:5–6	134
25	54		
51:34	202		

Haggai

1:7–11	24
2:6–9	24

Ezekiel

	74
29:3	202
32:2	202
32:6–15	71
37	50

Zechariah

8:9–13	24

Malachi

3:10	24

Daniel

	28, 45, 47
1–6	46
7–12	238
7	46–47
7:7–8	47
7:25	49
8	46–47
8:13–14	49
9:27	49
10–12	46–47, 244
10–11	49
11–12	47
12:1–3	49
12:2	50
12:3	221
12:11–12	49

~

Apocrypha

1 Maccabees

	27, 33, 42, 44, 56, 126–29, 136
1:56	92
1:57	92
2:42	44
7:12–16	44, 127
9:25	127
9:28–33	128
10:10–11	157
10:15—11:37	132
10:89	141
13–14	127
13:1–8	128
13:10	157
13:25–30	129
14:27–43	129, 156
14:29	129
14:48	77
16:23–24	157

Amos

2:6–8	34

Micah

1:3–4	54

Nahum

2:11–12	153
3:1	135

2 Maccabees

	42, 44
4:7–10	43
7	196
8:21–23	92
11:25	120

Sirach

	3, 27–30, 46, 61, 90–91, 203, 236–38
4:1–10	34
4:18	46
4:21	34, 46
6:34	29, 31, 36
7:14	29, 31, 36
7:29–31	32, 34
8:8	29, 36
9:17	31
10:1–3	31
13:18–23	35
15:5	36
21:17	36
24	91
24:1–22	40
24:23	91
25:1	38
25:8	38
25:13–15	38
25:16–26	38
25:24–26	38
26:1–9	38
26:13–18	38
29:1–20	34
29:2	91
29:9	91
30:27	31
32:14—33:3	90–91
33:19	31
34:5–7	46
34:24–27	34
35:1–12	34
35:6–12	32
38:1–8	37
38:24—39:5	28
38:32—39:1	173
38:32–34	36
38:32	34, 36
38:33	36
38:34—39:1	92
39:1–4	76
39:1–3	46
39:4	31, 36
39:31	45
42:16–17	45
42:18–19	46
42:19	46
43:1–33	36
43:2–5	45
43:6–8	45
43:9–12	45
43:17	45
43:32–33	46
44–50	31, 40
44–49	91
45:5	92
45:15–21	32
45:17	92
45:20–22	34
45:20–21	32
50	91
50:12–19	23

Pseudepigrapha

1 Enoch

	50, 216–21
1–16	42
12:3	50
15:1	50
37:2–5	218
38–44	218
38:1–4	219
39:4–5	221
39:7	221
41:2	221
42:1–2	219
45–57	218
45:4–5	219
46:8	220
47:1–4	220

53:1–7	220
53:1–2	220
53:7	220
54:2	220
56:5–7	218, 219
56:6	219
58–63	218
58:3	221
62:1—63:12	218
62:1	219
62:3	219
62:6	219
62:9	219
62:11	220
62:14	221
63:1	219
69:26–29	218
72–82	45, 74
85–90	19, 42, 45–47, 50, 53, 117, 191, 238, 244
85:3—89:8	51
89:9–38	51
89:28–36	53
89:50	52
89:54	52
89:56	52
89:59—90:19	51
89:66	52
89:73–74	52
90:2–4	52
90:6–19	52
90:6–9	52
90:6–9a	52
90:9b–10	52
90:11	52
90:12–16	52
90:12–13	52
90:16	52
90:17–19	52
90:17	52
90:20–25	53
90:26–27	53
90:28–29	53
92–104	204
104:1–6	50, 221

Jubilees

	60, 74–75, 94
2:24	75
4:15–19	50
6:22	75
30:10	75
36:1—38:14	138
38:1–14	138

Psalms of Solomon

	21, 200–205, 217, 219, 244
1	200, 202
1:4–8	202
2	202, 204
2:1–14	202
2:3–10	202
2:6	203
2:9	203
2:11–14	202
2:15–21	202
2:22–25	202
2:25–27	202
2:25	202
4:1	201
4:8	200
5:16–17	200
8	200, 202, 204
8:6–13	203
8:7	200, 203, 205
8:10–12	203
8:14–22	203
8:16	203
8:19	203
8:20	203
10:5–8	201
11	200, 204
11:14	202
12	201
14:1–2	200
17	200, 202, 205
17:5–6	204
17:7	204
17:9	204
17:11–20	204
17:11–13	204
17:16	201
17:17	204

Index of Ancient Documents

Psalms of Solomon *(continued)*

17:20	204
17:21–44	204
18	205

Testament of Moses

	45–46, 53–54, 216–17
5	54
6–7	54, 217
6:1	217
6:2–6	217
6:7	218
6:8–9	217
7:1–3	218
7:4	218
7:8	218
9	54
9:7	54
10	54
10:3–7	54

New Testament

Matthew

	ix, 12, 108, 223
12:9–13	222
15:1–9	222
22:15–22	222

Mark

	ix, 12, 223
1–2	87
3:1–6	222
7:1–13	222
12:13–17	222
12:28–34	101
12:29–30	210

Luke

	ix, 222–23
2:1	62
5:17	12

John

	222–23
7:32–48	222
11:45–48	222–23
12:42	223

Acts

5:33–39	228
23:1	120

Philippians

1:27	120

Revelation

21:1—22:5	53

Dead Sea Scrolls

1QpHab

2:8	135
8:4–13	134
9:5–12	134
12:2–9	134

1QS

	94, 96, 137
1:11–12	95
2:1–19	95
5–9	95
5:8–12	94
6:6–8	69–70, 95–96, 135

1QS^a

1:3–8	94

Index of Ancient Documents

4QMMT

137, 150

4Q169 (4QpNah)

	135
1:3–8	154
2:4–6	135
2:7–10	135
3:6–7	135
4:2–4	203
4:3–6	135

4Q171

	135
4:6–12	134–35

4Q173

135

11QT

60, 74–75, 94, 187

CD

	94, 134, 137
1:10	137
4:15–17	203
6:3–12	54
6:3–4	96
14:5–7	94
15:9–10	94

~

Josephus

Against Apion

	99
2.48	113
2.77	113
2.145–146	100
2.149	102
2.164–165	210
2.175	63, 102
2.178	63
2.184–187	102
2.204	63
2.291	100
2.293	100

Antiquities

	6–9, 97, 103, 108, 110, 118, 119, 126–27, 139, 151, 153, 161, 170, 195
1–4	210
1.6	100
1.10–25	132
1.25	97
3.84–321	97
3.86–87	97
3.93–94	97
3.99–187	98
4	98–99
4.180	98
4.184	98
4.196–319	97
4.196–197	99
4.198	97, 99
4.200	98
4.210	63
4.212	99
4.214	99
4.219	99
4.220	99
4.223–301	99
4.223	210
4.227	99
4.238	99
4.302	99
4.303–304	99
10.18–21	128
10.50	100
11.336	113
12.56	100
12.414	127
12.419	127
12.434	127
13	165

Antiquities (continued)

13.5	128
13.8	128
13.26–28	128
13.32–34	128
13.40–46	128
13.49–57	128
13.80–170	132
13.84	132
13.99–102	128
13.121	128
13.124	128
13.163	128
13.171–173	131–32
13.197–201	128
13.210–212	129
13.213–217	129
13.214	129
13.228–230	138
13.242–243	113
13.245	138
13.249	138
13.254–256	138
13.257–258	138
13.257	138
13.288	153
13.288a	139
13.294	233–34
13.299–300	137
13.299	153
13.301	151
13.318–319	151
13.320–347	151
13.320–322	162
13.331	183
13.356–371	151
13.372–373	25
13.372	151
13.373	152
13.374	152
13.377–378	152
13.379–380	25, 152
13.381–382	152
13.383	25, 152
13.394	153
13.395–397	153
13.395	153
13.399	153
13.401–404	153
13.408–414	163–64
13.416–417	165
13.417	163–64
13.428–429	164
13.430–432	165
14.8–20	169
14.57–70	203
14.58–71	170
14.65	100
14.71–76	170
14.79	203
14.91	171
14.105–110	171
14.113	171
14.119–120	171
14.127–157	171
14.158–180	172
14.163–170	172
14.167–180	172
14.172–174	172–73
13.174	173
14.175–176	182
14.175	173
14.176	173
14.177–184	173
14.271–276	211
14.272–276	174
14.274	174
14.275	174
14.294	175
14.302–304	175
14.324–326	175
14.327–329	175
14.334–364	176
14.384–389	176
14.470–486	176
14.475	204
14.487–491	204
15.2	176
15.3–4	172, 176, 182
15.5–10	178, 204
15.5	179
15.22–56	185
15.164–178	204
15.194–217	178
15.254	138
15.266–267	179

15.268–276	179	18.12–14	212–13
15.280–290	180	18.12	123
15.291	180	18.15	213
15.292–298	180	18.16–17	213
15.299–316	180	18.17	122
15.299–304	204	18.23–25	209
15.318–325	181	18.23	210
15.320	185	18.26	212
15.326	181	18.122	113
15.328	180	18.261–309	224
15.365	181	18.273–278	225
15.366–370	181	18.305	179
15.371–379	182	18.307	179
15.373–376	182–83	20.38	132
15.378–379	183	20.41	132
15.380–419	186	20.102	229
16.42	100	20.105–106	210
16.43	63	20.122–124	225
16.187	137	20.125–131	225
17.41–42	188	20.135	225
17.43–45	188–89	20.160–166	229
17.148–160	194–95	20.180–181	226
17.150	196	20.181	218
17.151	195	20.186	229
17.152–154	196	20.199–203	103, 233–34
17.157	196	20.200–202	172
17.158–159	197	20.205–207	226–27
17.161–163	197	20.206–207	218
17.164–167	197	20.208–210	230–31
17.171–171	197	20.211–212	227
17.174–181	197	20.266	137
17.191	197		
17.206–218	206		
17.254–264	217		

Life

7–8, 15, 97, 99, 107–10, 114–15, 119–24, 243

17.260–285	198		
17.289	217	1–9	127
17.95	217	1–7	137
17.345–348	192	2–12	122
17.346–347	183	9–12	132
18	122, 243	9	102
18.2–3	211	10–12	118, 120, 122–23
18.3	212	10	119
18.4–6	207	12	20, 119, 215
18.6–10	208	12a	120
18.6	212	12b	120, 121
18.12–25	131	17–19	110
18.12–17	243	21–28	114
18.12–15	122		

Life (continued)

21–23	110–11
21	112
28–29	114
28	111
29	111
62	172
64–69	118
189–335	115
189–192	104
191–192	115
194	116
197–198	115–16
258–262	121
274	119

War

	6, 8–11, 14–15, 100, 103, 108–10, 118, 126–27, 151, 153, 161, 164, 169, 195
1.54–56	138
1.61	138
1.65	139
1.67–68	139
1.67	153
1.68–69	137, 139
1.70	151
1.85–87	151
1.88	151
1.92–95	152
1.96–98	152
1.107–114	160–61
1.107–111	104
1.128–151	170
1.142–151	203
1.152–157	170
1.157	203
1.203–212	172
1.209	172
1.218–222	174
1.220–222	211
1.242	175
1.243–245	175
1.245–246	175
1.250–265	176
1.282–285	176
1.347–358	176
1.393–400	178
1.400	178
1.402–407	178
1.408–421	179
1.422–428	179
1.431–646	188
1.571	189
1.648–650	103, 194
2	111, 114
2.2–5	198
2.49–50	217
2.68	217
2.75	217
2.111	206
2.118	207
2.119–166	131, 212
2.120–161	191
2.122–127	214
2.139	101
2.162–166	214
2.162–165	212
2.162–164	104
2.163	211
2.184–203	224
2.197	113
2.200–202	225
2.223–227	210
2.254–256	229
2.257	231
2.265	231
2.408	232
2.409–417	111
2.409	112
2.411–417	112
2.411	112
2.412–413	113
2.417	112
2.418	114
2.422–425	232
2.426–427	63, 232
2.433–444	232
2.445	230
2.562–568	114
2.565	198
3.350–354	191
5.184–247	186
5.227–229	187
7.253	212
7.320–401	233

Philo

Embassy

115	63
210	63

Mishnah

Berakot

4:3	64

Bikkurim

3:7	64

Pirke Abot

1–2	58
1	177

Sanhedrin

1:5	187

Shebu'ot

2:2	187

Sukkah

3:10	64

Babylonian Talmud

Pesahim

57a	227

Qiddushin

66a	146–47, 151

Author Index

Applebaum, Shimon, 141, 156
Assmann, Jan, 67
Atkinson, Kenneth, 201–5
Attridge, Harold W., 119
Avigad, Nahman, 157, 226

Babota, Vasile, 127
Bartsch, Shadi, 110
Baumgarten, Albert I., 6, 10, 16, 131, 189
Baumgarten, J. M., 93, 137
Beard, Mary, 62
Bickerman, Elias, 42, 43
Blenkinsopp, Joseph, 88, 190
*Botha, Pieter J. J., 248
Bottero, Jean, 80
Bowman, Alan K., 62
Boyarin, Daniel, 14, 69
Broshi, Magen, 33

Camp, Claudia V., 38
Carr, David M., 38, 65, 67–68, 70, 84
Carruthers, Mary J., 69
Clanchy, M. T., 71
Cohen, Shaye J. D., 13, 17, 118, 139
Collins, John J., 46, 90, 91, 218
Cribiore, Raffaella, 67–68

Deines, Roland, 170
DiLella, Alexander A., 90

Finkelstein, Jacob, 80
Fitzmyer, Joseph A., 63
Foley, John Miles, 64
Fraade, Steven D., 94, 96

Gabba, Emilio, 179, 184, 186
Gamble, Harry Y., 63
Goodblatt, D., 6, 14, 213
Goodman, Martin, 18, 117
Grabbe, Lester L., 90
Graham, William A., 96
Green, William Scott, 68
Gruen, Erich, 142

Hanson, John S., 18, 174, 208
Harris, William V., 62
Hengel, Martin, 29, 170
Hezser, Catherine, 13, 62
Himmelfarb, Martha, 43
Horgan, Maurya P., 135
Horsley, Richard A., 17, 18, 28, 30, 35–36, 38, 42, 45–47, 50, 53, 62–63, 65–66, 68, 70, 76–77, 84, 110, 117, 127, 138, 174, 196, 198, 201–2, 208–9, 217–19, 221, 224, 229

Jaffee, Martin S., 59, 66, 68–69, 73, 105
James, M. R., 200,
Jones, Henry Scott, 120

Kasher, Aryeh, 138
Kautsky, John H., 33
Kelber, Werner H., 10, 19, 62, 64
Knight, Douglas A., 35, 80, 99

Lenski, Gerhard E., 30–34, 37, 39
Levine, Lee I., 13
Liddell, H. G., 120
Lieberman, Saul, 69, 77

Machinist, Peter, 84
Mason, Steve, 7–11, 102–3, 109, 111–12, 118–22, 131–32, 144, 146–47, 157–59, 161, 164, 176–77, 181–82, 188–90, 212–15
McKenzie, Roderick, 120
Miller, Shem, 70

Neusner, Jacob, 6–7, 10, 106, 108, 118, 146, 189
Nickelsburg, George W. E., 52, 196, 200, 218
Niditch, Susan, 71–73, 84
Noam, Vered, 145

Pedersén, Olaf, 84
Poirier, John C., 63
Popović, Mladen, 70
Portier-Young, Anathea, 28, 45

Redford, Donald B., 70
Regev, Eyal, 202
Rudich, Vasily, 109
Ryle, H. E., 200

Saldarini, Anthony J., 13, 17
Schäfer, Peter, 55, 151
Schalit, Abraham, 149, 154
Schaper, Joachim, 25
*Schatzman, Israel, 253
Schiffman, Lawrence H., 135–36
Schwartz, Daniel R., 5–6, 8, 10, 113, 137, 156

Schwartz, Seth, 17–18, 26, 42–43, 129, 140, 142
Scott, James C., 35, 77
Scott, Robert, 120
Sievers, Joseph, 130
Smelick, Willem, 63
Smith, Morton, 6, 10, 118
Speyer, Wolfgang, 84
Stern, Menahem, 170
Street, Brian V., 64

Talmon, Shemaryahu, 16
Tcherikover, Victor A., 42–43
Thackeray, H. St. John, 99, 103, 119–21, 144, 161, 163
Thatcher, Tom, 17
*Theissen, Gerd, 255
Thomas, Rosalind, 84–85
Tiller, Patrick A., 30
Toorn, Karel van der, 65, 85
Trafton, Joseph L., 200

Ulrich, Eugene, 4, 74, 76, 96
Unnik, W. C. van, 190

VanderKam, James C., 94, 218
Vermes, Geza, 69, 134

Watts, James W., 80, 88
*Weinfeld, Moshe, 255
Werline, Rodney A., 201
Wise, Michael Owen, 187
Woolf, Greg, 62

www.ingramcontent.com/pod-product-compliance
Lightning Source LLC
Chambersburg PA
CBHW022002220426
43663CB00007B/920